D0426207

A DOCUMENTARY HISTORY OF AMERICAN LIFE

General Editor: **David Donald,** *The Johns Hopkins University*

1. *Settlements to Society: 1584–1763*
JACK P. GREENE, *University of Michigan*

2. *Colonies to Nation: 1763–1789*
JACK P. GREENE, *University of Michigan*

3. *The Great Republic: 1789–1845*
WILSON SMITH, *University of California, Davis*

4. *Democracy on Trial: 1845–1877*
ROBERT W. JOHANNSEN, *University of Illinois*

5. *Shaping the Industrial Republic: 1877–1898*
ROBERT A. LIVELY, *Princeton University*

6. *Progressivism and Postwar Disillusionment: 1898–1928*
DAVID A. SHANNON, *University of Maryland*

7. *Depression, Recovery, and War: 1929–1945*
ALFRED B. ROLLINS, JR., *Harpur College, State University of New York*

8. *Anxiety and Affluence: 1945–1965*
ERNEST R. MAY, *Harvard University*

Depression, Recovery,

and War:

1929–1945

Edited by **ALFRED B. ROLLINS, JR.**

Harpur College,

State University of New York

Volume 7

A Documentary History of American Life

General Editor: **David Donald**

The Johns Hopkins University

McGRAW-HILL BOOK COMPANY

New York St. Louis San Francisco Toronto London Sydney

DEPRESSION, RECOVERY, AND WAR: 1929–1945

Library of Congress Catalog Card Number 66–14813

1234567890 HD 7321069876

FOREWORD

The history of the United States is more a matter of record than is that of any other major world power that has ever existed. The beginnings of our nation are not shrouded in myth or in medieval obscurity, for they can be traced in the precise and explicit directives which the English sovereigns gave their subjects who went to explore or inhabit the New World. At the other end of the time scale, the government of the United States has swiftly moved to declassify and to help publish even the "top secret" papers of World War II and after. For every intervening period the documentary record is voluminous and comprehensive.

A Documentary History of American Life presents an extensive, representative sampling of that vast record. It differs in a number of important ways from the several collections of documents already available to teachers and students. In the first place, it provides the most extensive coverage yet attempted for the entire history of America, from the first expedition of Walter Raleigh through the "Great Society" message to Congress by President Lyndon B. Johnson. The eight volumes of this series, containing approximately 2 million words, afford for the first time a canvas of sufficient size on which to present the panorama of the American past in its full complexity and detail. Moreover, the scope of the series allows the publication of all the significant portions of each document, not merely of selected snippets. Of course, not even a work of this size can include every document relating to American history, but for most students there is abundance here, and each teacher can choose those writings which best fit the needs of his particular courses.

A second major feature of the series is its variety. The seven editors, who have worked closely together during the preparation of these books, agree in rejecting the old notion that a document is necessarily a law, a treaty, or a Supreme Court decision. All these, to be sure, are here present, but so are diary accounts, contemporary letters, essays, poems, and cartoons. All the volumes include documents to illustrate our social, economic, and intellectual, as well as our political and diplomatic, history.

The series is further distinguished by its pedagogical usefulness. Teachers themselves, the seven editors are alert to the problems of college teaching in an age when classes are large and much of the actual instruction must be done by beginning instructors often only a few steps ahead of their pupils. Not just documents are needed, but documents whose relevance is explained and whose implications are explored. For each document, or group of documents, in this series, therefore, there is a full editorial introduction and a brief bibliographical note.

As a result, *A Documentary History of American Life* offers a rich fare to both beginning and advanced students who seek to know our country's history. The editors present these volumes in the profound conviction that only if our citizens understand the past can they intelligently face the future.

The Johns Hopkins University — *David Donald*

PREFACE

No era in American history has been more distinctly set off from the years surrounding it than the period 1929–1945. Depression and war destroyed comfortable habits, revealed ancient inequities, and compelled significant change. Most of the changes were rooted deeply in American traditions. Those which departed significantly from tradition were, nevertheless, designed to preserve the larger values of the old society. Some of the changes were inevitable; crisis merely hastened their occurrence.

This was an age of change in method. It was an age of conservatism in aim. The compulsion to act was tempered by the need to experiment. The American people were prepared for neither economic nor military crisis. They faced disaster without master plans. Only the largest and most general of goals were clearly seen: to bring economic recovery, to win the war.

New programs were devoted to the conservation of democracy, constitutionalism, and capitalism. The outcomes of these new programs were not at all clear during their evolution. But we can identify now a significant outgrowth of the Age of Herbert Hoover and Franklin D. Roosevelt: a mixed economy—much capitalism, some socialism; much regulation but great variety; considerable central guidance but not central management. The emergence of our mixed economy from the 1929–1945 period becomes even more significant when viewed in the light of the options cast aside by the American people at that time. Depression and war might have provided reason for revolution, for a complete restructuring of the economy and society. But Americans chose to save their system rather than scrap it. Under the whip of Depression and war, the nation might have destroyed democracy and the rule of law; it did not. Driven by fear, the nation might have choked off forever the traditions of free thought and discussion; it did not.

The American people determined never again to tolerate the indignities and desperation of economic collapse. It had become a major responsibility of national government to guard against economic catastrophe. Yet the power of economic decision remained widely spread throughout the economy. And there had been incurred a commitment to bigness that could never be reversed. It was war, more than anything else, that had created Big Government. But giant enterprise in business, labor, and agriculture had been created by technological and economic forces beyond the reach of governmental decision. The old dream of rural paradise and simple competition was dead. The new dreams of sophisticated affluence were tolerable only if the giants could be made to harness themselves and each other to the yoke of public responsibility.

While the techniques and scope of management were changing, the method and manner of politics were also changing. An urban trend to the Democratic party was clear as early as 1928, and the new political balances continued until they would tide Harry Truman through two terms in the White House and help to tip the scales for John F. Kennedy. New concepts of the Presidency grew, and the Constitution was adjusted to tolerate more expansive governmental responsibility.

Fundamental changes occurred in the nation's foreign policy. The United States emerged as one of the world's dominant powers; its people learned reluctantly that security demanded commitment. Old traditions were proved bankrupt, and war designed their replacements. World War II should not be underestimated. It may have been more significant than the Depression itself in shaping the economic and social life of the people as well as their fate in foreign affairs.

One looks, then, to the period 1929–1945 for the roots of much of contemporary life: governmental organization and political balance, economic activity and regulation, foreign policy, and social attitudes. The readings provided here constitute some of the most significant documents of the era and should help the reader to see clearly the most meaningful aspects of the period. They illustrate the variety, uncertainty, and experimentation which characterized this nation under stress.

Perhaps the most important thing that can be said about these years is that the American people did not, despite their travail, choose any *one* way. And there is no *one* set of documents to which one may refer as the pattern of the period. The selections included here, from the insights of poets, politicians, sociologists, diplomats, braintrusters, generals, and journalists who saw and helped to make the emerging patterns, should reveal the rich variety of America's responses to crisis.

Alfred B. Rollins, Jr.

CONTENTS

PART FOUR The Politics of Action

PART FIVE The Dynamic Constitution

PART SIX Reluctant Involvement: Foreign Policy, 1929–1938

PART SEVEN Shattered Illusions: Foreign Policy, 1938–1941

PART EIGHT War for the World

Indian Summer of American Prosperity

Although farmers, miners, and many others felt Depression in the early 1920s, middle-class and industrial America lived out the decade bathed in a narcotic haze of prosperity. In fact, it was only an Indian summer, bearing already an occasional hint of the disaster to come. But few could sense this. Prosperity appeared as a gift of the gods to an energetic nation. Only laxness, laziness, irresponsibility, it seemed, could destroy the dream.

Visitors to America often found the dream itself shabby. The values of culture and character were too often sacrificed to the endless compulsion of material achievement. The flapper and the gin mill were all too visible signs of a deep insecurity in middle-class America. A reborn Ku Klux Klan, gang wars in the streets, a general devotion to the mean clichés of racism and nativism bespoke a chaotic repudiation of both order and decency. But nothing appeared to stand so closely for American values as the dollar sign, which seemed, at moments, the sole measure of achievement.

If there was a naiveté regarding economic realities and a confusion regarding values, there was an even deeper confusion about the sense and significance of the decade. Some saw it as the prelude to a great new age of man in which the economic problems would be solved. Others saw it as a desperate era in which young America was destroying, with gay irresponsibility, the hallowed traditions of the nation. This was an age in which Herbert Hoover could speak piously of the "abolition of poverty" in America. But it was an age in which Sinclair Lewis could coin the character of Babbitt to become a synonym for phoniness and superficiality and Henry L. Mencken could clamor endlessly against the idiocies of the "boobocracy." It was also an age in which Bruce Barton could reinterpret Jesus Christ as the greatest business entrepreneur in human history, in which Andrew Mellon could be characterized as the "greatest Secretary of the Treasury since Alexander Hamilton," and in which Al Capone could become one of the most prominent, although not precisely the most admired, figures of the age.

Recent scholarship has begun to give new meaning to the 1920s. One of the most important books for an understanding of the period is Henry F. May's The End of American Innocence: A Study of the Years of Our Own Times, 1912–1917 *(1959). May demonstrates that the period between 1890 and 1920 was one in which the old America was repudiated. Deep questions were raised about the validity of the nation's assumptions regarding idealism, optimism, and culture. World War I, says May, came as a cataclysmic crisis, providing a bloody, violent repudiation of hopes and dreams already sadly undermined. In the light of Henry May's analysis, the decade of the 1920s begins to appear as a period not of either rebellion or reaction, but rather of searching transition. Facing new problems, men were inhibited by a system of values whose authority was deeply undermined. This was a decade for building new values and new institutions. It was certain to be a turbulent era.*

"The Money God": Sociologists Appraise Middle-class America, 1929

At the height of this dangerous decade, Robert and Helen Lynd undertook a pioneer sociological study of a "typical" small Midwestern city, Muncie, Indiana. They sought to reveal America through the community they called "Middletown." Their work, researched before the 1929 market crash, became a classic and also an academic best seller. They described, as no one else had been able to do, the structure and operation of American urban society. The Lynds' sprightly style and imagination made the city come alive. They provided a perceptive analysis of Middletown's trials and tensions, aspirations and dreams. In the brief excerpt which follows, the Lynds take a close look at the income structure of Middletown and its relations to the goals of her people. For the student thirty years later, they reveal a life in some ways familiar yet in some respects strangely different from his own. They reveal, in retrospect, a people both pathetic in their naive optimism and shocking in their provincial, impoverished concept of life.

An effective and scholarly summary of the 1920s is to be found in John Hicks, The Republican Ascendancy: 1921–1933 *(1960). William E. Leuchtenburg provides a brief but stimulating reinterpretation in* The Perils of Prosperity: 1914–1932 *(1958). George Soule analyzes the economic prospects and problems in* Prosperity Decade: From War to Depression, 1917–1929 *(1947). Frederick Lewis Allen's* Only Yesterday *(1931) was a popular, and readable, reflective memoir by a New York man of letters. It has become a classic; one suspects that it may always be read for its fresh reporting, even though specific statistics or interpretations may have become outdated. Arthur M. Schlesinger, Jr., has provided a somewhat different survey of the 1920s, looking at the decade as prelude to the New Deal in his* The Crisis of the Old Order *(1956). Important among the recent works challenging the traditional picture of the 1920s is Arthur Link, "What Happened to the Progressive Movement in the 1920s,"* American Historical Review, *volume 44, July, 1959, pages 833–851.*

The selection which follows is taken from Robert S. Lynd and Helen Merrell Lynd, Middletown, A Study in Contemporary American Culture *(New York: Harcourt, Brace & World, 1929), pages 80–89.*

For both working and business class no other accompaniment of getting a living approaches in importance the money received for their work. It is more this future, instrumental aspect of work, rather than the intrinsic satisfactions involved, that keeps Middletown working so hard as more and more of the activities of living are coming to be strained through the bars of the dollar sign. Among the business group, such things as one's circle of friends, the kind of car one drives, playing golf, joining Rotary, the church to which one belongs, one's political principles, the social position of one's wife apparently tend to be scrutinized somewhat more than formerly in Middletown for their instrumental bearing upon the main business of getting a living, while, conversely, one's status in these various other activities tends to be much influenced by one's financial position. As vicinage has decreased in its influence upon the ordinary social contacts of this group, there appears to be a constantly closer relation between the solitary factor of financial status and one's social status. A leading citizen presented this matter in a nutshell to a member of the research staff in discussing the almost universal local custom of "placing" newcomers in terms of where they live, how they live, the kind of car they drive, and similar externals: "It's perfectly natural. You see, they know money, and they don't know you."

This dominance of the dollar appears in the apparently growing tendency among younger working class men to swap a problematic future for immediate "big money." Foremen complain that Middletown boys entering the shops today are increasingly less interested in being moved from job to job until they have become all-round skilled workers, but want to stay on one machine and run up their production so that they may quickly reach a maximum wage scale.

The rise of large-scale advertising, popular magazines, movies, radio, and other channels of increased cultural diffusion from without are rapidly changing habits of thought as to what things are essential to living and multiplying optional occasions for spending money. Installment buying, which turns wishes into horses overnight, and the heavy increase in the number of children receiving higher education, with its occasions for breaking with home traditions, are facilitating this rise to new standards of living. In 1890 Middletown appears to have lived on a series of plateaus as regards standard of living; old citizens say there was more contentment with relative arrival; it was a common thing to hear a remark that so and so "is pretty good for people in our circumstances." Today the edges of the plateaus have been shaved off, and every one lives on a slope from any point of which desirable things belonging to people all the way to the top are in view.

This diffusion of new urgent occasions for spending money in every sector of living is exhibited by such new tools and services commonly used in Middletown today, but either unknown or little used in the nineties, as the following:

In the home—furnace, running hot and cold water, modern sanitation, electric appliances ranging from toasters to washing machines, telephone, refrigeration, green vegetables and fresh fruit all the year round, greater variety of clothing, silk hose and underwear, commercial pressing and cleaning of clothes, commercial laundering or use of expensive electrical equipment in the home, cosmetics, manicuring, and commercial hair-dressing.

In spending leisure time—movies (attendance far more frequent than at earlier cccasional "shows"), automobile (gas, tires, depreciation, cost of trips), phonograph, radio, more elaborate children's playthings, more club dues for more members of the family, Y.M.C.A. and Y.W.C.A., more formal dances and banquets, including a highly competitive series of "smartly appointed affairs" by high school clubs; cigarette smoking and expensive cigars.

In education—high school and college (involving longer dependence of children), many new incidental costs such as entrance to constant school athletic contests.

In the face of these rapidly multiplying accessories to living the "social problem" of "the high cost of living" is apparently envisaged by most people in Middletown as soluble if they can only inch themselves up a notch higher in the amount of money received for their work. Under these circumstances, why shouldn't money be important to people in Middletown? "The Bible never spoke a truer word," says the local paper in an editorial headed "Your Bank Account Your Best Friend," "than when it said: 'But money answereth all things.' . . . If it doesn't answer all things, it at least answers more than 50 per cent of them." And again, "Of our happy position in world affairs there need be no . . . further proof than the stability of our money system." One leading Middletown business man summed up this trend toward a monetary approach to the satisfactions of life in addressing a local civic club when he said, "Next to the doctor we think of the banker to help us and to guide us in our wants and worries today."

Money being, then, so crucial, how much money do Middletown people actually receive? The minimum cost of living for a "standard family of five" in Middletown in 1924 was $1,920.87. A complete distribution of the earnings of Middletown is not available. Twelve to 15 per cent of those getting the city's living reported a large enough income for 1923 to make the filing of a Federal income tax return necessary. Of the 16,000–17,000 people gainfully employed in 1923—including, however, somewhere in the neighborhood of a thousand married women, some of whom undoubtedly made joint returns with their husbands—210 reported net incomes (i.e., minus interest, contributions, etc.) of $5,000 or over, 999 more net incomes less than $5,000 but large enough to be taxable after subtracting allowed exemptions ($1,000 if single, $2,500 if married, and $400 per dependent), while 1,036 more filed returns but were not taxable after subtracting allowed deductions and exemptions. The other 85–88 per cent of those earning the city's living presumably received either less than $1,000 if single or less than $2,000 if married, or failed to make income tax returns. A cross section of working class earnings is afforded by the following distribution of 100 of the working class families interviewed according to their earnings in the preceding twelve months:

	Distribution of families by fathers' earnings only	*Distribution of families by total family earnings*
Total number of families	100	100
Earning less than minimum standard of $1,920.87		
Families of 5 members or more	42	39
Families of 4 or 3 members (including families of 2 foremen)	35	35
Earning more than minimum standard of $1,920.87		
Families of 5 members or more (including one foreman)	10	13
Families of 4 or 3 members (including 6 foremen)	13	13

The incomes of these 100 families range from $344.50 to $3,460.00, with the median at $1,494.75 and the first and third quartiles respectively at $1,193.63 and $2,006.00.

The relative earning power of males and females in Middletown is indicated by the fact that in a characteristic leading Middletown plant during the first six months of 1924 the weighted average hourly wage of all females (excluding office force and forewomen) was $0.31 and of all males (excluding office force and foremen) $0.55. The bulk of this plant is on a ten-hour basis, fifty-five hours per week, making the average annual income for fifty-two weeks, provided work is steady, $886.60 for females and $1,573.00 for males. In three other major plants similar average wages for males were $0.55, $0.54 and $0.59. In general, unskilled female labor gets $0.18 to $0.28 an hour and a few skilled females $0.30 to $0.50. Unskilled males receive $0.35 to $0.40 an hour and skilled males from $0.50 to $1.00 and occasionally slightly more.

As over against these wages of women in industry in Middletown in 1924, ranging from $10.00 to $18.00 a week in the main, the younger clerks in the leading department store received $10.00 a week, and more experienced clerks a flat rate from $8.00 to $17.00 a week plus a bonus, if earned—the whole amounting occasionally "when times are good" for a veteran clerk to $30.00 to $40.00 a week.

A detailed calculation of a cost of living index for Middletown in 1924 on the basis of the cost of living in 1891 reveals an increase of 117 per cent. A comparison of the average yearly earnings of the 100 heads of families in 1924 with available figures for 439 glass, wood, and iron and steel workers in Middletown in 1891 reveals an average of $1,469.61 in the former case and $505.65 in the latter, or an increase of 191 per cent today. Or if we take the earnings of school teachers as an index, probably conservative, of the trend in earnings, as against this rise of 117 per cent in the cost of living, it appears that the minimum salary paid to grade school teachers has risen 143 per cent and the maximum 159 per cent, and the minimum salary paid to high school teachers 134 per cent and the maximum 250 per cent. The median salary for grade school teachers in 1924 was $1,331.25, with the first and third quartiles at $983.66 and $1,368.00 respectively. The median salary for high school teachers was $1,575.00, with the first and third quartiles at $1,449.43 and $1,705.50 respectively. Substantial increases in the incomes of persons in certain other representative occupations are suggested by the fact that the salary of a bank teller has mounted from $50.00 or $65.00 a month in 1890 to $166.67 a month in 1924, that of an average male clerk in a leading men's clothing store from $12.00 a week in 1890 to $35.00 today; a doctor's fee for a normal delivery with the same amount of accompanying care in both periods has risen from $10.00 to $35.00, and for a house call from $1.00 to $3.00.

Thus this crucial activity of spending one's best energies year in and year out in doing things remote from the immediate concerns of living eventuates apparently in the ability to buy somewhat more than formerly, but both business men and working men seem to be running for dear life in this business of making the money they earn keep pace with the even more rapid growth of their subjective wants. A Rip Van Winkle who fell asleep in the Middletown of 1885 to awake today would marvel at the change as did the French economist Say when he revisited England at the close of the Napoleonic Wars; every one seemed to run intent upon his own business as though fearing to stop lest those behind trample him down. In the quiet county-seat of the middle eighties men lived relatively close to the earth and its products. In less than four decades, business class and working class, bosses and bossed, have been caught up by Industry, this new trait in the city's culture that is shaping the pattern of the whole of living. According to its needs, large numbers of people anxious to get their living are periodically stopped by the recurrent phenomenon of "bad times" when the machines stop running, workers are "laid off" by the hundreds, salesmen sell less, bankers call in loans, "credit freezes," and many Middletown families may take their children from school, move into cheaper homes, cut down on food, and do without many of the countless things they desire.

The working class is mystified by the whole fateful business. Many of them say, for instance, that they went to the polls and voted for Coolidge in November, 1924, after being assured daily by the local papers that "A vote for Coolidge is a vote for prosperity and your job"; puzzled as to why "times" did not improve after the overwhelming victory of Coolidge, a number of them asked the interviewers if the latter thought times would be better "after the first of the year"; the first of the year having come and gone, their question was changed to "Will business pick up in the spring?"

The attitude of the business men, as fairly reflected by the editorial pages of the press which today echo the sentiments heard at Rotary and the Chamber of Commerce, is more confident but confusing. Within a year the leading paper offered the following prescriptions for local prosperity: "The first duty of a citizen is to produce"; and later, "The American citizen's first importance to his country is no longer that of citizen but that of consumer. Consumption is a new necessity." "The way to make business boom is to buy." At the same time that the citizen is told to "consume" he is told, "Better start saving late than never. If you haven't opened your weekly savings account with some local bank, trust company, or building and loan, today's the day." Still within the same year the people of Middletown are told: "The only true prosperity is that for which can be assigned natural reasons such as good crops, a demand for building materials, . . . increased need for transportation," and ". . . advancing prices are due to natural causes which are always responsible for prices. . . . As all wealth comes from the soil, so does all prosperity, which is only another way of saying so does all business." But again, "natural causes" are apparently not the chief essential: "There can be no greater single contribution to the welfare of the nation than the spirit of hopefulness. . . ." "[This] will be a banner year because the people believe it will be, which amounts to the determination that it shall be. . . ." Still another solution for securing "good times" appears: "The most prosperous town is that in which the citizens are bound most closely together. . . . Loyalty to the home town . . . is intensely practical. . . . The thing we must get into our heads about this out-of-town buying business is that it hurts the individual who does it and his friends who live here. Spending your money at home in the long run amounts practically to spending it upon yourself, and buying away from home means buying the comforts and luxuries for the other fellow." "A dollar that is spent out of town never returns." One looking on at this procedure may begin to wonder if the business men, too, are not somewhat bewildered.

Although neither business men nor working men like the recurring "hard times," members of both groups urge the maintenance of the present industrial system. The former laud the group leaders who urge "normalcy" and "more business in government and less government in business," while the following sentences from an address by a leading worker, the president of the Trades Council, during the 1924 political campaign, sets forth the same faith in "free competition" on the part of the working class: "The important issue is the economic issue. We can all unite on that. We want a return to active free competition, so that prices will be lower and a man can buy enough for himself and his family with the money he makes." Both groups, as they order a lay-off, cut wages to meet outside competition, or, on the other hand, vote for La Follette in the hope of his being able to "do something to help the working man," appear to be fumbling earnestly to make their appropriate moves in the situation according to the rules of the game as far as they see them; but both appear to be bound on the wheel of this modern game of corner-clipping production. The puzzled observer may wonder how far any of them realizes the relation of his particular move to the whole function of getting a living. He might even be reminded of a picture appearing in a periodical circulated in Middletown during the course of the study: A mother leans over her two absorbed infants playing at cards on the floor and asks, "What are you playing, children?"

"We're playing 'Putcher,' Mamma. Bobby, putcher card down."

In the midst of such a partially understood but earnestly followed scheme of getting a living, the rest of living goes on in Middletown.

Debate with Disaster

In the early autumn of 1929, there came a series of economic disasters so intense, so pervasive, that they have dominated our thinking regarding the whole era. First, a series of steep breaks in the stock prices on the exchanges, then a collapse beyond all recall, then the mounting unemployment, deepening price cuts, the bankruptcies, bank closures—and suicides. And then, the thickening pall of chronic Depression to last, as it turned out, until the end of the next decade.

We know now that it was an economic collapse as fundamental as the crumbling of the nation's value structure a decade earlier. We know now that it brought a restructuring of economic and social and political institutions far beyond anything the nation had ever experienced or dreamed. But, as we look back upon the men and women of 1929, 1930, and 1931, we are struck by the fact that they had little comprehension of their situation and less conception of the institutional revolution it would create. They moved much like figures in a classic Greek tragedy, caught in the web of fate, and grasping on the momentary options between which they thought it was their power to choose. We see them as pitiable figures, trying to patch their ship when the hull was smashed beyond all repair, seeking to debate with fate itself when disaster left little room for argument.

In the White House, Herbert Hoover saw the situation as a temporary one. It was, he thought, merely a slightly more violent manifestation of the conventional and inevitable process of readjustment in a free economy. Outside the White House, Franklin D. Roosevelt, Governor of New York, like millions of others, would take over two long years before he would begin to grasp the enormity of what was happening.

The Market Crash: The "New York Times" Reports, 1929

October 24, 1929, was Black Thursday on the nation's stock markets. Thousands of small speculators saw their hopes withered, their security blasted in one rude day. It was, in fact, the beginning of a long, dark winter of despair. But most thought it a momentary matter. Only a few had been shrewd enough to sense the looming crisis and get out of the markets before the summer's end. A few more had noted the weakening of September and early October and, in escaping, had helped make the crash more violent. But most had been held then by the hysteria of optimism, and were caught still in a habit of boundless hope so numbing that disaster could only be recognized as temporary readjustment.

No source catches the drama and confusion of the moment more sharply than the New York Times. *Its terse but thorough story of the market on October 29 reflects both the desperation and the incorrigible optimism which marked the exchanges and the nation. The reporter's analysis of the roots and meaning of the crisis may be naive at points, but it reflects the popular understanding of the moment and sketches out the activities and anxieties of the third ghastly day of market disintegration, a day when some began to sense dimly the death of an entire era.*

Broadus Mitchell, The Depression Decade: From New Era through New Deal, 1929–1941 *(1947) provides a thorough survey of the forces and factors in crash and Depression. By far the most readable and suggestive book is, however, J. Kenneth Galbraith,* The Great Crash: 1929 *(1955). See also Murray Rothbard,* America's Great Depression *(1963).*

The following selection is from the New York Times, *October 30, 1929, page 1.*

Stock prices virtually collapsed yesterday, swept downward with gigantic losses in the most disastrous trading day in the stock market's history. Billions of dollars in open market values were wiped out as prices crumbled under the pressure of liquidation of securities which had to be sold at any price.

There was an impressive rally just at the close, which brought many leading stocks back from 4 to 14 points from their lowest points of the day.

Trading on the New York Stock Exchange aggregated 16,410,030 shares; on the Curb, 7,096,300 shares were dealt in. Both totals far exceeded any previous day's dealings.

From every point of view, in the extent of losses sustained, in total turnover, in the number of speculators wiped out, the day was the most disastrous in Wall Street's history. Hysteria swept the country and stocks went overboard for just what they would bring at forced sale.

Efforts to estimate yesterday's market losses in dollars are futile because of the vast number of securities quoted over the counter and on out-of-town exchanges on which no calculations are possible. However, it was estimated that 880 issues, on the New York Stock Exchange, lost between $8,000,000,000 and $9,000,000,000 yesterday. Added to that loss is to be reckoned the depreciation on issues on the Curb Market, in the over the counter market and on other exchanges.

There were two cheerful notes, however, which sounded through the pall of gloom which overhung the financial centres of the country. One was the brisk rally of stocks at the close, on tremendous buying by those who believe that prices have sunk too low. The other was that the liquidation has been so violent, as well as widespread, that many bankers, brokers and industrial leaders expressed the belief last night that it now has run its course.

A further note of optimism in the soundness of fundamentals was sounded by the directors of the United States Steel Corporation and the American Can Company, each of which declared an extra dividend of $1 a share at their late afternoon meetings.

Banking support, which would have been impressive and successful under ordinary circumstances, was swept violently aside, as block after block of stock, tremendous in proportions, deluged the market. Bid prices placed by bankers, industrial leaders and brokers trying to halt the decline were crashed through violently, their orders were filled, and quotations plunged downward in a day of disorganization, confusion and financial impotence.

That there will be a change today seemed likely from statements made last night by financial and business leaders. Organized support will be accorded to the market from the start, it is believed, but those who are staking their all on the country's leading securities are placing a great deal of confidence, too, in the expectation that there will be an overnight change in sentiment; that the counsel of cool heads will prevail and that the mob psychology which has been so largely responsible for the market's debacle will be broken.

The fact that the leading stocks were able to rally in the final fifteen minutes of trading yesterday was considered a good omen, especially as the weakest period of the day had developed just prior to that time and the minimum prices for the day had then been established. It was a quick run-up which followed the announcement that the American Can directors had declared an extra dividend of $1. The advances in leading stocks in this last fifteen minutes represented a measurable snapback from the lows. American Can gained 10; United States Steel common, 7½; General Electric, 12; New York Central, 14½; Anaconda Copper, 9½; Chrysler Motors, 5¼; Montgomery Ward, 4¼ and Johns Manville, 8. Even with these recoveries the losses of these particular stocks, and practically all others, were staggering.

Yesterday's market crash was one which largely affected rich men, institutions, investment trusts and others who participate in the stock market on a broad and intelligent scale. It was not the margin traders who were caught in the rush to sell, but the rich men of the country who are able to swing blocks of 5,000, 10,000 up to 100,000 shares of high-priced stocks. They went overboard with no more consideration than the little trader who was swept out on the first day of the market's upheaval, whose prices, even at their lowest of last Thursday, now look high in comparison.

The market on the rampage is no respecter of persons. It washed fortune after fortune away yesterday and financially crippled thousands of individuals in all parts of the world. It was not until after the market had closed that the financial district began to realize that a good-sized rally had taken place and that there was a stopping place on the downgrade for good stocks.

The market has now passed through three days of collapse, and so violent has it been that most authorities believe that the end is not far away. It started last Thursday, when 12,800,000 shares were dealt in on the Exchange and holders of stocks commenced to learn just what a decline in the market means. This was followed by a moderate rally on Friday and entirely normal conditions on Saturday, with fluctuations on a comparatively narrow scale and with the efforts of the leading bankers to stabilize the market evidently successful. But the storm broke anew on Monday, with prices slaughtered in every direction, to be followed by yesterday's tremendous trading of 16,410,030 shares.

Sentiment had been generally unsettled since the first of September. Market prices had then reached peak levels, and, try as they would, pool operators and other friends of the market could not get them higher. It was a gradual downward sag, gaining momentum as it went on, then to break out into an open market smash in which the good, the bad and indifferent stocks went down alike. Thousands of traders were able to weather the first storm and answered their margin calls; thousands fell by the wayside Monday and again yesterday, unable to meet the demands of their brokers that their accounts be protected.

There was no quibbling at all between customer and broker yesterday. In any case where margin became thin a peremptory call went out. If there was no immediate answer the stock was sold out "at the market" for just what it would bring. Thousands, sold out on the decline and amid the confusion, found themselves in debt to their brokers last night.

Three factors stood out most prominently last night after the market's close. They were:

Wall Street has been able to weather the storm with but a single Curb failure, small in size, and no member of the New York Stock Exchange has announced himself unable to meet commitments.

The smashing decline has brought stocks down to a level where, in the opinion of leading bankers and industrialists, they are a buy on their merits and prospects, and brokers have so advised their customers.

The very violence of the liquidation, which has cleaned up many hundreds of sore spots which honeycombed the market, and the expected ability of the market to right itself, since millions of shares of stock have passed to strong hands from weak ones.

One of the factors which Wall Street failed to take into consideration throughout the entire debacle was that the banking consortium has no idea of putting stocks up or to save any individuals from loss, but that its sole purpose was to alleviate the wave of financial hysteria sweeping the country and provide bids, at some price, where needed. It was pointed out in many quarters that no broad liquidating movement in the stock market has ever been stopped by so-called good buying. This is helpful, of course, but it never stops an avalanche of liquidation, as was this one.

There is only one factor, it was pointed out, which can and always does stop a down swing—that is, the actual cessation of forced liquidation. It is usually the case, too, that when the last of the forced selling has been completed the stock market always faces a wide-open gap in which there are practically no offerings of securities at all. When that point is reached, buying springs up from everywhere and always accounts for a sharp, almost perpendicular recovery in the best stocks. The opinion was widely expressed in Wall Street last night that that point has been reached, or at least very near reached.

The opening bell on the Stock Exchange released such a floor of selling as has never before been witnessed in this country. The failure of the market to rally consistently on the previous day, the tremendous shrinkage of open market values and the wave of hysteria which appeared to sweep the country brought an avalanche of stock to the market to be sold at whatever price it would bring.

From the very first quotation until thirty minutes after 10 o'clock it was evident that the day's market would be an unprecedented one. In that first thirty minutes of trading stocks were poured out in 5,000, 10,000, 20,000 and 50,000 share blocks at tremendous sacrifices as compared with the previous closing. The declines ranged from a point or so to as much as 29½ points, and the reports of opening prices brought selling into the market in confused volume that has never before been equaled.

In this first half hour of trading on the Stock Exchange a total of 3,259,800 shares were dealt in. The volume of the first twenty-six blocks of stock dealt in at the opening totaled more than 630,000 shares.

There was simply no near-by demand for even the country's leading industrial and railroad shares, and many millions of dollars in values were lost in the first quotations tapped out. All considerations other than to get rid of the stock at any price were brushed aside.

Wall Street was a street of vanished hopes, of curiously silent apprehension and of a sort of paralyzed hypnosis yesterday. Men and women crowded the brokerage offices, even those who have been long since wiped out, and followed the figures on the tape. Little groups gathered here and there to discuss the fall in prices in hushed and awed tones. They were participating in the making of financial history. It was the consensus of bankers and brokers alike that no such scenes ever again will be witnessed by this generation. To most of those who have been in the market it is all the more awe-inspiring because their financial history is limited to bull markets.

The machinery of the New York Stock Exchange and the Curb Market were unable to handle the tremendous volume of trading which went over them. Early in the day they kept up well, because most of the trading was in big blocks, but as on the previous big days of this week and last it was only by printing late quotations of stocks on the bond tickers and by the 10-minute flashes on stock prices put out by Dow, Jones & Co. and the Wall Street News Bureau that the financial district could get any idea of what was happening in the wild mob of brokers on the Exchange and the Curb.

In the afternoon trading the tickers got more than an hour behind. Current tape prices were 5, 10 and 20 points away from those on the floor of the Exchanges. The Exchange ticker did not tap out the final quotation on stock prices until 5:32 P.M. The Curb tickers completed their task at 6:17. In most cases no attempt was made to keep up records in the Exchange board rooms, and only the last prices received from the Exchange floor by the ticker services were posted. . . .

The bull market, the most extensive in the history of the country, started in the Coolidge Administration and reached its height with a tremendous burst of speculation in the public utility issues, the flames of speculation being fed by mergers, new groupings, combinations and good earnings.

The highest prices were reached in early September. At that time the market had a quick break and an equally rapid recovery. Then started a slow sag. Two developments, not considered important at the time, served to start the ball rolling downhill. The first of these was the refusal of the Massachusetts Public Service Commission to permit the Boston Edison Company to split its shares; the second was the collapse of a pool in International Combustion Engineering shares on the Stock Exchange, an over-exploited industrial which had been pushed across 100 by a pool and which crashed when the corporation passed its dividend.

In the meanwhile, the Hatry failure abroad had diverted a tremendous volume of selling to the United States, and under these influences the market continued to sag until it literally crumpled of its own weight.

The Reassuring Touch: President Hoover Speaks, 1931

Herbert Hoover (1874–1964) was one of the most dedicated and serious Presidents the nation has ever had. Yet fate and time turned a trick upon him which made this sensitive man seem, in his own time, the very prototype of irresponsibility and coldness. Elected in 1928 as the "great engineer," the master of prosperity, he was rudely forced to preside over the dissolution of his own dreams as well as the nation's. He was never quite able to rise above the shock. A certain tough detachment had once served him well in his crusade to feed the hungry during and after the First World War. But now the objective, analytical approach, which compelled him to turn away in cold logic from the most dramatic devices for relief, made him appear cruel and unthinking. Hoover's problem was not, in fact, coldness but rigidity. His deep anguish over his nation's trials was matched only by the inhibitions which bound him. His answer for the Depression was a continued application of the same policies which had helped to bring Depression: balanced budgets, high tariffs, tight money, governmental economy, and, above all, the relentless reminder that the people themselves, and not the government, must search out the way of escape.

Guided by a rigid social and political philosophy which he could not reexamine, even in crisis, Hoover found most options closed to him. It was the part of courage, he thought, to stand for the values of "character" and "ordered liberty" especially when they were under attack. But his words found little meaning for the hungry. To a later generation he would appear to have responded to need with clichés. When he did act, reluctantly, by supporting the creation of a Reconstruction Finance Corporation and a program to stabilize farm prices, the action was both limited and late.

But Herbert Hoover played out his chosen role with the valor of a hero. Relentlessly he spoke the words of encouragement to his despairing people. Symptomatic of his mood and manner were his words on Lincoln's birthday, 1931, in which he reasserted again his faith in the old ways.

Herbert Hoover's own views of the Depression are to be found in The Memoirs of Herbert Hoover: The Great Depression, 1929–1941 *(1952). The best general discussion of the problem is in Harris G. Warren,* Herbert Hoover and the Great Depression *(1959). See also, however, the pro–New Deal analysis in Arthur M. Schlesinger, Jr.,* The Crisis of the Old Order *(1956), and the pro-Hoover analysis in Carl Degler, "The Ordeal of Herbert Hoover,"* Yale Review, *volume 52 (1962–1963), pages 563–583.*

The text of this radio address by President Hoover is taken from the New York Times, *February 13, 1931, page 1.*

In Lincoln's day the dominant problem in our form of government turned upon the issue of States' rights. Though less pregnant with disaster, the dominant problem today in our form of government turns in large degree upon the issue of the relationship of Federal, State and local government responsibilities. We are faced with unceasing agitation that the Federal Government shall assume new financial burdens, that it shall undertake increased burdens in regulation of abuses and in the prosecution of crime.

It is true that since Lincoln's time many forces have swept across State borders and have become more potent than the State or local community can deal with alone either financially or by jurisdiction. Our concept of Federal, State and local responsibilities is possible of no unchangeable definitions and it must shift with the moving forces in the nation; but the time has come when we must have more national consideration and decision of the part which each shall assume in these responsibilities.

The Federal Government has assumed many new responsibilities since Lincoln's time, and will probably assume more in the future when the States and local communities cannot alone cure abuse or bear the entire cost of national programs, but there is an essential principle that should be maintained in these matters. I am convinced that where Federal action is essential, then in most cases it should limit its responsibilities to supplement the States and local communities, and that it should not assume the major role or the entire responsibility in replacement of the State or local government. To do otherwise threatens the whole foundations of local government, which is the very basis of self-government.

The moment responsibilities of any community, particularly in economic and social questions, are shifted from any part of the nation to Washington, then that community has subjected itself to a remote bureaucracy with its minimum of understanding and of sympathy. It has lost a large part of its voice and its control of its own destiny. Under Federal control the varied conditions of life in our country are forced into standard molds, with all their limitations upon life, either of the individual or the community. Where people divest themselves of local government responsibilities they at once lay the foundation for the destruction of their liberties.

And buried in this problem lies something even deeper. The whole of our governmental machinery was devised for the purpose that through ordered liberty we give incentive and equality of opportunity to every individual to rise to that highest achievement of which he is capable. At once when government is centralized there arises a limitation upon the liberty of the individual and a restriction of individual opportunity.

The true growth of the nation is the growth of character in its citizens. The spread of government destroys initiative and thus destroys character. Character is made in the community as well as in the individual by assuming responsibilities, not by escape from them. Carried to its logical extreme, all this shouldering of individual and community responsibility upon the government can lead but to the superstate, where every man becomes the servant of the State and real liberty is lost. Such was not the government that Lincoln sought to build.

There is an entirely different avenue by which we may both resist this drift to centralized government and at the same time meet a multitude of problems. That is to strengthen in the nation a sense and an organization of self-help and cooperation to solve as many problems as possible outside of government. We are today passing through a critical test in such a problem arising from the economic depression.

Due to lack of caution in business and to the impact of forces from an outside world, one-half of which is involved in social and political revolution, the march of our prosperity has been retarded. We are projected into temporary unemployment, losses and hardships. In a nation rich in resources, many people were faced with hunger and cold through no fault of their own. Our national resources are not only material supplies and material wealth but a spiritual and moral wealth in kindliness, in compassion, in a sense of obligation of neighbor to neighbor and a realization of responsibility by industry, by business, and the community for its social security and its social welfare.

The evidence of our ability to solve great problems outside of government action and the degree of moral strength with which we emerge from this period will be determined by whether the individuals and the local communities continue to meet their responsibilities.

Throughout this depression I have insisted upon organization of these forces through industry, through local government and through charity, that they should meet this crisis by their own initiative, by the assumption of their own responsibilities. The Federal Government has sought to do its part by example in the expansion of employment, by affording credit to drought sufferers for rehabilitation, and by cooperation with the community, and thus to avoid the opiates of government charity and the stifling of our national spirit of mutual self-help.

We can take courage and pride in the effective work of thousands of voluntary organizations for provision of employment, for relief of distress, that have sprung up over the entire nation. Industry and business have recognized a social obligation to their employes as never before. The State and local governments are being helpful. The people are themselves succeeding in this task. Never before in a great depression has there been so systematic a protection against distress; never before has there been so little social disorder; never before has there been such an outpouring of the spirit of self-sacrifice and service.

The ever-growing complexity of modern life, with its train of ever more perplexing and difficult problems, is a challenge to our individual characters and to our devotion to our ideals. The resourcefulness of America when challenged has never failed. Success is not gained by leaning upon government to solve all the problems before us. That way leads to enervation of will and destruction of character.

Victory over this depression and over our other difficulties will be won by the resolution of our people to fight their own battles in their own communities, by stimulating their ingenuity to solve their own problems, by taking new courage to be masters of their own destiny in the struggle of life. This is not the easy way, but it is the American way. And it was Lincoln's way.

The ultimate goal of the American social ideal is equality of opportunity and individual initiative. These are not born of bureaucracy. This ideal is the expression of the spirit of our people. This ideal obtained at the birth of the Republic. It was the ideal of Lincoln. It is the ideal upon which the nation has risen to unparalleled greatness.

We are going through a period when character and courage are on trial, and where the very faith that is within us is under test. Our people are meeting this test. And they are doing more than the immediate task of the day. They are maintaining the ideals of our American system. By their devotion to these ideals we shall come out of these times stronger in character, in courage and in faith.

SELECTION 4

Some Objections by Experts: Economists Oppose the Smoot-Hawley Tariff, 1930

The limitations of Hoover's policies were nowhere so clearly illustrated as in the Smoot-Hawley Tariff. The bill was a classic product of the lobbying system. It reflected a general abdication of responsibility by Congress to the special interests. More important, it marked the intellectual bankruptcy of the Hoover administration, for it offered answers to the Depression which were excessively rigid, which operated from false premises, and which were inconsistent with the administration's own analysis of the need for expanding markets overseas.

Congress passed the bill. But the President had to sign or veto it. Over one hundred economists, including most of the leaders in their field, rushed to petition Hoover to veto it. Their document presented the objections both thoroughly and dramatically. But the President signed.

The classic study of the Tariff Act of 1930 is Elmer E. Schattschneider, Politics, Pressures and the Tariff *(1935).*

The statement of the economists is republished here from the New York Times, *May 5, 1930, pages 1 and 4.*

The undersigned American economists and teachers of economics strongly urge that any measure which provides for a general upward revision of tariff rates be denied passage by Congress, or if passed, be vetoed by the President.

We are convinced that increased restrictive duties would be a mistake. They would operate, in general, to increase the prices which domestic consumers would have to pay. By raising prices they would encourage concerns with higher costs to undertake production, thus compelling the consumer to subsidize waste and inefficiency in industry.

At the same time they would force him to pay higher rates of profit to established firms which employed lower production costs. A higher level of duties, such as is contemplated by the Smoot-Hawley bill, would therefore raise the cost of living and injure the great majority of our citizens.

Few people could hope to gain from such a change. Miners, construction, transportation and public utility workers, professional people and those employed in banks, hotels, newspaper offices, in the wholesale and retail trades and scores of other occupations would clearly lose, since they produce no products which could be specially favored by tariff barriers.

The vast majority of farmers also would lose. Their cotton, pork, lard and wheat are export crops and are sold in the world market. They have no important competition in the home market. They cannot benefit, therefore, from any tariff which is imposed upon the basic commodities which they produce.

They would lose through the increased duties on manufactured goods, however, and in a double fashion. First, as consumers they would have to pay still higher prices for the products, made of textiles, chemicals, iron and steel, which they buy. Second, as producers their ability to sell their products would be further restricted by the barriers placed in the way of foreigners who wished to sell manufactured goods to us.

Our export trade, in general, would suffer. Countries cannot permanently buy from us unless they are permitted to sell to us, and the more we restrict the importation of goods from them by means of ever higher tariffs, the more we reduce the possibility of our exporting to them.

This applies to such exporting industries as copper, automobiles, agricultural machinery, typewriters and the like fully as much as it does to farming. The difficulties of these industries are likely to be increased still further if we pass a higher tariff.

There are already many evidences that such action would inevitably provoke other countries to pay us back in kind by levying retaliatory duties against our goods. There are few more ironical spectacles than that of the American Government as it seeks, on the one hand, to promote exports through the activity of the Bureau of Foreign and Domestic Commerce, while, on the other hand, by increasing tariffs it makes exportation ever more difficult.

We do not believe that American manufacturers, in general, need higher tariffs. The report of the President's Committee on Recent Economic Changes has shown that industrial efficiency has increased, that costs have fallen, that profits have grown with amazing rapidity since the end of the World War. Already our factories supply our people with over 96 per cent of the manufactured goods which they consume, and our producers look to foreign markets to absorb the increasing output of their machines.

Further barriers to trade will serve them not well but ill.

Many of our citizens have invested their money in foreign enterprises. The Department of Commerce has estimated that such investments, entirely aside from the war debts, amounted to between $12,555,000,000 and $14,555,000,000 on Jan. 1, 1929. These investors, too, would suffer if restrictive duties were to be increased, since such action would make it still more difficult for their foreign debtors to pay them the interest due them.

America is now facing the problem of unemployment. The proponents of higher tariffs claim that an increase in rates will give work to the idle. This is not true. We cannot increase employment by restricting trade. American industry, in the present crisis, might well be spared the burden of adjusting itself to higher schedules of duties.

Finally, we would urge our government to consider the bitterness which a policy of higher tariffs would inevitably inject into our international relations. The United States was ably represented at the world economic conference which was held under the auspices of the League of Nations in 1927. This conference adopted a resolution announcing that "the time has come to put an end to the increase in tariffs and to move in the opposite direction."

The higher duties proposed in our pending legislation violate the spirit of this agreement and plainly invite other nations to compete with us in raising further barriers to trade. A tariff war does not furnish good soil for the growth of world peace.

And Then Hunger: A Contemporary Report, 1933

The Depression was considerably more than a mere financial problem or an economic maladjustment which might be studied statistically and then remedied institutionally. It was disaster for people. Hoover's problem was partly that he never understood just how completely the human crisis had outmoded the institutions. It was a part of the public's problem, on the other hand, that, in hunger, it could not tolerate involved and time-consuming debates about the causes of hunger. People demanded action, without particular concern over the pattern or propriety of the action.

Fortune Magazine, *addressed to businessmen, announced: "No One Has Starved." But some had. No one saw this more clearly or recorded it so effectively as Mauritz Hallgren (1899–1956), a professional reporter. In the chapter provided below he tells the story of real people. There is more passion than balance here, and practically no objectivity. Hallgren could not be objective about hunger. And his age learned that in the mask of the Depression, the lines etched by starvation were the most provocative, the most dangerous, the most difficult to erase.*

There was a vast contemporary comment upon the social and personal impact of Depression. Without doubt one of the most important articles was by the editors of Fortune, *"No One Has Starved," volume 6, September, 1932, pages 19–28 and page 80. William Bilevitz described the shocking labor conditions in some of the garment factories in "The Connecticut Needle Trades,"* Nation, *volume 135, September 16, 1932, pages 475–477.*

The chapter provided here, entitled "A Word about Hunger," is from Mauritz Hallgren, Seeds of Revolt: A Study of American Life and the Temper of the American People during the Depression *(New York: Knopf, 1933), pages 3–12.*

Despite the calm assumption of many public men that there has been no real hunger in the United States at any time since the depression began, it is a fact that Ignatz Wlosinski starved to death. He had been missing from his home in Schenectady, New York, for more than a fortnight in the late autumn of 1932. His body was eventually found. The story is told by the Troy *Record,* a newspaper that has never shown any great sympathy for the unemployed.

> The body of a man found Wednesday morning huddled beneath a pile of straw in a barn at The Knolls [the *Record* reported] was identified yesterday as that of Ignatz Wlosinski of 148 Cork Street, Schenectady, missing since November 9. An autopsy revealed that the man had died of starvation and exposure. . . . Authorities believe Wlosinski had been on the road and had crawled into a pile of straw at the barn in an attempt to escape from Tuesday night's bitter cold. When found he was about four feet beneath the surface of the straw. He had removed his shoes which were later found in the straw pile. . . . The autopsy showed no trace of foul play, it was said. The victim was emaciated, his stomach and digestive tract were absolutely empty and had shriveled from disuse. A physician said the man had apparently been on a starvation diet for about three weeks.

There was also the unidentified man who stumbled for a moment and then fell to the ground in Grand Circus Park, Detroit, late in the summer of 1931. He was carried to a bench, and there he lay, murmuring half to himself: "I am hungry, I am hungry." An ambulance took him away to Receiving Hospital, where he died soon after. Reports immediately gained currency that people were dropping dead of hunger in the very streets of Detroit. Of course, the reports were just as promptly denied by the Board of Commerce, the municipal authorities, the press, and the pulpit. But sixteen persons had witnessed the incident in Grand Circus Park, and the sixteen were later willing to state upon legal oath that they had heard the man complaining of hunger as he lay upon the bench gasping for breath. One of the witnesses, a graduate nurse, swore that the man when she saw him was actually dying of starvation.

Of course, Chambers of Commerce and city officials will denounce such stories and seek to keep them off the public records. For the facts are too hard, too numerous. Yet this very practice has made it possible for supposedly reputable authorities like Dr. Louis I. Dublin of the Metropolitan Life Insurance Company to assert that "there is no evidence at all that anybody in these United States is starving." *Better Times,* the magazine of the Welfare Council of New York City, assigned Miss Eleanor Flexner to determine whether there was any truth in this statement. She discovered, as was to have been expected, that the records of the Bureau of Vital Statistics covering the year 1931 showed only two deaths from starvation in New York City. But she also discovered that on the records of the four largest hospitals of the city covering the same year there were listed ninety-five cases of starvation, frankly recorded as such. And of these ninety-five, twenty died in hospital.

So we cannot depend upon the public records. We must search elsewhere for this information. We must turn to the statements and reports of investigators like Miss Flexner, to the reports of social workers, trained journalists, neighborhood physicians, and other eyewitnesses. From them we can learn the history of the thousands of cases of starvation that have been found and competently verified. Not that they have been able to cover the field completely, for that has clearly been impossible. Moreover, as

Miss Flexner explained in her report, "a starvation case is more than likely to be suffering from an infection of some kind at the same time. If the starving person dies, death may be credited to pneumonia or some other disease, but none the less starvation is the primary cause." Nor would all of these cases find their way at once into the public records, for, as J. Prentice Murphy, a social worker of Philadelphia, pointed out to the Senate Committee on Manufactures, hungry people "do not die quickly. You can starve for a long while without dying."

Yet enough evidence has been uncovered to damn as falsehoods the absurd statements of United States senators and governors of various states that "nobody is suffering from hunger and cold." On the records of the Welfare Council of New York City, for example, appears the following report concerning a family in the Brownsville section of Brooklyn: "Family reported starving by neighbors. Investigator found five small children home while mother was out looking for vegetables under pushcarts. Family had moved into one room. Father sleeping at Municipal Lodging House because he could get more to eat there than at home and frequently brought food home from there in pockets for children and wife. Only other food they had for weeks came from under pushcarts." Again, in the same city, Patrolman Louis Lubliner, answering an emergency sick call at 194 Hull Street, Brooklyn, found a family of six "in destitute circumstances and without heat or food." Mrs. Henry Breuers of Staten Island was evicted from her home for nonpayment of rent, and as she stood outside the building, her belongings piled all around her, her ten-months-old baby died in her arms—from "malnutrition," the doctor said.

Joseph Gallagher, a jobless laborer of Fitchburg, Massachusetts, died in the police station at Greenfield "of heart trouble superinduced by hunger and privation." On one day in April 1932 there were thirteen unidentified bodies in the Boston city morgue—bodies of men who had died of hunger after collapsing on the streets or who had committed suicide in desperation, as Mayor James M. Curley frankly admitted. Social workers found Mrs. Jean Browne and her three children starving on Pittsburgh's north side. "She had sold the mattress from her bed and the carpets from the floor," according to the Federated Press. "The children beg potatoes from the neighbors to eat raw. . . . Having no carfare, she walks Pittsburgh's tremendous distances, up hill and down vale, looking for jobs, with her baby in her arms. There are no jobs." Michael McNulty, seven months old, also lived in Pittsburgh. His mother had gone without food for so many months that she could no longer nurse him. City Physician Evans was sent to the McNulty home, but the baby died soon after his arrival. "Starvation and malnutrition," the doctor wrote in his report. Mrs. Charles Schmidt was the mother of one of the eleven thousand families dropped from the food and milk list in the Detroit government's drive for municipal economy and a balanced budget during the summer of 1931. Her husband had been without work for thirteen months. Mrs. Schmidt took her son, Albert, five years old, into the kitchen and turned on the gas. Albert was dead, but she was still living when the police rescue squad broke into the house. "I don't know what I am going to give the children to eat," said a note she had written for her husband. "They are already half starved. I think it best to go into eternity and take little Albert along. Please do not take it too hard."

From Kentucky there have come across my desk scores of letters, all-too-human documents, of which the following is typical:

> We have been eating wild greens since January this year, such as Polk salad. Violet tops, wild onions. forget me-not wild lettuce and such weeds as cows eat as cows wont eat a poison weeds. Our family are in bad shape childrens need milk women need nurishments food shoes and dresses—that we cannot get. and there at least 10,000 hungry People in Harlan County daily. I know because I am one off them. . . . I would leave Harlan County if I only had $6.00 to send my wife and boy to Bristol-Va and I could walk away—But I cant clear a dollar per month that Is why I am here. that why houndreds are here they cant ship their family's home. But I am Glad we can find a few wild greens to eat. . . . I borrow this postage to send you this informations.

On the very day that Bishop Edwin Holt Hughes of the Chicago area of the Methodist Episcopal Church was declaring that the chief problem of the economic crisis was "not so much a matter of keeping the wolf from the home but keeping the wolf from the garage," John Reyee of Cicero, a suburb of Chicago, was arrested, to quote the Cicero *Herald,* "because he struck a man who tried to wedge into a food line at the garbage dump located at 32nd and Cicero Avenue. . . . Lines form every day at the garbage dump from eight in the morning to five in the afternoon, awaiting truckloads of city refuse that is dumped there daily. Men and women come there to see if they can't find food to carry back home with them. They get some, if they come early enough." And even nearer Bishop Hughes's front door is Chicago's new wholesale produce-distributing center, where, as described by the Federated Press, one could observe every afternoon, as the depression wore on, "hundreds of hungry workers, most of them ragged, bearing sacks, paper bags, small boxes. Some have two-wheeled carts. They are Americans, Mexicans, Poles—every nationality is represented. They are old and young, Negro and white. They are the scavengers of Chicago's model market. Hungrily they fill their receptacles with the refuse which they find in heaps in the alley, alongside trucks or under the loading platform. The food they pick out of the garbage heap is in various stages of decay. But hunger and pride do not go together—and parts of the decaying vegetables are edible. Some of the garbage they eat in the alley, biting into the rotten fruit with the eagerness of hungry people. Most of the garbage which they collect is put away in their bags for other hungry ones at home."

In the summer of 1932 Narcisso Sandoval, four years old, starved to death in Oakland, California. He died despite the explanation of the Associated Charities of Oakland that there was "no reason" why the children of Fidel Sandoval should have been hungry. "We sent them grocery orders right along," it was stated. "Of course, the orders were low because our funds have been low, but they should have been sufficient for a family of that size." But even the conservative San Francisco *Chronicle* could not accept this explanation.

> Failing to receive sufficient food from the Associated Charities [said the *Chronicle* on July 1, 1932], little Narcisso Sandoval, 4, who with four other members of his family had been subsisting on castaway food picked up near commission houses, was dead in Oakland last night. . . . The boy died in the Central Emergency Hospital from quick pneumonia, believed the result of malnutrition. His sister Anna, 12, is in the same hospital also believed to be dying. A third child, Margaret, 7, is in an adjoining bed, battling for her life. And from the lips of the distraught mother, Mrs. Fidel Sandoval, pours bitter accusation. . . .
>
> The woman speaks very little English, but through an interpreter she made herself clear to hospital attaches. "What we got from the Associated Charities was so little we were hungry all the time," she said. "We talked it over, my husband and myself—he said there was lots of good food back of commission houses, vegetables that fall from wagons. We went there and got those things. Sometimes we would get bread and meat in back of restaurants. . . . We were hungry. The children were hungry. We could not watch them cry. So we got the best we could find. Some of the meat was not always good, but sometimes we found very good vegetables."

One could go on citing similar cases almost without end. Or one could reproduce headlines telling of "THOUSANDS OF HUNGRY NEW YORKERS TURNED AWAY UNFED." Or Associated Press dispatches such as the following from Clinton, Massachusetts:

> More than 300 men, women, and crying children crowded the corridors of the Town Hall today appealing for food. The town treasury has been exhausted, banks have declined to lend Clinton money, and town officials were forced to turn the applicants away empty handed.

These are only a few instances of actual hunger and starvation taken at random. But they are sufficient to show the utter falsity of the common belief so often voiced by more comfortably circumstanced Americans that there has been no widespread privation and want in the country.

People You Really Know

Nor has hunger touched only those millions who normally stand at the lowest level of the economic scale. The proletarian class has always suffered from want, even in the heyday of our fabled prosperity, as we shall presently see. But the most significant social development of the crisis has been the economic collapse of the lower middle-class, of the countless thousands, if not millions, of petit-bourgeois families who have slid all the way to the bottom, having lost not only their jobs, but their homes, automobiles, furniture, radios, clothing, savings, and everything else—except their faith in the State, which has had and will continue to have an important bearing on the course of American politics.

Shortly before the bank panic of 1933 I received a letter from a man who was once an important newspaper executive, a former employer of mine, asking me where, in God's name, he could find a job. A few days later, while waiting for a train in the Pennsylvania Station in New York City, I was approached by a man who identified himself as an industrial chemist from Rockford, Illinois. He said he did not want charity, that he wasn't really hungry, though his appearance belied his words. He wanted only to know if I could help him. He showed me his credentials, talked about Rockford and Chicago. He said he had lost his home eighteen months before. In the previous two years and a half he had had only three weeks' work. Had he a family? Yes, a wife and two children; they were at home with her parents, or at least so he hoped. He had drifted for more than a year, had not written to his family for months, was ashamed to write home; they would not know where to find him. Again he spurned my charity. But was there no job anywhere in New York for an experienced chemist with two college degrees, for a man willing to take any kind of work?

Mrs. S— wrote to explain why she could not renew her magazine subscription. She said that her husband, an electrical engineer, had worked eighteen years for the General Electric Company—"the best years of his life"—only to be reduced when the hard times came to accepting a job as night fireman in an apartment house, thirteen hours of hard work every night, at seventy-five dollars a month, a small sum upon which to feed and clothe a family of four people who had been accustomed to a much higher standard of living. And this new job was to last only a few weeks longer. "I have tried in vain to get a job myself," Mrs. S— continued, "any kind of an honest job that I would be able to find, but because I have not been a servant before, and have no recommendations, I cannot get any. We have lost all, both position and hope, and worst of all our faith in human beings generally. People who have not tried it do not know what humiliations one is out for as unemployed. It feels like a crime one is innocent of."

Langlan Heinz, forty-four years old, told his story in the court of Magistrate Jacob Eilperin. He had been found asleep on a dump in Brooklyn and had been arrested on a charge of vagrancy. His bed he had made himself out of automobile parts and other junk. He was a university graduate who had worked for years as a construction engineer; for seven years he had been employed by the city of New York. Literally down to his last dime after months of unavailing search for work, he had come upon the dump pile in Brooklyn and had decided to make that his home. From this place of residence he departed early every morning to tramp the streets looking for a job. He said he averaged eighteen miles a day. When the arresting officer found him, he was sleeping under a blanket, and beside him was a bag of buns. The blanket had been given him by the firemen on duty at an engine-house nearby, and the buns had been brought to him by a group of students from James Madison High School.

But such tales as these, tragic individual and family histories of which I have personal knowledge, could be duplicated many times over. For unemployment, bank failures, the drop in security values, and the collapse of the suburban real-estate market have taken heavy toll in the middle class, have indeed reached up to the topmost level of that class to pull down by the thousands families who, whatever might happen to other people, thought themselves permanently secured against all the eccentricities of our economic system. As a writer in the *American Mercury* expressed it: "You used to think of unemployment as something that happened to your washerwoman's husband; now it's happening all about you, to people you really know!" and it is among these people you really know that there have been sowed the most fruitful seeds of revolt.

"The Farmers Go on Strike": A Sympathetic Account, 1932

Depression was most distressingly written on the faces of hungry children, most dishearteningly symbolized in the slumped shoulders and downcast eyes of the thousands on the breadlines. There was a tendency to identify with the city the dangers of instability, radicalism, and new ways. In fact, it was the farmer who had suffered longest. Farm misery was sometimes veiled from the uncritical outsider by the too obvious fact that a farmer could at least grow his own food, at least keep a roof over his head. By the summer of 1932 the veil had been rent. Tens of thousands of farmers, all over the country but especially in the wheat and corn belts of the Middle West, were losing their land by mortgage foreclosure and joining the swelling ranks of the rootless and harried wanderers of whom John Steinbeck was soon to write in The Grapes of Wrath.

If farm misery destroyed one romantic myth about industrial depression, the farmers' activities shattered another. For it was not the propertyless slum dweller but the American farmer, close to the soil, untouched by urban agitation and alien ideology, often a proud descendant of revolutionary or colonial families, who took the most radical action and demanded the most extreme policies. Donald Murphy's picture of direct farm tactics at Sioux City describes the nature of this direct action but merely suggests its scope. For broader-gauged descriptions of America's reaction to the Depression, see Dixon Wecter, The Age of the Great Depression: 1929–1941 *(1948), Arthur M. Schlesinger, Jr.,* Crisis of the Old Order *(1956), and David Shannon,* The Great Depression *(1960).*

The article printed below is by Donald R. Murphy, "The Farmers Go on Strike: Part I, The Blockade of Sioux City," New Republic, *volume 72, August 31, 1932, pages 66–68.*

On a paved road in northwestern Iowa, a truck loaded with cream cans bowls along. Suddenly a log-chain stretched between two trees bars the road.

From the sides of the highway, where they have been lounging under the trees in the tall grass, a dozen tanned men, the leader waving a red flag, bar the road. There are pitchforks handy for puncturing tires, rocks for cracking wind shields, clubs to persuade the truck driver.

"Where you bound?"

"Sioux City."

"What you got?"

"Cream."

"Turn around and git outa here. Don't you know the Farmers' Holiday is on?"

Usually the truck backs up. Sometimes the driver takes a chance and tries to break through. A few of these chance-takers have finally retreated with broken windshields and punctured tires. The cream has been dumped in the road.

This is a picture of the most dramatic phase of the Farmers' Holiday—the attempt of a group of Middle Western farmers to enforce a strike designed to stop the movement of all farm products to market.

In a dozen counties in northwestern Iowa, and to a lesser degree in other counties, farmers are picketing the roads and stopping shipments. In several small towns produce buyers have agreed to shut up shop during the holiday. Elevators are considering refusing to buy grain until the holiday is over. Up in the Sioux City area special deputies have been sworn in and are riding a few trucks daily through the picket line.

In some cases truck drivers and farmers refuse to accept protection by deputies and stay home. "I've got to stay on living here," said one. "I guess I'll leave the truck in the shed for a while." Leaders of the strike, disclaiming any desire to use violence, insist that social ostracism of strike breakers will hold farmers in line. A farmer with hostile neighbors is helpless at threshing and at silo-filling time.

The strike is the culmination of a growing sense of injustice by corn-belt farmers. Specifically it is the response to years of exhortation by Milo Reno, veteran leader of the Iowa Farmers' Union, and his associates. For years, Reno has told farmers that eventually they would have to go on strike and starve city people into giving the farmer a square deal. The farmers that are supporting the holiday have backed the old McNary-Haugen bill, the more recent Frazier bill to refinance farm mortgages at a low rate of interest and other farm legislation of a so-called "radical" type. They have seen these bills beaten and have watched farm prices go down and down since the big crash in 1920. For them the depression has lasted, not three years, but twelve.

This year farms are being taken over by mortgage holders at an increasing rate. Renters are finding that this year's crops will not pay cash rent. Farm buying power is down to 50 percent of the pre-war average.

To many farmers, it seemed that the time for direct action had come. Early this spring the Iowa Farmers' Union, traditional leader of left-wing movements in farm affairs, began to discuss plans for a Farmers' Holiday during which all farmers would be pledged to refuse to sell any farm products. The agitation was continued, mainly in Iowa but also in several other Midwestern states, through the summer. Organizers carried pledge cards for farmers to sign. Finally the Iowa strike was called to start August 8.

In a manifesto adopted by farmers from Iowa, North and South Dakota,

Illinois, Minnesota and Nebraska, at a meeting in Des Moines, August 15, the organizers of the movement said:

> Self-preservation is still the first law of nature and we agree to keep all of our products which can possibly be kept on the farms and hold same until the time shall have arrived when farm products shall bring a market price equal to the cost of production.
>
> We pledge ourselves to protect one another in the actual possession of our necessary homes, livestock and machinery as against all claimants.

What is "cost of production?" The Farmers' Union works it out this way: Allow the farmer 5 percent on his investment in real estate, 7 percent on investments in personal property and equipment and $100 a month for his own labor. To obtain this return, the union figures that on an average 160-acre Iowa farm with normal production, prices would have to be about as follows: ninety-two cents a bushel for corn, forty-nine cents a bushel for oats, $11.25 for hogs, thirty-five cents a dozen for eggs and sixty-two cents a pound for butter fat. On Monday, August 8, when the Farmers' Holiday was supposed to start, the farm prices on these products were: twenty-two cents for corn, eleven cents for oats, $3.85 for hogs, fifteen cents for eggs and eighteen cents for butter fat.

The call for the holiday directed farmers to stay off the market for thirty days or until prices reached "cost of production." Iowa was to start the ball rolling. Minnesota, Illinois and South Dakota were expected to come in the second or third week. North Dakota and Nebraska were also listed as prospects.

The first week of the strike in Iowa showed few results. Receipts of farm products at the different markets dropped off little if at all. In the second week, however, a new factor entered. The milk producers at Sioux City, who are getting only two cents a quart for whole milk, went on strike. These farmers began to hold up milk trucks and dump the milk.

The area around Sioux City has a good many Farmers' Union members and many more supporters of the Farmers' Holiday. These farmers seized the opportunity opened by the milk strike, joined the milk-strike pickets and began to stop, not only milk trucks, but trucks carrying any farm produce to town. The movement spread to an area including many of the counties in northwestern Iowa. Picketing, sometimes accompanied by mass action to turn back trucks, was common on many main highways. Even in northwestern Iowa, however, many towns were unaffected by the movement.

It is not entirely an accident that the area in which the Farmers' Holiday is strongest is roughly the same as the area of recent Bank Holidays. In this section lately, banks have adopted an extra-legal device to protect themselves against frightened depositors. They have persuaded the mayor in each town to declare a holiday, with all business houses closed, for a week or ten-day period. During this time, crews of business men have made the rounds of the depositors and obtained statements from them permitting the bank to retain the deposits for a period of some months, with the depositor not being allowed to check out any of his money except in specified small amounts.

The campaign to get these statements from depositors has been handled like the old Liberty Loan drives. Farmers reluctant to give up their deposits because they had been accumulated to meet interest or taxes, have been harassed by teams of solicitors until they signed. In cases where farmers have refused to sign, and banks have reopened, the banks have refused to let the non-signers have their money.

The Bank Holiday has furnished a fine argument for the backers of the Farmers' Holiday. They have used it vigorously. Even conservative farmers who take no part in the Farmers' Holiday movement seem pleased to see the bankers squirm when their own trick is turned against them.

Right now, in the third week of the Iowa strike, the usual guess is that the holiday will be confined to northwestern Iowa. The amount of produce going to market in that section is being cut down, but not enough to affect prices. If the balance of the state and other states join in, some real reduction in the flow of produce to market might be obtained. Of course, even if this should happen, the resultant rise in the price of farm products would hardly help the holiday supporters. The better prices would go to the farmers who continue to sell their products. As soon as the holiday backers would throw their products on the market again, any scarcity-induced rise in prices would collapse and the holiday backers would get the resulting low prices. The backers of the holiday claim that once higher prices are obtained they will be maintained by a system of feeding farm products into the market gradually.

In the long run the pledge of these farmers to protect each other against foreclosure may turn out to be more important than the strike. Certainly, even if the holiday ends with no real results, the irritation of farm people against low prices will not cease. There will be another outbreak. It may logically take the form of neighborhood defense against foreclosures. Such a program would have considerably more backing than the present strike. Even now, conservative farmers who see no success in the holiday movement express considerable sympathy for the project or for any project aimed at raising farm prices and keeping farmers on their own farms.

Farmers have submitted with surprising meekness to a long period of deflation. Orthodox and conservative, they have followed the conventional methods of trying to obtain reform by petitioning Congress for action. Instead of getting help, they have seen Coolidge veto two McNary-Haugen bills, and have seen Hoover block farm bills at the last session. Meanwhile farm prices have slipped lower and lower; farmer after farmer has met foreclosure, and no serious attempt—or so it seems to farmers—has been made by those in power to improve conditions. After twelve years of this, it relieves a farmer's feelings a good deal to throw a rock through a windshield or to take any positive step, no matter how futile it may ultimately prove to be, that seems to lead toward better prices.

The Farmers' Holiday will probably fail in obtaining any substantial reduction of the flow of farm products to market; it will undoubtedly fail in an attempt to affect prices to any extent. It remains, however, a significant symptom of the state of mind of a great conservative class which has borne depression for twelve years and which is finally ready to employ radical measures that seem to give it a chance to save itself from general bankruptcy. Unless farm prices go up this will not be the last outbreak in the corn belt.

SELECTION 

Challenge and Hope: Franklin D. Roosevelt's Speech at the Commonwealth Club, San Francisco, California, 1932

The American political calendar is sometimes almost unbearably rigid. So it seemed to many as 1930, 1931, and 1932 wore on. Whether Hoover was in part responsible for the origins and depths of the crisis was almost irrelevant. What was important was the general loss of confidence in his leadership. The 1932 election called, at last, for new options.

It fell to the Democratic party to furnish them. Republicans, caught by tradition and logic, were forced to the hapless expedient of renominating Herbert Hoover. The Depression gave the Democratic party its issues; it may have tipped the political balances to assure the nomination of a Franklin Roosevelt, rather than a John N. Garner or an Alfred E. Smith. And the Depression worked powerfully upon the candidate himself, driving him to a greater concern for the general welfare, to a larger concept of governmental power and presidential leadership, and to a more dynamic concept of politics than he had ever imagined. But much of this would appear only gradually throughout his four terms. For the moment, in the campaign of 1932, FDR worked joyously, but carefully, to create great national enthusiasm without unnecessarily dividing or alienating the massive support he had inherited from Hoover's misfortune. In the campaign there was much vagueness—glittering generalities for the farmers at Topeka—pious clichés for the workingmen at Detroit. And there was some inconsistency—the promise everywhere of grand new action against economic collapse, and the promise at Pittsburgh of balanced budgets and economy in government. In the welter of rhetoric there shows through one remarkable speech which must be read if all others must be left aside. It was remarkable because it was prophetic of the actual New Deal in ways that no other speech was. It was remarkable also because it betrayed clearly the fundamental, rather pessimistic assumptions upon which Roosevelt's concept of his evolving economic policy would be based.

For the 1932 campaign, see, in addition to Schlesinger's work, Frank Freidel, Franklin D. Roosevelt: The Triumph *(1956); James MacGregor Burns,* Roosevelt: The Lion and the Fox *(1956); and Alfred B. Rollins, Jr.,* Roosevelt and Howe *(1962).*

The Commonwealth Club speech may be found in Samuel Rosenman, (ed.), The Public Papers and Addresses of Franklin D. Roosevelt, Volume One: The Genesis of the New Deal, 1928–1932 *(New York: Random House, 1938), pages 742–756.*

I want to speak not of politics but of Government. I want to speak not of parties, but of universal principles. They are not political, except in that larger sense in which a great American once expressed a definition of politics, that nothing in all of human life is foreign to the science of politics.

I do want to give you, however, a recollection of a long life spent for a large part in public office. Some of my conclusions and observations have been deeply accentuated in these past few weeks. I have traveled far—from Albany to the Golden Gate. I have seen many people, and heard many things, and today, when in a sense my journey has reached the half-way mark, I am glad of the opportunity to discuss with you what it all means to me.

Sometimes, my friends, particularly in years such as these, the hand of discouragement falls upon us. It seems that things are in a rut, fixed, settled, that the world has grown old and tired and very much out of joint. This is the mood of depression, of dire and weary depression.

But then we look around us in America, and everything tells us that we are wrong. America is new. It is in the process of change and development. It has the great potentialities of youth, and particularly is this true of the great West, and of this coast, and of California.

I would not have you feel that I regard this as in any sense a new community. I have traveled in many parts of the world, but never have I felt the arresting thought of the change and development more than here, where the old, mystic East would seem to be near to us, where the currents of life and thought and commerce of the whole world meet us. This factor alone is sufficient to cause man to stop and think of the deeper meaning of things, when he stands in this community.

But more than that, I appreciate that the membership of this club consists of men who are thinking in terms beyond the immediate present, beyond their own immediate tasks, beyond their own individual interests. I want to invite you, therefore, to consider with me in the large, some of the relationships of Government and economic life that go deeply into our daily lives, our happiness, our future and our security.

The issue of Government has always been whether individual men and women will have to serve some system of Government or economics, or whether a system of Government and economics exists to serve individual men and women. This question has persistently dominated the discussion of Government for many generations. On questions relating to these things men have differed, and for time immemorial it is probable that honest men will continue to differ.

The final word belongs to no man; yet we can still believe in change and in progress. Democracy, as a dear old friend of mine in Indiana, Meredith Nicholson, has called it, is a quest, a never-ending seeking for better things, and in the seeking for these things and the striving for them, there are many roads to follow. But, if we map the course of these roads, we find that there are only two general directions.

When we look about us, we are likely to forget how hard people have worked to win the privilege of Government. The growth of the national Governments of Europe was a struggle for the development of a centralized force in the Nation, strong enough to impose peace upon ruling barons.

In many instances the victory of the central Government, the creation of a strong central Government, was a haven of refuge to the individual. The people preferred the master far away to the exploitation and cruelty of the smaller master near at hand.

But the creators of national Government were perforce ruthless men. They were often cruel in their methods, but they did strive steadily toward something that society needed and very much wanted, a strong central State able to keep the peace, to stamp out civil war, to put the unruly nobleman in his place, and to permit the bulk of individuals to live safely. The man of ruthless force had his place in developing a pioneer country, just as he did in fixing the power of the central Government in the development of Nations. Society paid him well for his services and its development. When the development among the Nations of Europe, however, had been completed, ambition and ruthlessness, having served their term, tended to overstep their mark.

There came a growing feeling that Government was conducted for the benefit of a few who thrived unduly at the expense of all. The people sought a balancing—a limiting force. There came gradually, through town councils, trade guilds, national parliaments, by constitution and by popular participation and control, limitations on arbitrary power.

Another factor that tended to limit the power of those who ruled, was the rise of the ethical conception that a ruler bore a responsibility for the welfare of his subjects.

The American colonies were born in this struggle. The American Revolution was a turning point in it. After the Revolution the struggle continued and shaped itself in the public life of the country. There were those who because they had seen the confusion which attended the years of war for American independence surrendered to the belief that popular Government was essentially dangerous and essentially unworkable. They were honest people, my friends, and we cannot deny that their experience had warranted some measure of fear. The most brilliant, honest and able exponent of this point of view was Hamilton. He was too impatient of slow-moving methods. Fundamentally he believed that the safety of the republic lay in the autocratic strength of its Government, that the destiny of individuals was to serve that Government, and that fundamentally a great and strong group of central institutions, guided by a small group of able and public spirited citizens, could best direct all Government.

But Mr. Jefferson, in the summer of 1776, after drafting the Declaration of Independence turned his mind to the same problem and took a different view. He did not deceive himself with outward forms. Government to him was a means to an end, not an end in itself; it might be either a refuge and a help or a threat and a danger, depending on the circumstances. We find him carefully analyzing the society for which he was to organize a Government. "We have no paupers. The great mass of our population is of laborers, our rich who cannot live without labor, either manual or professional, being few and of moderate wealth. Most of the laboring class possess property, cultivate their own lands, have families and from the demand for their labor, are enabled to exact from the rich and the competent such prices as enable them to feed abundantly, clothe above mere decency, to labor moderately and raise their families."

These people, he considered, had two sets of rights, those of "personal competency" and those involved in acquiring and possessing property. By "personal competency" he meant the right of free thinking, freedom of forming and expressing opinions, and freedom of personal living, each man according to his own lights. To insure the first set of rights, a Government must so order its functions as not to interfere with the individual. But even Jefferson realized that the exercise of the property rights might so interfere with the rights of the individual that the Government, without whose assistance the property rights could not exist, must intervene, not to destroy individualism, but to protect it.

You are familiar with the great political duel which followed; and how Hamilton, and his friends, building toward a dominant centralized power were at length defeated in the great election of 1800, by Mr. Jefferson's party. Out of that duel came the two parties, Republican and Democratic, as we know them today.

So began, in American political life, the new day, the day of the individual against the system, the day in which individualism was made the great watchword of American life. The happiest of economic conditions made that day long and splendid. On the Western frontier, land was substantially free. No one, who did not shirk the task of earning a living, was entirely without opportunity to do so. Depressions could, and did, come and go; but they could not alter the fundamental fact that most of the people lived partly by selling their labor and partly by extracting their livelihood from the soil, so that starvation and dislocation were practically impossible. At the very worst there was always the possibility of climbing into a covered wagon and moving west where the untilled prairies afforded a haven for men to whom the East did not provide a place. So great were our natural resources that we could offer this relief not only to our own people, but to the distressed of all the world; we could invite immigration from Europe, and welcome it with open arms. Traditionally, when a depression came a new section of land was opened in the West; and even our temporary misfortune served our manifest destiny.

It was in the middle of the nineteenth century that a new force was released and a new dream created. The force was what is called the industrial revolution, the advance of steam and machinery and the rise of the forerunners of the modern industrial plant. The dream was the dream of an economic machine, able to raise the standard of living for everyone; to bring luxury within the reach of the humblest; to annihilate distance by steam power and later by electricity, and to release everyone from the drudgery of the heaviest manual toil. It was to be expected that this would necessarily affect Government. Heretofore, Government had merely been called upon to produce conditions within which people could live happily, labor peacefully, and rest secure. Now it was called upon to aid in the consummation of this new dream. There was, however, a shadow over the dream. To be made real, it required use of the talents of men of tremendous will and tremendous ambition, since by no other force could the problems of financing and engineering and new developments be brought to a consummation.

So manifest were the advantages of the machine age, however, that the United States fearlessly, cheerfully, and, I think, rightly, accepted the bitter with the sweet. It was thought that no price was too high to pay for the advantages which we could draw from a finished industrial system. The history of the last half century is accordingly in large measure a history of a group of financial Titans, whose methods were not scrutinized with too much care, and who were honored in proportion as they produced the results, irrespective of the means they used. The financiers who pushed the railroads to the Pacific were always ruthless, often wasteful, and frequently corrupt; but they did build railroads, and we have them today. It has been estimated that the American investor paid for the American railway system more than three times over in the process; but despite this fact the net advantage was to the United States. As long as we had free land; as long as population was growing by leaps and bounds; as long as our industrial plants were insufficient to supply our own needs, society chose to give the ambitious man free play and unlimited reward provided only that he produced the economic plant so much desired.

During this period of expansion, there was equal opportunity for all and the business of Government was not to interfere but to assist in the development of industry. This was done at the request of business men themselves. The tariff was originally imposed for the purpose of "fostering our infant industry," a phrase I think the older among you will remember as a political issue not so long ago. The railroads were subsidized, sometimes by grants of money, oftener by grants of land; some of the most valuable oil lands in the United States were granted to assist the financing of the railroad which pushed through the Southwest. A nascent merchant marine was assisted by grants of money, or by mail subsidies, so that our steam shipping might ply the seven seas. Some of my friends tell me that they do not want the Government in business. With this I agree; but I wonder whether they realize the implications of the past. For while it has been American doctrine that the Government must not go into business in competition with private enterprises, still it has been traditional, particularly in Republican administrations, for business urgently to ask the Government to put at private disposal all kinds of Government assistance. The same man who tells you that he does not want to see the Government interfere in business—and he means it, and has plenty of good reasons for saying so—is the first to go to Washington and ask the Government for a prohibitory tariff on his product. When things get just bad enough, as they did two years ago, he will go with equal speed to the United States Government and ask for a loan; and the Reconstruction Finance Corporation is the outcome of it. Each group has sought protection from the Government for its own special interests, without realizing that the function of Government must be to favor no small group at the expense of its duty to protect the rights of personal freedom and of private property of all its citizens.

In retrospect we can now see that the turn of the tide came with the turn of the century. We were reaching our last frontier; there was no more free land and our industrial combinations had become great uncontrolled and irresponsible units of power within the State. Clear-sighted men saw with fear the danger that opportunity would no longer be equal; that the growing corporation, like the feudal baron of old, might threaten the economic freedom of individuals to earn a living. In that hour, our anti-trust laws were born. The cry was raised against the great corporations.

Theodore Roosevelt, the first great Republican Progressive, fought a Presidential campaign on the issue of "trust busting" and talked freely about malefactors of great wealth. If the Government had a policy it was rather to turn the clock back, to destroy the large combinations and to return to the time when every man owned his individual small business.

This was impossible; Theodore Roosevelt, abandoning the idea of "trust busting," was forced to work out a difference between "good" trusts and "bad" trusts. The Supreme Court set forth the famous "rule of reason" by which it seems to have meant that a concentration of industrial power was permissible if the method by which it got its power, and the use it made of that power, were reasonable.

Woodrow Wilson, elected in 1912, saw the situation more clearly. Where Jefferson had feared the encroachment of political power on the lives of individuals, Wilson knew that the new power was financial. He saw, in the highly centralized economic system, the despot of the twentieth century, on whom great masses of individuals relied for their safety and their livelihood, and whose irresponsibility and greed (if they were not controlled) would reduce them to starvation and penury. The concentration of financial power had not proceeded so far in 1912 as it has today; but it had grown far enough for Mr. Wilson to realize fully its implications. It is interesting, now, to read his speeches. What is called "radical" today (and I have reason to know whereof I speak) is mild compared to the campaign of Mr. Wilson. "No man can deny," he said, "that the lines of endeavor have more and more narrowed and stiffened; no man who knows anything about the development of industry in this country can have failed to observe that the larger kinds of credit are more and more difficult to obtain unless you obtain them upon terms of uniting your efforts with those who already control the industry of the country, and nobody can fail to observe that every man who tries to set himself up in competition with any process of manufacture which has taken place under the control of large combinations of capital will presently find himself either squeezed out or obliged to sell and allow himself to be absorbed." Had there been no World War—had Mr. Wilson been able to devote eight years to domestic instead of to international affairs—we might have had a wholly different situation at the present time. However, the then distant roar of European cannon, growing ever louder, forced him to abandon the study of this issue. The problem he saw so clearly is left with us as a legacy; and no one of us on either side of the political controversy can deny that it is a matter of grave concern to the Government.

A glance at the situation today only too clearly indicates that equality of opportunity as we have known it no longer exists. Our industrial plant is built; the problem just now is whether under existing conditions it is not overbuilt. Our last frontier has long since been reached, and there is practically no more free land. More than half of our people do not live on the farms or on lands and cannot derive a living by cultivating their own property. There is no safety valve in the form of a Western prairie to which those thrown out of work by the Eastern economic machines can go for a new start. We are not able to invite the immigration from Europe to share our endless plenty. We are now providing a drab living for our own people.

Our system of constantly rising tariffs has at last reacted against us to the point of closing our Canadian frontier on the north, our European markets on the east, many of our Latin-American markets to the south, and a goodly proportion of our Pacific markets on the west, through the retaliatory tariffs of those countries. It has forced many of our great industrial institutions which exported their surplus production to such countries, to establish plants in such countries, within the tariff walls. This has resulted in the reduction of the operation of their American plants, and opportunity for employment.

Just as freedom to farm has ceased, so also the opportunity in business has narrowed. It still is true that men can start small enterprises, trusting to native shrewdness and ability to keep abreast of competitors; but area after area has been preempted altogether by the great corporations, and even in the fields which still have no great concerns, the small man starts under a handicap. The unfeeling statistics of the past three decades show that the independent business man is running a losing race. Perhaps he is forced to the wall; perhaps he cannot command credit; perhaps he is "squeezed out," in Mr. Wilson's words, by highly organized corporate competitors, as your corner grocery man can tell you. Recently a careful study was made of the concentration of business in the United States. It showed that our economic life was dominated by some six hundred odd corporations who controlled two-thirds of American industry. Ten million small business men divided the other third. More striking still, it appeared that if the process of concentration goes on at the same rate, at the end of another century we shall have all American industry controlled by a dozen corporations, and run by perhaps a hundred men. Put plainly, we are steering a steady course toward economic oligarchy, if we are not there already.

Clearly, all this calls for a re-appraisal of values. A mere builder of more industrial plants, a creator of more railroad systems, an organizer of more corporations, is as likely to be a danger as a help. The day of the great promoter or the financial Titan, to whom we granted anything if only he would build, or develop, is over. Our task now is not discovery or exploitation of natural resources, or necessarily producing more goods. It is the soberer, less dramatic business of administering resources and plants already in hand, of seeking to reestablish foreign markets for our surplus production, of meeting the problem of underconsumption, of adjusting production to consumption, of distributing wealth and products more equitably, of adapting existing economic organizations to the service of the people. The day of enlightened administration has come.

Just as in older times the central Government was first a haven of refuge, and then a threat, so now in a closer economic system the central and ambitious financial unit is no longer a servant of national desire, but a danger. I would draw the parallel one step farther. We did not think because national Government had become a threat in the 18th century that therefore we should abandon the principle of national Government. Nor today should we abandon the principle of strong economic units called corporations, merely because their power is susceptible of easy abuse. In other times we dealt with the problem of an unduly ambitious central Government by modifying it gradually into a constitutional democratic

Government. So today we are modifying and controlling our economic units.

As I see it, the task of Government in its relation to business is to assist the development of an economic declaration of rights, an economic constitutional order. This is the common task of statesman and business man. It is the minimum requirement of a more permanently safe order of things.

Happily, the times indicate that to create such an order not only is the proper policy of Government, but it is the only line of safety for our economic structures as well. We know, now, that these economic units cannot exist unless prosperity is uniform, that is, unless purchasing power is well distributed throughout every group in the Nation. That is why even the most selfish of corporations for its own interest would be glad to see wages restored and unemployment ended and to bring the Western farmer back to his accustomed level of prosperity and to assure a permanent safety to both groups. That is why some enlightened industries themselves endeavor to limit the freedom of action of each man and business group within the industry in the common interest of all; why business men everywhere are asking a form of organization which will bring the scheme of things into balance, even though it may in some measure qualify the freedom of action of individual units within the business.

The exposition need not further be elaborated. It is brief and incomplete, but you will be able to expand it in terms of your own business or occupation without difficulty. I think everyone who has actually entered the economic struggle—which means everyone who was not born to safe wealth—knows in his own experience and his own life that we have now to apply the earlier concepts of American Government to the conditions of today.

The Declaration of Independence discusses the problem of Government in terms of a contract. Government is a relation of give and take, a contract, perforce, if we would follow the thinking out of which it grew. Under such a contract rulers were accorded power, and the people consented to that power on consideration that they be accorded certain rights. The task of statesmanship has always been the re-definition of these rights in terms of a changing and growing social order. New conditions impose new requirements upon Government and those who conduct Government.

I held, for example, in proceedings before me as Governor, the purpose of which was the removal of the Sheriff of New York, that under modern conditions it was not enough for a public official merely to evade the legal terms of official wrong-doing. He owed a positive duty as well. I said in substance that if he had acquired large sums of money, he was when accused required to explain the sources of such wealth. To that extent this wealth was colored with a public interest. I said that in financial matters, public servants should, even beyond private citizens, be held to a stern and uncompromising rectitude.

I feel that we are coming to a view through the drift of our legislation and our public thinking in the past quarter century that private economic power is, to enlarge an old phrase, a public trust as well. I hold that continued enjoyment of that power by an individual or group must depend upon the fulfillment of that trust. The men who have reached the summit of American business life know this best; happily, many of these urge the binding quality of this greater social contract.

The terms of that contract are as old as the Republic, and as new as the new economic order.

Every man has a right to life; and this means that he has also a right to make a comfortable living. He may by sloth or crime decline to exercise that right; but it may not be denied him. We have no actual famine or dearth; our industrial and agricultural mechanism can produce enough and to spare. Our Government formal and informal, political and economic, owes to everyone an avenue to possess himself of a portion of that plenty sufficient for his needs, through his own work.

Every man has a right to his own property; which means a right to be assured, to the fullest extent attainable, in the safety of his savings. By no other means can men carry the burdens of those parts of life which, in the nature of things, afford no chance of labor; childhood, sickness, old age. In all thought of property, this right is paramount; all other property rights must yield to it. If, in accord with this principle, we must restrict the operations of the speculator, the manipulator, even the financier, I believe we must accept the restriction as needful, not to hamper individualism but to protect it.

These two requirements must be satisfied, in the main, by the individuals who claim and hold control of the great industrial and financial combinations which dominate so large a part of our industrial life. They have undertaken to be, not business men, but princes of property. I am not prepared to say that the system which produces them is wrong. I am very clear that they must fearlessly and competently assume the responsibility which goes with the power. So many enlightened business men know this that the statement would be little more than a platitude, were it not for an added implication.

This implication is, briefly, that the responsible heads of finance and industry instead of acting each for himself, must work together to achieve the common end. They must, where necessary, sacrifice this or that private advantage; and in reciprocal self-denial must seek a general advantage. It is here that formal Government—political Government, if you choose—comes in. Whenever in the pursuit of this objective the lone wolf, the unethical competitor, the reckless promoter, the Ishmael or Insull whose hand is against every man's, declines to join in achieving an end recognized as being for the public welfare, and threatens to drag the industry back to a state of anarchy, the Government may properly be asked to apply restraint. Likewise, should the group ever use its collective power contrary to the public welfare, the Government must be swift to enter and protect the public interest.

The Government should assume the function of economic regulation only as a last resort, to be tried only when private initiative, inspired by high responsibility, with such assistance and balance as Government can give, has finally failed. As yet there has been no final failure, because there has been no attempt; and I decline to assume that this Nation is unable to meet the situation.

The final term of the high contract was for liberty and the pursuit of happiness. We have learned a great deal of both in the past century. We know that individual liberty and individual happiness mean nothing unless both are ordered in the sense that one man's meat is not another man's poison. We know that the old "rights of personal competency," the right to read, to think, to speak, to choose and live a mode of life, must be respected at all hazards. We know that liberty to do anything which deprives others of those elemental rights is outside the protection of any compact; and that Government in this regard is the maintenance of a balance, within which every individual may have a place if he will take it; in which every individual may find safety if he wishes it; in which every individual may attain such power as his ability permits, consistent with his assuming the accompanying responsibility.

All this is a long, slow talk. Nothing is more striking than the simple innocence of the men who insist, whenever an objective is present, on the prompt production of a patent scheme guaranteed to produce a result. Human endeavor is not so simple as that. Government includes the art of formulating a policy, and using the political technique to attain so much of that policy as will receive general support; persuading, leading, sacrificing, teaching always, because the greatest duty of a statesman is to educate. But in the matters of which I have spoken, we are learning rapidly, in a severe school. The lessons so learned must not be forgotten, even in the mental lethargy of a speculative upturn. We must build toward the time when a major depression cannot occur again; and if this means sacrificing the easy profits of inflationist booms, then let them go; and good riddance.

Faith in America, faith in our tradition of personal responsibility, faith in our institutions, faith in ourselves demand that we recognize the new terms of the old social contract. We shall fulfill them, as we fulfilled the obligation of the apparent Utopia which Jefferson imagined for us in 1776, and which Jefferson, Roosevelt and Wilson sought to bring to realization. We must do so, lest a rising tide of misery, engendered by our common failure, engulf us all. But failure is not an American habit; and in the strength of great hope we must all shoulder our common load.

In Defense of Tradition: Herbert Hoover's Speech at Detroit, 1932

Hoover was sadly disadvantaged in the campaign by his failure to resolve the Depression, by the immense rigidity of his own social philosophy, and not least by the traditionalism of his own campaign techniques. He refused to allow others to help with his addresses, had only contempt for a Roosevelt who could get drafts for his speeches from an assembly line and could play on his audience's emotions like a master organist at his instrument. Hoover's talks were dull and long and were entirely written by the President himself in longhand. But they were thorough, logical, and immensely serious, and they constitute an admirable analysis of the economic and political situation, if one can initially accept the premises upon which his thinking was based. If one cannot, they appear a well-meaning but tedious exercise in irrelevancy. Hoover's speeches were all closely related in logic and analysis, and his address at Detroit on October 22 summarizes effectively the whole burden of his campaign.

For Hoover's own picture of the campaign, see The Memoirs of Herbert Hoover: The Great Depression, 1929–1941 *(1952). For other sympathetic portraits, see Harris G. Warren,* Herbert Hoover and the Great Depression *(1959), and Edgar E. Robinson,* The Roosevelt Leadership *(1955). The classic contemporary study was by Roy V. Peel and Thomas C. Donnelly,* The 1932 Campaign: An Analysis *(1935).*

President Hoover's Detroit speech is taken from the New York Times, *October 23, 1932, page 28.*

The most important issue before the American people right now is to overcome this crisis.

What our people need is the restoration of their normal jobs, recovery of agricultural prices and business. They need help in the meantime to tide them over until these things are accomplished, that they may not go hungry nor lose their farms and homes.

I wish to present to you the evidence that the measures and policies of the Republican Administration are winning this major battle for recovery. They are taking care of distress in the meantime. It can be demonstrated that the tide has turned and the gigantic forces of depression are in retreat.

Our measures and policies have demonstrated their effectiveness. They have preserved the American people from certain chaos and have preserved a final fortress of stability in the world. Recovery would have been faster but for four months of paralysis during the Spring months while we were defeating proposals of the Democratic House of Representatives to increase governmental expenses by $3,500,000,000, the issue of fiat money and other destructive legislation.

The battle must be continued. We have yet to go a long way and capture many positions to restore agriculture and employment. But it can be made plain that if the stride we have established is maintained, and the battle not halted by a change in the midst of action, we shall win.

If we examine but a few indications we find that since it was known that the destructive proposals of the Democratic House were stopped, over $300,000,000 of gold has flowed into our country through restored confidence abroad. $250,000,000 of currency has returned from hoarding through restoration of confidence at home, the values of bonds have increased by 20 per cent, thus safeguarding every depositor in a savings bank and every policyholder in insurance companies.

Manufacturing production has increased by 10 per cent. Some groups, such as textiles, have increased over 50 per cent in activity.

Contrary to the usual seasonal trend, building contracts have steadily increased. The Department of Commerce shows that over 180,000 workers returned to the manufacturing industry in August, 360,000 more in September, and there is evidence of even a still larger number in October.

Car loadings have increased from 490,000 per week to 650,000 per week, showing the increased volume of materials moving. Exports and imports have increased nearly 23 per cent.

Agricultural prices, always the last to move, have improved from their low points, although they are still hideously low. Bank failures have almost ceased, credit has begun to expand. Every week some improvement is recorded somewhere.

As I have said, improvement would have begun four months earlier but for the fear of the destructive Democratic program.

We would be moving faster in the restoration of farm prices and employment but for the threat that these destructive measures will be revived by a change at this election. The Democratic candidate for President has refused to renounce or disavow these destructive measures, or to give the country the assurance it deserves that he will not be a party to these measures, including the prepayment of the bonus.

Observing this, and examining the dominant elements of his party under the leadership of the Vice Presidential candidate, we can only assume that this program is still in abeyance, to be produced by them if they shall come into power.

The Democratic candidate has devoted most of his speeches to presenting numerous faults and wrongdoings in our economic system, in which there is no new discovery. We may have much to do in the future to punish wrongdoing and correct weaknesses in the system, but these corrections have little bearing on our immediate national issue—that is, to restore employment, agricultural prices, relief of distress, so that fear and apprehension may be lifted from the homes of our people that they may be bright with hopes for the future. That is the first issue before the American people.

Before I discuss further the great and successful battle of the Republican Administration to meet a world-wide emergency and to restore economic life, I wish to deal with some of the statements made by the Democratic candidate upon economy and the fiscal policies of this administration.

I have on previous occasions repeatedly called attention to the vast increase in public expenditures, local, State and national, and the absolute necessity for their reduction as a fundamental part of national recovery.

The cost of all forms of government must be reduced. The burden of intolerable taxation must be lifted from the backs of men. While only thirty cents of the taxpayer's dollar of taxes goes to the Federal Government, I have worked hard to reduce this. Much has been accomplished, despite the opposition of selfish groups and sections of our country and the unwillingness of the Democratic House of Representatives. Much more must be done.

The Democratic candidate says that we have been extravagant and in his various statements implies that we should make a defense of our policies. There will be no defense; none is needed. The ordinary expenses of the Federal Government, except for relief purposes, have been reduced, while those of the government of New York State have been increased.

Moreover, there will be proof that the Governor of New York State, no doubt through ignorance of our fiscal system or through misinformation supplied to him, and totally ignoring the actions of the Democratic House of Representatives, has broadcast a misstatement of facts. In consequence, his conclusions are amazingly removed from the truth.

I live with these expenditures morning, noon and night. Not a day goes by that I do not have them before me for responsible action. There is not a year in the formulation of the budget when it is not a battle against selfish groups which would increase expenditures right and left. Not a session of Congress has convened that I have not had to veto increases in expenditures.

So few of the statements made by the Democratic candidate are in accordance with records of fact that it leaves me nonplussed where to begin. It would take hours to dissect his each line and paragraph, so I must confine myself to a few representative misstatements.

The Democratic candidate adopts the current method which I will follow, discussing expenditures not appropriations and of expressing expenditures in sums, less the postal receipts. The Governor also says he wants only to "compare the routine government outlay, the ordinary costs of conducting government" and excludes all extraordinary items in his comparisons.

On this basis he says we increased the routine ordinary cost of government by $1,000,000,000 between 1927 and 1931. I shall deal with that in a moment; but he omits to state that when the Republicans took office in 1921 Federal expenditures were still, three years after the war, at the rate of $5,500,000,000, and that by 1927 these were reduced to approximately $3,585,000,000, a reduction of nearly $2,000,000,000 a year.

The Governor states that, in order to arrive at a true representation of the ordinary expenditures of the government, he will deduct from each of these comparative years what he calls "an exceptional item"—that is, the reduction in interest and sinking fund on the public debt between the two periods, and that he will therefore deal with the residue. There was reduction of $368,000,000 in service on debts from 1927 to 1931. The Governor implies it is not fair to consider this as an economy. That is his first error, for it is a true economy in government. A large part of the reduction of the charge of the national debt was the result of many years of steady, painstaking refinancing to decrease interest and the application of other economies in expenditure to the reduction of the debt during Republican administrations. It can hardly be called an extravagance.

The actual expenditures for 1927 were $3,585,000,000. For 1931 they were $4,220,000,000, or an increase of $635,000,000. Bear in mind the Governor says he wants to compare the routine ordinary costs of conducting the government. He also says that he favors relief measures by the government.

He then neglects to inform the country that the increased expenditures for 1931 over and above those for 1927 were almost wholly for relief of the depression. These include an emergency increase over 1927 in public works and vessel construction, to relieve unemployment, of $335,900,000.

They include $243,600,000 of emergency relief to farmers. Beyond this they include $112,000,000 of emergency relief to the Postal Department because of falling off of receipts from the depression itself. They include a special payment to veterans on the bonus and other items of $124,000,000 as depression relief.

Thus we have a sum of emergency expenditures in relief of the depression of $815,500,000, and if we adopt the Governor's own definition of ordinary routine expenditures and deduct this sum, then the ordinary routine costs of government for 1931 were actually less than those of 1927, not one billion greater as he states.

The year 1927 was an especially low year, for reasons connected with census and national defense, and if the Governor wanted to be fair he could have adopted the year 1929, the last year before my administration, in which, you can be sure, there was no waste under President Coolidge. He not only practiced economy but gave the most practical demonstration ever seen in government.

Had the Governor adopted that year, with its total expenditures of $3,848,000,000, and deducted from 1931 the extraordinary expenditures due to relief, he would find there was an actual decrease in expenditures of upward of $300,000,000 in the ordinary conduct of government during my administration.

But of more importance, the Governor promises that he will reduce Federal expenditures a billion a year.

And now I would like to examine the record of the last session of Congress in its relation to economy as compared with the efforts of the Administration, for it is illuminating upon both the Democratic platform and the Governor's promises.

In October a year ago we prepared the budget, formulated before the crisis became completely acute, reducing expenditures by $369,000,000 over the previous year. The situation having grown more tense you will recollect that in a message to the Congress on December 8 I pointed out that revenues were falling steadily and then forecast a drop of $600,000,000, and that we must have even more definite and actual reduction in government expenditures than was possible by executive action, and again repeated my oft-made recommendations for legislative authority to effect further economies by consolidation, elimination of bureaus, &c.

As the situation became daily more tense you will recollect that I again, on Jan. 4, addressed the Congress and urged the growing seriousness of the situation demanded that we must have "further and more drastic economy in expenditure." On Feb. 17, you will recollect, I urged upon Congress again "the absolute necessity for most drastic economy," and proposed methods by which further economies could be brought about. The reply to this urging for economy was not economy, but the passage by the Democratic House on March 4 of the Gasque omnibus pension bill. I vetoed that bill.

On April 4, adequate action not yet having been taken by the Congress to reduce expenditures, you will recollect that I again addressed them, stating that the $369,000,000 of cuts originally recommended in the Executive budget were entirely inadequate to the growing situation, and proposed further savings which must have legislative authority. I pointed out the gravity of the situation and asked that a national committee of economy representing the Senate and the House and the Executive should be appointed to review the entire question.

The Democratic leaders denounced this suggestion as dictatorship. The House did appoint a committee. The administration at once recommended that legislative authority be given to effect certain positive economies amounting to $250,000,000 and certain indirect economies amounting to $50,000,000. At the same time we asked for more cuts by the Appropriations Committee.

By the time these recommendations had filtered through the Democratic committee and the Democratic House the economy bill had dwindled to savings of $40,000,000, although the Senate eventually restored part of them.

Again, as if in reply to my request for economies of April 13, a bill which was not economy was passed by the Democratic House setting up a train of large Indian claims which had been settled seventy-five years ago, which I was compelled to veto.

On May 31 I addressed the Senate in person, pointing out the disastrous effect of the failures of the Congress in effecting economies and to balance the budget without the shocks to the Federal credit and its responsibility for degeneration in the economic system, and I stated "the probable decrease in revenues by $1,700,000,000 necessitates absolute reduction in government expenditures" and I demanded as a first consideration that still more drastic economy be practiced. I asked for a total reduction of $400,000,000 in addition to my original proposal, the previous December, of $369,000,000, making a sum of nearly $800,000,000 of economies, and I pointed out where they could be obtained.

Despite the desperate situation of the country, the helpful reply of the Democratic House eight days later was not economy but the passage of the Garner-Rainey pork barrel bill, one portion of which called for increased expenditures of $1,200,000,000. I appealed for public support in protest and I am glad to say that the public so rallied that the bill practically died. Again showing their utter disregard of the nation's plight, on June 15 the Democratic House passed the Patman bill for the cash prepayment of the bonus, requiring the expenditure of $2,300,000,000. I again protested publicly and asked for public support in stopping this bill. It also died.

It would help if the Governor would state what year, and upon what theory, he proposed to use as a base for his reduction. It would appear from his adoption of the promise of the Democratic platform that he proposed to reduce the expenditures below the gross expenditures of all kinds for the year ending June, 1932. If he will compare these total expenditures for 1932 with the estimated total expenditures for the current fiscal year ending June, 1933, he will find a thing he may possibly know already, that his promised saving of a billion dollars has already been accomplished, even though we are still struggling with expenditures forced upon us by the Democratic House.

But, more than this, if the economies proposed by this administration had been accepted by the Democratic House there would have been for the current year a further saving of at least half a billion more.

If we are supported by the American people and if the Democratic

House will cooperate, I will make for the next fiscal year a reduction from the totals of 1932, not of a billion, but of $1,500,000,000.

If the Governor means to reduce government expenditures $1,000,000,000 below "ordinary routine" costs of government taking the present fiscal year 1933, which we are now in, as a base, as might be implied in any reasonable mind, it is only fair that the American people should know where and how he is going to accomplish it. If he is warranted in making such an assertion, then he must know the places where such reduction can be made.

To help him I may say that the "ordinary routine" expenditures for the current fiscal year are estimated at $3,647,000,000. Of these, $1,980,000,000 are for public debt and certain trust and refund services to which the government is obligated together with expenditures upon the army and navy. In the present disturbed state of the world we must not further reduce our defenses without a general agreement of reduction of arms.

Thus the Governor must find a cut of $1,000,000,000 out of the remaining $1,667,000,000 of ordinary routine government expenditures. Of this sum $946,000,000 is for veterans and $216,000,000 for ordinary public works, while all other costs of government are about $506,000,000. The last item includes the conduct of Congress, the judiciary, prisons, tax collection, accounting, foreign relations, public health, maintenance of lighthouses and airways, merchant marine, education, agriculture, various scientific bureaus, and a host of other critically important services.

Assuming the wildest estimate that these services could be reduced by one-half, that half the lighthouses could be extinguished, half the Federal prisoners turned loose on the public, the Governor would still have to find $750,000,000 of economy. Even if he stopped all public works he would finally have to take $500,000,000 of the $946,000,000 which the veterans receive. That would be a gross injustice. But that is where rash promises will inevitably lead.

The Governor points with satisfaction to the increase in expenditures of the Department of Commerce under my administration. He neglects to inform the American people that these increases were nearly all due to the transfer of bureaus to that department with corresponding decrease in expenditures in other departments.

Various conferences were carried on in an endeavor to arrive at an adequate relief bill, expending activities of reconstruction corporation but the Democratic leaders insisted not upon economy but upon inclusion in it of a new item of $322,000,000 of further expenditures from the Federal Treasury. Ultimately, this bill passed Congress, containing not only this provision but also measures putting the government into wholesale pawnbroking with unlimited use of Federal Government credit.

On July 11, I vetoed this bill and again protested about the item of $322,000,000, requesting at least that such a reservation be made as would hold back the expenditure until it could be determined if the budget be balanced. In order to secure the relief bill at all, with its very vital provisions in relief of distress, employment, and agriculture, I was compelled finally to accept it with inadequate safeguards to that $322,000,000, and this expenditure has been forced upon the government by the Democratic leaders.

If there is a deficit this year, it will be due to the Democratic members of Congress. We had a vast amount of oratory from the Democratic side on the subject of economy during the whole session. This oratory, instead of facts, seems to have lodged in the mind of the Democratic candidate.

And now these gentlemen arise to say that the Republican Administration is to blame if the budget is not precisely balanced. I am well aware that progress in a democracy requires cooperation and compromise on matters that do not involve great principle, but it is not for the Democratic leaders to rise now and talk of economy and reduction of government expenses after their attempts to foist $3,500,000,000 of further expenditures on the government, which we stopped, and after their failure to reduce expenses by some $200,000,000 to $300,000,000, which they refused, and after their forcing $322,000,000 new expenditures upon us after our most strenuous opposition. The expenditures for this fiscal year would be $500,000,000 less had our demands been heeded.

When our opponents rise and say that they are the party to be trusted with the reduction of governmental expenditures I recommend that you compare these promises with the actual performance of the body which, under the Constitution, initiates the fiscal policies of government, the House of Representatives.

Despite all this obstruction I propose to continue the fight for reduction of government expenditures, and if there is a fresh mandate from the people there will be no denying my recommendations.

The Governor involves himself in a labyrinth of inaccurate statements in trying to prove that the Secretary of the Treasury made errors in estimates of future revenue. He insists we should have increased taxation two years earlier than was done. He ignores the fact that Federal budget estimates are made in October for the year beginning the following July. He would appear to expect that by crystal gazing or by astrology the Secretary would have been able to prophesy the revenues a year ahead in the midst of the greatest crisis in history and to have thus anticipated the effect of every crash in the world upon our revenues.

I wish it were possible for human beings to predict the action of a Democratic House a year or two in advance. If we had been able to do this, we could have interpreted the effect on the revenues and budget of the actions of the last Congress and their disturbances in the whole economic system and their foray on the Treasury.

In this particular the Governor might be interested to know that certain Democratic leaders in Congress publicly protested that no taxes should be imposed at all or that they should be delayed still another year, and that we should continue to live off our fat. The administration was the first to insist that the undermined revenues of the country should be increased as a fundamental necessity to the maintenance of stability of the United States Government.

The Governor implies that as the result of failure to read the crystal of the future we have jeopardized the credit of the Federal Government. The answer is that the Governor does not know that only ten days ago the Treasury sold $500,000,000 of notes at 3 per cent interest. There is no government in the world financing upon such a confidence in its stability.

The Governor's labored charge that for some sinister purpose the facts were misrepresented or concealed from the people is too silly to merit serious consideration. The actual Federal expenditures and receipts are issued to the public every day in the year at 9:30 o'clock in the morning.

Now I want to address myself to the constructive policies of my administration and the Republican party, and in addressing myself to this task I want to address myself to the man who has a job, to the man who has no job and is looking for one, to the farmer and the business man who are in difficulty.

After all, the thing which is of real importance is not the misinformation furnished to the Democratic candidate or the promises of that party but the actual measures and forces which we have in motion to restore jobs, agriculture and business.

It has been my fate to have been born and raised in contact with the problems that come from distress and striving to maintain a fireside and home for loved ones. And I can say without challenge that a large part of my life has been spent in contact with and in efforts to solve human difficulties.

Therefore I wish to discuss with you the emergency program which we have put into action and propose for overcoming this crisis and to compare it with the Democratic program as made evident by the last Congress and with some suggestions by the Democratic candidate.

In a previous address I have traced the origins of this depression. I have spoken of the forces which dragged down the prosperity of our people and brought suffering, distress and fear into American homes.

The first stage of the depression in this country was a reaction from the mania of speculation and flotation of 1929. I have traced the measures we initiated to increase employment, to hold wages, to assist agriculture, to prevent distress and the gradual recovery of the country from the domestic phase a year later.

I have pictured the dreadful calamity which then interrupted our recovery through the tremendous earthquake whose origins were in the World War and its aftermath and the strains which it had placed upon the nations of Europe.

As the result of these they collapsed one by one, finally culminating, at the end of September last year when Great Britain abandoned the gold standard and was followed by a score of other nations with financial panics, overthrown governments and revolutions.

In other places I have discussed the methods by which this tremendous world crisis was transmitted to the United States. At the moment I desire only to point out to you the effect. In weeks following abandonment of the gold standard in England, the bank failures measured in deposits rose to over $250,000,000 per week and hoarding rose to over $100,000,000 a week. Foreigners, fearing that even we might be engulfed, drew out $725,000,000 in gold from us in six weeks.

We met the situation promptly. On Oct. 3 a year ago I secured from the bankers of the country the establishment of the National Credit Association with $500,000,000 with which to support the financial situation. On Oct. 6 I called a meeting of the political leaders of both parties and secured a declaration of unity of national action in the face of national danger.

The ship began to right itself. But, again, at the end of November it became evident that the forces moving against us were more powerful than could be stopped by these measures. Bank failures and hoarding increased, with a thousand other effects in increased unemployment and decreasing farm prices.

We were faced with three great perils.

The first was that through the losses and decrease in profits of business there was a sharp drop in Federal tax revenues of $1,700,000,000 or nearly one-half the whole. We were faced with inability to pay our expenses of government except by an increase in taxes or alternatively by enormous borrowings.

Second—The integrity of the monetary system was increasingly threatened by the terrible impact of foreign gold withdrawals and our own hoarding and the inflexibility of the Federal Reserve act.

Third—The whole private credit machinery of the country was so paralyzed that credit was practically impossible to obtain, business dried up and demands were made right and left upon debtors to force them to raise cash upon their property in diminished or non-existent markets. Unless these forces could be stopped the whole nation was in the gravest danger.

I should like for a moment to review the whole program we proposed and have largely established to meet this emergency. Some of its effectiveness was lost by delays in placing these weapons in our hands, for in battle much depends upon being there on time.

Some part of the losses, in failures, bankruptcies, falls in farm prices, increases in unemployment, were due to these delays. Some of the delays were the result of the slow moving of democracy, much of it, and refusal to enact some measures, were in consequence of destructive Democratic opposition. And again I wish to state that certain members of that party did cooperate with us and to them I pay tribute for their patriotism.

You will recollect my recommendations to the Congress in my message of last Dec. 8:

First—Drastic reduction in government expenses.

Second—By this and an increase in revenues to balance the budget, thus to hold the impregnability of the credit of the Federal Government.

Third—The strengthening of the capital of the Federal Land Banks by $125,000,000 in order to relieve the pressure upon farmers to repay their mortgages.

Fourth—Creation of the Reconstruction Finance Corporation with $2,000,000,000 of reserves in order that, having maintained national credit, we should thrust the full resources of public credit behind the private credit system of the country in order to re-establish and maintain it in an unassailable position.

That with the backing of Federal credit it should protect the depositors in savings banks, insurance policy holders, the leaders and borrowers in building and loan associations.

That it should through existing agencies expand the funds available for loans to merchants, manufacturers, farmers, agricultural marketing associations.

That it should protect the railways from receivership in order that in turn the railroad securities in the insurance companies and savings banks might be protected and the employes of the railways and a score of other services.

Fifth—Extension of authority of the Federal Reserve Board to meet the danger to our gold standard and to expand credit in counteraction to the strangulation due to hoarding and foreign withdrawal.

Sixth—Creation of the Home Loan Discount Banks with resources of several hundred millions to give home owners a chance to hold their homes from foreclosure and to furnish credit to create new homes and to expand employment.

Seventh—An authority by which we could secure early liquidation of deposits in closed banks that we might relieve the distress of millions of depositors.

Eighth—Revision of our banking laws.

Ninth—Continuation of the public works program of some $600,000,000 per annum to aid employment.

Later in the session of Congress, I expanded these emergency recommendations to include:

Tenth—Authority to the Reconstruction Finance Corporation to loan up to $300,000,000 to the States whose resources had been exhausted for relief of distress.

Eleventh—Loans by the Reconstruction Corporation up to $1,500,000,000 for the undertaking of great works which would add to employment and from their own earnings repay the outlay.

Twelfth—The erection of a new system of agricultural credit banks with indirect resources of $300,000,000.

Thirteenth—The extension of credits through the Reconstruction Corporation for movement of agricultural commodities.

And may I add to these measures others which we have in motion to aid in this emergency:

Fourteenth—To maintain the protective tariff as the first safeguard of every manufacturer and every workman and every farmer in the United States. Never has this been so vital as in this emergency when twenty countries are suffering from depreciated currencies and their standards of living and wages are so low. The danger of flooding our markets with foreign goods was never greater than at this moment.

A week ago, in Cleveland, I showed that wages in foreign countries would buy only from one-eighth to one-third as much bread and butter as could be bought by the wage in America today.

In the face of these standards of living the Democratic party proposes to lower tariffs. In this emergency as never before we require the preservation of our non-partisan tariff commission, by which this flood can be prevented and through which, if tariffs should become too high, they can be lowered without all the disruption and logrolling of Congressional action. Our opponents propose to destroy this function.

Fifteenth—The prevention of immigration during this emergency except for relatives of those already resident in the United States. This is vital to hold for our people the jobs which they have.

Sixteenth—The mobilization and support of all private relief agencies as we have done over the past three years in order that we may have the fullest care and support given to those who are ill and in distress and that we may maintain a sense of responsibility of every man to his neighbor.

Seventeenth—The mobilization of our business men, our labor and agricultural leaders to carry on their present cooperative activities and initiate new activities for increasing employment and aids to agriculture.

Eighteenth—The vigorous consummation of results from the world economic conference with a view to relieving the pressures from the outside and preventing recurrences of this distress in the future. The continuation of our negotiations for reduction of armament in order to reduce our own expense and to relieve the world of fear and political instability.

This is the constructive program proposed by the Republican Administration and largely adopted for relief of this emergency. The reform of banking and relief to depositors of closed banks were not secured. We have other measures to propose at the next Congress, especially for further relief of farm mortgages. Our program has conformed with American practice, American experience and American common sense.

It is proving that every day. It prevented national chaos.

It is today producing national recovery.

The first series of these measures was proposed on Dec. 8, but the Congress concluded, against my appeal to its leaders, to adjourn for the Christmas holidays, and only one of them was enacted until February.

Coincident with the passage of the principal of these measures, in the middle of last February, the ship began to right itself. The country began to show the resilience in its resources and courage, increased employment, upward trend of prices of agricultural products and to give signs of again resuming its activities.

There then supervened a whole period of obstructive and destructive actions by the Democratic House of Representatives which I will elaborate a little later as showing their real program.

It is now taken for granted that this Republican program has come of its natural self because in retrospect there is such universal recognition of its necessity. On the contrary, it has been wrought out of the fiery ordeal of hard and honest thought, the facing of the facts when loose thinking of frightened men offered every temptation of specious panaceas. It was wrought against the heart-breaking obstructions and delays of the Democratic House.

But it has in the main been established. It is working every minute.

Practically the only evidence of the attitude of the Democratic candidate upon this program is the sneer that it has been designed to help banks and corporations; that it has not helped the common man.

He knows full well that the only purpose of helping an insurance company is to protect the policyholder. He knows full well that the only purpose in a bank is to protect the depositor and the borrower. He knows full well that the only purpose of helping a farm mortgage company is to enable the farmer to hold his farm. He knows full well that the only purpose of helping the building and loan associations is to protect savings and homes.

He knows full well that in sustaining the business man it maintains the worker in his job. He knows full well that in loans to the States it protects the families in distress.

Millions of men and women are employed today because there has been restored to his employers the ability to borrow the money to buy raw materials and pay labor and thus keep his job.

If he be a farmer, it has restored his ability to secure credit upon which to produce his crops and live stock. If be a home owner or a farm owner in jeopardy of foreclosure of his mortgage, it now gives him a chance.

If he had borrowed for any purpose he has not been forced to the wall by bankruptcy through inability to instantly meet his debt. If he has savings in the bank it has protected him and removed his anxieties. If he has an insurance policy it has preserved the validity of that policy. If he be a merchant it has stopped the calling of his loans and today enables him again to borrow to purchase his stock and thus start employment.

If he be unemployed it is making hundreds of thousands of jobs. If he be in distress it enables his State or city to secure the money which assures him that he will not suffer hunger and cold.

Those who are in distress in this city are today receiving their bread and their rent from the result of these measures. But beyond this it is today creating new jobs and giving to the whole system a new breadth of life. Nothing has ever been devised in our history which has done more for those whom Mr. Coolidge has aptly called the common run of men and women.

Now I wish to turn for a moment to the specific Democratic program for this emergency as shown by their actions in the House of Representatives. I have only to repeat and enumerate them. I hope by this time you are familiar with them. I can remember them by the dates when they were passed by the House of Representatives.

Jan. 9, 1932: The Collier bill was passed by the Democratic House providing for destruction of the effective powers of the Tariff Commission. It also provided for an international conference to help us lower American tariffs. It also proposed reciprocal tariffs, and in vetoing it I stated that "no concessions other than those on agricultural tariffs would be of importance to other nations."

March 4, 1932: The Gasque omnibus pension bill was passed by the House. As I have said, I vetoed it.

March 7, 1932: The revenue bill, introduced by the non-partisan Ways and Means Committee, was torn to pieces on the floor of the Democratic House. It had to be sent back to committee, and an inadequate patchwork bill was substituted and passed. Long and harmful delays resulted. The injustices in that bill are yet to be remedied.

April 13, 1932: As I have said, I vetoed a bill passed by the Democratic House that would have set in train the opening of large Indian claims settled over seventy-five years ago. This was not in accordance with Democratic claims of economy.

May 2, 1932: The Democratic House passed a bill ordering the Federal Reserve System and the Treasury to fix prices at the average prevailing during the years 1921–1929 by control of the volume of currency and credit. As no mortal man could accomplish this end, both these agencies promptly denied they could produce this rubber dollar.

May 3, 1932: The House committees and the Democratic House refused to pass the economies originally proposed by the administration for $250,000,000 and reduced them to less than $50,000,000.

June 7, 1932: The Democratic Garner-Rainey bill was passed by the House, one section of which provided for increased expenditures by the taxpayer of $1,200,000,000. This was the pork-barrel bill. This bill did not get through the Senate because of public protest. The Democratic Vice Presidential candidate still advocates it.

June 15, 1932: The Patman bill was passed by the Democratic House, providing for the cash payment of adjusted service certificates to veterans, requiring the immediate expenditure of $2,300,000,000.

June 15, 1932: The Democratic House passed a provision for the issuance of $2,300,000,000 of fiat money—a form of currency inflation best exemplified by the similar action by the German Government in issuing paper marks in 1922. Had this measure ever become law, every farmer and every workman would be paying penalties for it today.

July 7, 1932: The Democratic House passed the Rainey bill, including a provision for injecting the Federal Government into direct personal banking. In vetoing that measure I stated it would mean loans for every conceivable purpose on every conceivable security to any one who wants money. It would place the government in private banking in such fashion as to violate every principle of public relations on which we have builded our nation and would render insecure its very foundations.

July 13, 1932: The House passed the relief bill, but insisted upon injecting $322,000,000 of expenditures upon the taxpayer against my protests. These are by no means all the Democratic House did, but they indicate the controlling elements of that party.

I now wish to discuss a proposal of the Democratic candidate himself.

Early in September there appeared among the unemployed in some of our cities reproductions of a letter from Governor Roosevelt which read:

Mr. Lowe Shearon,
358 Front Street,
New York, N. Y.

In accordance with your request, I shall be glad to have you quote me as follows:

I believe in the inherent right of every citizen to employment at a living wage and pledge my support to whatever measures I may deem necessary for inaugurating self-liquidating public works, such as utilization of our water resources, flood control and land reclamation to provide employment for all surplus labor at all times.

Yours very sincerely,
FRANKLIN D. ROOSEVELT.

This did not appear in the press until Oct. 13, when it was published in a leading New York journal. It was republished on the 14th, and on the 15th it was again published with the statement, quoted from Governor Roosevelt, that it was substantially correct.

There can be only one conclusion from this statement. It is a hope held out to the 10,000,000 men and women now unemployed and suffering that they will be given jobs by the government. It is a promise no government could fulfill. It is utterly wrong to delude suffering men and women with such assurances.

The most menacing condition in the world today is the lack of confidence and faith. It is a terrible thing to increase this undermining effect by holding out, for political purposes, promises to 10,000,000 men which can not be kept and must end in leaving them disillusioned.

There are a score of reasons why this whole plan is fantastic.

These 10,000,000 men, nor any appreciable fraction of them, can not be provided with jobs in this fashion. The only way is by healing the wounds of the economic system to restore them to their normal jobs.

There are many reasons why all this is true. To give a living wage to these 10,000,000 men, either through employing them directly on such works or indirectly in the furnishing of supplies and services, would cost the government from nine to twelve billion dollars a year. The borrowing of this amount of money would suck the resources from industry and commerce and cause unemployment to other millions. It would destroy government and private credit on which all present employment is built and upon which all hope of future employment rests.

There are not in the United States enough of these self-liquidating projects to employ but a small fraction of this total, and the Reconstruction Corporation is today engaged in considering and authorizing all such available projects. If there were any beyond their resources it would require at least a year or two years of technical preparation to get any of them into action before any one could be employed.

To increase land reclamation would hugely increase agricultural production at a time when our farmers are already paralyzed by enormous surpluses. It would erect the most gigantic bureaucracy in all history.

But, above all, I ask you whether or not such frivolous promises and dreams should be held out to suffering unemployed people. Is this the new deal? I may reiterate again that the only method by which we can stop suffering and unemployment is by returning people to their normal jobs in their normal homes, carrying on their normal functions of life. This can only be done by sound processes of protecting and stimulating the existing economic system which we have in action today.

I have tonight confined myself to the measures which we have taken to save this country from a gigantic disaster and which are in action to overcome the present emergency. I have not attempted to cover the long-view program of the administration and the Republican party. That I will do upon some other occasion.

In dealing with the present emergency I have insisted that we shall as a nation rely upon the initiative and responsibilities of our citizens, of our institutions and of our fabric of local government; that the full powers of the Federal Government shall be used for the protection of our people in this emergency; that the great instrumentalities and the measures which we have erected shall be conducted without interruption and with constantly inspiring vigorous action until restoration is completed; and above all, that they shall be used in such a manner as to sustain these fundamentals which are the real spirit of our national life.

Your purpose and my purpose is to protect the American home with all of its precious blessings, and to protect our children in their rightful heritage of job and hope and opportunity, and thus hand on to them the ideals and aspirations which we have received from our fathers. As a nation we have many labors before us when this emergency is past; the strengthening of the home; the more adequate protection of our people; better regulation of public service; improvement of our banking and credit systems; the development of a better scheme of agriculture and of industry; and a score of other pressing duties.

And there is one inspiration for this emergency and for the future of this nation that transcends all others. That inspiration we shall continue to discover in the schools and churches of this land and in communion with the great searcher of all souls. Our nation has survived thus far because it was founded in the favor of God by men and women who were more concerned with His will than they were with selfish aggrandizement and material acquisitions. The ultimate sources of great constructive measures of government and law are in the moral and spiritual impulses.

These are the beliefs and the convictions which necessarily come to me from vivid association with these currents and with the forces of the office which I have occupied, its invisible presence of those many men who before me have fought and builded for these ideals.

No man can be President without looking back upon the effort given to the country by the thirty Presidents who in my case have preceded me. No man of imagination can be President without thinking of what shall be the course of his country under the thirty more Presidents who will follow him. He must think of himself as a link in the long chain of his country's destiny, past and future. That future is in your hands. By your action on Nov. 8 you will determine whether we shall go on in the orderly adaptation of our old American ways to new needs, whether we shall build on the foundations laid by our forefathers over the past century and a half, or whether you will let momentary despair lead you to give the country a new and untried direction.

I can well understand that my countrymen are weary and sore and tired. I can well understand that part of this weariness comes from the exhaustion of a long battle. But in the battle we have carried the first line trenches. It is of transcendent importance that there shall be no interruption; that there shall be no change in the strategy and tactics used in the midst of victorious movement. The essentials of American life must not be broken down in chaos and in peril.

These are questions which the American people must weigh and weigh heavily in the next two weeks. What you will determine on Nov. 8 will be much more than a change of individuals, of even more importance than merely making a choice between the ways of coming out of this emergency. More than all that, it will determine the permanent course of the country.

The future of individuals is of no great importance in the life-stream of the nation. No one of us has the right to stand in the light of the nation's progress. Change in my personal position from command to the ranks is of trifling importance in the life of this nation. What is of vast importance is the measures and policies you adopt by your vote, and the men and the forces who in front and behind the scenes will dominate our national life.

I am anxious to see that these present sound policies and measures shall be continued only because I am anxious to see that my country shall come safely into the harbor from the dangers that but few men not occupying my responsibilities will ever appreciate. Following will-o'-the-wisps is not progressive. That is not being liberal. Rather it is driving slowly to the tyranny which means the extinction under bureaucracy of liberty and hope and opportunity.

In conclusion, I declare again that it is the high resolve of my administration, it is the historic determination of the Republican party, to preserve the nation for our children with its American system of liberty intact, its American free opportunity and its equal opportunity still open, moving ever forward in accord with these principles; its American government forever in the hands of men who believe that our fathers builded well when for 150 years they strove with brain and brawn to make this the greatest land that ever free man loved.

A Total Alternative: The Platform of the Socialist Party, 1932

Franklin D. Roosevelt has so much preempted the stage in our history of the 1930s that we are tempted to forget the other options open to the American people. While Roosevelt offered a stratagem of reform with extremism eschewed, but the details quite vague, the gradualist Socialist party, led by Norman Thomas (1884–   ), proposed what for many appeared a completely viable and more realistic alternative. A reading of the Socialist party platform indicates that this was no violent or reckless movement. It was built upon the American tradition of reform. The Socialist party came nowhere near victory. They could not even claim, in such a landslide as Roosevelt's, to have affected the result. However, the sharp increase in their vote and its considerable total stood as warning that a significant group of Americans had come to question the entire social system.

David Shannon, The Socialist Party of America: A History *(1955) is the standard work. See also Murray B. Seidler,* Norman Thomas: Respectable Rebel *(1961). The Socialist platform has been taken from the* Congressional Record, *Seventy-second Congress, first session, volume 75, part 13, pages 14702–14703.*

We are facing a breakdown of the capitalist system. This situation the Socialist Party has long predicted. In the last campaign it warned the people of the increasing insecurity in American life and urged a program of action which, if adopted, would have saved millions from their present tragic plight.

To-day in every city of the United States jobless men and women by the thousands are fighting the grim battle against want and starvation while factories stand idle and food rots on the ground. Millions of wage earners and salaried workers are hunting in vain for jobs while other millions are only partly employed.

Unemployment and poverty are inevitable products of the present system. Under capitalism the few own our industries. The many do the work. The wage earners and farmers are compelled to give a large part of the product of their labor to the few. The many in the factories, mines, shops, offices, and on the farms obtain but a scanty income and are able to buy back only a part of the goods that can be produced in such abundance by our mass industries.

Goods pile up. Factories close. Men and women are discharged. The Nation is thrown into a panic. In a country with natural resources, machinery, and trained labor sufficient to provide security and plenty for all, masses of people are destitute.

Capitalism spells not only widespread economic disaster but class strife. It likewise carries with it an ever-present threat of international war. The struggle of the capitalist class to find world markets and investment areas for their surplus goods and capital was a prime cause of the World War. It is to-day fostering those policies of militarism and imperialism which, if unchecked, lead to another world conflict.

From the poverty, insecurity, unemployment, the economic collapse, the wastes, and the wars of our present capitalistic order only the united efforts of workers and farmers, organized in unions and cooperatives and, above all, in a political party of their own, can save the Nation.

The Republican and Democratic Parties, both controlled by the great industrialists and financiers, have no plan or program to rescue us from the present collapse. In this crisis their chief purpose and desire has been to help the railroads, banks, insurance companies, and other capitalist interests.

The Socialist Party is to-day the one democratic party of the workers whose program would remove the causes of class struggles, class antagonisms, and social evils inherent in the capitalist system.

It proposes to transfer the principal industries of the country from private ownership and autocratic, cruelly inefficient management to social ownership and democratic control. Only by these means will it be possible to organize our industrial life on a basis of planned and steady operation, without periodic breakdowns and disastrous crises.

It proposes the following measures:

Unemployment and Labor Legislation

1. A Federal appropriation of $5,000,000,000 for immediate relief for those in need, to supplement State and local appropriations.

2. A Federal appropriation of $5,000,000,000 for public works and roads, reforestation, slum clearance, and decent homes for the workers, by Federal Government, States, and cities.

3. Legislation providing for the acquisition of land, buildings, and equip-

ment necessary to put the unemployed to work producing food, fuel, and clothing and for the erection of houses for their own use.

4. The 6-hour day and the 5-day week without a reduction of wages.
5. A comprehensive and efficient system of free public employment agencies.
6. A compulsory system of unemployment compensation with adequate benefits, based on contributions by the Government and by employers.
7. Old-age pensions for men and women 60 years of age and over.
8. Health and maternity insurance.
9. Improved systems of workmen's compensation and accident insurance.
10. The abolition of child labor.
11. Government aid to farmers and small-home owners to protect them against mortgage foreclosures and a moratorium on sales for nonpayment of taxes by destitute farmers and unemployed workers.
12. Adequate minimum wage laws.

Social Ownership

1. Public ownership and democratic control of mines, forests, oil, and power resources; public utilities dealing with light and power, transportation and communication, and of all other basic industries.
2. The operation of these publicly owned industries by boards of administration on which the wageworker, the consumer, and the technician are adequately represented; the recognition in each industry of the principles of collective bargaining and civil service.

Banking

Socialization of our credit and currency system and the establishment of a unified banking system, beginning with the complete governmental acquisition of the Federal reserve banks and the extension of the services of the postal savings banks to cover all departments of the banking business and the transference of this department of the post office to a Government-owned banking corporation.

Taxation

1. Steeply increased inheritance taxes and income taxes on the higher incomes and estates of both corporations and individuals.
2. A constitutional amendment authorizing the taxation of all Government securities.

Agriculture

Many of the foregoing measures for socializing the power, banking, and other industries, for raising living standards among the city workers, etc., would greatly benefit the farming population.

As special measures for agricultural upbuilding we propose:

1. The reduction of tax burdens by a shift from taxes on farm property to taxes on incomes, inheritances, excess profits, and other similar forms of taxation.

2. Increased Federal and State subsidies to road building and educational and social services for rural communities.

3. The creation of a Federal marketing agency for the purchase and marketing of agricultural products.

4. The acquisition by bona fide cooperative societies and by governmental agencies of grain elevators, stockyards, packing houses, and warehouses and the conduct of these services on a nonprofit basis. The encouragement of farmers' cooperative societies and of consumers' cooperatives in the cities, with a view of eliminating the middleman.

5. The socialization of Federal land banks and the extension by these banks of long-term credit to farmers at low rates of interest.

6. Social insurance against losses due to adverse weather conditions.

7. The creation of national, regional, and State land utilization boards for the purpose of discovering the best uses of the farming land of the country, in view of the joint needs of agriculture, industry, recreation, water supply, reforestation, etc., and to prepare the way for agricultural planning on a national and, ultimately, on a world scale.

Constitutional Changes

1. Proportional representation.
2. Direct election of the President and Vice President.
3. The initiative and referendum.
4. An amendment to the Constitution to make constitutional amendments less cumbersome.
5. Abolition of the power of the Supreme Court to pass upon the constitutionality of legislation enacted by Congress.
6. The passage of the Socialist Party's proposed workers' rights amendment to the Constitution empowering Congress to establish national systems of unemployment, health and accident insurance and old age pensions, to abolish child labor, establish and take over enterprises in manufacture, commerce, transportation, banking, public utilities, and other business and industries to be owned and operated by the Government and, generally, for the social and economic welfare of the workers of the United States.

(The plank dealing with prohibition has been submitted to a referendum of the party membership.)

Civil Liberties

1. Federal legislation to enforce the first amendment to the Constitution so as to guarantee freedom of speech, press, and assembly, and to penalize officials who interfere with the civil rights of citizens.

2. The abolition of injunctions in labor disputes, the outlawing of "yellow-dog" contracts and the passing of laws enforcing the rights of workers to organize into unions.

3. The immediate repeal of the espionage law and other repressive legislation, and the restoration of civil and political rights to those unjustly convicted under wartime laws.

4. Legislation protecting aliens from being excluded from this country or from citizenship or from being deported on account of their political, social, or economic beliefs, or on account of activities engaged in by them which are not illegal for citizens.

5. Modification of the immigration laws to permit the reuniting of families and to offer a refuge to those fleeing from political or religious persecution.

The Negro

The enforcement of constitutional guarantees of economic, political, and legal equality for the Negro.

The enactment and enforcement of drastic antilynching laws.

International Relations

While the Socialist Party is opposed to all war, it believes that there can be no permanent peace until socialism is established internationally. In the meanwhile, we will support all measures that promise to promote good will and friendship among the nations of the world, including:

1. The reduction of armaments, leading to the goal of total disarmament by international agreement, if possible; but, if that is not possible, by setting an example ourselves. Soldiers, sailors, and workers unemployed by reason of disarmament to be absorbed, where desired, in a program of public works, to be financed in part by the savings due to disarmament. The abolition of conscription, of military training camps and the Reserve Officers' Training Corps.

2. The recognition of the Soviet Union and the encouragement of trade and industrial relations with that country.

3. The cancellation of war debts due from the allied governments as part of a program for wiping out war debts and reparations, provided that such cancellation does not release money for armaments but promotes disarmament.

4. The entrance of the United States into the World Court.

5. The entrance of the United States into the League of Nations under conditions which will make it an effective instrument for world peace and renewed cooperation with the working-class parties abroad to the end that the league may be transformed from a league of imperialist powers to a democratic assemblage representative of the aspirations of the common people of the world.

6. The creation of international economic organizations on which labor

is adequately represented, to deal with problems of raw material, investments, money, credit, tariffs, and living standards from the viewpoint of the welfare of the masses throughout the world.

7. The abandonment of every degree of military intervention by the United States in the affairs of other countries. The immediate withdrawal of military forces from Haiti and Nicaragua.

8. The withdrawal of United States military and naval forces from China and the relinquishment of American extraterritorial privileges.

9. The complete independence of the Philippines and the negotiation of treaties with other nations safeguarding the sovereignty of these islands.

10. Prohibition of the sales of munitions to foreign powers.

Committed to this constructive program, the Socialist Party calls upon the Nation's workers and upon all fair-minded and progressive citizens to unite with it in a mighty movement against the present drift into social disaster and in behalf of sanity, justice, peace, and freedom.

PART **THREE**

The New Deal: Experiment with Hope

Varied Approaches

Basic Charters

Appraisal

The New Deal is a term which crept almost accidentally into the nation's political vocabulary. It has become the label by which we tie together the intricate political history of the prewar Roosevelt years (1933–1940). In retrospect we can define it. It was the set of programs produced in those years: National Recovery Administration, Agricultural Adjustment Administration, Civilian Conservation Corps, and the rest. But the use of the term should not be easily assumed to imply that the Roosevelt administration had a consistent philosophy, or definitive directions, or specific, firmly agreed programs when it came into office.

In fact, if there was *a New Deal in prospect in March, 1933, it was a matter of mood and manner, rather than of substance. Certain goals were clearly set by the situation. It was necessary to promote economic recovery, to do it quickly and dramatically. It was necessary to develop reforms appropriate to the removal of certain dramatically exposed abuses—reforms for the situation on the stock exchange, for example. Beyond this there was little certainty, aside from three propositions. The New Deal meant, first, the determination to make the solution of national social and economic problems the major business of government; second, the conscious decision to arrive at policies through experimentation; and finally, the firm and irrevocable presumption that there was hope.*

On the early New Deal one should certainly read Arthur M. Schlesinger,

Jr., The Coming of the New Deal *(1958), and William E. Leuchtenburg,* Franklin D. Roosevelt and the New Deal *(1963). Among the memoirs, perhaps the most interesting are Raymond Moley,* After Seven Years *(1939); Frances Perkins,* The Roosevelt I Knew *(1946); and Eleanor Roosevelt,* Autobiography *(1961), as well as the careful blend of memoir and scholarship provided by John Blum in* From the Morgenthau Diaries: 1928–1938 *(1959).*

SELECTION 10

Challenge and Promise: Franklin D. Roosevelt's Inaugural Address, 1933

During the winter of 1932 and 1933 the mood was anticlimax and the manner confusion. The people had spoken in November, and yet a repudiated President Hoover must somehow hold the reins of responsibility until March. The people had spoken clearly, and yet, as a President-elect without power or direct responsibility, Franklin Roosevelt would husband his advantages, avoid premature and divisive maneuvers. He would wait while the crisis deepened. He would wait while repudiated Republicans and enthusiastic but undisciplined Democrats created a deepening shadow of confusion. He must *wait, although more people were hungry, more violence threatened, more danger of institutional collapse loomed than ever before.*

Perhaps partly because of the long and desperate waiting period, the coming of the new administration was a riotous term of action, a remarkable exercise of human faith. The future had turned, and the turning point had been almost too dramatically FDR's First Inaugural Address, delivered on March 4. Here the reader will find a general forecast of the New Deal and also Roosevelt's own appraisal of the dimensions and possibilities of the crisis.

The First Inaugural Address is to be found in Samuel Rosenman (ed.), The Public Papers and Addresses of Franklin D. Roosevelt, Volume Two: Year of Crisis, 1933 *(New York: Random House, 1938), pages 11–16.*

I am certain that my fellow Americans expect that on my induction into the Presidency I will address them with a candor and a decision which the present situation of our Nation impels. This is preeminently the time to speak the truth, the whole truth, frankly and boldly. Nor need we shrink from honestly facing conditions in our country today. This great Nation will endure as it has endured, will revive and will prosper. So, first of all, let me assert my firm belief that the only thing we have to fear is fear itself—nameless, unreasoning, unjustified terror which paralyzes needed efforts to convert retreat into advance. In every dark hour of our national life a leadership of frankness and vigor has met with that understanding and support of the people themselves which is essential to victory. I am convinced that you will again give that support to leadership in these critical days.

In such a spirit on my part and on yours we face our common difficulties. They concern, thank God, only material things. Values have shrunken to fantastic levels; taxes have risen; our ability to pay has fallen; government of all kinds is faced by serious curtailment of income; the means of exchange are frozen in the currents of trade; the withered leaves of industrial enterprise lie on every side; farmers find no markets for their produce; the savings of many years in thousands of families are gone.

More important, a host of unemployed citizens face the grim problem of existence, and an equally great number toil with little return. Only a foolish optimist can deny the dark realities of the moment.

Yet our distress comes from no failure of substance. We are stricken by no plague of locusts. Compared with the perils which our forefathers conquered because they believed and were not afraid, we have still much to be thankful for. Nature still offers her bounty and human efforts have multiplied it. Plenty is at our doorstep, but a generous use of it languishes in the very sight of the supply. Primarily this is because rulers of the exchange of mankind's goods have failed through their own stubbornness and their own incompetence, have admitted their failure, and have abdicated. Practices of the unscrupulous money changers stand indicted in the court of public opinion, rejected by the hearts and minds of men.

True they have tried, but their efforts have been cast in the pattern of an outworn tradition. Faced by failure of credit they have proposed only the lending of more money. Stripped of the lure of profit by which to induce our people to follow their false leadership, they have resorted to exhortations, pleading tearfully for restored confidence. They know only the rules of a generation of self-seekers. They have no vision, and when there is no vision the people perish.

The money changers have fled from their high seats in the temple of our civilization. We may now restore that temple to the ancient truths. The measure of the restoration lies in the extent to which we apply social values more noble than mere monetary profit.

Happiness lies not in the mere possession of money; it lies in the joy of achievement, in the thrill of creative effort. The joy and moral stimulation of work no longer must be forgotten in the mad chase of evanescent profits. These dark days will be worth all they cost us if they teach us that our true destiny is not to be ministered unto but to minister to ourselves and to our fellow men.

Recognition of the falsity of material wealth as the standard of success goes hand in hand with the abandonment of the false belief that public office and high political position are to be valued only by the standards of pride of place and personal profit; and there must be an end to a conduct in banking and in business which too often has given to a sacred trust the likeness of callous and selfish wrongdoing. Small wonder that confidence languishes, for it thrives only on honesty, on honor, on the sacredness of obligations, on faithful protection, on unselfish performance; without them it cannot live.

Restoration calls, however, not for changes in ethics alone. This Nation asks for action, and action now.

Our greatest primary task is to put people to work. This is no unsolvable problem if we face it wisely and courageously. It can be accomplished in part by direct recruiting by the Government itself, treating the task as we would treat the emergency of a war, but at the same time, through this employment, accomplishing greatly needed projects to stimulate and reorganize the use of our natural resources.

Hand in hand with this we must frankly recognize the overbalance of population in our industrial centers and, by engaging on a national scale in a redistribution, endeavor to provide a better use of the land for those best fitted for the land. The task can be helped by definite efforts to raise the values of agricultural products and with this the power to purchase the output of our cities. It can be helped by preventing realistically the tragedy of the growing loss through foreclosure of our small homes and our farms. It can be helped by insistence that the Federal, State, and local governments act forthwith on the demand that their cost be drastically reduced. It can be helped by the unifying of relief activities which today are often scattered, uneconomical, and unequal. It can be helped by national planning for and supervision of all forms of transportation and of communications and other utilities which have a definitely public character. There are many ways in which it can be helped, but it can never be helped merely by talking about it. We must act and act quickly.

Finally, in our progress toward a resumption of work we require two safeguards against a return of the evils of the old order: there must be a strict supervision of all banking and credits and investments, so that there will be an end to speculation with other people's money; and there must be provision for an adequate but sound currency.

These are the lines of attack. I shall presently urge upon a new Congress, in special session, detailed measures for their fulfillment, and I shall seek the immediate assistance of the several States.

Through this program of action we address ourselves to putting our own national house in order and making income balance outgo. Our international trade relations, though vastly important, are in point of time and necessity secondary to the establishment of a sound national economy. I favor as a practical policy the putting of first things first. I shall spare no effort to restore world trade by international economic readjustment, but the emergency at home cannot wait on that accomplishment.

The basic thought that guides these specific means of national recovery is not narrowly nationalistic. It is the insistence, as a first consideration, upon the interdependence of the various elements in and parts of the United States—a recognition of the old and permanently important manifestation of the American spirit of the pioneer. It is the way to recovery. It is the immediate way. It is the strongest assurance that the recovery will endure.

In the field of world policy I would dedicate this Nation to the policy of the good neighbor—the neighbor who resolutely respects himself and, because he does so, respects the rights of others—the neighbor who respects his obligations and respects the sanctity of his agreements in and with a world of neighbors.

If I read the temper of our people correctly, we now realize as we have never realized before our interdependence on each other; that we cannot merely take but we must give as well; that if we are to go forward, we must move as a trained and loyal army willing to sacrifice for the good of a common discipline, because without such discipline no progress is made, no leadership becomes effective. We are, I know, ready and willing to submit our lives and property to such discipline, because it makes possible a leadership which aims at a larger good. This I propose to offer, pledging that the larger purposes will bind upon us all as a sacred obligation with a unity of duty hitherto evoked only in time of armed strife.

With this pledge taken, I assume unhesitatingly the leadership of this great army of our people dedicated to a disciplined attack upon our common problems.

Action in this image and to this end is feasible under the form of government which we have inherited from our ancestors. Our Constitution is so simple and practical that it is possible always to meet extraordinary needs by changes in emphasis and arrangement without loss of essential form. That is why our constitutional system has proved itself the most superbly enduring political mechanism the modern world has produced. It has met every stress of vast expansion of territory, of foreign wars, of bitter internal strife, of world relations.

It is to be hoped that the normal balance of Executive and legislative authority may be wholly adequate to meet the unprecedented task before us. But it may be that an unprecedented demand and need for undelayed action may call for temporary departure from that normal balance of public procedure.

I am prepared under my constitutional duty to recommend the measures that a stricken Nation in the midst of a stricken world may require. These measures, or such other measures as the Congress may build out of its experience and wisdom, I shall seek, within my constitutional authority, to bring to speedy adoption.

But in the event that the Congress shall fail to take one of these two courses, and in the event that the national emergency is still critical, I shall not evade the clear course of duty that will then confront me. I shall ask the Congress for the one remaining instrument to meet the crisis—broad Executive power to wage a war against the emergency, as great as the power that would be given to me if we were in fact invaded by a foreign foe.

For the trust reposed in me I will return the courage and the devotion that befit the time. I can do no less.

We face the arduous days that lie before us in the warm courage of national unity; with the clear consciousness of seeking old and precious moral values; with the clean satisfaction that comes from the stern performance of duty by old and young alike. We aim at the assurance of a rounded and permanent national life.

We do not distrust the future of essential democracy. The people of the United States have not failed. In their need they have registered a mandate that they want direct, vigorous action. They have asked for discipline and direction under leadership. They have made me the present instrument of their wishes. In the spirit of the gift I take it.

In this dedication of a Nation we humbly ask the blessing of God. May He protect each and every one of us. May He guide me in the days to come.

SELECTION 11

The Need to Plan: Rexford G. Tugwell on "Getting What We Want from Industry," 1927

The broad accomplishments and challenges of the early New Deal were suggested by the President's Inaugural Address. Yet the immediate steps, and even the general philosophy to guide and the techniques for achieving the goals, were at best fuzzy in Roosevelt's mind. He was not himself a thinker; he was not himself an architect of programs. He was preeminently an able politician, a fact which meant that he must turn to others for ideas. He must himself specialize in adapting those ideas to reality, in selling them to the public, in finding and supporting the men who could make facts from the dreams. Part of Roosevelt's difficulty, and at the same time part of his strength, lay in the fact that he had a mixed team of warring advisers about him. He seldom followed a line charted by prior agreement within his camp. He would spend much of his time maneuvering and navigating among the varied, often sharply antithetical points of view represented by the loyal Roosevelt henchmen and the ambitious Roosevelt braintrusters within his team.

Among the original braintrusters, the speechwriters and academic advisers of the presidential campaign years, no one was more vigorous in his drive for action, more imaginative in his ideas than Professor Rexford G. Tugwell, a forty-two-year-old political scientist. Tugwell had joined the loosely organized volunteer team of advisers which his Columbia University colleague, Raymond Moley, had organized for Governor Roosevelt long before the actual preconvention campaign had begun. He had helped to "educate" Roosevelt before and during the campaign. After they moved to Washington, he sought to help guide the directions of Roosevelt's program. Like other advisers he found himself a good deal less influential after the election than he had been before, and he spent the twelve years of the Roosevelt Era in constant warfare with other Roosevelt partisans who stood for differing techniques. His career carried him from a post as Assistant Secretary of Agriculture through a final assignment as Governor of Puerto Rico. But he stood throughout the whole era as the signal advocate of organized planning, of cooperative enterprise, of the use of governmental power to guide the direction of American growth. Not a socialist by any means, he had nevertheless a firm commitment to the concept that capitalism must learn to live with a new social responsibility. The people, he believed, must learn to accept, to benefit from, and to manage the new capitalistic giantism which American enterprise had evolved. Tugwell was always controversial; his thinking represents one of the disparate lines of advice in the Roosevelt camp, that line which led backward to Theodore Roosevelt's "New Nationalism" and forward toward the "welfare state." The excerpt quoted here from one of his early books suggests the direction and dimensions of his thinking.

Tugwell became in later years an historian of the New Deal. His own view of the era is laid out in his valuable book, half memoir, half history, The Democratic Roosevelt *(1957). Bernard Sternsher has recently completed an extensive study,* Rexford G. Tugwell and the New Deal *(1964).*

The selections given here are from Rexford G. Tugwell, "Getting What We Want from Industry," in Industry's Coming of Age *(New York: Columbia University Press, 1927), pages 245–246, 255–257, 260, 262–267.*

It has been the thesis here that industry is coming to maturity, that it has reached the stretches of its career when what has hitherto been haphazard growth, tortured by the uncertainties of adolescence, ought to become a mature career determined by a program of progress, encouraged by a sense of achievement. So far, this career has had its successes, but also its failures; so that none of us knows certainly for the future whether we shall be present at a cultural tragedy or whether we shall see the newest, and, perhaps, the most lusty youth of the race, come into the full powers of his strength intelligently disciplined for a place in the world, or whether we shall see in him a gradual disorganization and a drift into futility. . . . It is not motives which have changed, but the world in which they operate. Private selfishness can no longer by economic legerdemain be erected into a desirable social policy.

It is not a wrong thing but a right one that people should want to provide for themselves and those whom they love. The difference is that the way to provide now is through coöperation, not, as it once was, by exclusively individual effort and by a competitive struggle which wore most of the aspects of war. We still retain the old motives, which are good, but we have developed a means of attaining their ends which is bad. We need, then, somehow, to get our motives to work for us rather than against us.

We are only now beginning to see the relevancy of the curious modern inversion of the psychological stresses of normal living. The desirable ways of living and qualities of behavior observable in less complex economies are here distorted out of all semblance to their origins. In a simpler existence those persons are revered—and thus set the fashion for conduct—who serve their neighbors best, economically and socially. For an illustration of this way of life and mode of conduct we may use the country doctor of a generation or two ago. Others might be chosen, but none perhaps which would be still personally familiar to so many of us. What kind of pay was it that he demanded for his services? Was it money, the power to command wealth? We know that it was not. His pay was mostly in some such sort as a gratefully wrung hand and a later saying in the mouths of people, his neighbors. How would this plain, rough, bearded man appear, fitted out with the trappings of the modern wealthy? Surely the meaning of the contrast between the fundamental motivations of life is plain enough in the mere stating. The fact is that the country-doctor sort of person in the environment which produced him neither could nor wished to become rich. If there were no other reason, there is explanation enough in the resentment of neighbors. The fact is that, in a simple economy, people see that the getting rich of neighbors is accomplished at the general expense, and they will not tolerate it. There is a remainder of that feeling still so far as some professional classes are concerned, and a faint survival of the notion that great wealth must have been acquired dishonorably.

It may very well be asked why, in the case of the modern rich, we tend to ape their extravagances and at the same time to consider their gains dishonorable, as we undoubtedly do. This feeling of the dishonor attached to wealth may be taken as a survival of the morality of simpler economies which has refused to change as economic conditions permitting such great aggregations of wealth have developed. Competition worked to keep a certain equality in the old system as it does not work now. And we have not come to the point of adopting new controls for leveling incomes although we still retain vestiges of the old morality. This is one of those cases in which we exhibit a confusion of moral ideas. The very wealth we deplore on moral grounds, and the very people we despise for having it are the stimulus for emulation. We want what is undoubtedly dishonorable, but that seems to cause very little diminution in the strength of our desire. . . .

Modes of conduct are not, as we supposed a few years ago, fixed and inflexible. New habit patterns may be constructed which have the force of will in them; but to ask that habit patterns be built up which require an indifference to the approvals of the social group in which one lives would raise other questions quite as vexing. An indifference in one respect involves indifferences in other respects, for instance, and the immense moral force of social pressure is at once lost. Surely this cannot be the answer to the problem that is posed by distortions of economic incentive. We do not want men to be insensitive to group morals. Rather, we want an increased sensitivity.

But if we are to keep men responsive to social approvals, they must yield better fruits than they are now producing. Some moral controls over the immense and increasing spending power of our age must be constructed so that the first recourse of persons who come into money, as we say, will not be to barbaric ostentation and all the silly vanities of competitive consumption. It ought to be wrong to squander wealth, and only right to use it wisely and well. We have got to give up trying to make of every day a Roman holiday; we must sometimes remember to celebrate the appointed feasts of reason. . . .

If we see what it is that we want from industry in the way of goods and in decent kinds of work, and if we see how it is that our best motives become perverted, we are in a much better position to get what we want than we are if we register only uncertainty when we are confronted with these questions. It is most of all necessary to see that without moral decisions even industrial life cannot be trusted to operate well.

We cannot treat either our morals or our industrial arrangements as absolutes and expect to progress very rapidly. We must at least be willing to let them become accommodated to each other. Which will be required to change most seems unimportant. The real necessity is for fusion. And this fusion can be accomplished only on the basis of expediency. An illustration or two may make this clearer. . . .

The recent adoption by the Ford interests of the five-day week raised a whole storm of discussion among business leaders. Mr. Ford was roundly condemned and his five-day week bitterly objected to by a considerable number of his contemporaries. A sophisticated bystander could guess what arguments would be used. And as would have been expected, they were motivated by a defense of already assumed positions, in their industries, not in Mr. Ford's. Whether it was expedient for Mr. Ford was a consideration which was entirely neglected.

Many similar illustrations from industrial life might be adduced. We are for or against one party to an industrial dispute not because we know the situation and what it requires, but because one settlement conforms to our moral notions and the other does not. We want the coal industry to come under governmental control because we favor governmental control, not because we think it will work well for producing coal; or we do not favor it because we want the government "kept out of business." We favor high or low tariffs, or one form of taxation as against another, with very similar influences shaping the opinion.

It is my belief that we cannot get anywhere in the guidance of industry on an idealistic basis of this sort. But the motives involved are not to be impugned. They are perfectly good human motives. We are trying all the time to be moral conformers. We have only to realize that we cannot get what we want in that way. How this realization can be made general and so change our concrete attitudes toward the making of decisions is not an easy question to answer. Perhaps only the long and slow processes of education will train us to substitute expediency for ideals, the scientific attitude for received dogma, openmindedness for conventional decisions. I am inclined to that view. But that is perhaps because I am an educator. There may be other ways. But I am perfectly sure of the necessity for escaping from emotional or moralistic attitudes and replacing them by the tests of experience. And this involves the making of decisions rather than accepting traditions.

It might be well to point out, too, that we move within certain rather well-defined limits in getting industry to provide us with goods of the quality and kinds we want. Not to recognize these limits is to become an out-and-out Utopian. For instance, it seems quite clear that we are committed to large-scale organization, to the minute division of tasks, and to the more and more complete machinization of factory work. And it will not do us much good to complain about these things. . . .

My own idea is that we might grow away from poverty and the other ugly concomitants of industrialism and toward something better, though not, indeed, like Athens or Florence or any of Mr. Wells' Utopias. And that we might accomplish this by taking industry as we find it and shaping it reasonably and slowly but also forcefully toward what seem, for the time being, better arrangements. This would be done in great decisions and in small ones, by consumers and producers each in their own way; but it would be better done if we worked to some plan, some expectation by which results could be judged. The first condition of achieving such a plan, however, seems to me, as I have implied, the recognition of present trends so that we may have some assurance that we are working for an attainable result and not wasting effort on Utopian aircastles.

These trends are so important that, unless I am utterly mistaken, they will result in an almost complete remaking of American economic life. In the clear view of them which is emerging all the plans for our future must be made.

SELECTION 12

"Keep Open the Path of Opportunity": Louis D. Brandeis on the Problems of Bigness

Tugwell represented only one of several disparate views in the administration. Not all of FDR's advisers had been inspired by Theodore Roosevelt. Some had worked with Woodrow Wilson. Not all of them looked forward to the planned management of interests in an age of economic giants. Some looked back with fondness to the age of competitive enterprise, to the simple, small-scaled rivalries of the rural economy. Best known and most influential of these was Louis Dembitz Brandeis (1865–1941), crusader against the money trust and for labor regulation in the Age of Taft, schoolmaster to candidate Woodrow Wilson, and an associate justice of the United States Supreme Court since 1916.

Brandeis could not meddle with policy directly from his position on the bench. But he could and did indirectly, through his disciple Felix Frankfurter, a close Roosevelt adviser, and later a master employment manager for the New Deal. Brandeis also exercised influence through young and ebullient White House aides like Thomas Corcoran and Benjamin Cohen. Roosevelt did not heed him slavishly, but he respected deeply this old "Isaiah," as he called Brandeis. The influence of Brandeis's attitudes seemed to become greater as the National Recovery Administration foundered on the shoals of administrative confusion and staling enthusiasm. Some historians have even come to see the period from 1935 through 1937 as a distinctive "second New Deal," characterized sharply by Brandeisian "atomism" rather than by Tugwell's "corporatism."

As the first of the following selections makes clear, Brandeis was unwilling to accept as inevitable or desirable the growth of economic monopolies. But it is equally clear that he was arguing neither for "do nothing" government nor for a naive return to the crossroads store or the blacksmith shop as the basic unit of economic activity. What Brandeis wanted, from 1912 when he wrote the first of these excerpts until 1931 when he wrote the second of them, was a government strong enough and enlightened enough to do two important things. It must prevent the growth of irresponsible monopoly, standing in this way as a representative of the public interest. Second, it must experiment constantly to maintain realistic and reasonable ground rules for an economic competition which would "keep open the path of opportunity" and keep alive the regulatory activity of the marketplace. What he did not *want was an easy reliance upon giant government to regulate the private economic giants. He could bring himself to trust neither completely.*

On Brandeis's influence see Arthur M. Schlesinger, Jr., The Politics of Upheaval *(1960), as well as Alpheus T. Mason,* Brandeis: A Free Man's Life *(1946). Fascinating in its insights to both the "New Freedom" and the "New Deal" is Harlan Phillips (ed.),* Felix Frankfurter Reminisces *(1960).*

The first excerpt provided here is "The Regulation of Competition against the Regulation of Monopoly," an essay written in 1912 when Brandeis was evolving the philosophy which he was to carry with him until the end of his career. It was published in Louis D. Brandeis, The Curse of Bigness *(New York: Viking, 1934), pages 109–111. The second excerpt is from Brandeis's dissenting opinion in* New State Ice Co. v. Liebmann, *285 U.S. 280ff. (1931), in which he argues that government should be allowed to play an active and an experimental role in guiding the economy and also points out some of the difficulties involved. These two essays suggest the boundaries of the approach to economic problems which Brandeis and his admirers pressed upon Roosevelt as an alternative to completely unbridled competition, also to total social planning.*

THE DANGER OF MONOPOLY, 1912

A large part of the American people realize today that competition is in no sense inconsistent with large-scale production and distribution. They realize that the maintenance of competition does not necessarily involve destructive and unrestrained competition, any more than the maintenance of liberty implies license or anarchy. We learned long ago that liberty could be preserved only by limiting in some way the freedom of action of individuals; that otherwise liberty would necessarily lead to absolutism and in the same way we have learned that unless there be regulation of competition, its excesses will lead to the destruction of competition, and monopoly will take its place.

A large part of our people have also learned that efficiency in business does not grow indefinitely with the size of the business. Very often a business grows in efficiency as it grows from a small business to a large business; but there is a unit of greatest efficiency in every business at any time, and a business may be too large to be efficient, as well as too small. Our people have also learned that these profits are not due in the main to efficiency but are due to control of the market, to the exercise by a small body of men of the sovereign taxing power. Nothing has helped so much to make this clear to our people as an incident in the life of the Tobacco Trust. When the Spanish War came on and we needed additional revenue, Congress properly increased the tax on tobacco products. Three years later, when our country no longer needed that additional revenue, Congress sought to remove the burden which it had placed upon the people, but Congress found itself powerless to remove the burden it had imposed. And when Congress reduced the tax, the effect was merely to transfer, from the Treasury of the United States to the treasury of the Trust, the several millions of dollars a year which represented the reduction in the tax; because the tobacco-products market was controlled by the Trust, which held the selling price practically unchanged.

The history of the Tobacco Trust also showed in the history of its detailed operations how control made for profit, for the degree of control exercised by that great Trust was very different in the various departments of its business and, as the commissioner of corporations found, the ratio of profit was ordinarily in direct relation to the ratio of control. Where the trusts had a high degree of control, the profits were great; where they had a small degree of control the profits were small. In the cigar business, in which the Trust had no control of the market, in which it was merely a large concern, doing perhaps one-eighth of the cigar business of the country, the Trust's profits were not only small, but they were very much smaller than would be satisfactory to the ordinary manufacturer. In the same year in which some of the subsidiary corporations of the Trust were earning fifty, sixty, eighty, or one hundred per cent upon the tangible assets, the Trust was earning in its cigar department only four to six per cent, although the ultimate management of all departments of the Trust's business rested with the same able men and was supplied with the same great resources. Such facts as these have made men realize that while trusts are sometimes efficient, it is not their efficiency but the fact that they control the market, that accounts for the huge profits of trusts.

And people have learned also another fact of perhaps even greater importance. They have come to realize the effect of monopoly in arresting progress, arresting that advance in industry without which a great industrial future is unattainable.

What America needs is not that we do anything for these, our fellow citizens, but that we keep open the path of opportunity to enable them to do for themselves. When these Americans come to do for themselves they find this situation: The trust is not merely a capitalistic control of men. It is the worst form of capitalistic control. One hundred and fifty thousand persons are said to be interested as stockholders in the Steel Trust. The Steel Trust is a conspicious instance of ownership separated from responsibility. The Steel Trust presents a condition similar to that which led to the demoralization of Ireland—the condition of absentee landlordism. The managers may be good men and true, but the permanent separation of ownership from control must prove fatal to the public interest. The responsibility of ownership is lacking. If there had been responsibility of ownership in the Steel Trust it would have been impossible that with the huge profits of the corporation—which the commissioner of corporations found to be $650,000,000 in ten years, far in excess of a fair return upon the capital originally invested in that concern—men would have been compelled to work twelve hours a day, seven days in a week, and at such low wages that even if they had worked 365 days in a year, seven days a week, the year's earnings would have been less than was necessary, less than the minimum amount necessary in the city of Pittsburgh for the support of a man, his wife, and three children with the minimum of decency, alas!

THE DANGER OF INACTION, 1931

The people of the United States are now confronted with an emergency more serious than war. Misery is widespread, in a time, not of scarcity, but of overabundance. The long continued depression has brought unprecedented unemployment, a catastrophic fall in commodity prices and a volume of economic losses which threatens our financial institutions.

Some people believe that the existing conditions threaten even the stability of the capitalistic system. Economists are searching for the causes of this disorder and are reexamining the bases of our industrial structure. Business men are seeking possible remedies. Most of them realize that failure to distribute widely the profits of industry has been a prime cause of our present plight. But rightly or wrongly, many persons think that one of the major contributing causes has been unbridled competition. Increasingly, doubt is expressed whether it is economically wise, or morally right, that men should be permitted to add to the producing facilities of an industry which is already suffering from overcapacity. In justification of that doubt, men point to the excess capacity of our productive facilities resulting from their vast expansion without corresponding increase in the consumptive capacity of the people. They assert that through improved methods of manufacture, made possible by advances in science and invention and vast accumulation of capital, our industries have become capable of producing from 30 to 100 percent more than was consumed even in days of vaunted prosperity; and that the present capacity will, for a long time, exceed the needs of business. All agree that irregularity in employment—the greatest of our evils—cannot be overcome unless production and consumption are more nearly balanced. Many insist there must be some form of economic control. There are plans for proration. There are many proposals for stabilization. And some thoughtful men of wide business experience insist that all projects for stabilization and proration must prove futile unless, in some way, the equivalent of the certificate of public convenience and necessity is made a prerequisite to embarking new capital in an industry in which the capacity already exceeds the production schedules.

Whether that view is sound nobody knows. The objections to the proposal are obvious and grave. The remedy might bring evils worse than the present disease. The obstacles to success seem insuperable. The economic and social sciences are largely uncharted seas. We have been none too successful in the modest essays in economic control already entered upon. The new proposal involves a vast extension of the area of control. Merely to acquire the knowledge essential as a basis for the exercise of this multitude of judgments would be a formidable task; and each of the thousands of these judgments would call for some measure of prophecy. Even more serious are the obstacles to success inherent in the demands which execution of the project would make upon human intelligence and upon the character of men. Man is weak and his judgment is at best fallible.

Yet the advances in the exact sciences and the achievements in invention remind us that the seemingly impossible sometimes happens. There are many men now living who were in the habit of using the age-old expression: "It is as impossible as flying." The discoveries in physical science, the triumphs in invention, attest the value of the process of trial and error. In large measure, these advances have been due to experimentation. In those fields experimentation has, for two centuries, been not only free but encouraged. Some people assert that our present plight is due, in part, to the limitations set by courts upon experimentation in the fields of social and economic science; and to the discouragement to which proposals for betterment there have been subjected otherwise. There must be power in the states and the nation to remold, through experimentation, our economic practices and institutions to meet changing social and economic needs. I cannot believe that the framers of the Fourteenth Amendment, or the states which ratified it, intended to deprive us of the power to correct the evils of technological unemployment and excess productive capacity which have attended progress in the useful arts.

To stay experimentation in things social and economic is a grave responsibility. Denial of the right to experiment may be fraught with serious consequences to the nation. It is one of the happy incidents of the federal system that a single courageous state may, if its citizens choose, serve as a laboratory, and try novel social and economic experiments without risk to the rest of the country. This Court has the power to prevent an experiment. We may strike down the statute which embodies it on the ground that, in our opinion, the measure is arbitrary, capricious or unreasonable We have the power to do this, because the due-process clause has been held by the Court applicable to matters of substantive law as well as to matters of procedure. But in the exercise of this high power, we must be ever on our guard, lest we erect our prejudices into legal principles. If we would guide by the light of reason, we must let our minds be bold.

The Need to Share What We Have: Senator Hugo Black Advocates the Thirty-hour Week, 1933

The options open to the Roosevelt administration were not always charted by long-term planning or fundamental philosophy. Some were expedients suggested by the immediate crisis. One such was the plan of Senator Hugo Black of Alabama (1886–   ) and some others to spread the available work. This plan, born in Congress before Roosevelt had been inaugurated, was pressed upon the President throughout the spring of 1933. It moved in a sharply different direction from the ideas of a Tugwell or a Brandeis, and it was not adopted by the administration, but it suggests the variety of stresses under which the administration labored. It had its influence, since the National Industrial Recovery Act (NRA) was developed at least in part to offset more simplistic or extreme plans for economic stabilization like those of Black. And at least some of the sentiment for a maximum-hours law, which later became part of the Fair Labor Standards Act, originated with Black and his friends.

The excerpt given here is Senator Black's explanation of his proposal and is to be found in the Congressional Record, *Seventy-second Congress, second session, volume 76, part 4, 4304–4305.*

Mr. President, I desire to discuss at this time a bill which I have introduced to prohibit the use of interstate commerce for the transportation of goods manufactured or mined in establishments where employees work longer than five days per week and six hours per day. . . .

It is my sincere belief that the prompt enactment of this measure into law would bring about the quick employment of millions of jobless Americans and at the same time actually benefit legitimate industry and languishing agriculture. The bill is not offered as a cure for all our economic ills but as a major part of an imperatively necessary program for national readjustment and recovery.

There are, of course, other pressing problems of vital importance. Without attempting to enumerate all of them, but on account of their fundamental nature, might be mentioned farm-mortgage indebtedness and, indeed, all kinds and forms of our crushing load of debts, low farm commodity prices, the unstable and shifting value of our dollar, and our lost foreign trade.

To-day, however, I wish to present this one measure, relating directly to the one subject of hours of labor in industry, and attempt to show that it has an indirect bearing upon all other phases of trade and commerce, and indeed is a subject that can not and must not be ignored in any comprehensive plan to restore normal business activities and bring about that economic justice upon which the domestic tranquility of our people depends. . . .

It is my belief that this measure should be speedily enacted into law. Among other important effects, the evidence before our committee indicates it would have the following results:

> First. The adoption of the 5-day week and 6-hour day would bring about the employment of approximately six and one-half million of our present army of jobless and despairing citizens within a comparatively short period of time.
>
> Second. It would aid the farmers and business enterprises of the Nation by greatly increasing the aggregate purchasing power of the people.
>
> Third. The absorption of the vast number of unemployed in useful labor would aid in the reestablishment of confidence and would be a long step toward a restoration of normal business conditions and would aid in relieving the widespread misery and distress abroad throughout the land.

It is my belief that American industry working its employees five days a week and six hours per day, can produce all that is needed in times of prosperity to satisfy the demands of both our foreign and domestic commerce. The marvelous advances in machinery and efficient mass production support this statement. It is difficult to understand how any thinking person can deny this development who has given proper weight to the evidence around him and the facts available to all who seek reliable information. The fallacy of the economic dogma that the niggardliness of nature and the insatiability of human wants justify long hours in order to produce a limitless supply of ever-increasing commodities, has been exposed and disproven by the inventive genius of man. Dogmatic assertions of economic laws that can not survive the test of workability are not sound.

New principles recognize the lavish generosity of nature. The problem in our complex age is one of satisfying human wants through a proper system of distribution. That is our task to-day.

SELECTION **14**

To Feed the Hungry: Senator Robert F. Wagner Argues for Direct Federal Relief, 1933

None of the plans pressed upon Roosevelt by expediency was more important, or more irresistible, than those for direct Federal relief expenditures. Democratic Senator Robert F. Wagner of New York (1877–1949) had been arguing for such expenditures for many months before the end of the Hoover administration and spoke particularly strongly during the lame duck session of January and February, 1933. One of his speeches during this session is reported in part below. Wagner and others made eloquent pleas, but Hoover resisted, feeling that direct relief went beyond the powers of the Federal government and invaded the area of local responsibility. The drying up of state funds, the deepening crisis, the passionate eloquence and tough political influence of men like Wagner all made certain that the Roosevelt administration must turn to direct relief, and at once. This tactic became one of the basic weapons of the New Deal against the economic crisis, although it had no particular bearing upon the philosophical questions raised by Tugwell and Brandeis.

This excerpt is taken from the Congressional Record, *Seventy-second Congress, second session, volume 76, part 4, pages 4315–4316 and 4318–4320.*

Mr. President, I sometimes wonder whether all of us have yet realized the extent and the depth of the present crisis in the lives of the people of the United States; whether we all know that in every large city large numbers of upstanding, sturdy, and splendid men and women are being destroyed by a poverty so grim that the like of it has never been seen in this country. In this day and age of plenty, hundreds and thousands of people in the congested areas of population are living on city refuse like the beasts of the jungle. Homeless, cheerless, hopeless, half starved, and cold, these American families are being crushed into the very earth.

I marvel at the general complacency in the presence of these facts. Can it be that in so short time we have come to accept such conditions as normal and proper? Are we blind to the demoralization which is in progress to the obliteration of all standards of living for a large portion of our population? Are we unaware that these inhuman conditions are placing the fate of America in jeopardy?

What is the situation with respect to relief? The known facts can be stated simply. The need for the relief of destitution is to-day greater than it has been at any time during the depression, and it is still growing. The rising curve of destitution is graphically illustrated in the chart which I have before me, prepared by the Children's Bureau of the Department of Labor, and appearing in its January, 1933, relief bulletin. That chart, Mr. President, shows only the growth in the amount of money expended for relief; it does not reveal, and we have no means of knowing, the even greater spread of want, dependence, and destitution.

It is not difficult to see why the need for relief should be increasing. Basically, of course, the reason is that unemployment is still spreading. In his testimony before the subcommittee of the Banking and Currency Committee which held hearings upon my bill, Mr. Edward McGrady, representing the American Federation of Labor, expressed that fundamental fact effectively. He said:

> I might call your attention to the fact, Senator, that on the 1st of February you reached the all-time peak of unemployment. You have crossed the 12,000,000 line for the first time, and, as I understand it, that is more unemployed than we have records for in any other country of the world that keeps records, and it is getting worse. . . . In addition, . . . 9,000,000 more are now getting only part-time work.

The full significance of this startling figure is not understood unless it is considered in the light of the long duration of the depression. In the course of four cruel winters private resources have been exhausted, savings-bank accounts have been depleted to the extent of three and one-half billion dollars in a single year, life-insurance policies have been borrowed against to the limit, homes have been abandoned, private possessions sold. No wonder that the case load of relief agencies is to-day growing at a more rapid pace than unemployment itself. Examine the Red Cross figures. They tell a burning story of American tragedy which ought to leave no heart unmoved, no act undone to stop or, at least, to mitigate the ravages of the prevailing distress. According to the report of the Red Cross as of December 31, 1932, 4,750,000 separate families have applied for flour and almost as many for clothing.

It seems to me that on the basis of this evidence there is ample justification for the estimate made by one of the witnesses before the Banking and Currency Committee that "there are no less than 45,000,000 people living in poverty," of which "15,000,000 are existing only with the help of charity, without which they would perish."

These facts and figures offer a challenge to American leadership which has thus far not been met, and I say to those who have continuously resisted and checked every effort to meet it that if they persist they will endanger the very existence of the most cherished American institutions and inflict a blow from which the American people will not fully recover for generations to come.

We are not in a mere business recession. We are not undergoing a so-called depression. We are in a life and death struggle with the forces of social and economic dissolution, and it is our responsibility to throw all the resources of our people and our Government into the fray on the side of humanity to prevent the disintegration which is in progress before our very eyes.

The most immediate objective and the most crucial is to provide adequate relief upon a standard of decency for all those who are in need of assistance. No one whose conscience has been penetrated by the prevailing scene of desolation questions that assertion.

How shall we provide the necessary relief? Private charity has reached the peak of its efforts and has begun to decline. A steadily increasing proportion of relief has come from governmental sources. Most of the States and municipalities have reached the limit of their capacity and are not likely to increase their commitments for relief, except by diverting sums from normal and essential functions.

If proof of these declarations is necessary, it is readily accessible. Mr. Ralph G. Hurlin testified before the Committee on Manufactures that the community-chest campaign in 150 communities succeeded in raising for 1933 only 77 per cent of the amount collected for 1932. When last we considered relief legislation it was commonly accepted that of the relief money then expended, 30 per cent came from private sources. The January bulletin of the Children's Bureau discloses that the ratio has changed. To-day only 12 per cent has its origin in private contributions, 88 per cent in public funds. There is no explanation for that shift except the obvious fact that whereas the need for relief has been expanding the capacity of private contributors has been declining.

Now we face the further fact that the resources of States and municipalities are no longer capable of meeting the enlarged need. We recognized that fact when Congress passed the emergency relief and construction act. It is far truer to-day. The situation was well summarized by Prof. Sumner Slichter, of Harvard, a very careful investigator. I quote him:

> But the ability of the cities (and the counties) to raise funds by taxation is shrinking, because about nine-tenths of their income is derived from the taxation of real estate which, even before the depression, was heavily overtaxed relative to other sources of income. Falling rents and a rising percentage of vacancies are steadily reducing the ability of real estate to bear the burden of relief. All this is reflected in the mounting tax delinquencies. Last year Detroit imposed a levy of $76,000,000, of which it failed to collect $18,000,000. Pittsburgh had a levy of $22,594,000, of which over $3,000,000 was delinquent. In Cleveland nearly 19 per cent of the county taxes are delinquent and about 50 per cent of the special-assessment taxes. Particularly important is the fact that ability to give relief has diminished most of all in precisely those communities where unemployment is greatest. For a few months relief may be financed by borrowing, but city after city has now reached the point where further borrowing is impossible.

There is but one conclusion that can possibly be drawn from the facts I have so briefly sketched, and that is that the Federal Government must assume a much larger and direct responsibility in meeting the relief and employment obligations of the current emergency. . . .

Mr. President, what has been done under the emergency relief and construction act is cruelly little, but let it be said now that it is the only emergency action taken which has directly contributed to the preservation of life and has kept at least some men at work in their normal occupations and has sustained their morale, their purchasing power, and their citizenship.

It seems to be beyond dispute that we shall not start a single force for recovery by pursuing a policy of slow national starvation and attrition until declining production overtakes vanishing consumption. That is the course of self-imposed poverty and deliberate national deterioration. In so far as recovery can be promoted by domestic efforts, it must have as its focus the expansion, not the contraction, of activity; the spread of purchasing power, not its further destruction. The only line of fruitful activity which will not serve to increase the very surplus of unsalable commodities is the construction of necessary projects which are in the public interest.

Beyond this central fact there are additional pertinent factors which deserve consideration and fortify the wisdom of pursuing that course. First, construction is the most severely deflated of American industries. The decline in wage payments in that industry has been in excess of 75 per cent as compared with 1929, and the volume of construction contracts awarded has shrunk from an average of $550,000,000 a month in 1928 to about $110,000,000 a month in 1932. Second, construction costs have fallen to so low a level that, in the interests of genuine economy and the saving of the taxpayers' money both now and in the future, it is desirable to prosecute every needful construction or reconstruction project at the present time. Third, the expansion of construction through Reconstruction Finance Corporation financing gives us the necessary means of releasing the right kind of inflation—credit inflation—through the creation of job-giving activities for the production of genuine wealth of permanent value. I have, as the Senate knows, long advocated the advance planning of public construction as a method of helping to stabilize employment. The policy of advance planning was, after much effort, written into the law in February, 1931.

I have before me a very interesting calculation prepared by the Director of the Federal Employment Stabilization Board which indicates that proper allocation of all public construction between 1925 and 1929 would have left almost $4,000,000,000 for construction activity in 1931 and 1932. That would have been enough, practically, to take up the slack in that industry. . . .

Mr. President, I do not believe there is any serious division of opinion respecting the proposal that every effort be made to open up employment opportunities through the initiation of necessary construction projects. That proposal is the policy we adopted in the emergency relief and construction act of 1932. The reasons for the meager performance under that measure are to be found both in the restrictive language of the act as now written, as well as in the ultraconservative policy pursued by the Reconstruction Finance Corporation. It was the common opinion expressed at the hearings before the subcommittee of the Banking and Currency Committee that the two chief obstacles to the initiation of job-giving projects under the emergency relief and construction act were, first, the rigorous definition of a self-liquidating project; and, second, the high interest rates required by the Reconstruction Finance Corporation. In both respects the bill which I present provides what I regard as the necessary remedy. So far as public construction by local governmental bodies is concerned, the requirement that a project be self-liquidating is entirely abandoned. In lieu of that requirement the bill would provide a new standard that any project initiated by a public body shall be eligible for a loan if it is needful and in the public interest. The rate of interest to be charged on construction loans by the Reconstruction Finance Corporation is fixed at a rate not to exceed one-half per cent above the rate carried on the last issue of Federal bonds immediately preceding the making of the loan. These are the principal changes. They will, in my judgment, permit the Reconstruction Finance Corporation to function in the manner in which it was intended to function, namely, as an agency to promote recovery, to provide employment, and to stimulate business, industry, and agriculture. . . .

Mr. President, as we consider the questions of depression and relief, as we fix our attention upon statistical tables showing the rise and fall of business, we sometimes forget the individual who has borne the brunt of the long economic struggle. Undoubtedly every portion of the population has suffered in the general deflation of values and shrinkage of income, but I submit that the heavy end of the load has been carried by the men and women who work on the farm and in the factory to earn their daily bread. And not only is that true but it is also a fact that during the days of prosperity they did not enjoy the same relative increase in earnings that was enjoyed by the investor. . . .

It is about time that we turned our attention in the direction of the wage earner who did not enjoy, relatively, the benefits of prosperity and who is to-day the chief sufferer of the consequences of depression. Out of his labor we reared the industrial greatness of America. That greatness can not endure unless we restore him to gainful employment.

A Plan for National Mobilization: The National Industrial Recovery Act, 1933

When the administration came to act, the precise nature of the situation, the problems of administration and politics added new dimensions to the theoretical arguments which had raged about the President's desk. The National Recovery Administration (NRA) was a case in point. It became the landmark of the first New Deal, the great experiment in cooperative, planned recovery. It was based upon a stimulating assumption: the deep interdependence of all elements of the economy—labor, management, investor, consumer. It was launched with drama, carried on for some months with flair. It was ambitious in its conception, logical in its development. And it collapsed after slightly over two years.

In 1935, the Supreme Court declared this act unconstitutional as an excessive delegation of congressional responsibility and power. The Court also rejected the concept of interstate commerce as a broad process, a concept upon which the NRA's authority over industry completely depended (A. L. A. Schechter Corporation v. United States, *reprinted later in this book as Selection 35). Yet the NRA collapsed not because of the adverse Supreme Court ruling but because the administrative, public-relations, and economic challenges it had set itself had far outrun the imagination, talents, and techniques of the society. It was never a real test of an idea; it was simply an unhappy commentary upon the inadequacy of man's knowledge and techniques at that point. Its impact was sharply debated; did it actually bring recovery? Yet it clearly made contributions; it became a vast rallying ground for the renewed hopes and determinations of a people; it provided experience of incalculable value to economic management in World War II; it helped reverse the precedents in labor matters; it cleared the decks for yet another experiment in trust-busting. Because the NRA represented a sharp démarche from much of the American tradition, the full statute is provided below, with only administrative trivia removed.*

On NRA, in addition to the work of Schlesinger and Leuchtenburg, one should study Leverett S. Lyon et al., The National Recovery Administration *(1935); Sidney Fine,* The Automobile under the Blue Eagle *(1963); and Hugh Johnson,* The Blue Eagle from Egg to Earth *(1935).*

The National Industrial Recovery Act, Title I, of June 16, 1933, is to be found in U.S. Statutes at Large, *volume 48, pages 195–200.*

Declaration of Policy

Section 1. A national emergency productive of widespread unemployment and disorganization of industry, which burdens interstate and foreign commerce, affects the public welfare, and undermines the standards of living of the American people, is hereby declared to exist. It is hereby declared to be the policy of Congress to remove obstructions to the free flow of interstate and foreign commerce which tend to diminish the amount thereof; and to provide for the general welfare by promoting the organization of industry for the purpose of cooperative action among trade groups, to induce and maintain united action of labor and management under adequate governmental sanctions and supervision, to eliminate unfair competitive practices, to promote the fullest possible utilization of the present productive capacity of industries, to avoid undue restriction of production (except as may be temporarily required), to increase the consumption of industrial and agricultural products by increasing purchasing power, to reduce and relieve unemployment, to improve standards of labor, and otherwise to rehabilitate industry and to conserve natural resources.

Administrative Agencies

Sec. 2. (a) To effectuate the policy of this title, the President is hereby authorized to establish such agencies, to accept and utilize such voluntary and uncompensated services, to appoint, without regard to the provisions of the civil service laws, such officers and employees, and to utilize such Federal officers and employees, and, with the consent of the State, such State and local officers and employees, as he may find necessary, to prescribe their authorities, duties, responsibilities, and tenure, and, without regard to the Classification Act of 1923, as amended, to fix the compensation of any officers and employees so appointed.

(b) The President may delegate any of his functions and powers under this title to such officers, agents, and employees as he may designate or appoint, and may establish an industrial planning and research agency to aid in carrying out his functions under this title. . . .

Codes of Fair Competition

Sec. 3. (a) Upon the application to the President by one or more trade or industrial associations or groups, the President may approve a code or codes of fair competition for the trade or industry or subdivision thereof, represented by the applicant or applicants, if the President finds

(1) that such associations or groups impose no inequitable restrictions on admission to membership therein and are truly representative of such trades or industries or subdivisions thereof, and (2) that such code or codes are not designed to promote monopolies or to eliminate or oppress small enterprises and will not operate to discriminate against them, and will tend to effectuate the policy of this title: *Provided,* That such code or codes shall not permit monopolies or monopolistic practices: *Provided further,* That where such code or codes affect the services and welfare of persons engaged in other steps of the economic process, nothing in this section shall deprive such persons of the right to be heard prior to approval by the President of such code or codes. The President may, as a condition of his approval of any such code, impose such conditions (including requirements for the making of reports and the keeping of accounts) for the protection of consumers, competitors, employees, and others, and in furtherance of the public interest, and may provide such exceptions to and exemptions from the provisions of such code, as the President in his discretion deems necessary to effectuate the policy herein declared.

(b) After the President shall have approved any such code, the provisions of such code shall be the standards of fair competition for such trade or industry or subdivision thereof. Any violation of such standards in any transaction in or affecting interstate or foreign commerce shall be deemed an unfair method of competition in commerce within the meaning of the Federal Trade Commission Act, as amended; but nothing in this title shall be construed to impair the powers of the Federal Trade Commission under such Act, as amended.

(c) The several district courts of the United States are hereby invested with jurisdiction to prevent and restrain violations of any code of fair competition approved under this title; and it shall be the duty of the several district attorneys of the United States, in their respective districts, under the direction of the Attorney General, to institute proceedings in equity to prevent and restrain such violations.

(d) Upon his own motion, or if complaint is made to the President that abuses inimical to the public interest and contrary to the policy herein declared are prevalent in any trade or industry or subdivision thereof, and if no code of fair competition therefor has theretofore been approved by the President, the President, after such public notice and hearing as he shall specify, may prescribe and approve a code of fair competition for such trade or industry or subdivision thereof, which shall have the same effect as a code of fair competition approved by the President under subsection (a) of this section.

(e) On his own motion, or if any labor organization, or any trade or industrial organization, association, or group, which has complied with the provisions of this title, shall make complaint to the President that any article or articles are being imported into the United States in substantial quantities or increasing ratio to domestic production of any competitive article or articles and on such terms or under such conditions as to render ineffective or seriously to endanger the maintenance of any code or agreement under this title, the President may cause an immediate investigation to be made by the United States Tariff Commission, which shall give precedence to investigations under this subsection, and if, after such investigation and such public notice and hearing as he shall specify, the President shall find the existence of such facts, he shall, in order to effectuate the policy of this title, direct that the article or articles concerned shall be permitted entry into the United States only upon such terms and conditions and subject to the payment of such fees and to such limitations in the total quantity which may be imported (in the course of any specified period or periods) as he shall find it necessary to prescribe in order that the entry thereof shall not render or tend to render ineffective any code or agreement made under this title. In order to enforce any limitations imposed on the total quantity of imports, in any specified period or periods, of any article or articles under this subsection, the President may forbid the importation of such article or articles unless the importer shall have first obtained from the Secretary of the Treasury a license pursuant to such regulations as the President may prescribe. Upon information of any action by the President under this subsection the Secretary of the Treasury shall, through the proper officers, permit entry of the article or articles specified only upon such terms and conditions and subject to such fees, to such limitations in the quantity which may be imported, and to such requirements of license, as the President shall have directed. The decision of the President as to facts shall be conclusive. Any condition or limitation of entry under this subsection shall continue in effect until the President shall find and inform the Secretary of the Treasury that the conditions which led to the imposition of such condition or limitation upon entry no longer exists.

(f) When a code of fair competition has been approved or prescribed by the President under this title, any violation of any provision thereof in any transaction in or affecting interstate or foreign commerce shall be a misdemeanor and upon conviction thereof an offender shall be fined not more than $500 for each offense, and each day such violation continues shall be deemed a separate offense.

Agreements and Licenses

Sec. 4. (a) The President is authorized to enter into agreements with, and to approve voluntary agreements between and among, persons engaged in a trade or industry, labor organizations, and trade or industrial organizations, associations, or groups, relating to any trade or industry, if in his judgment such agreements will aid in effectuating the policy of this title with respect to transactions in or affecting interstate or foreign commerce, and will be consistent with the requirements of clause (2) of subsection (a) of section 3 for a code of fair competition.

(b) Whenever the President shall find that destructive wage or price cutting or other activities contrary to the policy of this title are being practiced in any trade or industry or any subdivision thereof, and, after such public notice and hearing as he shall specify, shall find it essential to license business enterprises in order to make effective a code of fair competition or an agreement under this title or otherwise to effectuate the policy of this title, and shall publicly so announce, no person shall, after a date fixed in such announcement, engage in or carry on any business, in or affecting interstate or foreign commerce, specified in such announcement, unless he shall have first obtained a license issued pursuant to such regulations as the President shall prescribe. The President may suspend or revoke any such license, after due notice and opportunity for hearing, for violations of the terms or conditions thereof. Any order of the President suspending or revoking any such license shall be final if in accordance with law. Any person who, without such a license or in violation of any condition thereof, carries on any such business for which a license is so required, shall, upon conviction thereof, be fined not more than $500, or imprisoned not more than six months, or both, and each day such violation continues shall be deemed a separate offense. Notwithstanding the provisions of section 2 (c), this subsection shall cease to be in effect at the expiration of one year after the date of enactment of this Act or sooner if the President shall by proclamation or the Congress shall by joint resolution declare that the emergency recognized by section 1 has ended.

Sec. 5. While this title is in effect (or in the case of a license, while section 4 (a) is in effect) and for sixty days thereafter, any code, agreement, or license approved, prescribed, or issued and in effect under this title, and any action complying with the provisions thereof taken during such period, shall be exempt from the provisions of the antitrust laws of the United States.

Nothing in this Act, and no regulation thereunder, shall prevent an individual from pursuing the vocation of manual labor and selling or trading the products thereof; nor shall anything in this Act, or regulation thereunder, prevent anyone from marketing or trading the produce of his farm.

Limitations upon Application of Title

Sec. 6. (a) No trade or industrial association or group shall be eligible to receive the benefit of the provisions of this title until it files with the President a statement containing such information relating to the activities of the association or group as the President shall by regulation prescribe.

(b) The President is authorized to prescribe rules and regulations designed to insure that any organization availing itself of the benefits of this title shall be truly representative of the trade or industry or subdivision thereof represented by such organization. Any organization violating any such rule or regulation shall cease to be entitled to the benefits of this title.

(c) Upon the request of the President, the Federal Trade Commission shall make such investigations as may be necessary to enable the President to carry out the provisions of this title, and for such purposes the Commission shall have all the powers vested in it with respect of investigations under the Federal Trade Commission Act, as amended.

Sec. 7. (a) Every code of fair competition, agreement, and license approved, prescribed, or issued under this title shall contain the following conditions: (1) That employees shall have the right to organize and bargain collectively through representatives of their own choosing, and shall be free from the interference, restraint, or coercion of employers of labor, or their agents, in the designation of such representatives or in self-organization or in other concerted activities for the purpose of collective bargaining or other mutual aid or protection; (2) that no employee and no one seeking employment shall be required as a condition of employment to join any company union or to refrain from joining, organizing, or assisting a labor organization of his own choosing; and (3) that employers shall comply with the maximum hours of labor, minimum rates of pay, and other conditions of employment, approved or prescribed by the President.

(b) The President shall, so far as practicable, afford every opportunity to employers and employees in any trade or industry or subdivision thereof with respect to which the conditions referred to in clauses (1) and (2) of subsection (a) prevail, to establish by mutual agreement, the standards as to the maximum hours of labor, minimum rates of pay, and such other conditions of employment as may be necessary in such trade or industry or subdivision thereof to effectuate the policy of this title; and the standards established in such agreements, when approved by the President, shall have the same effect as a code of fair competition, approved by the President under subsection (a) of section 3.

(c) Where no such mutual agreement has been approved by the President he may investigate the labor practices, policies, wages, hours of labor, and conditions of employment in such trade or industry or subdivision thereof; and upon the basis of such investigations, and after such hearings as the President finds advisable, he is authorized to prescribe a limited code of fair competition fixing such maximum hours of labor, minimum rates of pay, and other conditions of employment in the trade or industry or subdivision thereof investigated as he finds to be necessary to effectuate the policy of this title, which shall have the same effect as a code of fair competition approved by the President under subsection (a) of section 3. The President may differentiate according to experience and skill of the employees affected and according to the locality of employment; but no attempt shall be made to introduce any classification according to the nature of the work involved which might tend to set a maximum as well as a minimum wage. . . .

Oil Regulation

Sec. 9. (a) The President is further authorized to initiate before the Interstate Commerce Commission proceedings necessary to prescribe regulations to control the operations of oil pipe lines and to fix reasonable, compensatory rates for the transportation of petroleum and its products by pipe lines, and the Interstate Commerce Commission shall grant preference to the hearings and determination of such cases.

(b) The President is authorized to institute proceedings to divorce from any holding company any pipe-line company controlled by such holding company which pipe-line company by unfair practices or by exorbitant rates in the transportation of petroleum or its products tends to create a monopoly.

(c) The President is authorized to prohibit the transportation in interstate and foreign commerce of petroleum and the products thereof produced or withdrawn from storage in excess of the amount permitted to be produced or withdrawn from storage by any State law or valid regulation or order prescribed thereunder, by any board, commission, officer, or other duly authorized agency of a State. Any violation of any order of the President issued under the provisions of this subsection shall be punishable by fine of not to exceed $1,000, or imprisonment for not to exceed six months, or both.

Rules and Regulations

Sec. 10. (a) The President is authorized to prescribe such rules and regulations as may be necessary to carry out the purposes of this title, and fees for licenses and for filing codes of fair competition and agreements, and any violation of any such rule or regulation shall be punishable by fine of not to exceed $500, or imprisonment for not to exceed six months, or both.

(b) The President may from time to time cancel or modify any order, approval, license, rule, or regulation issued under this title; and each agreement, code of fair competition, or license approved, prescribed, or issued under this title shall contain an express provision to that effect.

A Sample Charter: The Code of Fair Competition for the Automobile Manufacturing Industry, 1933

It is difficult to visualize from the broad terms of the statute itself even the dreams of the National Recovery Administration planners, to say nothing of the actual development of the administration. A closer look at one of the actual codes of fair competition can provide a sharper image not only of what was proposed, but also of some of the problems which might have been expected to arise. It must be remembered, however, that the codes varied immensely in terms of the problems of the industry involved in each case, the effectiveness of the particular administrators involved in NRA, and the degree of political pressure which could be brought to bear upon the industry. It should also be remembered that even the code gives only the bare outline of the proposition. What actually happened was a matter of dynamic interaction of particular people in complicated and fluid administrative situations. Most of the detailed NRA operations have not yet been examined with care. But one can see the outlines of its major difficulties in careful studies such as the following: Sidney Fine, "President Roosevelt and the Automobile Code," Mississippi Valley Historical Review, *volume 45 (1958–1959) pages 23–50; Gerald Nash, "Experiments in Industrial Mobilization: W.I.B. and N.R.A.,"* Mid-America, *volume 45 (1963), pages 157–174; and William H. Wilson, "How the Chamber of Commerce Viewed the N.R.A.: A Reexamination,"* Mid-America, *volume 44 (1962), pages 95–108. Various NRA codes may be found in Lewis Mayer (ed.),* A Handbook of N.R.A. *(2d ed., 1934).*

The automobile code was Executive Order 6258-A, issued on August 26, 1933. Section I, consisting of definitions, has been omitted.

The following provisions are established as a Code of Fair Competition for the automobile manufacturing industry:

II. Wages

On and after the effective date, and to and until the expiration date:

The minimum wages of factory employes covered hereby shall be at the following hourly rates regardless of whether the employe is compensated on the basis of time rate or piece rate or otherwise:

In cities having 500,000 population or over, 43 cents; in cities having 250,000 and less than 500,000 population, 41½ cents; in cities or towns having less than 250,000 population, 40 cents.

Provided, however, that apprentices and learners and females not doing the same work as adult males shall be paid not less than 87½ per cent of said minimums, but the number of such apprentices and learners and females not doing the same work as adult males, employed by any employer, shall not exceed 5 per cent of the total number of factory employes of such employer, including subsidiary and affiliated companies.

Equitable adjustment in all pay schedules of factory employes above the minimums shall be made on or before Sept. 15, 1933, by any employers who have not heretofore made such adjustments and the first monthly reports of wages required to be filed under this code shall contain all wage increases made since May 1, 1933.

The minimum wages of office and salaried employes covered hereby shall not be less than the following weekly rates:

In cities having 500,000 population or over, at the rate of $15 per week; in cities having 250,000 and less than 500,000 population, at the rate of $14.50 per week; in cities or towns having less than 250,000 population, at the rate of $14 per week.

III. Hours

There are substantial fluctuations in the rate of factory production throughout each year, due mainly to the concentration of a large part of the annual demand for cars within a few months, and also to the slowing down of employment in connection with changes in models and other causes beyond the industry's control.

To lessen the effect on employment of these conditions, it has been the policy of the industry to adjust working hours, in order to retain the greatest number of employes and, so far as practicable, adjust the manufacturing schedules of component parts to allow a more uniform schedule of hours. The industry will continue this policy.

The progressive falling off of retail sales during the years of depression, resulting in the necessity of repeated adjustments downward in production schedules, had its important influence in causing an abnormal fluctuation in employment schedules.

Before the presentation of this code the industry had gone far in spreading available work to relieve unemployment, and under this code it proposes to spread the work as far as practicable in its judgment, consistent with the policy of giving each employe a reasonable amount of work in each year.

For this purpose it is made a provision of this code that employers shall so operate their plants that the average employment of all factory employes (with the exceptions stated below) shall not exceed thirty-five hours per week for the period from the effective date to the expiration date, and the hours of each individual employe shall so far as practicable conform with this average and shall in no case exceed the same by more than 3 per cent.

In order to give to employes such average of thirty-five hours per week it will be necessary at times to operate for substantially longer hours, but no employe shall be employed for more than six days or forty-eight hours in any one week, and all such peaks shall be absorbed in such average.

In order that production and employment for the main body of employes may be maintained with as few interruptions as possible, it is necessary, and it is a part of this code, that the supervisory staff and employes engaged in the preparation, care and maintenance of plant machinery and facilities of and for production, shall be exempt from the weekly limitations above provided, but the hours of employment of any such exempted employe engaged in the preparation, care and maintenance of factories and machinery of and for production shall not exceed forty-two hours per week averaged on an annual basis.

Office and other salaried employes, covered hereby, receiving less than $35 per week shall not work more than forty-eight hours in any one week and not more than an average of forty hours per week for the period from the effective date to the expiration date. Employes receiving more than $35 per week and executives and managerial and supervisory staffs are not subject to any hourly limitations.

The industry recognizes the serious problem of major fluctuations in production due to concentrated seasonal customer demand and changes in the rate of production caused by changes in models, which changes are necessary. The chamber pledges itself to make a further study of this problem in an effort to develop any further practical measures which can be taken to provide more stable and continuous employment and to reduce to a minimum the portion of employes temporarily employed and to submit a report thereon to the administrator by Dec. 1, 1933.

IV. Child Labor

Employers in the industry shall not employ any person under the age of 16 years. The chamber states that child labor has at no time been a factor in the automobile industry.

V. Reports and Statistics

Each employer engaged in the industry will furnish to the chamber as herein below provided, approximately every four weeks, duly certified reports in such form as may hereafter be provided showing actual hours worked by the various occupational groups of employes and wages paid.

VI. Administration

For the purpose of supplying the President and the administrator with requisite data as to the observance and effectiveness of this code and the administration thereof, the chamber is hereby designated—

(a) To collect from the members of the industry all data and statistics called for by this code, or required by the President, or reasonably pertinent to the effectuation of Title I of the National Industrial Recovery Act, and compile the same, and disseminate among the members of the industry summaries thereof, all in such form and manner as the chamber shall reasonably prescribe subject to approval by the Administrator.

(b) To represent the industry in conference with the administrator with respect to the application of this code and of said act and any regulations issued thereunder; provided, however, that as regards all matters mentioned in this paragraph (b), the chamber shall have no power to bind the industry or any subdivision thereof. The President or the administrator may designate a representative to participate in such conferences, who shall have access to all data and statistics collected by the chamber as above provided. The chamber or its authorized committee or agent shall hold itself in readiness to assist and keep the administrator fully advised, and to meet with the administrator's representative from time to time as required to consider and study any suggestions or proposals presented upon behalf of the administrator or any member of the industry regarding the operation, observance or administration of this code.

(c) The duties of the chamber above referred to shall be exercised by the chamber by its board of directors, which may delegate any of said duties to such agents and committees as it may appoint whose personnel, duties and power may be changed.

VII. Collective Bargaining

Employers in this industry shall comply with the following requirements of Section 7 (a) of Title I of the National Industrial Recovery Act.

Employes shall have the right to organize and bargain collectively through representatives of their own choosing, and shall be free from the interference, restraint, or coercion of employers of labor, or their agents, in the designation of such representatives or in self-organization or in other concerted activities for the purpose of collective bargaining or other mutual aid or protection; (2) no employe and no one seeking employment shall be required as a condition of employment to join any company union or to refrain from joining, organizing, or assisting a labor organization of his own choosing; and (3) employers shall comply with the maximum hours of labor, minimum rates of pay, and other conditions of employment, approved or prescribed by the President.

Without in any way attempting to qualify or modify, by interpretation, the foregoing requirements of the National Industrial Recovery Act, employers in this industry may exercise their right to select, retain or advance employes on the basis of individual merit, without regard to their membership or non-membership in any organization.

VIII. Modifications

As required by Section 10 (b) of Title I of the National Industrial Recovery Act, the following provision is contained in this code. The President may from time to time cancel or modify any order, approval, license, rule or regulation issued under said title.

IX. Right to Object to Modifications

By presenting this code the chamber and others assenting hereto do not thereby consent to any modification thereof and they reserve the right to object individually or jointly to any such modifications.

X. Supplementary Provisions

Such provisions of this code as are not required to be included therein by the National Industrial Recovery Act may, upon the application of the industry or a subdivision thereof and with the approval of the President, be modified or eliminated. It is contemplated that from time to time supplementary provisions to this code or additional codes may be submitted in behalf of the industry or various subdivisions thereof for the approval of the President.

Too Great a Blessing: An Answer to Overproduction, the Agricultural Adjustment Act, 1933

Roosevelt was able to serve up during the campaign a bland and inoffensive farm speech which had been put together by over thirty conflicting advisers and said little. In office, however, he had to decide among the plans, and soon. The result of the complicated maneuvering in the spring of 1933 was a farm bill which hopefully combined crop controls (designed to cut production and *increase prices) with conservation practices (designed to restore the soil) and incentive payments (planned in order to reduce the surpluses of the future). The issue was a complex one at best. It was confused at once by the emergency action which destroyed crops and pigs, since, for the first year, the legislation had been passed too late to prevent production in advance. Here was dramatic, emotional material for those who saw a "policy of scarcity" as a departure from moral law. The constitutional issues were grave and controversial. When the statute printed below was declared unconstitutional by the Supreme Court (*Butler v. United States, *1936), the administration resorted to a Soil Conservation and Domestic Allotment Act which carried the policy along on a halting basis. In 1938 a new, and constitutional, Agricultural Adjustment Act set the basis for farm policy until the end of the war, and after. There was much experiment with specific techniques, in the face of raging debates and of farmers' ingenuity in increasing production despite controls. But the initial act provided below makes clear the general tenor of the New Deal's agricultural policy.*

A rich literature has developed on the matter of Roosevelt's farm policy. Especially interesting are Christina Campbell, The Farm Bureau Federation and the New Deal *(1962); Dean Albertson,* Roosevelt's Farmer: Claude R. Wickard in the New Deal *(1961); Murray R. Benedict,* Farm Policies of the United States: 1790–1950 *(1953); Gilbert C. Fite,* George H. Peek and the Fight for Farm Parity *(1954) and "Farmer Opinion and the Agricultural Adjustment Act of 1933,"* Mississippi Valley Historical Review, *volume 48 (1961–1962), pages 656–673; and Edwin G. Nourse et al.,* Three Years of the Agricultural Adjustment Act *(1937).*

Title I of the Act itself is to be found in U.S. Statutes at Large, *volume 48, pages 31–38.*

DECLARATION OF EMERGENCY

That the present acute economic emergency being in part the consequence of a severe and increasing disparity between the prices of agricultural and other commodities, which disparity has largely destroyed the purchasing power of farmers for industrial products, has broken down the orderly exchange of commodities, and has seriously impaired the agricultural assets supporting the national credit structure, it is hereby declared that these conditions in the basic industry of agriculture have affected transactions in agricultural commodities with a national public interest, have burdened and obstructed the normal currents of commerce in such commodities, and render imperative the immediate enactment of title I of this Act.

DECLARATION OF POLICY

Sec. 2. It is hereby declared to be the policy of Congress—

(1) To establish and maintain such balance between the production and consumption of agricultural commodities, and such marketing conditions therefor, as will reestablish prices to farmers at a level that

will give agricultural commodities a purchasing power with respect to articles that farmers buy, equivalent to the purchasing power of agricultural commodities in the base period. The base period in the case of all agricultural commodities except tobacco shall be the prewar period, August 1909-July 1914. In the case of tobacco, the base period shall be the postwar period, August 1919-July 1929.

(2) To approach such equality of purchasing power by gradual correction of the present inequalities therein at as rapid a rate as is deemed feasible in view of the current consumptive demand in domestic and foreign markets.

(3) To protect the consumers' interest by readjusting farm production at such level as will not increase the percentage of the consumers' retail expenditures for agricultural commodities, or products derived therefrom, which is returned to the farmer, above the percentage which was returned to the farmer in the prewar period, August 1909–July 1914.

Part 1—Cotton Option Contracts

. . . *Sec. 6.* (a) The Secretary of Agriculture is hereby authorized to enter into option contracts with the producers of cotton to sell to any such producer an amount of cotton to be agreed upon not in excess of the amount of reduction in production of cotton by such producer below the amount produced by him in the preceding crop year, in all cases where such producer agrees in writing to reduce the amount of cotton produced by him in 1933, below his production in the previous year, by not less than 30 per centum, without increase in commercial fertilization per acre.

(b) To any such producer so agreeing to reduce production the Secretary of Agriculture shall deliver a nontransferable-option contract agreeing to sell to said producer an amount, equivalent to the amount of his agreed reduction, of the cotton in the possession and control of the Secretary.

(c) The producer is to have the option to buy said cotton at the average price paid by the Secretary for the cotton procured under section 3, and is to have the right at any time up to January 1, 1934, to exercise his option, upon proof that he has complied with his contract and with all the rules and regulations of the Secretary of Agriculture with respect thereto, by taking said cotton upon payment by him of his option price and all actual carrying charges on such cotton; or the Secretary may sell such cotton for the account of such producer, paying him the excess of the market price at the date of sale over the average price above referred to after deducting all actual and necessary carrying charges: *Provided,* That in no event shall the producer be held responsible or liable for financial loss incurred in the holding of such cotton or on account of the carrying charges therein: *Provided further,* That such agreement to curtail cotton production shall contain a further provision that such cotton producer shall not use the land taken out of cotton production for the production for sale, directly or indirectly, of any other nationally produced agricultural commodity or product.

(d) If any cotton held by the Secretary of Agriculture is not disposed of under subsection (c), the Secretary is authorized to enter into similar option contracts with respect to such cotton, conditioned upon a like reduction of production in 1934, and permitting the producer in each case to exercise his option at any time up to January 1, 1935.

Sec. 7. The Secretary shall sell the cotton held by him at his discretion, but subject to the foregoing provisions: *Provided,* That he shall dispose of all cotton held by him by March 1, 1936: *Provided further,* That the Secretary shall have authority to enter into additional option contracts for so much of such cotton as is not necessary to comply with the provisions of section 6, in combination with benefit payments as provided for in part 2 of this title.

Part 2—Commodity Benefits

General Powers

Sec. 8. In order to effectuate the declared policy, the Secretary of Agriculture shall have power—

(1) To provide for reduction in the acreage or reduction in the production for market, or both, of any basic agricultural commodity, through agreements with producers or by other voluntary methods, and to provide for rental or benefit payments in connection therewith or upon that part of the production of any basic agricultural commodity required for domestic consumption, in such amounts as the Secretary deems fair and reasonable, to be paid out of any moneys available for such payments. . . .

(2) To enter into marketing agreements with processors, associations of producers, and others engaged in the handling, in the current of interstate or foreign commerce of any agricultural commodity or product thereof, after due notice and opportunity for hearing to interested parties. The making of any such agreement shall not be held to be in violation of any of the antitrust laws of the United States, and any such agreement shall be deemed to be lawful. . . .

(3) To issue licenses permitting processors, associations of producers, and others to engage in the handling, in the current of interstate or foreign commerce, of any agricultural commodity or product thereof, or any competing commodity or product thereof. Such licenses shall be subject to such terms and conditions, not in conflict with existing Acts of Congress or regulations pursuant thereto, as may be necessary to eliminate unfair practices or charges that prevent or tend to prevent the effectuation of the declared policy and the restoration of normal economic conditions in the marketing of such commodities or products and the financing thereof. The Secretary of Agriculture may suspend or revoke any such license, after due notice and opportunity for hearing, for violations of the terms or conditions thereof. Any order of the Secretary suspending or revoking any such license shall be final if in accordance with law. Any such person engaged in such handling without a license as required by the Secretary under this section shall be subject to a fine of not more than $1,000 for each day during which the violation continues.

(4) To require any licensee under this section to furnish such reports as to quantities of agricultural commodities or products thereof bought and sold and the prices thereof, and as to trade practices and charges, and to keep such systems of accounts, as may be necessary for the purpose of part 2 of this title. . . .

Processing Tax

Sec. 9. (a) To obtain revenue for extraordinary expenses incurred by reason of the national economic emergency, there shall be levied processing taxes as hereinafter provided. When the Secretary of Agriculture determines that rental or benefit payments are to be made with respect to any basic agricultural commodity, he shall proclaim such determination, and a processing tax shall be in effect with respect to such commodity from the beginning of the marketing year therefor next following the date of such proclamation. The processing tax shall be levied, assessed, and collected upon the first domestic processing of the commodity, whether of domestic production or imported, and shall be paid by the processor. The rate of tax shall conform to the requirements of subsection (b). Such rate shall be determined by the Secretary of Agriculture as of the date the tax first takes effect, and the rate so determined shall, at such intervals as the Secretary finds necessary to effectuate the declared policy, be adjusted by him to conform to such requirements. The processing tax shall terminate at the end of the marketing year current at the time the Secretary proclaims that rental or benefit payments are to be discontinued with respect to such commodity. . . .

(b) The processing tax shall be at such rate as equals the difference between the current average farm price for the commodity and the fair exchange value of the commodity; except that if the Secretary has reason to believe that the tax at such rate will cause such reduction in the quantity of the commodity or products thereof domestically consumed as to result in the accumulation of surplus stocks of the commodity or products thereof or in the depression of the farm price of the commodity, then he shall cause an appropriate investigation to be made and afford due notice and opportunity for hearing to interested parties. If thereupon the Secretary finds that such result will occur, then the processing tax shall be at such rate as will prevent such accumulation of surplus stocks and depression of the farm price of the commodity. In computing the current average farm price in the case of wheat, premiums paid producers for protein content shall not be taken into account.

(c) For the purposes of part 2 of this title, the fair exchange value of a commodity shall be the price therefor that will give the commodity the same purchasing power, with respect to articles farmers buy, as such commodity had during the base period specified in section 2; and the current average farm price and the fair exchange value shall be ascertained by the Secretary of Agriculture from available statistics of the Department of Agriculture. . . .

(e) When any processing tax, or increase or decrease therein, takes effect in respect of a commodity the Secretary of Agriculture, in order to prevent pyramiding of the processing tax and profiteering in the sale of the products derived from the commodity, shall make public such information as he deems necessary regarding (1) the relationship between the processing tax and the price paid to producers of the commodity, (2) the effect of the processing tax upon prices to consumers of products of the commodity, (3) the relationship, in previous periods, between prices paid to the producers of the commodity and prices to consumers of the products thereof, and (4) the situation in foreign countries relating to prices paid to producers of the commodity and prices to consumers of the products thereof. . . .

Sec. 10.

. . . (b) The Secretary of Agriculture is authorized to establish, for the more effective administration of the functions vested in him by this title, State and local committees, or associations of producers, and to permit cooperative associations of producers, when in his judgment they are qualified to do so, to act as agents of their members and patrons in connection with the distribution of rental or benefit payments. . . .

Commodities

Sec. 11. As used in this title, the term "basic agricultural commodity" means wheat, cotton, field corn, hogs, rice, tobacco, and milk and its products, and any regional or market classification, type, or grade thereof; but the Secretary of Agriculture shall exclude from the operation of the provisions of this title, during any period, any such commodity or classification, type, or grade thereof if he finds, upon investigation at any time and after due notice and opportunity for hearing to interested parties, that the conditions of production, marketing, and consumption are such that during such period this title can not be effectively administered to the end of effectuating the declared policy with respect to such commodity or classification, type, or grade thereof.

The Cooperative Commonwealth: The Tennessee Valley Act, 1933

None of the New Deal legislation was so specifically forecast by the campaign as the Tennessee Valley Act, but none was more controversial. It not only suggested a dramatic new extension of the use of Federal government power; it also put government squarely into a "business" which produced and distributed goods (electricity and fertilizer). The specific situation which made

TVA possible was a relatively narrow one, the government construction of a hydroelectric dam on the Tennessee River at Muscle Shoals during World War I. The dam had not been completed in time to lend its electrical power to the nitrates factory being built nearby for the production of explosives, and after the war the whole elaborate structure had become a vast white elephant. The Coolidge and Hoover administrations found the mere possession of it embarrassing in the light of their strong advocacy of private enterprise. Progressive Congressman George Norris of Nebraska worked hard throughout the 1920s to prevent its being turned over to some private interest. Norris's persistency, Roosevelt's election, and the whiplash of the Depression made it possible to see Muscle Shoals as an asset rather than a liability for the American people.

The administration's approach to the problem was hardly narrow. In fact, it represents one of the genuinely new and imaginative devices in modern government. The Tennessee Valley Authority was to be a regional development project, with a variety of interlocking objectives. It was not to suffer the irrelevant inhibitions of state boundaries, and it was to be an independent operation, a government-owned corporation. Once started, it would conduct its own operations, repay Congress's investment and plow its "profits" back into further development. It would be dependent upon neither the state legislatures nor the Congress for the year-by-year financing (and control) which had generally characterized government business operations.

In the circumstances, it was necessary to devote a significant part of the legislation to the matter of establishing ethical guides and constitutional bases for such a unique situation; the TVA was certain to become controversial. It was attacked as a symbol of socialism, especially by the electric power companies and many of the politicians of the region who feared its competition and resented its independence. It was plagued also by internal dissensions over the relationships of its many roles. Without doubt, it has become one of the most nearly permanent and one of the most generally significant of the New Deal innovations, although the hope that it would be widely imitated in dealing with other river valleys has been consistently frustrated.

David Lilienthal, T.V.A.: Democracy on the March *(1944), an excerpt from which is printed later as Selection 22, is the classic explanation and defense of the authority by its most dynamic and imaginative director. Lilienthal's* The Journals of David E. Lilienthal *(1964), two volumes, is an almost uniquely frank diary which reveals much of the inside story of the great experiment. On Roosevelt's interests in conservation generally, see Edgar B. Nixon (ed.),* Franklin D. Roosevelt and Conservation: 1911–1945 *(1957).*

The text of the act is taken from U.S. Statutes at Large, *volume 48, pages 58–69 and 71.*

Be it enacted . . . , That for the purpose of maintaining and operating the properties now owned by the United States in the vicinity of Muscle Shoals, Alabama, in the interest of the national defense and for agricultural and industrial development, and to improve navigation in the Tennessee River and to control the destructive flood waters in the Tennessee River and Mississippi River Basins, there is hereby created a body corporate by the name of the "Tennessee Valley Authority" (hereinafter referred to as the "Corporation"). The board of directors first appointed shall be deemed the incorporators, and the incorporation shall be held to have been effected from the date of the first meeting of the board. This Act may be cited as the "Tennessee Valley Authority Act of 1933."

Sec. 2. (a) The board of directors of the Corporation (hereinafter referred to as the "board") shall be composed of three members, to be appointed by the President, by and with the advice and consent of the Senate. In appointing the members of the board, the President shall designate the chairman. All other officials, agents, and employees shall be designated and selected by the board.

(b) The terms of office of the members first taking office after the approval of this Act shall expire as designated by the President at the time of nomination, one at the end of the third year, one at the end of the sixth year, and one at the end of the ninth year, after the date of approval of this Act. . . .

(e) Each of the members of the board shall be a citizen of the United States, and shall receive a salary at the rate of $10,000 a year, to be paid by the Corporation as current expenses. . . . No member of said board shall, during his continuance in office, be engaged in any other business, but each member shall devote himself to the work of the Corporation.

(f) No director shall have financial interest in any public-utility corporation engaged in the business of distributing and selling power to the public nor in any corporation engaged in the manufacture, selling, or distribution of fixed nitrogen or fertilizer, or any ingredients thereof, nor shall any member have any interest in any business that may be adversely affected by the success of the Corporation as a producer of concentrated fertilizers or as a producer of electric power.

(g) The board shall direct the exercise of all the powers of the Corporation.

(h) All members of the board shall be persons who profess a belief in the feasibility and wisdom of this Act.

Sec. 3. The board shall without regard to the provisions of Civil Service laws applicable to officers and employees of the United States, appoint such managers, assistant managers, officers, employees, attorneys, and agents, as are necessary for the transaction of its business, fix their compensation, define their duties, require bonds of such of them as the board may designate, and provide a system of organization to fix responsibility and promote efficiency. Any appointee of the board may be removed in the discretion of the board. No regular officer or employee of the Corporation shall receive a salary in excess of that received by the members of the board.

All contracts to which the Corporation is a party and which require the employment of laborers and mechanics in the construction, alteration, maintenance, or repair of buildings, dams, locks, or other projects shall contain a provision that not less than the prevailing rate of wages for work of a similar nature prevailing in the vicinity shall be paid to such laborers or mechanics.

In the event any dispute arises as to what are the prevailing rates of wages, the question shall be referred to the Secretary of Labor for determination, and his decision shall be final. In the determination of such prevailing rate or rates, due regard shall be given to those rates which have been secured through collective agreement by representatives of employers and employees.

Where such work as is described in the two preceding paragraphs is done directly by the Corporation the prevailing rate of wages shall be paid in the same manner as though such work had been let by contract.

Insofar as applicable, the benefits of the Act entitled "An Act to provide compensation for employees of the United States suffering injuries while in the performance of their duties, and for other purposes," approved September 7, 1916, as amended, shall extend to persons given employment under the provisions of this Act.

Sec. 4. Except as otherwise specifically provided in this Act, the Corporation—

(a) Shall have succession in its corporate name.

(b) May sue and be sued in its corporate name.

(c) May adopt and use a corporate seal, which shall be judicially noticed.

(d) May make contracts, as herein authorized.

(e) May adopt, amend, and repeal bylaws.

(f) May purchase or lease and hold such real and personal property as it deems necessary or convenient in the transaction of its business, and may dispose of any such personal property held by it. . . .

(g) Shall have such powers as may be necessary or appropriate for the exercise of the powers herein specifically conferred upon the Corporation.

(h) Shall have power in the name of the United States of America to exercise the right of eminent domain, and in the purchase of any real estate or the acquisition of real estate by condemnation proceedings, the title to such real estate shall be taken in the name of the United States of America, and thereupon all such real estate shall be entrusted to the Corporation as the agent of the United States to accomplish the purposes of this Act.

(i) Shall have power to acquire real estate for the construction of dams, reservoirs, transmission lines, power houses, and other structures, and navigation projects at any point along the Tennessee River, or any of its tributaries, and in the event that the owner or owners of such property shall fail and refuse to sell to the Corporation at a price deemed fair and reasonable by the board, then the Corporation may proceed to exercise the right of eminent domain, and to condemn all property that it deems necessary for carrying out the purposes of this Act, and all such condemnation proceedings shall be had pursuant to the provisions and requirements hereinafter specified, with reference to any and all condemnation proceedings.

(j) Shall have power to construct dams, reservoirs, power houses, power structures, transmission lines, navigation projects, and incidental works in the Tennessee River and its tributaries, and to unite the various power installations into one or more systems by transmission lines.

Sec. 5. The board is hereby authorized—

(a) To contract with commercial producers for the production of such fertilizers or fertilizer materials as may be needed in the Government's program of development and introduction in excess of that produced by Government plants. Such contracts may provide either for outright purchase of materials by the board or only for the payment of carrying charges on special materials manufactured at the board's request for its program.

(b) To arrange with farmers and farm organizations for large-scale practical use of the new forms of fertilizers under conditions permitting an accurate measure of the economic return they produce.

(c) To cooperate with National, State, district, or county experimental stations or demonstration farms, for the use of new forms of fertilizer or fertilizer practices during the initial or experimental period of their introduction.

(d) The board in order to improve and cheapen the production of fertilizer is authorized to manufacture and sell fixed nitrogen, fertilizer, and fertilizer ingredients at Muscle Shoals by the employment of existing facilities, by modernizing existing plants, or by any other process or processes that in its judgment shall appear wise and profitable for the fixation of atmospheric nitrogen or the cheapening of the production of fertilizer.

(e) Under the authority of this Act the board may make donations or sales of the product of the plant or plants operated by it to be fairly and equitably distributed through the agency of county demonstration agents, agricultural colleges, or otherwise as the board may direct, for experimentation, education, and introduction of the use of such products in cooperation with practical farmers so as to obtain information as to the value, effect, and best methods of their use.

(f) The board is authorized to make alterations, modifications, or improvements in existing plants and facilities, and to construct new plants.

(g) In the event it is not used for the fixation of nitrogen for agricultural purposes or leased, then the board shall maintain in stand-by condition nitrate plant numbered 2, or its equivalent, for the fixation of atmospheric nitrogen, for the production of explosives in the event of war or a national emergency, until the Congress shall by joint resolution release the board from this obligation, and if any part thereof be used by the board for the manufacture of phosphoric acid or potash, the balance of nitrate plant numbered 2 shall be kept in stand-by condition.

(h) To establish, maintain, and operate laboratories and experimental plants, and to undertake experiments for the purpose of enabling the Corporation to furnish nitrogen products for military purposes, and nitrogen and other fertilizer products for agricultural purposes in the most economical manner and at the highest standard of efficiency. . . .

(m) No products of the Corporation shall be sold for use outside of the United States, its Territories and possessions, except to the United States Government for the use of its Army and Navy, or to its allies in case of war. . . .

Sec. 6. In the appointment of officials and the selection of employees for said Corporation, and in the promotion of any such employees or officials, no political test or qualification shall be permitted or given consideration, but all such appointments and promotions shall be given and made on the basis of merit and efficiency. Any member of said board who is found by the President of the United States to be guilty of a violation of this section shall be removed from office by the President of the United States, and any appointee of said board who is found by the board to be guilty of a violation of this section shall be removed from office by said board.

Sec. 7. In order to enable the Corporation to exercise the powers and duties vested in it by this Act—

(a) The exclusive use, possession, and control of the United States nitrate plants numbered 1 and 2, including steam plants, located, respectively, at Sheffield, Alabama, and Muscle Shoals, Alabama, together with all real estate and buildings connected therewith, all tools and machinery, equipment, accessories, and materials belonging thereto, and all laboratories and plants used as auxiliaries thereto; the fixed-nitrogen research laboratory, the Waco limestone quarry, in Alabama, and Dam Numbered 2, located at Muscle Shoals, its power house, and all hydroelectric and operating appurtenances (except the locks), and all machinery, lands, and buildings in connection therewith, and all appurtenances thereof, and all other property to be acquired by the Corporation in its own name or in the name of the United States of America, are hereby intrusted to the Corporation for the purposes of this Act. . . .

Sec. 9. (a) The board shall file with the President and with the Congress, in December of each year, a financial statement and a complete report as to the business of the Corporation covering the preceding governmental fiscal year. This report shall include an itemized statement of the cost of power at each power station, the total number of employees and the names, salaries, and duties of those receiving compensation at the rate of more than $1,500 a year.

(b) The Comptroller General of the United States shall audit the transactions of the Corporation at such times as he shall determine, but not less frequently than once each governmental fiscal year, with personnel of his selection. . . .

Sec. 10. The board is hereby empowered and authorized to sell the surplus power not used in its operations, and for operation of locks and other works generated by it, to States, counties, municipalities, corporations, partnerships, or individuals, according to the policies hereinafter set forth; and to carry out said authority, the board is authorized to enter into contracts for such sale for a term not exceeding twenty years, and in the sale of such current by the board it shall give preference to States, counties, municipalities, and cooperative organizations of citizens or farmers, not organized or doing business for profit, but primarily for the purpose of supplying electricity to its own citizens or members: *Provided,* That all contracts made with private companies or individuals for the sale of power, which power is to be resold for a profit, shall contain a provision authorizing the board to cancel said contract upon five years' notice in writing, if the board needs said power to supply the demands of States, counties, or municipalities. In order to promote and encourage the fullest possible use of electric light and power on farms within reasonable distance of any of its transmission lines the board in its discretion shall have power to construct transmission lines to farms and small villages that are not otherwise supplied with electricity at reasonable rates, and to make such rules and regulations governing such sale and distribution of such electric power as in its judgment may be just and equitable: *Provided further,* That the board is hereby authorized and directed to make studies, experiments, and determinations to promote the wider and better use of electric power for agricultural and domestic use, or for small or local industries, and it may cooperate with State governments, or their subdivisions or agencies, with educational or research institutions, and with cooperatives or other organizations, in the application of electric power to the fuller and better balanced development of the resources of the region.

Sec. 11. It is hereby declared to be the policy of the Government so far as practical to distribute and sell the surplus power generated at Muscle Shoals equitably among the States, counties, and municipalities within transmission distance. This policy is further declared to be that the projects herein provided for shall be considered primarily as for the benefit of the people of the section as a whole and particularly the domestic and rural consumers to whom the power can economically be made available, and accordingly that sale to and use by industry shall be a secondary purpose, to be utilized principally to secure a sufficiently high load factor and revenue returns which will permit domestic and rural use at the lowest possible rates and in such manner as to encourage increased domestic and rural use of electricity. It is further hereby declared to be the policy of the Government to utilize the Muscle Shoals properties so far as may be necessary to improve, increase, and cheapen the production of fertilizer and fertilizer ingredients by carrying out the provisions of this Act.

Sec. 12. In order to place the board upon a fair basis for making such contracts and for receiving bids for the sale of such power, it is hereby expressly authorized, either from appropriations made by Congress or from funds secured from the sale of such power, or from funds secured by the sale of bonds hereafter provided for, to construct, lease, purchase, or authorize the construction of transmission lines within transmission distance from the place where generated, and to interconnect with other systems. The board is also authorized to lease to any person, persons, or corporation the use of any transmission line owned by the Government and operated by the board, but no such lease shall be made that in any way interferes with the use of such transmission line by the board: *Provided,* That if any State, county, municipality, or other public or cooperative organization of citizens or farmers, not organized or doing business for profit, but primarily for the purpose of supplying electricity to its own citizens or members, or any two or more of such municipalities or organizations, shall construct or agree to construct and maintain a properly designed and built transmission line to the Government reservation upon which is located a Government generating plant, or to a main transmission line owned by the Government or leased by the board and under the control of the board, the board is hereby authorized and directed to contract with such State, county, municipality, or other organization, or two or more of them, for the sale of electricity for a term not exceeding thirty years; and in any such case the board shall give to such State, county, municipality, or other organization ample time to fully comply with any local law now in existence or hereafter enacted providing for the necessary legal authority for such State, county, municipality, or other organization to contract with the board for such power: *Provided further,* That all contracts entered into between the Corporation and any municipality or other political subdivision or cooperative organization shall provide that the electric power shall be sold and distributed to the ultimate consumer without discrimination as between consumers of the same class, and such contract shall be voidable at the election of the board if a discriminatory rate, rebate, or other special concession is made or given to any consumer or user by the municipality or other political subdivision or cooperative organization: *And provided further,* That as to any surplus power not so sold as above provided to States, counties, municipalities, or other said organizations, before the board shall sell the same to any person or corporation engaged in the distribution and resale of electricity for profit, it shall require said person or corporation to agree that any resale of such electric power by said person or corporation shall be made to the ultimate consumer of such electric power at prices that shall not exceed a schedule fixed by the board from time to time as reasonable, just, and fair; and in case of any such sale, if an amount is charged the ultimate consumer which is in excess of the price so deemed to be just, reasonable, and fair by the board, the contract for such sale between the board and such distributor of electricity shall be voidable at the election of the board: *And provided further,* That the board is hereby authorized to enter into contracts with other power systems for the mutual exchange of unused excess power upon suitable terms, for the conservation of stored water, and as an emergency or break-down relief.

Sec. 13. Five per centum of the gross proceeds received by the board for the sale of power generated at Dam Numbered 2, or from any other hydropower plant hereafter constructed in the State of Alabama, shall be paid to the State of Alabama; and 5 per centum of the gross proceeds from the sale of power generated at Cove Creek Dam, hereinafter provided for, or any other dam located in the State of Tennessee, shall be paid to the State of Tennessee. . . .

Sec. 15. In the construction of any future dam, steam plant, or other facility, to be used in whole or in part for the generation or transmission of electric power the board is hereby authorized and empowered to issue on the credit of the United States and to sell serial bonds not exceeding $50,000,000 in amount, having a maturity not more than fifty years from the date of issue thereof, and bearing interest not exceeding 3½ per centum per annum. Said bonds shall be issued and sold in amounts and prices approved by the Secretary of the Treasury, but all such bonds as may be so issued and sold shall have equal rank. None of said bonds shall be sold below par, and no fee, commission, or compensation whatever shall be paid to any person, firm, or corporation for handling, negotiating the sale, or selling the said bonds. . . .

Sec. 20. The Government of the United States hereby reserves the right, in case of war or national emergency declared by Congress, to take possession of all or any part of the property described or referred to in this Act for the purpose of manufacturing explosives or for other war purposes. . . .

Sec. 23. The President shall, from time to time, as the work provided for in the preceding section progresses, recommend to Congress such legislation as he deems proper to carry out the general purposes stated in said section, and for the especial purpose of bringing about in said Tennessee drainage basin and adjoining territory in conformity with said general purposes (1) the maximum amount of flood control; (2) the maximum development of said Tennessee River for navigation purposes; (3) the maximum generation of electric power consistent with flood control and navigation; (4) the proper use of marginal lands; (5) the proper method of reforestation of all lands in said drainage basin suitable for reforestation; and (6) the economic and social well-being of the people living in said river basin.

Sec. 26. The net proceeds derived by the board from the sale of power and any of the products manufactured by the Corporation, after deducting the cost of operation, maintenance, depreciation, amortization, and an amount deemed by the board as necessary to withhold as operating capital, or devoted by the board to new construction, shall be paid into the Treasury of the United States at the end of each calendar year.

A Turning Point: Franklin D. Roosevelt's Annual Message, 1935

Some historians distinguish two New Deals. The first is said to have run from March, 1933, through the Congressional elections of 1934. It was characterized by the cooperative and regulatory approach of the National Recovery Administration and the Agricultural Adjustment Administration, the brief experiments with price raising through monetary manipulation, and, of course, the emergency relief appropriations. After the election of 1934, Roosevelt found Congress newly rigid and resistant to his pressure for legislation. The second New Deal, presumably conceived during the difficult congressional session of 1935 and coming to fruition in the summer of 1936, appeared to have abandoned the generalized concept of "public interest" and national cooperation and to have retreated to the narrower ground occupied by special interests, labor, farmers, certain minority groups. Roosevelt's Annual Message of January 4, 1935, is thought by some historians to be a trumpet which sounded the beginning of this second New Deal. Certainly FDR drafted his message to suggest a new stress on reform, on the social obligations of government. Whether it in fact introduced a sharp change in the New Deal—and there is much dispute about this—the message does appear to have marked out a heavier and more systematic reliance upon spending as the basic device of recovery.

For various discussions of this turning point, see Arthur M. Schlesinger, Jr., The Politics of Upheaval *(1960); James M. Burns,* Roosevelt: the Lion and the Fox *(1956); and Basil Rauch,* The History of the New Deal: 1933–1938 *(1944).*

The annual Message may be found in Samuel Rosenman (ed.), The Public Papers and Addresses of Franklin D. Roosevelt, Volume Four: The Court Disapproves, 1935 *(New York: Random House, 1938), pages 15–25.*

The constitution wisely provides that the Chief Executive shall report to the Congress on the state of the Union, for through you, the chosen legislative representatives, our citizens everywhere may fairly judge the progress of our governing. I am confident that today, in the light of the events of the past two years, you do not consider it merely a trite phrase when I tell you that I am truly glad to greet you and that I look forward to common counsel, to useful cooperation, and to genuine friendships between us.

We have undertaken a new order of things; yet we progress to it under the framework and in the spirit and intent of the American Constitution. We have proceeded throughout the Nation a measurable distance on the road toward this new order. Materially, I can report to you substantial benefits to our agricultural population, increased industrial activity, and profits to our merchants. Of equal moment, there is evident a restoration of that spirit of confidence and faith which marks the American character. Let him, who, for speculative profit or partisan purpose, without just warrant would seek to disturb or dispel this assurance, take heed before he assumes responsibility for any act which slows our onward steps.

Throughout the world, change is the order of the day. In every Nation economic problems, long in the making, have brought crises of many kinds for which the masters of old practice and theory were unprepared. In most Nations social justice, no longer a distant ideal, has become a definite goal, and ancient Governments are beginning to heed the call.

Thus, the American people do not stand alone in the world in their desire for change. We seek it through tested liberal traditions, through processes which retain all of the deep essentials of that republican form of representative government first given to a troubled world by the United States.

As the various parts in the program begun in the Extraordinary Session of the 73rd Congress shape themselves in practical administration, the unity of our program reveals itself to the Nation. The outlines of the new economic order, rising from the disintegration of the old, are apparent. We test what we have done as our measures take root in the living texture of life. We see where we have built wisely and where we can do still better.

The attempt to make a distinction between recovery and reform is a narrowly conceived effort to substitute the appearance of reality for reality itself. When a man is convalescing from illness, wisdom dictates not only cure of the symptoms, but also removal of their cause.

It is important to recognize that while we seek to outlaw specific abuses, the American objective of today has an infinitely deeper, finer and more lasting purpose than mere repression. Thinking people in almost every country of the world have come to realize certain fundamental difficulties with which civilization must reckon. Rapid changes—the machine age, the advent of universal and rapid communication and many other new factors—have brought new problems. Succeeding generations have attempted to keep pace by reforming in piecemeal fashion this or that attendant abuse. As a result, evils overlap and reform becomes confused and frustrated. We lose sight, from time to time, of our ultimate human objectives.

Let us, for a moment, strip from our simple purpose the confusion that results from a multiplicity of detail and from millions of written and spoken words.

We find our population suffering from old inequalities, little changed by past sporadic remedies. In spite of our efforts and in spite of our talk, we have not weeded out the overprivileged and we have not effectively lifted up the underprivileged. Both of these manifestations of injustice have retarded happiness. No wise man has any intention of destroying what is known as the profit motive; because by the profit motive we mean the right by work to earn a decent livelihood for ourselves and for our families.

We have, however, a clear mandate from the people, that Americans must forswear that conception of the acquisition of wealth which, through excessive profits, creates undue private power over private affairs and, to our misfortune, over public affairs as well. In building toward this end we do not destroy ambition, nor do we seek to divide our wealth into equal shares on stated occasions. We continue to recognize the greater ability of some to earn more than others. But we do assert that the ambition of the individual to obtain for him and his a proper security, a reasonable leisure, and a decent living throughout life, is an ambition to be preferred to the appetite for great wealth and great power.

I recall to your attention my message to the Congress last June in which I said: "among our objectives I place the security of the men, women and children of the Nation first." That remains our first and continuing task; and in a very real sense every major legislative enactment of this Congress should be a component part of it.

In defining immediate factors which enter into our quest, I have spoken to the Congress and the people of three great divisions:

1. The security of a livelihood through the better use of the national resources of the land in which we live.
2. The security against the major hazards and vicissitudes of life.
3. The security of decent homes.

I am now ready to submit to the Congress a broad program designed ultimately to establish all three of these factors of security—a program which because of many lost years will take many future years to fulfill.

A study of our national resources, more comprehensive than any previously made, shows the vast amount of necessary and practicable work which needs to be done for the development and preservation of our natural wealth for the enjoyment and advantage of our people in generations to come. The sound use of land and water is far more comprehensive than the mere planting of trees, building of dams, distributing of electricity or retirement of sub-marginal land. It recognizes that stranded populations, either in the country or the city, cannot have security under the conditions that now surround them.

To this end we are ready to begin to meet this problem—the intelligent care of population throughout our Nation, in accordance with an intelligent distribution of the means of livelihood for that population. A definite program for putting people to work, of which I shall speak in a moment, is a component part of this greater program of security of livelihood through the better use of our national resources.

Closely related to the broad problem of livelihood is that of security against the major hazards of life. Here also, a comprehensive survey of what has been attempted or accomplished in many Nations and in many States proves to me that the time has come for action by the national Government. I shall send to you, in a few days, definite recommendations based on these studies. These recommendations will cover the broad subjects of unemployment insurance and old age insurance, of benefits for children, for mothers, for the handicapped, for maternity care and for other aspects of dependency and illness where a beginning can now be made.

The third factor—better homes for our people—has also been the subject of experimentation and study. Here, too, the first practical steps can be made through the proposals which I shall suggest in relation to giving work to the unemployed.

Whatever we plan and whatever we do should be in the light of these three clear objectives of security. We cannot afford to lose valuable time in haphazard public policies which cannot find a place in the broad outlines of these major purposes. In that spirit I come to an immediate issue made for us by hard and inescapable circumstance—the task of putting people to work. In the spring of 1933 the issue of destitution seemed to stand apart; today, in the light of our experience and our new national policy, we find we can put people to work in ways which conform to, initiate and carry forward the broad principles of that policy.

The first objectives of emergency legislation of 1933 were to relieve destitution, to make it possible for industry to operate in a more rational and orderly fashion, and to put behind industrial recovery the impulse of large expenditures in Government undertakings. The purpose of the National Industrial Recovery Act to provide work for more people succeeded in a substantial manner within the first few months of its life, and the Act has continued to maintain employment gains and greatly improved working conditions in industry.

The program of public works provided for in the Recovery Act launched the Federal Government into a task for which there was little time to make preparation and little American experience to follow. Great employment has been given and is being given by these works.

More than two billions of dollars have also been expended in direct relief to the destitute. Local agencies of necessity determined the recipients of this form of relief. With inevitable exceptions the funds were spent by them with reasonable efficiency and as a result actual want of food and clothing in the great majority of cases has been overcome.

But the stark fact before us is that great numbers still remain unemployed.

A large proportion of these unemployed and their dependents have been forced on the relief rolls. The burden on the Federal Government has grown with great rapidity. We have here a human as well as an economic problem. When humane considerations are concerned, Americans give them precedence. The lessons of history, confirmed by the evidence immediately before me, show conclusively that continued dependence upon relief induces a spiritual and moral disintegration fundamentally destructive to the national fibre. To dole out relief in this way is to administer a narcotic, a subtle destroyer of the human spirit. It is inimical to the dictates of sound policy. It is in violation of the traditions of America. Work must be found for able-bodied but destitute workers.

The Federal Government must and shall quit this business of relief.

I am not willing that the vitality of our people be further sapped by the giving of cash, of market baskets, of a few hours of weekly work cutting grass, raking leaves or picking up papers in the public parks. We must preserve not only the bodies of the unemployed from destitution but also their self-respect, their self-reliance and courage and determination. This decision brings me to the problem of what the Government should do with approximately five million unemployed now on the relief rolls.

About one million and a half of these belong to the group which in the past was dependent upon local welfare efforts. Most of them are unable for one reason or another to maintain themselves independently—for the most part, through no fault of their own. Such people, in the days before the great depression, were cared for by local efforts—by States, by counties, by towns, by cities, by churches and by private welfare agencies. It is my thought that in the future they must be cared for as they were before. I stand ready through my own personal efforts, and through the public influence of the office that I hold, to help these local agencies to get the means necessary to assume this burden.

The security legislation which I shall propose to the Congress will, I am confident, be of assistance to local effort in the care of this type of case. Local responsibility can and will be resumed, for, after all, common sense tells us that the wealth necessary for this task existed and still exists in the local community, and the dictates of sound administration require that this responsibility be in the first instance a local one.

There are, however, an additional three and one half million employable people who are on relief. With them the problem is different and the responsibility is different. This group was the victim of a nation-wide depression caused by conditions which were not local but national. The Federal Government is the only governmental agency with sufficient power and credit to meet this situation. We have assumed this task and we shall not shrink from it in the future. It is a duty dictated by every intelligent consideration of national policy to ask you to make it possible for the United States to give employment to all of these three and one half million employable people now on relief, pending their absorption in a rising tide of private employment.

It is my thought that with the exception of certain of the normal public building operations of the Government, all emergency public works shall be united in a single new and greatly enlarged plan.

With the establishment of this new system we can supersede the Federal Emergency Relief Administration with a coordinated authority which will be charged with the orderly liquidation of our present relief activities and the substitution of a national chart for the giving of work.

This new program of emergency public employment should be governed by a number of practical principles.

1. All work undertaken should be useful—not just for a day, or a year, but useful in the sense that it affords permanent improvement in living conditions or that it creates future new wealth for the Nation.

2. Compensation on emergency public projects should be in the form of security payments which should be larger than the amount now received as a relief dole, but at the same time not so large as to encourage the rejection of opportunities for private employment or the leaving of private employment to engage in Government work.

3. Projects should be undertaken on which a large percentage of direct labor can be used.

4. Preference should be given to those projects which will be self-liquidating in the sense that there is a reasonable expectation that the Government will get its money back at some future time.

5. The projects undertaken should be selected and planned so as to compete as little as possible with private enterprises. This suggests that if it were not for the necessity of giving useful work to the unemployed now on relief, these projects in most instances would not now be undertaken.

6. The planning of projects would seek to assure work during the coming fiscal year to the individuals now on relief, or until such time as private employment is available. In order to make adjustment to increasing private employment, work should be planned with a view to tapering it off in proportion to the speed with which the emergency workers are offered positions with private employers.

7. Effort should be made to locate projects where they will serve the greatest unemployment needs as shown by present relief rolls, and the broad program of the National Resources Board should be freely used for guidance in selection. Our ultimate objective being the enrichment of human lives, the Government has the primary duty to use its emergency expenditures as much as possible to serve those who cannot secure the advantages of private capital.

Ever since the adjournment of the 73d Congress, the Administration has been studying from every angle the possibility and the practicability of new forms of employment. As a result of these studies I have arrived at certain very definite convictions as to the amount of money that will be necessary for the sort of public projects that I have described. I shall submit these figures in my budget message. I assure you now they will be within the sound credit of the Government.

The work itself will cover a wide field including clearance of slums, which for adequate reasons cannot be undertaken by private capital; in rural housing of several kinds, where, again, private capital is unable to function; in rural electrification; in the reforestation of the great watersheds of the Nation; in an intensified program to prevent soil erosion and to reclaim blighted areas; in improving existing road systems and in constructing national highways designed to handle modern traffic; in the elimination of grade crossings; in the extension and enlargement of the successful work of the Civilian Conservation Corps; in non-Federal works, mostly self-liquidating and highly useful to local divisions of Government; and on many other projects which the Nation needs and cannot afford to neglect.

This is the method which I propose to you in order that we may better meet this present-day problem of unemployment. Its greatest advantage is that it fits logically and usefully into the long-range permanent policy of providing the three types of security which constitute as a whole an American plan for the betterment of the future of the American people.

I shall consult with you from time to time concerning other measures of national importance. Among the subjects that lie immediately before us are the consolidation of Federal regulatory administration over all forms of transportation, the renewal and clarification of the general purposes of the National Industrial Recovery Act, the strengthening of our facilities for the prevention, detection and treatment of crime and criminals, the restoration of sound conditions in the public utilities field through abolition of the evil features of holding companies, the gradual tapering off of the emergency credit activities of Government, and improvement in our taxation forms and methods.

We have already begun to feel the bracing effect upon our economic system of a restored agriculture. The hundreds of millions of additional income that farmers are receiving are finding their way into the channels of trade. The farmers' share of the national income is slowly rising. The economic facts justify the widespread opinion of those engaged in agriculture that our provisions for maintaining a balanced production give at this time the most adequate remedy for an old and vexing problem. For the present, and especially in view of abnormal world conditions, agricultural adjustment with certain necessary improvements in methods should continue.

It seems appropriate to call attention at this time to the fine spirit shown during the past year by our public servants. I cannot praise too highly the cheerful work of the Civil Service employees, and of those temporarily working for the Government. As for those thousands in our various public agencies spread throughout the country who, without compensation, agreed to take over heavy responsibilities in connection with our various loan agencies and particularly in direct relief work, I cannot say too much. I do not think any country could show a higher average of cheerful and even enthusiastic team-work than has been shown by these men and women.

I cannot with candor tell you that general international relationships outside the borders of the United States are improved. On the surface of things many old jealousies are resurrected, old passions aroused; new strivings for armament and power, in more than one land, rear their ugly heads. I hope that calm counsel and constructive leadership will provide the steadying influence and the time necessary for the coming of new and more practical forms of representative government throughout the world wherein privilege and power will occupy a lesser place and world welfare a greater.

I believe, however, that our own peaceful and neighborly attitude toward other Nations is coming to be understood and appreciated. The maintenance of international peace is a matter in which we are deeply and unselfishly concerned. Evidence of our persistent and undeniable desire to prevent armed conflict has recently been more than once afforded.

There is no ground for apprehension that our relations with any Nation will be otherwise than peaceful. Nor is there ground for doubt that the people of most Nations seek relief from the threat and burden attaching to the false theory that extravagant armament cannot be reduced and limited by international accord.

The ledger of the past year shows many more gains than losses. Let us not forget that, in addition to saving millions from utter destitution, child labor has been for the moment outlawed, thousands of homes saved to their owners and most important of all, the morale of the Nation has been restored. Viewing the year 1934 as a whole, you and I can agree that we have a generous measure of reasons for giving thanks.

It is not empty optimism that moves me to a strong hope in the coming year. We can, if we will, make 1935 a genuine period of good feeling, sustained by a sense of purposeful progress. Beyond the material recovery, I sense a spiritual recovery as well. The people of America are turning as never before to those permanent values that are not limited to the physical objectives of life. There are growing signs of this on every hand. In the face of these spiritual impulses we are sensible of the Divine Providence to which Nations turn now, as always, for guidance and fostering care.

Labor's Charter: The National Labor Relations (Wagner) Act, 1935

The demise of the National Recovery Administration left labor without even the experimental guarantees of rights to organize, bargain, and strike which had been embedded in Section 7(a). More important, the bankruptcy of the NRA idea had left the administration without a basic philosophy of intervention. In 1933, Roosevelt had hoped to spark a kind of self-regulation by industry which would balance against each other the claims of labor, management, owner, and consumer and would bring about a consensus for voluntary compliance. This lost, the President turned increasingly to a more crudely and toughly attained balance. If management would not cooperate, as he thought to be the case, then perhaps it was the proper role of government to arm the weaker elements in the economic structure so that they might them-

selves provide a check against economic arrogance. That this might also be politically sound was evident at a glance.

The National Labor Relations Act was not the creation of the President. It had been forced through much of the congressional machinery by New York Senator Robert F. Wagner (1877–1949) and his friends, without aid or comfort from FDR. Yet the President adopted it, suddenly and firmly, in the early summer of 1935. It was soon through Congress. He signed it with a flourish as part of the Independence Day celebration, and he was happy to boast it as a cornerstone of his new approach to the nation's economic problems.

On labor problems in the New Deal, see especially Irving Bernstein, The New Deal Collective Bargaining Policy *(1950); Milton Derber and Edwin Young (eds.),* Labor and the New Deal *(1957); and Frances Perkins,* The Roosevelt I Knew *(1946).*

The Wagner Act of July 5, 1935 is in U.S. Statutes at Large, *volume 49, pages 445–455.*

Findings and Policy

Section 1. The denial by employers of the right of employees to organize and the refusal by employers to accept the procedure of collective bargaining lead to strikes and other forms of industrial strife or unrest, which have the intent or the necessary effect of burdening or obstructing commerce by (a) impairing the efficiency, safety, or operation of the instrumentalities of commerce; (b) occurring in the current of commerce; (c) materially affecting, restraining, or controlling the flow of raw materials or manufactured or processed goods from or into the channels of commerce, or the prices of such materials or goods in commerce; or (d) causing diminution of employment and wages in such volume as substantially to impair or disrupt the market for goods flowing from or into the channels of commerce.

The inequality of bargaining power between employees who do not possess full freedom of association or actual liberty of contract, and employers who are organized in the corporate or other forms of ownership association substantially burdens and affects the flow of commerce, and tends to aggravate recurrent business depressions, by depressing wage rates and the purchasing power of wage earners in industry and by preventing the stabilization of competitive wage rates and working conditions within and between industries.

Experience has proved that protection by law of the right of employees to organize and bargain collectively safeguards commerce from injury, impairment, or interruption, and promotes the flow of commerce by removing certain recognized sources of industrial strife and unrest, by encouraging practices fundamental to the friendly adjustment of industrial disputes arising out of differences as to wages, hours, or other working conditions, and by restoring equality of bargaining power between employers and employees.

It is hereby declared to be the policy of the United States to eliminate the causes of certain substantial obstructions to the free flow of commerce and to mitigate and eliminate these obstructions when they have occurred by encouraging the practice and procedure of collective bargaining and by protecting the exercise by workers of full freedom of association, self-organization, and designation of representatives of their own choosing, for the purpose of negotiating the terms and conditions of their employment or other mutual aid or protection. . . .

National Labor Relations Board

Sec. 3. (a) There is hereby created a board, to be known as the "National Labor Relations Board" (hereinafter referred to as the "Board"), which shall be composed of three members, who shall be appointed by the President, by and with the advice and consent of the Senate. One of the original members shall be appointed for a term of one year, one for a term of three years, and one for a term of five years, but their successors shall be appointed for terms of five years each, except that any individual chosen to fill a vacancy shall be appointed only for the unexpired term of the member whom he shall succeed. The President shall designate one member to serve as chairman of the Board. Any member of the Board may be removed by the President, upon notice and hearing, for neglect of duty or malfeasance in office, but for no other cause. . . . Nothing in this Act shall be construed to authorize the Board to appoint individuals for the purpose of conciliation or mediation (or for statistical work), where such service may be obtained from the Department of Labor. . . .

Rights of Employees

Sec. 7. Employees shall have the right to self-organization, to form, join, or assist labor organizations, to bargain collectively through representatives of their own choosing, and to engage in concerted activities, for the purpose of collective bargaining or other mutual aid or protection.

Sec. 8. It shall be an unfair labor practice for an employer—

(1) To interfere with, restrain, or coerce employees in the exercise of the rights guaranteed in section 7.

(2) To dominate or interfere with the formation or administration of any labor organization or contribute financial or other support to it: *Provided,* That subject to rules and regulations made and published by the Board pursuant to section 6 (a), an employer shall not be prohibited from permitting employees to confer with him during working hours without loss of time or pay.

(3) By discrimination in regard to hire or tenure of employment or any term or condition of employment to encourage or discourage membership in any labor organization: *Provided,* That nothing in this Act, or in the National Industrial Recovery Act (U. S. C., Supp. VII, title 15, secs. 701–712), as amended from time to time, or in any code or agreement approved or prescribed thereunder, or in any other statute of the United States, shall preclude an employer from making an agreement with a labor organization (not established, maintained, or assisted by

any action defined in this Act as an unfair labor practice) to require as a condition of employment membership therein, if such labor organization is the representative of the employees as provided in section 9 (a), in the appropriate collective bargaining unit covered by such agreement when made.

(4) To discharge or otherwise discriminate against an employee because he has filed charges or given testimony under this Act.

(5) To refuse to bargain collectively with the representatives of his employees, subject to the provisions of Section 9 (a).

Representatives and Elections

Sec. 9. (a) Representatives designated or selected for the purposes of collective bargaining by the majority of the employees in a unit appropriate for such purposes, shall be the exclusive representatives of all the employees in such unit for the purposes of collective bargaining in respect to rates of pay, wages, hours of employment, or other conditions of employment: *Provided,* That any individual employee or a group of employees shall have the right at any time to present grievances to their employer.

(b) The Board shall decide in each case whether, in order to insure to employees the full benefit of their right to self-organization and to collective bargaining, and otherwise to effectuate the policies of this Act, the unit appropriate for the purposes of collective bargaining shall be the employer unit, craft unit, plant unit, or subdivision thereof.

(c) Whenever a question affecting commerce arises concerning the representation of employees, the Board may investigate such controversy and certify to the parties, in writing, the name or names of the representatives that have been designated or selected. In any such investigation, the Board shall provide for an appropriate hearing upon due notice, either in conjunction with a proceeding under section 10 or otherwise, and may take a secret ballot of employees, or utilize any other suitable method to ascertain such representatives.

(d) Whenever an order of the Board made pursuant to section 10 (c) is based in whole or in part upon facts certified following an investigation pursuant to subsection (c) of this section, and there is a petition for the enforcement or review of such order, such certification and the record of such investigation shall be included in the transcript of the entire record required to be filed under subsections 10 (e) or 10 (f), and thereupon the decree of the court enforcing, modifying, or setting aside in whole or in part the order of the Board shall be made and entered upon the pleadings, testimony, and proceedings set forth in such transcript.

Prevention of Unfair Labor Practices

Sec. 10. (a) The Board is empowered, as hereinafter provided, to prevent any person from engaging in any unfair labor practice (listed in section 8) affecting commerce. This power shall be exclusive, and shall not be affected by any other means of adjustment or prevention that has been or may be established by agreement, code, law, or otherwise.

(b) Whenever it is charged that any person has engaged in or is engaging in any such unfair labor practice, the Board, or any agent or agency designated by the Board for such purposes, shall have power to issue and cause to be served upon such person a complaint stating the charges in that respect, and containing a notice of hearing before the Board or a member thereof, or before a designated agent or agency, at a place therein fixed, not less than five days after the serving of said complaint. Any such complaint may be amended by the member, agent, or agency conducting the hearing or the Board in its discretion at any time prior to the issuance of an order based thereon. The person so complained of shall have the right to file an answer to the original or amended complaint and to appear in person or otherwise and give testimony at the place and time fixed in the complaint. In the discretion of the member, agent or agency conducting the hearing or the Board, any other person may be allowed to intervene in the said proceeding and to present testimony. In any such proceeding the rules of evidence prevailing in courts of law or equity shall not be controlling.

(c) The testimony taken by such member, agent or agency or the Board shall be reduced to writing and filed with the Board. Thereafter, in its discretion, the Board upon notice may take further testimony or hear argument. If upon all the testimony taken the Board shall be of the opinion that any person named in the complaint has engaged in or is engaging in any such unfair labor practice, then the Board shall state its findings of fact and shall issue and cause to be served on such person an order requiring such person to cease and desist from such unfair labor practice, and to take such affirmative action, including reinstatement of employees with or without back pay, as will effectuate the policies of this Act. Such order may further require such person to make reports from time to time showing the extent to which it has complied with the order. If upon all the testimony taken the Board shall be of the opinion that no person named in the complaint has engaged in or is engaging in any such unfair labor practice, then the Board shall state its findings of fact and shall issue an order dismissing the said complaint.

(d) Until a transcript of the record in a case shall have been filed in a court, as hereinafter provided, the Board may at any time, upon reasonable notice and in such manner as it shall deem proper, modify or set aside, in whole or in part, any finding or order made or issued by it.

(e) The Board shall have power to petition any circuit court of appeals of the United States (including the Court of Appeals of the District of Columbia), or if all the circuit courts of appeals to which application may be made are in vacation, any district court of the United States (including the Supreme Court of the District of Columbia), within any circuit or district, respectively, wherein the unfair labor practice in question occurred or wherein such person resides or transacts business, for the enforcement of such order and for appropriate temporary relief or restraining order, and shall certify and file in the court a transcript of the entire record in the proceeding, including the pleadings and testimony upon which such order was entered and the findings and order of the Board. Upon such filing, the court shall cause notice thereof to be served upon such person, and thereupon shall have jurisdiction of the proceeding and of the question determined therein, and shall have power to grant such temporary relief or restraining order as it deems just and proper, and to make and enter upon the pleadings, testimony, and proceedings set forth in such transcript a decree enforcing, modifying, and enforcing as so modified, or setting aside in whole or in part the order of the Board. No objection that has not been urged before the Board, its member, agent or agency, shall be considered by the court, unless the failure or neglect to urge such objection shall be excused because of extraordinary circumstances. The findings of the Board as to the facts, if supported by evidence, shall be conclusive. If either party shall apply to the court for leave to adduce additional evidence and shall show to the satisfaction of the court that such additional evidence is material and that there were reasonable grounds for the failure to adduce such evidence in the hearing before the Board, its member, agent, or agency, the court may order such additional evidence to be taken before the Board, its member, agent, or agency, and to be made a part of the transcript. The Board may modify its findings as to the facts, or make new findings, by reason of additional evidence so taken and filed, and it shall file such modified or new findings, which, if supported by evidence, shall be conclusive, and shall file its recommendations, if any, for the modification or setting aside of its original order. The jurisdiction of the court shall be exclusive and its judgment and decree shall be final, except that the same shall be subject to review by the appropriate circuit court of appeals if application was made to the district court as hereinabove provided, and by the Supreme Court of the United States. . . .

(f) Any person aggrieved by a final order of the Board granting or denying in whole or in part the relief sought may obtain a review of such order in any circuit court of appeals of the United States in the circuit wherein the unfair labor practice in question was alleged to have been engaged in or wherein such person resides or transacts business, or in the Court of Appeals of the District of Columbia, by filing in such court a written petition praying that the order of the Board be modified or set aside. A copy of such petition shall be forthwith served upon the Board, and thereupon the aggrieved party shall file in the court a transcript of the entire record in the proceeding, certified by the Board, including the pleading and testimony upon which the order complained of was entered and the findings and order of the Board. Upon such filing, the court shall proceed in the same manner as in the case of an application by the Board under subsection (e), and shall have the same exclusive jurisdiction to grant to the Board such temporary relief or restraining order as it deems just and proper, and in like manner to make and enter a decree enforcing, modifying, and enforcing as so modified, or setting aside in whole or in part the order of the Board; and the findings of the Board as to the facts, if supported by evidence, shall in like manner be conclusive.

(g) The commencement of proceedings under subsection (e) or (f) of this section shall not, unless specifically ordered by the court, operate as a stay of the Board's order. . . .

The New Deal: Experiment with Hope—Appraisal

"... the lamps are out": A Sensitive Observer Sees the South, 1936

The New Deal was recovery, for some people; relief, for some; reform, for certain others. And for some it was only that remnant of the National Recovery Administration, the fading Blue Eagle on dirty shop windows in town, or the distant, alien voice of FDR on the barroom radio, a promise without relevance to them. James Agee and Walker Evans found many such when they went deep into the cotton South with pen and camera to record the impact of the New Deal in 1936. Agee (1909–1955) proved himself not merely a sensitive and keen reporter but also an artist with language hardly matched in our century. Three brief disparate flashes from their book, Let Us Now Praise Famous Men, *catch something of the hapless misery they found in the clay country and along the bayous of the South.*

Another picture of the same situation is to be found in Arthur F. Raper and Ira De A. Reid, Sharecroppers All *(1941). An interesting special study is M. K. Venkatarami, "Norman Thomas, Arkansas Sharecroppers and the Roosevelt Agricultural Policies, 1933–1937,"* Mississippi Valley Historical Review, *volume 47 (1960–1961), pages 225–246. John Steinbeck's classic picture of the impoverished on the move is* The Grapes of Wrath *(1939).*

The selections provided here are from James Agee and Walker Evans, Let Us Now Praise Famous Men *(Boston: Houghton Mifflin, 1941), pages 44–45, 80–81, 116–119.*

All over Alabama, the lamps are out. Every leaf drenches the touch; the spider's net is heavy. The roads lie there, with nothing to use them. The fields lie there, with nothing at work in them, neither man nor beast. The plow handles are wet, and the rails and the frogplates and the weeds between the ties: and not even the hurryings and hoarse sorrows of a distant train, on other roads, is heard. The little towns, the county seats, house by house white-painted and elaborately sawn among their heavy and dark-lighted leaves, in the spaced protections of their mineral light they stand so prim, so voided, so undefended upon starlight, that it is inconceivable to despise or to scorn a white man, an owner of land; even in Birmingham, mile on mile, save for the sudden frightful streaming, almost instantly diminished and silent, of a closed black car, and save stone lonesome sinister heelbeats, that show never a face and enter, soon, a frame door flush with the pavement, and ascend the immediate lightless staircase, mile on mile, stone, stone, smooth charted streams of stone, the streets under their lifted lamps lie void before eternity. New Orleans is stirring, rattling, and sliding faintly in its fragrance and in the enormous richness of its lust; taxis are still parked along Dauphine Street and the breastlike, floral air is itchy with the stilettos and embroiderings above black blood drumthroes of an eloquent cracked indiscoverable cornet, which exists only in the imagination and somewhere in the past, in the broken heart of Louis Armstrong; yet even in that small portion which is the infested genitals of that city, never free, neither of desire nor of waking pain, there are the qualities of the tender desolations of profoundest night. Beneath, the gulf lies dreaming, and beneath, dreaming, that woman, that id, the lower American continent, lies spread before heaven in her wealth. The parks of her cities are iron, loam, silent, the sweet fountains shut, and the pure façades, embroiled, limelike in street light are sharp, are still: . . .

* * *

How did we get caught? Why is it things always seem to go against us? Why is it there can't ever be any pleasure in living? I'm so tired it don't seem like I ever could get rest enough. I'm as tired when I get up in the morning as I am when I lay down at night. Sometimes it seems like there wouldn't never be no end to it, nor even a let-up. One year it'll look like things was going to be pretty good; but you get a little bit of money saved, something always happens.

I tell you *I* won't be sorry when I die. I wouldn't be sorry this minute if it wasn't for Louise and Squinchy-here. Rest vmd git along all right:

(But *I* am young; and I am young, and strong, and in good health; and I am young, and pretty to look at; and I am too young to worry; and so am I, for my mother is kind to me; and we run in the bright air like animals, and our bare feet like plants in the wholesome earth: the natural world is around us like a lake and a wide smile and we are growing: one by one we are becoming stronger, and one by one in the terrible emptiness and the leisure we shall burn and tremble and shake with lust, and one by one we shall loosen ourselves from this place, and shall be married, and it will be different from what we see, for we will be happy and love each other, and keep the house clean, and a good garden, and buy a cultivator, and use a high grade of fertilizer, and we will know how to do things right; it will be very different:) (? :)

((?)) :)

How were we caught?

What, what is it has happened? What is it has been happening that we are living the way we are?

The children are not the way it seemed they might be:

She is no longer beautiful:

He no longer cares for me, he just takes me when he wants me:

There's so much work it seems like you never see the end of it:

I'm so hot when I get through cooking a meal it's more than I can do to sit down to it and eat it:

How was it we were caught?

And seeing the multitudes, he went up into a mountain; and when he was set, his disciples came unto him:
And he opened his mouth and taught them, saying: . . .

* * *

Woods and Ricketts own no home and no land, but Woods owns one mule and Ricketts owns two, and they own their farming implements. Since they do not have to rent these tools and animals, they work under a slightly different arrangement. They give over to the landlord only a third of their cotton and a fourth of their corn. Out of their own parts of the crop, however, they owe him the price of two thirds of their cotton fertilizer and three fourths of their corn fertilizer, plus interest; and, plus interest, the same debts on rations money.
Woods and Ricketts are tenants: they work on third and fourth.

A very few tenants pay cash rent: but these two types of arrangement, with local variants (company stores; food instead of rations money; slightly different divisions of the crops) are basic to cotton tenantry all over the South.

From March through June, while the cotton is being cultivated, they live on the rations money.
From July through to late August, while the cotton is making, they live however they can.

From late August through October or into November, during the picking and ginning season, they live on the money from their share of the cottonseed.
From then on until March, they live on whatever they have earned in the year; or however they can.

During six to seven months of each year, then—that is, during exactly such time as their labor with the cotton is of absolute necessity to the landlord—they can be sure of whatever living is possible in rations advances and in cottonseed money.

During five to six months of the year, of which three are the hardest months of any year, with the worst of weather, the least adequacy of shelter, the worst and least of food, the worst of health, quite normal and inevitable, they can count on nothing except that they may hope least of all for any help from their landlords.

Gudger—a family of six—lives on ten dollars a month rations money during four months of the year. He has lived on eight, and on six. Woods—a family of six—until this year was unable to get better than eight a month during the same period; this year he managed to get it up to ten. Ricketts—a family of nine—lives on ten dollars a month during this spring and early summer period.

This debt is paid back in the fall at eight per cent interest. Eight per cent is charged also on the fertilizer and on all other debts which tenants incur in this vicinity.

At the normal price, a half-sharing tenant gets about six dollars a bale from his share of the cottonseed. A one-mule, half-sharing tenant makes on the average three bales. This half-cropper, then, Gudger, can count on eighteen dollars, more or less, to live on during the picking and ginning: though he gets nothing until his first bale is ginned.

Working on third and fourth, a tenant gets the money from two thirds of the cottonseed of each bale: nine dollars to the bale. Woods, with one mule, makes three bales, and gets twenty-seven dollars. Ricketts, with two mules, makes and gets twice that, to live on during the late summer and fall.

What is earned at the end of a given year is never to be depended on and, even late in a season, is never predictable. It can be enough to tide through the dead months of the winter, sometimes even better: it can be enough, spread very thin, to take through two months, and a sickness, or six weeks, or a month: it can be little enough to be completely meaningless: it can be nothing: it can be enough less than nothing to insure a tenant only of an equally hopeless lack of money at the end of his next year's work: and whatever one year may bring in the way of good luck, there is never any reason to hope that that luck will be repeated in the next year or the year after that.

The best that Woods has ever cleared was $1300 during a war year. During the teens and twenties he fairly often cleared as much as $300; he fairly often cleared $50 and less; two or three times he ended the year in debt. During the depression years he has more often cleared $50 and less; last year he cleared $150, but serious illness during the winter ate it up rapidly.

The best that Gudger has ever cleared is $125. That was in the plow-under year. He felt exceedingly hopeful and bought a mule: but when his landlord warned him of how he was coming out the next year, he sold it. Most years he has not made more than $25 to $30; and about one year in three he has ended in debt. Year before last he wound up $80 in debt; last year, $12; of Boles, his new landlord, the first thing he had to do was borrow $15 to get through the winter until rations advances should begin.

Years ago the Ricketts were, relatively speaking, almost prosperous.

Besides their cotton farming they had ten cows and sold the milk, and they lived near a good stream and had all the fish they wanted. Ricketts went $400 into debt on a fine young pair of mules. One of the mules died before it had made its first crop; the other died the year after; against his fear, amounting to full horror, of sinking to the half-crop level where nothing is owned, Ricketts went into debt for other, inferior mules; his cows went one by one into debts and desperate exchanges and by sickness; he got congestive chills; his wife got pellagra; a number of his children died; he got appendicitis and lay for days on end under the ice cap; his wife's pellagra got into her brain; for ten consecutive years now, though they have lived on so little rations money, and have turned nearly all their cottonseed money toward their debts, they have not cleared or had any hope of clearing a cent at the end of the year.

But for Some There Is Hope: David Lilienthal's Appraisal of TVA, 1944

In the South, as elsewhere, despair was mixed with hope. Hope seemed nowhere quite so promising as it did along the reaches of the Tennessee Valley. Although the Tennessee Valley Authority never lived up to its billing as a master planning agency, and although it never concerned itself quite as effectively with personal problems of poverty as it did with the mighty problems of power, yet it made a large and permanent difference in the economy and the life of the mid-Southern states

David Lilienthal (1889–) was from 1933 to 1945 one of its directors, perhaps the most influential and best known. Of course his evaluation is not an objective one, but this is not to say that it is inaccurate. Lilienthal believed in TVA and was committed to it. His appraisal not only provides some of the incontrovertible facts of the case but also relates something of the spirit of the TVA crusaders. When it was written, it constituted in itself a widely influential wartime document, for it made TVA more popular by linking it with the war effort. Its statement of Lilienthal's beliefs in democracy became for many a convincing explanation of why the nation fought.

This excerpt is drawn from David Lilienthal, T.V.A.: Democracy on the March *(New York: Harper & Row, 1944), pages 34–40.*

The story thus far as I have recounted it has been chiefly one of physical changes in the Tennessee Valley. But what has been the yield to the people—to those who live in the region, and to the people of the country as a whole who advanced most of the funds?

First of all, the level of income of the region's people is definitely rising. By 1940, and before the effect of war expansion, the per capita income had increased in the seven valley states 73 per cent over the level of 1933; while for the same period the increase in the country as a whole was only 56 per cent. The same trend is reflected in income payment statistics. Between 1933 and 1943 the seven valley states show an increase in per capita income payments which substantially exceeds the index for the country as a whole. The rate of increase in each of the seven valley states is above the index for the country. The same is true of total income payments: the rate of increase for all the valley states, and for each of the states, exceeds the national index of rate of increase. Bank deposits increased 76 per cent between 1933 and 1939 compared to 49 per cent in the country, and retail sales increased 81 per cent compared to 71 per cent for the country.

All the available figures—and the evidence of one's eyes—show that our income level is rising. But the Tennessee Valley is still a region of low income, about half the United States average.

What has happened to the businesses of the people? Farming is the most important private enterprise in this region; that business, as I have indicated, is moving upward as the fruitfulness and stability of the land increase. What of business in the industrial sense? That too is developing, and at a rapid rate. Even before the war the valley saw the addition or expansion of several large industries devoted to the basic materials of modern industry, such as aluminum, ferro-silicon, heavy chemicals; these included two of the largest phosphatic chemical works in the country.

The war has added mightily to the list. For reasons of security little of this expansion can now be told. But when the full story of a once industrially laggard valley's part in production for war can be revealed, it will rank as one of the miracles of American enterprise, the kind of miracle that is marvelled at when it occurs across the seas, rarely comprehended close at home.

At least as important as these heavy industries is the rise of new light industries and the expansion of plants that existed before 1933. The industries added since 1933 range from those for the processing of frozen foods and the production of cheese to the manufacture of aircraft and mattresses, bottle washers, stoves, flour, inlaid wood, barrel heads and staves, electric water heaters, furniture, hats and shoes, pencils, carbon electrodes, boats, horse collars, ground mica, oxygen and acetylene, metal dies, ax handles, and barites. Many new small industries are the immediate result of opportunities for profit provided by the chain of lakes that make the Tennessee River a new arc of beauty through the countryside.

We have a long way yet to go in the valley. There are many factories yet to be built, in an area with such great potential wealth and with less than its economic share of the nation's industry and manufacturing. There are many new jobs to be created by the laboratories and businessmen out of the region's dormant resources. There are millions of acres yet to be restored to full productiveness. When TVA began its work in 1933, of the total of eight and a half million acres of cultivated land in the valley, erosion in varying degrees had damaged seven million acres. On more than a million acres the top soil had entirely disappeared. There are more trees to plant, houses, schools, roads, and hospitals to build. Many new skills have been learned—among farmers, industrial workers in the new factories, the tens of thousands of men and women who have added to their skills in the course of their work for the TVA—but lack of training is still a heavy handicap to be overcome. The task is barely begun—but the Tennessee Valley is on its way.

Democracy is on the march in this valley. Not only because of the physical changes or the figures of increased income and economic activity. My faith in this as a region with a great future is built most of all upon what I have come to know of the great capacities and the spirit of the people. The notion that has been expressed that the region's problem, as one commentator has put it, is one of "human salvage" completely misses the mark. The human resources of this valley are its greatest asset and advantage. The people have seized upon these modern tools of opportunity and have raised up their own leadership. They have shown an ability to hold themselves to tough assignments with a singleness of purpose and a resourcefulness in doing much with little that will be difficult to match anywhere in the country.

This advent of opportunity has brought with it the rise of a confident, sure, chesty feeling. The evidence is everywhere. It is epitomized in an editorial in the Decatur, Alabama, *Daily* for May 18, 1943. The editor, a community leader, candidly relates the doleful past and contrasts it with the optimistic and fruitful present. Seven years ago Decatur was in great trouble; today it is one of the most enterprising and promising small cities in the interior United States. "What has happened in these seven years?" he asks, and then he answers:

> We can write of great dams . . . of the building of home-grown industry and of electricity at last coming to the farms of thousands of farm people in the Valley. *Yet the significant advance has been made in the thinking of a people.* They are no longer afraid. *They have caught the vision of their own powers.* They can stand now and talk out in meeting and say that if industry doesn't come into the Valley from other sections, then we'll build our own industry. This they are doing today.

These changes of a decade were not, of course, wrought by TVA alone: in point of fact, the very essence of TVA's method in the undertaking, as I shall later indicate in detail, was at every hand to minimize what it was to do directly and to encourage and stimulate the broadest possible *coalition* of all forces. Private funds and private efforts, on farms and in factories; state funds and state activities; local communities, clubs, schools, associations, co-operatives—all have had major roles. Moreover, scores of federal agencies co-operated—the Civilian Conservation Corps; the Department of Agriculture through such agencies as the Farm Security Administration, the Rural Electrification Administration, the scientific research bureaus, the Agricultural Adjustment Administration, the Commodity Credit Corporation, the co-operative loan banks and the Forest Service; the Public Health Service; the Army Corps of Engineers which prior to 1933 had prepared a preliminary survey of the Tennessee River widely known as "House Document 328"; the Coast Guard; the Public Works Administration; several of the bureaus of the Interior Department, the Bureau of Reclamation which prepared designs for early Norris and Wheeler dams, the Geological Survey, the Bureau of Mines, the Bureau of Fish and Wildlife Service, the National Park Service; the Geodetic Survey and the Weather Bureau—and so on; the list, if complete, would include most national agencies.

How much of the public's money has the TVA spent in these ten years? Has it been worth that cost as measured in dividends to the people?

It is as important that a public enterprise should produce benefits and values as great as or greater than their cost as it is when the undertaking is a private one. And, to those who are studying the feasibility of developments of a comparable character, the question of cost and the balancing of investment of materials and manpower against the yield the investment produces are considerations of the first consequence.

I shall not, of course, go into all the possible technical refinements of TVA's financial affairs, since they are of little interest to the general reader. The facts are all readily available in TVA's financial statements, in its annual reports to Congress, in thousands of pages of testimony before Congressional committees, and in technical books and writings on the subject. I shall here only summarize the basic facts and the considerations that may be useful in judging the significance of those facts.

The funds used by the TVA have all been advanced from funds appropriated by Congress with two major exceptions: 65 millions of TVA bonds and about 50 millions supplied by electric rate-payers and reinvested in dams and equipment. To avoid unduly complicating the statement, however, I shall treat the funds expended as if they *all* had been advanced directly from the federal treasury; the exceptions do not affect the principles. The American people who advanced these funds are entitled to a return from them.

In judging whether they have received such a return and whether the product of TVA's investment of the people's money has been worth the outlay, it must be remembered that much of the return, to the Tennessee Valley and the nation, is in benefits which cannot be exactly measured. It is only the investment in power facilities that yields the federal taxpayers a return in dollars in addition to other benefits. For power is the only major product of the TVA investment that is sold for dollars. For the other expenditures little if any of the return is in dollars, but instead is realized in benefits to citizens and their communities and business enterprises.

The benefits of a navigable channel, for example, go to shippers, to industries using the channel, to consumers of grain, oil, gasoline, and so on. This is true, of course, not only on the Tennessee but also on the Ohio, the Illinois, the Missouri, all of the many rivers where millions of federal funds have been expended for a century and more. So it is not possible to record the same precise dollar measure of navigation benefits as it is with power. But simply because they do not appear on TVA's books as income does not mean, of course, that there are no benefits.

Likewise, the benefits of flood control produced by these dams extend all the way down the Mississippi River to the mouth of the Red. But since TVA is not paid for those benefits in dollars, the taxpayers' return cannot be measured in that way. And so it is with TVA's expenditures to produce phosphate plant food, and to demonstrate its use to control soil erosion not only in the Tennessee Valley but in Minnesota, Wisconsin, New York, Iowa, and seventeen other states outside this region. So with forestry, industrial research, mapping.

The *cost* of such development work appears on *TVA's books as a net expense; but the benefits appear on the balance sheet of the region and of the nation.* And, as with public improvement expenditures generally the country over, it was anticipated that such expenditures would be repaid to the taxpayers not directly in dollars, but indirectly in benefits.

Turning now to TVA's expenditures, and first the cost of developing the river: TVA's financial balance sheet shows that to provide a 650-mile navigable channel, flood protection, and power supply, the TVA has an investment in completed plant as of June 30, 1943, totaling about $475,000,000. By the end of 1944, when several dams now (September, 1943) under construction will be completed and in use, the figure will be in the neighborhood of $700,000,000. Of this amount approximately 65 per cent, or $450,000,000, will represent the power investment. The river control works will then be substantially completed.

What dividends for the people does this investment yield? Do the expenditures yield a product that justifies this cost?

As to power the answer is a relatively easy one, since the power is sold and the revenues provide a dollar measurement, and one that is reassuring. In the fiscal year ended June 30, 1943, the sale of power yielded revenues to TVA in excess of $31,500,000. Operating expenses to produce that power, including about $2,000,000 of tax payments and about $6,000,000 (or almost 20 per cent of each dollar of revenue) in depreciation charges, left a surplus of revenue over cost of more than $13,000,000.

Actual earnings in the first months of the current fiscal year indicate that the total net income from power since the beginning of the TVA in 1933 to June 30, 1944, will be well over $40,000,000. This substantial surplus will have been accumulated in only five or six years, for between 1933 and 1937 the TVA was not a going power concern; the system was incomplete and operations were beset by a multiplicity of lawsuits and injunctions which prevented the normal sale of the power produced by the river. The size of this net income indicates pretty clearly that the power asset of the Tennessee River certainly is worth its cost.

These calculations take into account only dollar returns to TVA, and none of the indirect benefits. But such benefits are many. Among them are the $10,000,000 annual savings to consumers as a result of greatly reduced rates, the effects on the region's business enterprises of large amounts of low-cost power, the benefits that have resulted to business in other regions of the country, as well as the fact that 80 per cent of the equipment and materials purchased by TVA were produced in factories located in regions outside the Tennessee Valley. Nor do they seek to measure the value to the country of the fact that it was largely because of power from this river that in 1943 America was able to build huge fleets of bombers to send over Europe and the South Pacific.

SELECTION 23

". . . they are just like the rest of us": Harry Hopkins Speaks on Relief, 1936

One of the inevitable assaults against the New Deal was the claim that it took money from the provident with which to mollycoddle the incompetent and the lazy. Another series of charges dealt with the supposed inefficiency, waste, and corruption of the government. Harry Hopkins (1890–1946), because he became the chief spender of the administration, bore the brunt of these attacks more frequently than did others, and his agencies, the Federal Emergency Relief Administration (FERA), the Civil Works Administration (CWA), and later the Works Progress Administration (WPA) were more sharply criticized than others. Some waste and some apparent silliness were certain to result when the prime need was to feed people in a hurry. Hopkins was not disturbed by the leaf-raking projects when they were the best work at hand. He thought it more important to see that people were fed. But he did become irritated on occasion with the relentless criticism his programs attracted. The following excerpt from one of his speeches suggests some of his answers to these stock charges.

Hopkins was one of the people who remained influential throughout the entire Roosevelt Era. A social worker, he had been FDR's emergency relief administrator in New York before coming to Washington to manage FERA. In 1938 he became Secretary of Commerce. During the war, he was Roosevelt's most intimate adviser, handling many significant matters of diplomacy and military planning. Searle F. Charles traces the relief programs and Hopkins's role in them in Minister of Relief: Harry Hopkins and the Depression *(1963).*

The reading provided here, a selection from a 1936 speech, has been drawn from the most significant source on Hopkins's work, Robert Sherwood, Roosevelt and Hopkins: An Intimate History *(New York: Harper & Row, 1948), pages 83–85.*

I am getting sick and tired of these people on the W.P.A. and local relief rolls being called chiselers and cheats. It doesn't do any good to call these people names, because they are just like the rest of us. They don't drink any more than the rest of us, they don't lie any more, they're no lazier than the rest of us—they're pretty much a cross section of the American people. . . .

I want to finish by saying two things. I have never liked poverty. I have never believed that with our capitalistic system people have to be poor. I think it is an outrage that we should permit hundreds and hundreds of thousands of people to be ill clad, to live in miserable homes, not to have enough to eat; not to be able to send their children to school for the only reason that they are poor. I don't believe ever again in America are we going to permit the things to happen that have happened in the past to people. We are never going back again, in my opinion, to the days of putting the old people in the alms houses, when a decent dignified pension at home will keep them there. We are coming to the day when we are going to have decent houses for the poor, when there is genuine and real security for everybody. I have gone all over the moral hurdles that people are poor because they are bad. I don't believe it. A system of government on that basis is fallacious. I think further than that, that this economic system of ours is an ideal instrument to increase this national income of ours, not back to 80 billion where it was, but up to 100 billion or 120 billion. The capitalistic system lends itself to providing a national income that will give real security for all.

Now I want to say this, I have been at this thing for three and a half years. I have never been a public official before. I was brought up in that school of thought that believed that no one went on the public payroll except for political purposes or because he was incompetent or unless he had a job that he didn't work at. One of the most insidious things is the propaganda that something is wrong about one that works for the people. I have learned something in these three and a half years. I have taken a look at a lot of these public servants. I have seen these technical fellows working for three or four thousand a year—not working seven hours a day but working fifteen hours a day. I have seen these fellows in the Army engineer corps. The motivation can't be money—they don't get very much. I have seen them work just as hard as any engineers in America and just as qualified and just as competent, and I have come to resent an attitude on the part of some people in America that you should never be part of this business of public service. I am proud of having worked for the Government. It has been a great experience for me. I have signed my name to about $6,000,000,000 in the last three and a half years. None of it has stuck to the fingers of our administrators. You might think some of it has been wasted. If it has been wasted it was in the interest of the unemployed. You might say we have made mistakes. I haven't a thing to apologize for about our so-called mistakes. If we have made mistakes we made them in the interests of the people that were broke.

When this thing is all over and I am out of the Government the things I am going to regret are the things I have failed to do for the unemployed. I don't know whether you would have liked the job. Every night when you went home and after you got home and remembered there was a telegram you didn't answer, the fact that you failed to answer the telegram and the telephone call may have resulted in somebody not eating. That is the kind of a job I have had for the last three and a half years, and still have. When it is all over, the thing I am going to be proudest of are the people all over America, public officials, volunteers, paid workers, thousands of people of all political and religious faiths who joined in this enterprise of taking care of people in need. It has been a great thing. I am not ashamed of one of them and I hope when I am through they are not going to be ashamed of me, and as I go around this country and see the unemployment and see the people who are running this show of ours, I am tremendously proud of this country of ours and I am tremendously proud that I am a citizen of it. Thank you very much.

SELECTION 24

"Anyone who's sure of his next meal, raise your hand!": "Waiting for Lefty," 1935

For labor also, the returns of the New Deal were slow in coming, painful in their impact. Section 7(a) had not been much more than a gesture. Even the Wagner Act provided only a more friendly milieu within which to bargain and fight. For many, the moderation, cooperation, and general peacefulness of FDR's approach seemed misleading, or worse, and they called for direct action. Some, but by no means all, of the activists were communists, and the argument over tactics sometimes sketched the boundaries between liberalism and radicalism. But the inadequacy of the New Deal and the plain fact of hunger were also issues. Clifford Odets (1906–1963) was one of the most brilliant of the American authors who created a new literature of social realism and provided an artistic vehicle for the Marxist message. Odets' best-known work was the play Waiting for Lefty, *which introduced the Broadway theater public to the trauma and tensions of the union hall and the picket line. The brief opening colloquy in the first act between Harry Fatt and Joe suggests some of the varied responses one could find among workingmen to the programs of the New Deal and to the problems of making a living wage. Some of these problems were mildly alleviated by the passage of the Fair Labor Standards Act in 1937, providing minimum wage and maximum hours protection for workers in areas affecting interstate commerce.*

Irving Howe and Lewis Coser, The American Communist Party *(1957) is one of the standard sources on the subject. The socially conscious theater is investigated with both authority and interest by Morgan Y. Himelstein in* Drama Was a Weapon: The Left-wing Theater in New York, 1929–1941 *(1963).*

The excerpt below is from Clifford Odets, Waiting for Lefty, *in* Six Plays of Clifford Odets *(New York: Random House, 1939), pages 5–7.*

As the curtain goes up we see a bare stage. On it are sitting six or seven men in a semi-circle. Lolling against the proscenium down left is a young man chewing a toothpick: a gunman. A fat man of porcine appearance is talking directly to the audience. In other words he is the head of a union and the men ranged behind him are a committee of workers. They are now seated in interesting different attitudes and present a wide diversity of type, as we shall soon see. The fat man is hot and heavy under the collar, near the end of a long talk, but not too hot: he is well fed and confident. His name is HARRY FATT.

FATT: You're so wrong I ain't laughing. Any guy with eyes to read knows it. Look at the textile strike—out like lions and in like lambs. Take the San Francisco tie-up—starvation and broken heads. The steel boys wanted to walk out too, but they changed their minds. It's the trend of the times, that's what it is. All we workers got a good man behind us now. He's top man of the country—looking out for our interests—the man in the White House is the one I'm referrin' to. That's why the times ain't ripe for a strike. He's working day and night—

VOICE: *(from the audience):* For who? *(The* GUNMAN *stirs himself.)*

FATT: For you! The records prove it. If this was the Hoover régime, would I say don't go out, boys? Not on your tin-type! But things is different now. You read the papers as well as me. You know it. And that's why I'm against the strike. Because we gotta stand behind the man who's standin' behind us! The whole country——

ANOTHER VOICE: Is on the blink! *(The* GUNMAN *looks grave.)*

FATT: Stand up and show yourself, you damn red! Be a man, let's see what you look like! *(Waits in vain.)* Yellow from the word go! Red and yellow makes a dirty color, boys. I got my eyes on four or five of them in the union here. What the hell'll they do for you? Pull you out and run away when the trouble starts. Give those birds a chance and they'll have your sisters and wives in the whore houses, like they done in Russia. They'll tear Christ off his bleeding cross. They'll wreck your homes and throw your babies in the river. You think that's bunk? Read the papers! Now listen, we can't stay here all night. I gave you the facts in the case. You boys got hot suppers to go to and——

ANOTHER VOICE: Says you!

GUNMAN: Sit down, Punk!

ANOTHER VOICE: Where's Lefty? *(Now this question is taken up by the others in unison.* FATT *pounds with gavel.)*

FATT: That's what I wanna know. Where's your pal, Lefty? You elected him chairman—where the hell did he disappear?

VOICES: We want Lefty! Lefty! Lefty!

FATT *(pounding):* What the hell is this—a circus? You got the committee here. This bunch of cowboys you elected. *(Pointing to man on the extreme right end.)*

MAN: Benjamin.

FATT: Yeah, Doc Benjamin. *(Pointing to other men in circle in seated order):* Benjamin, Miller, Stein, Mitchell, Phillips, Keller. It ain't my fault Lefty took a run-out powder. If you guys——

A GOOD VOICE: What's the committee say?

OTHERS: The committee! Let's hear from the committee! (FATT *tries to quiet the crowd, but one of the seated men suddenly comes to the front. The* GUNMAN *moves over to center stage, but* FATT *says:)*

FATT: Sure, let him talk. Let's hear what the red boys gotta say! *(Various shouts are coming from the audience.* FATT *insolently goes back to his seat in the middle of the circle. He sits on his raised platform and relights his cigar. The* GUNMAN *goes back to his post.* JOE, *the new speaker, raises his hand for quiet. Gets it quickly. He is sore.)*

JOE: You boys know me. I ain't a red boy one bit! Here I'm carryin' a shrapnel that big I picked up in the war. And maybe I don't know it when it rains! Don't tell me red! You know what we are? The black and blue boys! We been kicked around so long we're black and blue from head to toes. But I guess anyone who says straight out he don't like it, he's a red boy to the leaders of the union. What's this crap about goin' home to hot suppers? I'm asking to your faces how many's got hot suppers to go home to? Anyone who's sure of his next meal, raise your hand! A certain gent sitting behind me can raise them both. But not in front here! And that's why we're talking strike—to get a living wage!

VOICE: Where's Lefty?

JOE: I honest to God don't know, but he didn't take no run-out powder. That Wop's got more guts than a slaughter house. Maybe a traffic jam got him, but he'll be here. But don't let this red stuff scare you. Unless fighting for a living scares you. We gotta make up our minds. My wife made up my mind last week, if you want the truth. It's plain as the nose on Sol Feinberg's face we need a strike. There's us comin' home every night—eight, ten hours on the cab. "God," the wife says, "eighty cents ain't money—don't buy beans almost. You're working for the company," she says to me, "Joe! you ain't workin' for me or the family no more!" She says to me, "If you don't start . . . "

"The conflicting and confusing character of the early Roosevelt program . . .": An Economist Looks at the New Deal, 1936

Reactions to the New Deal were as varied as the specific measures one might have in mind or the interests and experience one might bring to the judgment. Businessmen quite generally insisted it had been a tragic, unnecessary failure. Presuming that business confidence was the only stimulator of economic activity, they noted their own lack of confidence as the best evidence of both the fact of failure and the reason for it. They called attention to the continued high level of unemployment, to the mounting government deficits, negligible by later standards, but alarming as compared with past traditions. Although national income had leaped from about 40 billion dollars in 1932 to over 71 billion in 1937, it was frequently charged that this was a "phony" recovery, kept going only by continued transfusions from deficit spending.

Both businessmen and the President worried about inflation by the winter of 1936–1937, and industrial leaders were particularly incensed by the sharp increase in strikes and labor "instability" in the wake of the Wagner Act. When Roosevelt sought to take anti-inflationary measures by cutting back sharply on government expenditures, there ensued, between August and December, 1937, one of the most abrupt recessions in the nation's history. After some reluctance and considerable uncertainty, Roosevelt returned to heavy deficit spending. Indices of economic activity and health began to rise sharply again, a trend which continued until the essential defense and war expenditures of the post-Munich period began to assure an unprecedented prosperity.

The business community generally insisted thereafter that Roosevelt's policies had actually prevented healthy recovery by the persistent use of crutches. The recession of 1937–1938, they said, merely showed what would happen when crutches were removed without rebuilding the confidence of investors through conservative policies. Former President Hoover continued to repeat the most extreme version of this analysis, as he insisted that prosperity had actually been building in the winter of 1932–1933, only to be destroyed by Roosevelt's policies.

At the opposite extreme many New Dealers such as Harry Hopkins, Marriner Eccles, head of the Federal Reserve Board, or Secretary of the Interior Harold Ickes, claimed that the New Deal policies had been effective, and that what relative failures there had been could be laid at the doors of uncooperative businessmen. They noted that recession came almost immediately upon the retrenchment in spending of early 1937, and that recovery began again with the resumption of spending. They called attention to the strong reassertion of corporate profits between 1933 and 1937 and some, notably Ickes, insisted that there had been an actual business conspiracy to destroy the New Deal.

Since no one can really know what amount of recovery would have come without Roosevelt's program, judgments about his success are likely to depend upon the economic views of the judge. Followers of John Maynard Keynes, believing that government must compensate for the weaknesses of an economy at any given point, will insist that the administration was on the right track, but clumsy, uncertain, inconsistent in many of its actions. Pre-Keynesian economists with an ideological devotion to laissez faire *will conclude the Roosevelt experiments to have been a failure, as they must have been, by definition, for this school of economists.*

The difficulties are two. The war intervened before it was possible to know whether the administration's policies could have produced a definitive recovery. Further, the administration did not follow any set line of policy consistently and thoroughly enough so that it could be credited with the success, or blamed for the failure. Spending and economy, inflationary and deflationary policies, promonopoly and antimonopoly policies were all tried, and often in overlapping ways. It was an open-ended experiment conducted on several different levels at once and never quite finished. It was sparked by necessity rather than by any thoroughgoing ideology. In retrospect, it looked vaguely Keynesian, but the ideas of John Maynard Keynes became known in the United States only late in the Depression, long after the policy commitments had been made.

Most historians agree in retrospect that economic recovery did not come fully until World War II, but that, despite all its confusions and uncertainties, the New Deal undoubtedly contributed heavily to recovery. It can *be said that relief was provided for millions of people, that the general confidence of the country was restored (even though that of the business community would wane after mid-1933), that levels of economic activity* did *rise sharply. And it can be said, in the light of modern economics, that many of the policies the administration followed were the logically correct ones.*

One of the most nearly objective and thorough among the contemporary analyses was that of a group of scholars at the Brookings Institution in Washington. A part of their appraisal of the effect of the New Deal upon economic recovery follows. Although their statements are open to argument at points, they suggest some of the complex questions which must be faced in any estimate of the age.

Among the later studies which might well be consulted are the following: H. V. Hodson, Slump and Recovery: 1929–1937 *(1938); Kenneth Roose,* The Economics of Recession and Revival *(1954); Lewis Kimmel,* Federal Budget and Fiscal Policy: 1789–1958 *(1959).*

The contemporary estimate reprinted here is from Harold G. Moulton et al., The Recovery Problem in the United States *(Washington: The Brookings Institution, 1936), pages 451–460.*

It is readily apparent that certain phases of the early Roosevelt program were fundamentally incompatible: (1) the efforts to re-establish business confidence through the reconstruction of the credit system and the reduction of expenditures by the regular federal departments were in large measure nullified by the uncertainty arising out of the program of dollar devaluation and currency management. (2) The authorization of billions of dollars for public works was seen as a menace to the program of fiscal stability. (3) The currency policy necessitated independent national action, and it thus disrupted the World Economic Conference and deferred the program intended to mitigate trade barriers and reopen the channels of international commerce. (4) The sharp increase in industrial prices fostered by the NRA program of increasing wages and shortening hours worked directly at cross purposes with the AAA policy of restoring price parity between agriculture and industry. It should also be noted that some of the permanent reform implications of the Administration's general program—however meritorious they may be—inevitably occasioned uneasiness and hence served to impede the recovery program.

The changes which occurred during the second stage (1934–36) served to eliminate some of the major conflicts within the program. The abandonment of currency management carried with it an abandonment of the policy of economic isolation, and paved the way for the reopening of negotiations intended to encourage international trade development. The dissolution of the National Recovery Administration eliminated the program of progressively raising industrial costs and prices, and thus removed a serious obstacle to the restoration of agricultural and industrial price parity.

The new policy of promoting recovery through vast governmental expenditures presented, however, a fresh complication. The rapidly increasing public indebtedness was viewed as a menace to the stability of public credit, and thus to the stability of the dollar. In other words, while the reduction of the value of the dollar as a matter of definite policy had apparently been abandoned, it was feared that currency stability might be undermined in another—and less controllable—way. The great question became whether the stimulus resulting from government expenditures might generate a sufficient expansion in business activity to make possible in good season a restoration of fiscal equilibrium. No one could definitely forecast the outcome.

Because of the complex factors involved in the process of economic recovery, it is difficult to establish conclusively whether government policies as a whole have been a stimulating or retarding influence. The available evidence does, however, definitely enable one to limit the area of doubt and to indicate whether the policies pursued were of decisive importance, one way or the other. To throw light on the issue thus raised we may compare the time and extent of recovery in the United States with that in other countries and also indicate how closely the degree of actual recovery in the United States at various stages articulated with the recovery program that was being evolved.

In the first place, it is clear that the recovery in this country has been part of a world movement . . . that the bottom of the depression in general was reached in the summer of 1932, and that the slow, if halting, process of recovery was under way in the second half of that year. Even in the United States the lowest level of industrial output was reached in July 1932. The index of industrial production rose from 48.7 in that month to about 56 in the late autumn, only to decline again to 49.6 at the time of the banking crisis in March 1933. During this period industrial production in Great Britain rose from about 78 to 85; in Sweden from 67 to 81; in Germany from 51 to 57; and in Japan from 95 to 117. The monthly data indicate that the new American decline in the first quarter of 1933 exercised a restraining influence upon, but did not altogether check the advance elsewhere.

In the light of these facts, it seems a fair presumption that as soon as the American banking crisis was cleared up a new advance in the United States would have begun, even had no further governmental action been taken. The question remains, however, whether other policies may not have accelerated the forward movement. In attempting to throw light on this issue, it will be necessary to divide the period of recovery into several segments.

The first period is the three-month interval from March to May 1933. The most significant developments in these months were the reopening of the banks, the setting up of the Agricultural Adjustment Administration, the emphasis upon a balanced budget, and the gradual downward drift of the dollar in the foreign exchanges. It should be borne in mind that a definite decision to devalue the currency had not yet been reached, and that the National Industrial Recovery Act was still only in the stages of preliminary discussion.

During this period the index of industrial production in the United States showed a marked rise, from 49.6 in March to 65.5 in May. Meanwhile, industrial output in Great Britain, Germany, Sweden, and Japan, showed little change. During these three months the American recovery movement may be said to have caught up with, and even passed, that of other leading countries. It is impossible to assign responsibility for this strong upward surge to any single development; it would probably be safest to attribute it to a combination of factors, including the new spirit of hopefulness engendered by the President.

The next period to be considered separately is June and July 1933. It was in the former month that the policy of depreciating the currency was definitely adopted and that the National Industrial Recovery program was announced. Industrial production jumped sharply, from 65 in May to 84 in July. Meanwhile, in Germany, Great Britain, Japan, and Sweden there was little change in the level of output. One must conclude, therefore, that the policies of the United States government were a powerful stimulus at this particular juncture. The prospect of substantially higher costs and prices, arising from monetary and industrial code policies, led to a rapid expansion of output in anticipation of the changes to come.

In the following months there was a sharp reversal of trend, the index of industrial production declining from 84.0 in July to 60.5 in November—well below the level of May. This period was one of liquidation of excessive inventories accumulated in anticipation of the new level of costs. During these months, however, there was a strong advance in other countries. Measured from the low point of the depression to December 1933 the degree of recovery in the United States had been somewhat less than that in Great Britain, Germany, Sweden, and Japan.

The next period requiring scrutiny is the first eleven months of the year 1934. The index of industrial output in the United States fluctuated between about 60 and 72. It stood at 65.5 in January, reached a high of 72.3 in May, and then declined to an average of about 61.0 in September, October, and November. This was just about the level of the preceding autumn. Meanwhile, there was a further advance of over 10 per cent in the level of production in Great Britain, Germany, Sweden, and Japan.

A rather sharp recovery occurred in December 1934 and January 1935. For the first half of 1935 as a whole, however, the index of industrial production was only about four points above the level of the first half of 1934. It is of interest to note also that in June 1935 the level of industrial output was below that of June 1933 and materially below the peak reached in July of that year. Moreover, the degree of recovery by June 1935 had been less than that in any of the other countries with which we are here making comparisons.

Since the middle of 1935 there has been a fairly steady and strong forward movement. The index of industrial output advanced from 72.3 in June 1935 to 86.6 in June 1936 and to 91.6 in September of this year. This advance has been somewhat more pronounced that that in most other countries. At the present time, however, the degree of recovery in the United States is still considerably less than that in various other countries.

The best-sustained recovery movement thus began shortly after the National Industrial Recovery Act was declared unconstitutional. It is evident that the grave fears entertained that the abandonment of the codes would lead to a new period of business disorganization were not well founded. It should be observed in this connection, however, that the ensuing improvement in business did not result from downward wage readjustments—for the fact is that wage rates have tended to rise rather than fall.

One would not be justified in attributing all of the improvement which has occurred since the middle of 1935 to the disappearance of the codes. Other factors have doubtless played a part, such as the relative increase in farm income, the increasing confidence resulting from the modification of government policy with respect to currency, and the continued forward movement in other countries. Moreover, recovery is ordinarily a cumulative process and in the absence of definitely retarding influences one would expect to find an expanding volume of production as the months pass.

When the degree of recovery is considered more broadly, in relation to the two phases of the Roosevelt recovery program, a conclusion of primary significance may be drawn. It will be recalled that in the first stage of the recovery program the internal inconsistencies were much greater than in the second stage. These conflicts of policy manifested themselves most strikingly during the first year or so; and it was during this period that the recovery movement was most halting, and most uneven in character. One may fairly conclude, therefore, that the conflicting and confusing character of the early Roosevelt program tended on the whole to retard the recovery program.

It is interesting to note in this connection that the two measures which gave the greatest initial impetus to industrial expansion, namely, dollar depreciation and the anticipation of the NRA program to raise costs and price, were the very measures which in the end threatened to undermine the whole recovery program. Dollar depreciation not only engendered fear over the future stability of values, but it produced serious international complications which impeded the recovery of world trade. The NRA not only became administratively impossible and a source of endless confusion and controversy, but it failed to increase the real income of the laboring classes as a whole, and tended to checkmate the policy of increasing the real purchasing power of the agricultural population.

During the second phase of the government's recovery effort, the spending program came to occupy a place of primary importance. It is impossible to gauge accurately the bearing of this policy upon recovery, for one cannot segregate its effects from those of other factors in the situation. It may be pointed out that the spending program was vigorously pushed throughout the year 1934 and that it was not until after the middle of 1935 that a strong forward movement began. Was this simply a natural lag, or does it suggest rather that the benefits were for the time being nullified by the adverse effects of other phases of the government program? No one can answer this question conclusively.

It is evident, however, that the spending program operated as a sort of two-edged sword. On the one hand, it undoubtedly served as a direct stimulus to retail trade, and through retail trade to the processes of production. On the other hand, it produced uneasiness with reference to the future stability of the dollar, and thus militated against long-term credit operations. A considerable period of time elapsed before the fears resulting alike from the devaluation and budget unbalancing programs subsided; and it was not until 1935 that long-term credit operations—even refunding operations—were resumed on any considerable scale.

The effects of the spending program on business activity, however, tended to be cumulative in character. At the outset the influence was exerted chiefly in the markets for consumers' goods; but as time passed the expansion movement gradually extended to the field of capital construction. It is possible that an earlier and more rapid expansion might have occurred had confidence not been impaired by fiscal policy; but one cannot tell from any available evidence.

In considering the influence of the spending program on recovery, it will be helpful again to make comparisons with the experience of other countries. Both Great Britain and Sweden have attained a greater degree of recovery than has the United States, and neither has permitted any material increase in the public debt. It is evidently possible, therefore, to have recovery, even from a world depression, without vast outlays of public funds.

However, it must also be noted that Germany and Japan have had an even greater degree of expansion than Great Britain, and that their budgets have been even more seriously unbalanced than has that of the United States. It is clearly evident, therefore, that an unbalanced budget is not an insurmountable barrier to recovery. But at the same time there is no doubt that if recovery is achieved without a piling up of government indebtedness there exists a much sounder basis for enduring prosperity. Unbalanced budgets and public debts leave an aftermath of complications which threaten both financial and economic stability.

In connection with these international comparisons it must be borne in mind that the comparisons are not between one country in which vigorous efforts were made by the government to promote recovery and other countries in which economic trends were allowed to run a normal course uninfluenced by government policy. All countries endeavored in one way or another to use the powers of government in promoting business revival. We must therefore repeat here what was said at the close of that chapter, namely, that it is impossible to make a simple direct comparison of results in countries which invoked the powers of government with the outcome in countries following a policy of strict laissez faire—for there were none of the latter.

Sociologists Study the Problem: Middletown Revisited, 1937

In the mid-1930s Robert and Helen Lynd returned to the Midwestern city which they had studied so extensively at the peak of prosperity. They found Muncie, Indiana, citizens now confused and troubled, although conscious both of the disaster and of some progress made upon the road to recovery. Perhaps the largest surprise was the fact that the extended crisis had shaken the value structure so little. There had been no revolution in middle-class attitudes. A part of the Lynds's classic study follows. It is reprinted from Robert S. Lynd and Helen Merrell Lynd, Middletown in Transition: A Study in Cultural Conflicts *(New York: Harcourt, Brace & World, 1937), pages 19–27.*

The first definite intimation of what was to give the coup de grâce to local confidence came in April, 1932, when a four-inch article on an inner page of the afternoon paper announced that the local branch of General Motors would "be affected by changes proposed," followed in a day or so by the announcement that part of the plant might be moved away to another city. Now a latent tendency to apprehension appeared in renewed strength. As a businessman described it: "People would go around saying in low tones, 'Have you heard that they're boarding up the so-and-so plant?' And a few days later, 'Have you heard that so-and-so-many trucks of machinery were moved out of town today? They say that half the floor at the plant is stripped already.' It got on our nerves as this went on!" And by late summer General Motors had stripped its floors and moved away, lock, stock, and barrel. A delegation of local businessmen went to Detroit and persuaded the company not to board up the empty plant because of the bad publicity it would give the city owing to the plant's prominent location on the through railroad line that crosses the city.

By this time, despite the running in the paper of a "Bright Spots in Business" department every few days citing hopeful signs over the United States, editorial optimism was becoming sobered to the grim and more cautious reassurance that "The pendulum cannot swing forever in one direction. It must swing back." And the editor of the evening paper so far let himself slip from the officially correct attitude of Middletown papers as to qualify his congratulation of Middletown banks for their sound condition by the acid comment: "Far be it from this column to laud banks unduly. In general its opinion of them is not so high." This remark literally could not have appeared in either of Middletown's dailies in 1925.

Among the casualties of the black days of 1932–33 were some of the small factories of younger businessmen. These men, fighting ahead under the American formula of "a little credit and a lot of hard work," included some of the growing business leaders of the city. As will be pointed out in a later chapter the unseating of these potential independent leaders has operated to tighten the grip of the central group of elder businessmen, who in 1935 appeared so markedly to control the city.

Over against this loss of struggling young factories must be set the widespread inventiveness in earning money in small ways that cropped up. All over town, with the exception of the more exclusive residential neighborhoods, one sees evidences of this ingenuity. Little signs in yards announce the presence of household beauty parlors and cleaning and pressing businesses; grocery stores have been opened in cottage front rooms or in additions to residences built out flush with the street; some houses on prominent corners have installed on the corner of the lot little ice-cream and soft-drink booths in the form of spotless ice-cream freezers twelve feet high and eight feet in diameter; others have cashed in on the forced sales of old farms in this section of the state by opening household antique shops; while one woman whose husband's flourishing meat market went under is serving well-appointed dinners in her home to local women's clubs and sororities.

During the dark days of 1933 the city wrestled with the unprecedented problem of relief which was costing in excess of $1,000 a day. Radicalism was in the wind, though it never attained any large proportions locally. The substantial businessfolk were envisioning the possibility of a general collapse of their world. As one of these people laughingly remarked in 1935:

> We all laugh about it now, but it was no joke then! At the time of the national bank crisis in 1933, when it seemed for a while that everything might collapse, many of us bought a great deal of canned food and stored it in our cellars, fearing a possible siege. One family I know bought enough for more than five years. People in our set were talking to each other about how long the city could get along on its available food supply if transportation and communication broke down, where we'd buy candles, and all that sort of thing.

There was no revival of business until late in 1934, and even then the city's mood was that of grasping at straws of hope rather than the welcoming of large reality. Middletown's leading department store went under in April, 1934. But from late 1933 on, Federal farm subsidies, for wheat acreage reduction at the beginning and later for corn and hogs, began to give a lift to the constricted flow of money as the farmers from the rich counties around Middletown brought in their Federal checks and took away clothing, home furnishings, and farm supplies. The return of legal beer is regarded by one banker as having had a symbolic value operating to cheer people up, though other local persons doubt that this significance attached to the end of prohibition. Federal relief helped some, and the city grasped all it could get. During 1934, moreover, one local plant secured new capital and moved to larger quarters; an automotive-parts plant had a big year; fruit jars continued to boom; and two local glass plants added the production of beer bottles to their schedules. The industrial gears were beginning to catch again.

But the turn in the tide came psychologically in 1935. One of the city's largest plants, manufacturing automotive parts, passed its all-time employment peak early in the year. And then, in April, came the heady news that put Middletown "over the top" emotionally: General Motors was moving back to Middletown! And, as, with the lifting of the smallpox quarantine in 1893, local morale had surged back with "General jollification, assemblies of people on streets, blowing of horns, burning of red fire," so in June, 1935, Middletown called in the governor of the state and celebrated the return of good times with a great public dinner. As one businessman said: "We were joking earlier this year when we talked about the 'past' depression, but now we mean it!" Later in 1935, heavy production in the city's automotive-parts plants kept the big drum booming. The Borg-Warner unit broke ground for an enlargement of its plant and in November announced its "all-time high" in local employment; while the Delco-Remy plant manufacturing motor batteries reached in November "the highest daily production in the history of the [Middletown] unit, or four times its daily output in 1928 when Plant No. 9 moved to [Middletown]." Early in October the National Retail Credit Association reported that Middletown had led the country in September with its 30 per cent increase in its retail credit collections.

A factor in this business-class jollification was "the end of N.R.A." Local businessmen do not like to recall now the eagerness with which they turned to the Federal Government in the crisis of 1933, and little is said of the now inconsistent fact that they still utilize all the Federal relief money the city can get. Since the first flush of emotional relief in the late spring of 1933, Middletown's reaction to the Roosevelt administration and its New Deal have been uneven and sharply marked by class differences. As noted elsewhere, the New Deal legislation has driven a wedge between business- and working-class attitudes toward the national governmental machinery. A local banker commented in 1935: "Our local workingmen are for the New Deal and our businessmen are against it. While our workingmen are beginning to feel that Roosevelt has let them down in his promises to further labor organization, their attitude has been and still is that the people in Washington had a pretty good idea and they knew what they were doing. But our businessmen hate Roosevelt's guts and his whole New Deal!" "[Middletown] is so rock-ribbed Republican," commented another businessman, "that our best people around here are unwilling to give the New Deal type of thinking and planning an even and candid break."

But the political label of an administration has been of trivial concern as compared with the possibility of the return of prosperity, so Middletown's businessmen ate political crow during 1933–34 in the hope of eating economic turkey. After insisting to Middletown before the 1932 election that ruin would be the only possible outcome of electing a Democratic President, the local press expressed the hope after the election that "the public, regardless of partisan politics, [would] give the new administration a 'break.' " When the business leaders met at the Chamber of Commerce to organize the local code authorities, an officer of the Chamber is reported to have expressed the prevailing sentiment in opening the proceedings by exclaiming, "God damn Roosevelt and the N.R.A.!"—but Middletown's businessmen drove ahead with as much of the N.R.A. as they could stomach. In October, 1933, they actually staged an enthusiastic N.R.A. parade which the press described as "the greatest peacetime parade in Middletown's history: distinctly big-town stuff!" Simultaneously, "a permanent [Middletown] National Recovery Crusade Board" was organized, composed chiefly of the presidents of local civic clubs, "to convince people that there is a way out"; and the public was urged to "Get behind the N.R.A. until something better comes along."

But as the fall and winter wore on, N.R.A. became troublesome to one group or another to the extent that it really began to operate. Labor began to organize under Section 7a of the Recovery Act. Some local plants eagerly took advantage of N.R.A. wage rates to drive down Middletown's always relatively low wages. Where local business could, it did what big business was doing widely elsewhere under the codes, and the headlines read: "Bids for School Coal Are Same; [School] Board Is Irate." Attached to each of the nine bids by local coal dealers, according to the press report, was "the usual affidavit stating that there had been no collusion among dealers, but to each form affidavit had been added the words, 'except as required by the compliance agreement of the retail solid-fuel industry.' "

As the halo around the New Deal wore off with the non-appearance of prosperity, local protest over these complications mounted. While the local business leaders and their newspapers set the direction and dictated the slogans, much of the sustaining weight of the thrust behind this local protest came from that section of Middletown's business largely outside the great industrial codes. Aside from the heads of half-a-dozen major industries, Middletown's businessmen regard themselves proudly as "small businessmen," who, their traditions have taught them, are the purest strain of our American democratic economy. One cannot understand the reaction of Middletown to the N.R.A., "bureaucracy," "organized labor," and to Middletown's other political and economic devils apart from the American conception of the "small businessman." Perched on his toe hold of advantage in the economic system, intent on climbing higher, he believes with the intensity of single-track conviction that Western economy was made "of, by, and for" individual strivers such as he. To this "small-businessman" culture—a culture stressing "Every tub on its own bottom," "You win if you're any good and your winnings are caused by you and belong to you," and "If a man doesn't make good it's his own fault"—one must look for much of the sustaining support for the outspoken, bitter resentment of bureaucracy and social legislation by Middletown businessmen in 1935. As the owner of a small non-manufacturing business remarked, "We small businessmen resent the way we've been soaked in the New Deal." A businessman went dramatically to his file and held up a folder: "See that? It's a pension plan for our two [Middletown businesses], all worked out. Now"—with a disgusted gesture—"it's just shelved, with the Wagner bill passed!" A banker, a man of great ability and breadth of outlook, voiced the same disgusted protest when he said: "We object to our bank's being taxed to pay for industrial security when we don't have any unemployment at the bank. We actually take on extra help in the summer so that our people can have their vacations."

Middletown banks are reported to have quietly sabotaged the Federal Home Owners' Loan Corporation, after unloading some of their poorer risks on it; while N.R.A., A.A.A., C.W.A., the Securities Act, and social-security legislation are all now looked upon by many businessmen as unwarranted interferences with "the normal functioning of business."

Everywhere in Middletown one sees these small businessmen looking out at social change with the personal resentment of one who by long defensive training asks first of every innovation, "What will it do for (or to) me?" The resulting tendency is to stress the negative aspects of new proposals and for local opinion to dwell upon and to crystallize around extremes of possible abuse which might occur. It is typical of this tendency that a local banker warned Middletown regarding the proposed child-labor amendment to the Federal Constitution that: "If it is carried to the logical extremes now discussed, it may not only disturb us economically but throw a very serious social problem on our hands in the activities of the young people not allowed to work."

The tendency noted here is not so much a commentary upon the kinds of people Middletown's businessmen are as upon the kind of culture in which they have grown up and to which they must largely conform if they are to survive. They live in a culture built around competition, the private acquisition of property, and the necessity for eternal vigilance in holding on to what one has. In such an exposed situation, rife with threats and occasions for personal tension, human beings tend to react primitively in the direction of warding off threats and seeking to conserve whatever stability they have personally been able to wrest from their environment.

Across the railroad tracks from this world of businessmen is the other world of wage earners—constituting a majority of the city's population, nurtured largely in the same habits of thought as the North Side, but with less coherence, leadership, and morale.

Among these people the New Deal fanned briskly for a brief period the faintly smoldering ashes of local labor organization. Middletown was in the 1890's "one of the best organized cities in the United States." The new workers pouring into the city with the gas boom had come heavily from already industrialized areas rather than off the farm, and they had brought a faith in labor organization. By 1925 this earlier fabric of organization had long since largely raveled away, and the lethargy as regards labor organization observed in 1925 not only continued but was even increased by the early years of the depression. Middletown entered the depression as an industrially open-shop town. Seven of its sixteen active unions affiliated with the Central Labor Union were in the building trades, and one more in the printing trades; six of the remaining eight were in a straggling group of barbers, musicians, motion-picture operators, postal carriers, and two groups of railway workers. The great metal-working industries comprising Middletown's leading group of factories—the automotive-parts plants and foundries—were unrepresented save for small molders' and pattern-makers' unions. The glass industry, the second group of industries in local importance, was totally unorganized.

The significance of the wave of labor organization encouraged by the N.R.A. lies not so much in the number of new unions it brought as in the momentary vitality it gave to the whole local labor movement by reason of the fact that it advanced straight on the two central strongholds of the open shop in Middletown: the automotive machine shops and the glass plants. Four of the ten new unions organized in 1933–34 aimed at the metal-working industries, while a fifth sought to awaken the moribund glass unions, once strong in Middletown, and to organize the X plant.

Middletown's working class in recent years has been heavily recruited from first- and second-generation farm stock. These men share the prevailing philosophy of individual competence. Working in an open-shop city with its public opinion set by the business class, and fascinated by a rising standard of living offered them on every hand on the installment plan, they do not readily segregate themselves from the rest of the city. They want what Middletown wants, so long as it gives them their great symbol of advancement—an automobile. Car ownership stands to them for a large share of the "American dream"; they cling to it as they cling to self-respect, and it was not unusual to see a family drive up to the relief commissary in 1935 to stand in line for its four- or five-dollar weekly food dole. "It's easy to see why our workers don't think much about joining unions," remarked a union official in 1935. He then went on to use almost the same words heard so often in 1925: "So long as they have a car and can borrow or steal a gallon of gas, they'll ride around and pay no attention to labor organization; and if they can't get gas, they're busy trying to figure out some way to get it."

To men in this mood, the depression came as an individual calamity. Like the businessmen across the tracks, their attention was focused on the place where the shoe pinched and they were initially disinclined to take either a broad or a long-term view of the situation. As one looks at the upsurge and abrupt subsidence of union activity under the New Deal—the "newness" of which to Middletown's working class as to its business class lay in its being a personal life line rather than a commitment to social change—one must bear constantly in mind the personal and institutional frictions against which labor organization in Middletown operated. The opposition of employers and the press to organized labor was of long standing and without subtlety in its expression and operation. To which should be added the following four deterrents to local labor organization, as listed by an officer of the local Central Labor Union in 1935:

1. Men who have jobs are afraid of losing them if they organize.
2. They can't pay union dues in bad times, for some of them are unemployed; and, while some are employed, they are on wages of only $10–$12 a week part time, or $16–$17 a week full time.
3. Some plants are still importing Kentucky and Tennessee hillbillies. These hillbillies can be educated into joining the union, but as soon as they do, they lose their jobs and drift off.
4. As long as a man has any morale left he will do anything, even leave his union and accept any wages and hours, in order to stay off the relief rolls.

And to this list should be added yet another factor stressed by a local carpenter and probably widely operating: "Men's families press them hard from behind to work for anything they can get, regardless of union rates."

Middletown had in 1929 roughly 900 union members out of a total of approximately 13,000 persons of both sexes gainfully employed in working-class occupations. Early in 1933, before the advent of the New Deal, the total of union members had shrunk by "a couple of hundred." At the peak in 1934 the total stood at 2,800, and by the end of 1935 it had wasted back to 1,000.

"Have you seen men handed refusals . . . ?": Carl Sandburg in Anger, 1936

Depression, like other facets of human experience, appeared to the artist more clearly, struck him more violently than it did most people. The artists of the 1930s responded vigorously, toughly, in anger always, although sometimes the anger was direct and sometimes it was clothed in irony or masked with cynicism. Carl Sandburg, the Chicago poet, preferred his anger straight. His long poem The People Yes *was published at the depths of the Depression. It was not a polite book, but it was powerful—powerful as a paean to democracy and powerful as a bludgeon attack upon privilege and fakery, the twin enemies of a people in distress. The brief excerpt below tells a lesson that middle-class Americans were only beginning to learn in 1936, despite six years of major Depression. It also stands as a brief introduction to the monumental work of Carl Sandburg (1878–   ), the poet of people, of cities, of toughness and reality, of twentieth-century life as it actually is. Sandburg is one of the literary giants of his age. But he has also become both a great honest critic of his society and a great romanticizer. His verse, starting with* Chicago Poems *in 1915, has been his major vehicle. It is often sharp and critical. But his massive biography of Abraham Lincoln is a romantic interpretation of one of the great heroes. And his* American Songbag *helps to recreate the romantic folk music of the nation.*

The verse printed here was published in 1936 and is from Carl Sandburg, "The People Yes," in Complete Poems *(New York: Harcourt, Brace & World, 1950), pages 484–485.*

Have you seen men handed refusals
  till they began to laugh
  at the notion of ever landing a job again—
Muttering with the laugh,
  "It's driving me nuts and the family too,"
Mumbling of hoodoos and jinx,
  fear of defeat creeping in their vitals—
Have you never seen this?
  or do you kid yourself
  with the fond soothing syrup of four words
  "Some folks won't work"??
Of course some folks won't work—
  they are sick or wornout or lazy
  or misled with the big idea
the idle poor should imitate the idle rich.

Have you seen them with savings gone
  step out and hustle for the family
  some in night life on the streets
  some fighting other women and kids
  for the leavings of fruit and vegetable markets
  or searching alleys and garbage dumps for scraps?

Have you seen them with savings gone
  furniture and keepsakes pawned
  and the pawntickets blown away in cold winds?
  by one letdown and another ending
  in what you might call slums—

To be named perhaps in case reports
and tabulated and classified
among those who have crossed over
from the employables into the *un*employables?

What is the saga of the employables?
what are the breaks they get?
What are the dramas of personal fate
spilled over from industrial transitions?
what punishments handed bottom people
who have wronged no man's house
or things or person?

Stocks are property, yes.
Bonds are property, yes.
Machines, land, buildings, are property, yes.
A job is property,
no, nix, nah nah.

The rights of property are guarded
by ten thousand laws and fortresses.
The right of a man to live by his work—
what is this right?
and why does it clamor?
and who can hush it
so it will stay hushed?
and why does it speak
and though put down speak again
with strengths out of the earth?

"If you can't eat you got to . . .": E. E. Cummings Writes as Anger Turns to Ennui, 1940

It was not simply that many were hungry; it was just as bad that many were bored with failure, were ready to give up. E. E. Cummings (1894–1962) spoke more often in symbols than did Sandburg; he ranged his words about in the manner of a nonobjective painter, seeking patterns in letters and punctuation points, welding the ring of words, the look of words, the sense of words to serve the steel-hard point of an idea. Always he spoke with the bitter sarcasm which frustration had taught his age to savor. Sandburg blasted out for all to see the great, rough chasms of discontent; Cummings etched upon their rugged walls the sharp epigrams which drew an end to old clichés and marked the boundaries of a great crisis in values. The verse which follows operates on two levels. At one it raises a physical image of a hedonist in retreat from reality; at the other it plumbs the utter pointlessness which seemed for many sensitive people the ultimate meaning of their age.

The verse below was first published in 1940 as a part of 50 Poems *and has been taken from E. E. Cummings,* Poems: 1923–1954 *(New York: Harcourt, Brace & World, 1954), page 353.*

If you can't eat you got to

smoke and we aint got
nothing to smoke: come on kid

let's go to sleep
if you can't smoke you got to

Sing and we aint got

nothing to sing; come on kid
let's go to sleep

if you can't sing you got to
die and we aint got

Nothing to die, come on kid

let's go to sleep
if you can't die you got to

dream and we aint got
nothing to dream (come on kid

Let's go to sleep)

PART FOUR

The Politics of Action

The promise of Roosevelt's New Deal was action without revolution, recovery without total upheaval. Yet certain dangers were posed by such a moderate approach to monstrous problems. The faltering first steps toward recovery and reform might lead to more expansive demands for action which a mere President could no longer manage. On the other hand, the patent failure to meet the problems of many large groups of Americans, the promise of hope without fulfillment, might make the time ripe for demagoguery.

Always controversial, Roosevelt was attacked with particular vigor during 1934, 1935, and 1936, from the right and from the left. Sometimes the two merged so closely it was difficult at best to attach a label to the assault. In general, FDR's politics in the face of attack involved holding the central position in both publicity and policy. He made the most of the substantive accomplishments of the New Deal and of his own salesmanship. He gradually drew away from the businessmen who had deserted his ambitious concept of a common front. He moved slightly more vigorously with social welfare legislation as the 1936 campaign approached, in order to encourage the people in their natural rejection of the extremists. His great victory of 1936 sealed for this crisis the fate of the extremists. He then moved on to attempt to weed from his own party the well-placed conservative elements in Congress. In this he failed during the 1938 primaries. Yet he succeeded in his larger objective during the campaign and election of 1940. Even though FDR's own personal majorities declined, the Republican candidate, Wendell Willkie, adopted much of Roosevelt's program. Herein lay evidence of FDR's most significant political achievement, the adoption into the national consciousness of the substantial core of the New Deal.

A useful summary of Roosevelt's approach to campaigns is Harold Gosnell, Champion Campaigner: Franklin D. Roosevelt *(1952). On the Republican politics of the period see George H. Mayer,* The Republican Party: 1854–1964 *(1964). Donald R. McCoy investigates a variety of the pressures exerted upon Roosevelt in* Angry Voices: Left of Center Politics in the New Deal Era *(1958). Right-wing pressures have been explored by George Wolfskill in* The Revolt of the Conservatives: A History of the American Liberty League, 1934–1940 *(1962).*

SELECTION 

The Way of the Demagogue: The "Share the Wealth" Plan of Huey P. Long, 1935

As the luster of the first New Deal dimmed, the danger of a shift to an extreme became more and more pressing. The nation abounded in aspiring candidates for the command. The "radio priest," Father Charles E. Coughlin, bound an expansive national following in a spell of personal magnetism and political and social utopianism which aroused the increasing concern of moderate leaders. Dr. Francis E. Townsend dotted the countryside with clubs devoted to his remarkably simplistic and appealing program for total security for the aged. But no leader was more effective, more outrageous in his promises, more potentially dangerous than Huey P. Long (1893–1935) the Democratic Senator from Louisiana. A product of the provincial hill country of his state, Long had risen to power and notoriety by an inspired combination of tough machine tactics, folksy, rumpled personal appeal, solid accomplishment, and uninhibited hill-country oratory. It was Long who predicted coolly that fascism might come to the United States, but in the guise of antifascism. It was Long, the man who brought better schools and good roads to Louisiana, who could keep his hat on in the President's office and could call irascible Secretary of the Interior Harold Ickes the "Chicago Cinchbug." And it was Long who, more than anyone else, engaged the deepest fears of Roosevelt and his associates.

Long's principal device for building a national following was his "Share the Wealth Clubs." His letter to potential members not only makes clear the nature of his appeal but also provides a case study in the pattern of demagoguery in the United States. His career, and Roosevelt's fears, were both destroyed by the assassin's bullets which cut down Senator Long in the Louisiana State House on September 8, 1935. But it is significant that it was an accident of a personal vendetta, rather than the substantial political processes of the country, which destroyed Long. It is significant also that Long spoke to and for large groups in American society which maintained well beyond his death the power to demand a reckoning. Many historians feel that Long played a significant role in pushing the New Deal farther than it otherwise might have gone, and in dramatizing by practice the dangers inherent in American democracy in time of crisis.

Huey Long's career is described in Allan P. Sindler, Huey Long's Louisiana: State Politics, 1920–1952 *(1956), and in two popular works: Harnett Kane,* Louisiana Hayride: The American Rehearsal for Dictatorship, 1928–1940 *(1941), and Robert Penn Warren,* All the King's Men *(1946). Important scholarly reappraisals are T. Harry Williams, "Gentleman from Louisiana: Demagogue or Democrat?"* Journal of Southern History, *volume 26 (1960), pages 3–21; and V. O. Key, Jr.,* Southern Politics in State and Nation *(1949), pages 156–182. The Rev. Charles E. Coughlin's career has been recently examined in Charles J. Tull,* Father Coughlin and the New Deal *(1965), and in James Shenton, "Fascism and Father Coughlin,"* Wisconsin Magazine of

History, *volume 44, August, 1960, pages 6–11. See also Alexander Holtzman,* The Townsend Movement *(1963).*

Long's own description of the "Share the Wealth Clubs," embodied in a letter to potential members, is taken from the Congressional Record, *Seventy-fourth Congress, first session, volume 79, part 7, pages 8040–8043.*

T*o members and well-wishers of the Share Our Wealth Society:*

For 20 years I have been in the battle to provide that, so long as America has, or can produce, an abundance of the things which make life comfortable and happy, that none should own so much of the things which he does not need and cannot use as to deprive the balance of the people of a reasonable proportion of the necessities and conveniences of life. The whole line of my political thought has always been that America must face the time when the whole country would shoulder the obligation which it owes to every child born on earth—that is, a fair chance to life, liberty, and happiness.

I had been in the United States Senate only a few days when I began my effort to make the battle for a distribution of wealth among all the people a national issue for the coming elections. On July 2, 1932, pursuant to a promise made, I heard Franklin Delano Roosevelt, accepting the nomination of the Democratic Party at the Chicago convention for President of the United States, use the following words:

"Throughout the Nation, men and women, forgotten in the political philosophy of the Government for the last years, look to us here for guidance and for a more equitable opportunity to share in the distribution of the national wealth."

It therefore seemed that all we had to do was to elect our candidate and that then my object in public life would be accomplished.

But a few nights before the Presidential election I listened to Mr. Herbert Hoover deliver his speech in Madison Square Garden, and he used these words:

"My conception of America is a land where men and women may walk in ordered liberty, where they may enjoy the advantages of wealth, not concentrated in the hands of a few, but diffused through the lives of all."

So it seems that so popular had become the demand for a redistribution of wealth in America that Mr. Hoover had been compelled to somewhat yield to that for which Mr. Roosevelt had previously declared without reservation.

It is not out of place for me to say that the support which I brought to Mr. Roosevelt to secure his nomination and election as President—and without which it was hardly probable he would ever have been nominated —was on the assurances which I had that he would take the proper stand for the redistribution of wealth in the campaign. He did that much in the campaign; but after his election, what then? I need not tell you the story. We have not time to cry over our disappointments, over promises which others did not keep, and over pledges which were broken.

We have not a moment to lose.

It was after my disappointment over the Roosevelt policy, after he became President, that I saw the light. I soon began to understand that, regardless of what we had been promised, our only chance of securing the fulfillment of such pledges was to organize the men and the women of the United States so that they were a force capable of action, and capable of requiring such a policy from the lawmakers and from the President after they took office. That was the beginning of the Share Our Wealth Society movement.

Let me say to the members and well-wishers that in this movement, the principles of which have received the endorsement of every leader of this time, and of other times, I am not concerned over my personal position or political fortune; I am only interested in the success of the cause; and on any day or at any time when, by our going for any person or for any party, we can better, or more surely or more quickly secure home, comfort, education, and happiness for our people, that there is no ambition of mine which will stand in the way. But there can be no minimum of success until every child in this land is fed, clothed, and housed comfortably and made happy with opportunity for education and a chance in life.

Even after the present President of the United States had thrown down the pledge which he had made time after time, and rather indicated the desire, instead, to have all the common people of America fed from a half-starvation dole, while the plutocrats of the United States were allowed to wax richer and richer, even after that, I made the public proposition that if he would return to his promise and carry out the pledge given to the people and to me that, regardless of all that had passed, I would again support his administration to the limit of my ability.

Of course, however, I was not blind; I had long since come to the understanding that he was chained to other purposes and to other interests which made impossible his keeping the words which he uttered to the people.

I delayed using this form of call to the members and well-wishers of the Share Our Wealth Society until we had progressed so far as to convince me that we could succeed either before or in the next national election of November 1936. Until I became certain that the spirit of the people could be aroused throughout the United States, and that, without any money— because I have none, except such little as I am given—the people could be persuaded to perfect organizations throughout the counties and communities of the country, I did not want to give false hopes to any of those engaged with me in this noble work. But I have seen and checked back enough, based upon the experiences which I have had in my public career, to know that we can, with much more ease, win the present fight, either between now and the next national campaign, or else in the next national campaign—I say with much more ease than many other battles which I have won in the past but which did not mean near so much.

We now have enough societies and enough members, to say nothing of the well-wishers who—if they will put their shoulders to the wheel and give us one-half of the time which they do not need for anything else—can force the principles of the Share Our Wealth Society to the forefront, to where no person participating in national affairs can ignore them further.

Now, here is what I ask the officers and members and well-wishers of all the Share Our Wealth Societies to do—two things, to wit:

First. If you have a Share Our Wealth Society in your neighborhood—or, if you have not one, organize one—meet regularly, and let all members, men and women, go to work as quickly and as hard as they can to get every person in the neighborhood to become a member and to go out with them to get more members for the society. If members do not want to go into the society already organized in their community, let them organize another society. We must have them as members in the movement, so that, by having their cooperation, on short notice we can all act as one person for the one object and purpose of providing that in the land of plenty there shall be comfort for all. The organized 600 families who control the wealth of America have been able to keep the 125,000,000 people in bondage because they have never once known how to effectually strike for their fair demands.

Second. Get a number of members of the Share Our Wealth Society to immediately go into all other neighborhoods of your county and into the neighborhoods of the adjoining counties, so as to get the people in the other communities and in the other counties to organize more Share Our Wealth Societies there; that will mean we can soon get about the work of perfecting a complete, unified organization that will not only hear promises but will compel the fulfillment of pledges made to the people.

It is impossible for the United States to preserve itself as a republic or as a democracy when 600 families own more of this Nation's wealth—in fact, twice as much—as all the balance of the people put together. Ninety-six percent of our people live below the poverty line, while 4 percent own 87 percent of the wealth. America can have enough for all to live in comfort and still permit millionaires to own more than they can ever spend and to have more than they can ever use; but America cannot allow the multi-millionaires and the billionaires, a mere handful of them, to own everything unless we are willing to inflict starvation upon 125,000,000 people.

We looked upon the year 1929 as the year when too much was produced for the people to consume. We were told and we believed that the farmers raised too much cotton and wool for the people to wear and too much food for the people to eat. Therefore, much of it went to waste, some rotted, and much of it was burned or thrown into the river or into the ocean. But, when we picked up the bulletin of the Department of Agriculture for that year 1929, we found that, according to the diet which they said everyone should eat in order to be healthy, multiplying it by 120,000,000, the number of people we had in 1929, had all of our people had the things which the Government said they should eat in order to live well, we did not have enough even in 1929 to feed the people. In fact, these statistics show that in some instances we had from one-third to one-half less than the people needed, particularly of milk, eggs, butter, and dried fruits.

But why in the year 1929 did it appear we had too much? Because the people could not buy the things they wanted to eat, and needed to eat. That showed the need for and duty of the Government then and there, to have forced a sharing of our wealth, and a redistribution, and Roosevelt was elected on the pledge to do that very thing.

But what was done? Cotton was plowed under the ground. Hogs and cattle were burned by the millions. The same was done to wheat and corn, and farmers were paid starvation money not to raise and not to plant because of the fact that we did not want so much because of people having no money with which to buy. Less and less was produced, when already there was less produced than the people needed if they ate what the Government said they needed to sustain life. God forgive those rulers who burned hogs, threw milk in the river, and plowed under cotton while little children cried for meat and milk and something to put on their naked backs!

But the good God who placed this race on earth did not leave us without an understanding of how to meet such problems; nor did the Pilgrim fathers who landed at Plymouth in 1620 fail to set an example as to how a country and a nation of people should act under such circumstances, and our great statesmen like Thomas Jefferson, Daniel Webster, Abraham Lincoln, Theodore Roosevelt, and Ralph Waldo Emerson did not fail to explain the need and necessity for following the precedents and purposes, which are necessary, even in a land of abundance, if all the people are to share the fruits produced therein. God's law commanded that the wealth of the country should be redistributed ever so often, so that none should become too rich and none should become too poor; it commanded that debts should be canceled and released ever so often, so that the human race would not be loaded with a burden which it could never pay. When the Pilgrims landed at Plymouth in 1620, they established their law by compact, signed by everyone who was on board the *Mayflower,* and it provided that at the end of every 7 years the finances of their newly founded country would be readjusted and that all debts would be released and property redistributed, so that none should starve in the land of plenty, and none should have an abundance of more than he needed. These principles were preserved in the Declaration of Independence, signed in 1776, and in our Constitution. Our great statesmen, such men as James Madison, who wrote the Constitution of the United States, and Daniel Webster, its greatest exponent, admonished the generations of America to come that they must never forget to require the redistribution of wealth if they desired that their Republic should live.

And, now, what of America? Will we allow the political sports, the high heelers, the wiseacres, and those who ridicule us in our misery and poverty to keep us from organizing these societies in every hamlet so that they may bring back to life this law and custom of God and of this country? Is there a man or woman with a child born on the earth, or who expects ever to have a child born on earth, who is willing to have it raised under the present-day practices of piracy, where it comes into life burdened with debt, condemned to a system of slavery by which the sweat of its brow throughout its existence must go to satisfy the vanity and the luxury of a leisurely few, who can never be made to see that they are destroying the root and branch of the greatest country ever to have risen? Our country is calling; the laws of the Lord are calling; the graves of our forefathers would open today if their occupants could see the bloom and flower of their creation withering and dying because the greed of the financial masters of this country has starved and withheld from mankind those things produced by his own labor. To hell with the ridicule of the wise street-corner politician. Pay no attention to any newspaper or magazine that has sold its columns to perpetuate this crime against the people of America. Save this country. Save mankind. Who can be wrong in such a work, and who cares what consequences may come following the mandates of the Lord, of the Pilgrims, of Jefferson, Webster, and Lincoln? He who fails in this fight falls in the radiance of the future. Better to make this fight and lose than to be a party to a system that strangles humanity.

It took the genius of labor and the lives of all Americans to produce the wealth of this land. If any man, or 100 men, wind up with all that has been produced by 120,000,000 people, that does not mean that those 100 men produced the wealth of the country; it means that those 100 men stole, directly or indirectly, what 125,000,000 people produced. Let no one tell you that the money masters made this country. They did no such thing. Very few of them ever hewed the forest; very few ever hacked a crosstie; very few ever nailed a board; fewer of them ever laid a brick. Their fortunes came from manipulated finance, control of government, rigging of markets, the spider webs that have grabbed all businesses; they grab the fruits of the land, the conveniences and the luxuries that are intended for 125,000,000 people, and run their heelers to our meetings to set up the cry, "We earned it honestly." The Lord says they did no such thing. The voices of our forefathers say they did no such thing. In this land of abundance, they have no right to impose starvation, misery, and pestilence for the purpose of vaunting their own pride and greed.

Whenever any newspaper or person, whether he be a private individual or an officer of the Government, says that our effort to limit the size of fortunes is contrary to the principles of our Government, he is too ignorant to deserve attention. Either he knows that what he says is untrue or else he is too ignorant to know what the truth is.

We can go further than that: Whenever any person says that he is following any Christian religion; or, if he be a Jew, if he says he is following the religion of the Jews; or even if he be a Chinaman, if he is following the teachings of Confucius, he cannot say that he thinks his own religion is sound unless he is willing to follow the principles to share the wealth of the land. Such is taught and required in the lines of the Bible, both in the New Testament and in the Old Testament, and the divine warning of those pages, repeated time and again, is that unless there is a comfortable living guaranteed to the man at the bottom, and unless the size of the big man's fortune is so limited as to allow the common run of people a fair share of the earth's fruits and blessings, that a race of people cannot survive.

If a man declare himself to be an American, and a believer in the American principles, then from the day that this country was founded until the present time, whether it be by the French or by the English, he must profess the share-our-wealth principles, or else he is not following the American doctrine. When the Pilgrims landed at Plymouth, here was a part of their compact and law:

> 5. That at ye end of ye 7 years, ye capital & profits, viz., the houses, lands, goods, and chatles, be equally devided betwixte ye adventurers, and planters; wch done, every man shall be free from other of them of any debt or detrimente concerning this adventure.

When the Declaration of Independence was written in 1776, here was a part of that immortal document:

> We hold these truths to be self evident, that all men are created equal, that they are endowed by their Creator with certain inalienable rights, that among these are life, liberty, and the pursuit of happiness. That to secure these rights (of life, liberty, and happiness), governments are instituted among them, deriving their power from the consent of the governed. That whenever any form of government becomes destructive of these ends (of life, liberty, and happiness), it is the right of the people to alter or to abolish it; and to institute new government, laying its foundation on such principles and organizing its power in such form, as to them shall seem most likely to effect their safety and happiness.

When James Madison, the father of the Constitution of this country, looked over the situation, here is what he said:

> We are free today substantially, but the day will come when our Republic will be an impossibility. It will be an impossibility because wealth will be concentrated in the hands of a few. A republic cannot stand upon bayonets, and when that day comes, when the wealth of the Nation will be in the hands of a few, then we must rely upon the wisdom of the best elements in the country to adjust the laws of the Nation to the changed conditions.

When the greatest exponent of our Constitution and of our Union, Daniel Webster, spoke of this principle, he said this:

> The freest government, if it could exist, would not be long acceptable if the tendencies of the law were to create a rapid accumulation of property in few hands and to render the great mass of the population dependent. Universal suffrage, for example, could not long exist in a community where there was a great inequality of property. In the nature of things, those who have not property and see their neighbors possess much more than they think them to need cannot be favorable to laws made for the protection of property.

And so, even if this principle born of the Creator when he placed the first man on earth, reaffirmed by Christ and the Apostles, and which was made a part of this country from the day that the Pilgrims first landed, is now to be cast aside, if it is to be misrepresented by some of the newspapers and magazines and by bought-out politicians and hired perverters of the truth, none the less the common run of mankind cannot escape the calamity unless the wealth of our land is distributed. To see men, politicians, and journals engaged in a business to betray mankind, to spread untruths and ridicule so that men and women may be lowered into the turmoil of distress, misery, and death; to see people with talent willing to sell their genius and to use their efforts to curse and destroy their fellow beings, is almost inconceivable in the sight of God and man. Nevertheless, the greatest institution of America today is that concerted group of multi-millionaire and billionaire families, whose organization has written "liar" across the heart of men of ability, of whom they make use to thwart justice, equity, and mercy among mankind.

We are calling upon people whose souls cannot be cankered by the lure of wealth and corruption. We are calling upon people who have at heart, above their own nefarious possessions, the welfare of this country and of its humanity. We are calling upon them, we are calling upon you, we are calling upon the people of America, upon the men and women who love this country, and who would save their children and their neighbors from calamity and distress, to call in the people whom they know, to acquaint them with the purposes of this society and secure organization and co-operation among everyone willing to lend his hand to this worthy work. Fear of ridicule? Fear of reprisal? Fear of being taken off of the starvation dole? It is too late for our people to have such fears. I have undergone them all. There is nothing under the canopy of heaven which has not been sent to ridicule and embarrass my efforts in this work. And yet, despite such ridicule, face to face in any argument I have yet to see the one of them who dares to gainsay the principle to share our wealth. On the contrary, when their feet are put to the fire, each and every one of them declare that they are in favor of sharing the wealth, and the redistribution of wealth. But then some get suddenly ignorant and say they do not know how to do it. Oh, ye of little faith! God told them how. Apparently they are too lazy in mind or body to want to learn, so long as their ignorance is for the benefit of the 600 ruling families of America who have forged chains of slavery around the wrists and ankles of 125,000,000 free-born citizens. Lincoln freed the black man, but today the white and the black are shackled far worse than any colored person in 1860.

The debt structure alone has condemned the American people to bondage worse than the Egyptians ever forged upon the Israelites. Right now America's debts, public and private, are $262,000,000,000, and nearly all of it has been laid on the shoulders of those who have nothing. It is a debt of more than $2,000 to every man, woman, or child. They can never pay it. They never have paid such debts. No one expects them to pay it. But such is the new form of slavery imposed upon the civilization of America; and the street-corner sports and hired political tricksters, with the newspapers whom they have perverted, undertake to laugh to scorn the efforts of the people to throw off this yoke and bondage; but we were told to do so by the Lord, we were told to do so by the Pilgrim Fathers, we were guaranteed such should be done by our Declaration of Independence and by the Constitution of the United States.

Here is the whole sum and substance of the share-our-wealth movement:

1. Every family to be furnished by the Government a homestead allowance, free of debt, of not less than one-third the average family wealth of the country, which means, at the lowest, that every family shall have the reasonable comforts of life up to a value of from $5,000 to $6,000. No person to have a fortune of more than 100 to 300 times the average family fortune, which means that the limit to fortunes is between $1,500,000 and $5,000,000, with annual capital levy taxes imposed on all above $1,000,000.

2. The yearly income of every family shall be not less than one-third of the average family income, which means that, according to the estimates of the statisticians of the United States Government and Wall Street, no family's annual income would be less than from $2,000 to $2,500. No yearly income shall be allowed to any person larger than from 100 to 300 times the size of the average family income, which means that no person would be allowed to earn in any year more than from $600,000 to $1,800,000, all to be subject to present income-tax laws.

3. To limit or regulate the hours of work to such an extent as to prevent overproduction; the most modern and efficient machinery would be encouraged, so that as much would be produced as possible so as to satisfy all demands of the people, but to also allow the maximum time to the workers for recreation, convenience, education, and luxuries of life.

4. An old-age pension to the persons over 60.

5. To balance agricultural production with what can be consumed according to the laws of God, which includes the preserving and storage of surplus commodities to be paid for and held by the Government for the emergencies when such are needed. Please bear in mind, however, that when the people of America have had money to buy things they needed, we have never had a surplus of any commodity. This plan of God does not call for destroying any of the things raised to eat or wear, nor does it countenance wholesale destruction of hogs, cattle, or milk.

6. To pay the veterans of our wars what we owe them and to care for their disabled.

7. Education and training for all children to be equal in opportunity in all schools, colleges, universities, and other institutions for training in the professions and vocations of life; to be regulated on the capacity of children to learn, and not on the ability of parents to pay the costs. Training for life's work to be as much universal and thorough for all walks in life as has been the training in the arts of killing.

8. The raising of revenue and taxes for the support of this program to come from the reduction of swollen fortunes from the top, as well as for the support of public works to give employment whenever there may be any slackening necessary in private enterprise.

I now ask those who read this circular to help us at once in this work of giving life and happiness to our people—not a starvation dole upon which someone may live in misery from week to week. Before this miserable system of wreckage has destroyed the life germ of respect and culture in our American people let us save what was here, merely by having none too poor and none too rich. The theory of the Share Our Wealth Society is to have enough for all, but not to have one with so much that less than enough remains for the balance of the people.

Please, therefore, let me ask you who read this document—please help this work before it is too late for us to be of help to our people. We ask you now, (1) help to get your neighbor into the work of this society and (2) help get other Share Our Wealth societies started in your county and in adjoining counties and get them to go out to organize other societies.

To print and mail out this circular costs about 60 cents per hundred, or $6 per thousand. Anyone who reads this who wants more circulars of this kind to use in the work, can get them for that price by sending the money to me, and I will pay the printer for him. Better still, if you can have this circular reprinted in your own town or city.

Let everyone who feels he wishes to help in our work start right out and go ahead. One man or woman is as important as any other. Take up the fight! Do not wait for someone else to tell you what to do. There are no high lights in this effort. We have no State managers and no city managers. Everyone can take up the work, and as many societies can be organized as there are people to organize them. One is the same as another. The reward and compensation is the salvation of humanity. Fear no opposition. "He who falls in this fight falls in the radiance of the future!"

Yours sincerely,
HUEY P. LONG,
United States Senator, Washington, D. C.

A Bid for Socialism in California: "The EPIC Plan," 1935

Long's appeal, like that of Coughlin or Townsend, was pragmatic rather than ideological. It was extreme, but it was based upon the immediate pressures of poverty and prospects for power. Even the old Socialists had learned to be pragmatic in terms of judging their immediate tactics and first steps, but they presented a more systematic and philosophically based program. One of the most successful of these was the novelist Upton Sinclair (1878–). Sinclair came closer than did any other American Socialist to major political success with his campaign for the California governorship in 1934. His program was called EPIC (End Poverty in California). It looked in the direction of public ownership of the means of production, exchange, and distribution of goods. But it was more akin to the New Deal itself than to utopian socialism in the limits it suggested to the immediate social responsibility of the state. And there are distinct relationships between Sinclair's 1935 revision of his plan, printed below, and the various native American traditions represented by the Populists, the Single Taxers, and the Townsend Movement. One interesting examination of Sinclair's activities is Charles E. Larsen, "The Epic Campaign of 1934," Pacific Historical Review, *volume 27 (1958), pages 127–147.*

The document provided here is taken from Upton Sinclair, "The EPIC Plan (revised, 1935)," in I, Candidate for Governor: And How I Got Licked *(Pasadena, Calif.: privately printed, 1935), pages viii–ix.*

1. A legislative enactment for the establishment of State land colonies, whereby the unemployed may become self-sustaining and cease to be a burden upon the taxpayers. A public body, the California Authority for

Land (the CAL) will rent or purchase idle land, and land sold for taxes and at foreclosure sales, and erect dormitories, kitchens, cafeterias, and social rooms, and cultivate the land, using modern machinery under the guidance of experts.

2. A public body entitled the California Authority for Production (the CAP), will be authorized to rent or purchase production plants whereby the unemployed may produce the basic necessities required for themselves and for the land colonies, and to operate these factories and house and feed and care for the workers. CAL and CAP will maintain a distribution system for the exchange of each other's products. The industries will include laundries, bakeries, canneries, clothing and shoe factories, cement-plants, brick-yards, lumber yards, thus constituting a complete industrial system, a new and self-sustaining world for those our present system cannot employ.

3. A public body entitled the California Authority for Barter (the CAB) will devise and issue warehouse receipts, certificates of service, credit accounts, and other means of exchanging the products within the system. It will also issue bonds to cover the purchase of land and factories, the erection of buildings and the purchase of machinery.

4. An act of the legislature repealing the present sales tax on the necessities of life.

5. An act of the legislature providing for a State income tax graduated after the fashion of the Federal tax, but preceding that tax.

6. An increase in the State inheritance tax, steeply graduated and applying to all property in the State regardless of where the owner may reside.

7. A law increasing the taxes on privately owned public utility corporations and banks.

8. A constitutional amendment revising the tax code of the State, providing that cities and counties shall exempt from taxation the first $1000 of assessment on homes occupied by the owners and ranches cultivated by the owners. This exemption later to be increased to $3000.

9. A constitutional amendment providing for a State land tax upon unimproved building land and agricultural land which is not under cultivation. The first $1000 of assessed valuation to be exempt, and the tax to be graduated according to the value of land held by the individual. Provision to be made for a state building loan fund for those who wish to erect homes.

10. A law providing for the payment of a pension of $50 per month to every needy person over sixty years of age who has lived in the State of California three years prior to the date of the coming into effect of the law.

A law providing for the payment of $50 per month to all persons who are blind, or who by medical examination are proved to be physically unable to earn a living; these persons also having been residents of the State for three years.

12. A pension of $50 per month to all widowed women who have dependent children; if the children are more than two in number, the pension to be increased by $25 per month for each additional child. These also to have been residents three years in the State.

SELECTION 31

Return to the Barricades: Herbert Hoover Assails the National Recovery Administration, 1935

Herbert Hoover remained, in retirement, the unrelenting critic of the New Deal. He was particularly bitter in his commentary upon the NRA. Herein lay an irony, since NRA had been planned to seek with governmental authority many of the objectives which Hoover himself as Secretary of Commerce had once encouraged upon private trade associations.

Hoover's commentary ran along two lines. It measured the idea *of the NRA against the formulas of* laissez faire *and states' rights which had become the landmarks of Hoover's philosophy. It also measured the* accomplishments *of NRA. In both cases it found the experiment not merely wanting but even dangerously defective and subversive of the "truth." But Hoover spoke not merely for himself. His views were particularly significant because they reflected the rumbling, widespread discontent with NRA which disturbed the administration during its third year.*

Well to the "right" of Hoover were the sharp critics in the American Liberty League, financed by millionaires and fronted, among others, by Alfred E. Smith. The work of the League is carefully analyzed and well told in George Wolfskill, The Revolt of the Conservatives: A History of the American Liberty League, 1934–1940 *(1962), and in Frederick Rudolph, "The American Liberty League, 1934–1940,"* American Historical Review, *volume 56 (1950–1951), pages 19–33.*

The comments of Herbert Hoover used here are from "The NRA: Reply to Press Inquiry," Palo Alto (May 15, 1935), in Addresses upon the American Road, 1933–1938 *(New York: Scribner, 1938), pages 45–47.*

In reply to your question, the one right answer by the House of Representatives to the Senate's action extending the life of the NRA is to abolish it entirely.

Present NRA proposals are as bad, in many ways, as the original. With its continuation until the next Congress and with Federal agents putting pressure on State legislatures to get them to enact State laws in support of NRA, it is evident that there has been no real retreat.

This whole idea of ruling business through code authorities with delegated powers of law is un-American in principle and a proved failure in practice. The codes are retarding recovery. They are a cloak for conspiracy against the public interest. They are and will continue to be a weapon of bureaucracy, a device for intimidation of decent citizens.

To the customary answer of "destructive criticism" or the other question "what substitute is offered?" I suggest that the only substitute for an action that rests on definite and proved economic error is to abandon it. We do not construct new buildings on false foundations, and we cannot build a Nation's economy on a fundamental error.

The beneficent objectives of a greater social justice and the prevention of sweating, child labor and abuse in business practices should be and can be better attained by specific statutory law.

There are already sufficient agencies of government for enforcement of the laws of the land. Where necessary those laws should be strengthened, but not replaced with personal government.

The prevention of waste in mineral resources should be carried out by the States operating under Federally encouraged interstate compacts. That is an American method of eradicating economic abuses and wastes, as distinguished from Fascist regimentation.

The multitude of code administrators, agents or committees has spread into every hamlet, and, whether authorized or not, they have engaged in the coercion and intimidation of presumably free citizens. People have been sent to jail, but far more have been threatened with jail. Direct and indirect boycotts have been organized by the bureaucracy itself. Many are being used today. Claiming to cure immoral business practices, the codes have increased them a thousandfold through "chiseling." They have not protected legitimate business from unfair competition but they have deprived the public of the benefits of fair competition.

This whole NRA scheme has saddled the American people with the worst era of monopolies we have ever experienced. However monopoly is defined, its objective is to fix prices or to limit production or to stifle competition. Any one of those evils produces the other two, and it is no remedy to take part of them out. These have been the very aim of certain business elements ever since Queen Elizabeth. Most of the 700 NRA codes effect those very purposes.

Exactly such schemes to avoid competition in business were rejected by my Administration because they are born from a desire to escape the anti-trust laws. If the anti-trust laws had not been effective in a major way, there would have been no such desire to escape them. If they do not meet modern conditions, they should be openly amended or circumvented.

My investigations over the country show that the codes have increased costs of production and distribution, and therefore prices. Thus they have driven toward decreased consumption and increased unemployment. They have increased the cost of living, and placed a heavier burden on the American farmer.

NRA codes have been crushing the life out of small business, and they are crushing the life out of the very heart of the local community body. There are 1,500,000 small businesses in this country, and our purpose should be to protect them.

The codes are preventing new enterprises. In this they deprive America's youth of the opportunity and the liberty to start and build their independence, and thus stop the men and women of tomorrow from building soundly toward a true social security.

Publishers have had to resist arduously the encroachment of these NRA codes upon such fundamental, constitutionally guaranteed American liberties as free speech.

The whole concept of NRA is rooted in a regimented "economy of scarcity"—an idea that increased costs, restricted production and hampered enterprise will enrich a Nation. That notion may enrich a few individuals and help a few businesses, but it will impoverish the nation and undermine the principles of real social justice upon which this Nation was founded.

If the NRA has increased employment, it is not apparent. If we subtract the persons temporarily employed by the coded industries as the direct result of the enormous Government expenditures, we find that the numbers being employed are not materially greater than when it was enacted. NRA's pretended promises to labor were intentionally vague and have never been clarified. They have only promoted conflict without establishing real rights.

That original ballyhoo used to hypnotize and coerce the people into acquiescence is now gone. Most of the originally grandiose schemes now are conceded to be a violation of the spirit and the letter of the American Constitution.

Some business interests already have established advantages out of the codes, and therefore seek the perpetuation of NRA. Even these interests should recognize that in the end they themselves will become either the pawns of a bureaucracy that they do not want or the instruments of a bureaucracy the American people do not want.

Action Challenged: Alfred M. Landon Speaks at Madison Square Garden, 1936

The Republican party chose in 1936 to make the issue clear, to chart out again the options between Rooseveltian activism and experiment, Republican traditionalism and "soundness." The candidate was Alfred M. Landon (1887–   ), Governor of Kansas. Personally liberal in his instincts, Landon was forced to dampen his own predilections and run on a platform more reminiscent of Hoover than hopeful of the future. He conjured up an image of Rooseveltian uncertainty, confusion, recklessness, deviousness. He offered as alternative a return to "sound" and ancient principles. Landon was a vigorous candidate, and personally appealing. He sketched the alternatives boldly. The fact that he was defeated more disastrously than any other Republican presidential candidate marked clearly the general repudiation of the traditions and the rigidity for which he formally stood in the campaign. Nowhere was his program more clearly stated or his charges against Roosevelt more dramatically drawn than in his climactic address of the campaign at Madison Square Garden on October 29, 1936.

There is no good biography of Alfred M. Landon. Malcolm Moos, The Republicans: A History of Their Party *(1956) discusses the 1936 election and Landon's problem, as does George H. Mayer,* The Republican Party: 1854–1964 *(1964).*

Landon's speech is taken from the New York Times, *October 30, 1936, page 16.*

We are drawing to the end of a great campaign—a campaign that transcends all party lines. Tonight I am here not alone as the representative of a great party; I am here as the representative of a great cause—a cause in which millions of my fellow-citizens are joined—a cause in which Democrats, independents and Republicans are fighting shoulder to shoulder.

Let me begin by restating the basic principles of my political creed.

I believe in our constitutional form of government—a government established by the people, responsible to the people and alterable only in accordance with the will of the people.

I believe in our indivisible union of undestructible States.

I believe in the American system of free enterprise regulated by law.

I believe in the liberty of the individual as guaranteed by the Constitution.

I believe in the rights of minorities as protected by the Constitution.

I believe in the liberties secured by the Bill of Rights and in their maintenance as the best protection against bigotry and all intolerance, whether of race, color or creed.

I believe in an independent Supreme Court and judiciary, secure from executive or legislative invasion.

I believe that in the future, as in the past, the hopes of our people can best be realized by following the American way of life under the American Constitution.

I believe in the principles of civic righteousness exemplified by Theodore Roosevelt and I pledge myself to go forward along the trail he blazed.

In the light of this creed I have already outlined my stand on the chief issues of the campaign. Tonight I am going to review my position and contrast it with that of my opponent.

It is fitting that I should start with the problem of agriculture. Your City of New York is the greatest market for farm products in the country. As consumers you want an ample supply of food at fair prices. As wage-earners you need the buying power of a prosperous farm population.

The welfare of agriculture is also the welfare of industry. A fair adjustment between the two is not a matter of politics, it is a matter of national necessity.

Now let us look at the record.

In direct defiance of the 1932 Democratic platform, which condemned the unsound policy of crop restriction, the Triple A was enacted. The Triple A restricted agricultural production by 36,000,000 acres.

This administration has rewarded scarcity and penalized plenty. Not only has it failed to correct the basic ills of agriculture, it has added to them. I am from a great agricultural State and I know.

I know how this program dislocated our agricultural system. I know, for instance, that almost overnight it forced the Southern farmer out of cotton into crops competing with the North and West. It led him into dairy farming and the raising of livestock. This affected not only the farmer of the North and West. It also affected the farmer of the South, who lost a large part of his cotton export market.

Luckily for this administration, the full damage of its program has been hidden by the droughts.

Government has a moral obligation to help repair the damage caused to the farmer by this administration's destructive experiments. Farming, by its very nature, cannot readjust itself as rapidly as industry to the after-effects of economic planning. During the period of readjustment, and until foreign markets are reopened, the government must help the farmer.

We can do this without violating the Constitution. We can do this without imposing such burdens as the processing tax upon the consumer. We can do this within the limits of a balanced budget. And don't forget I am going to balance the budget.

The Republican party also proposes a sound long-term program of conservation and land use. This is the only permanent solution of the farm problem and is essential to the preservation of the nation's land resources. We propose to stop muddling and meddling and to begin mending.

And what does the President mean to do for agriculture? Is he going to continue the policy of scarcity?

The answer is: No one can be sure.

Now let us turn to industry. What was the basic declaration of the Democratic platform of 1932? It was that the anti-trust laws—the laws protecting the little fellow from monopoly—should be strengthened and enforced.

And what did the administration do? It created the NRA. This law gave the sanction of government to private monopoly. It endorsed the vicious policy of price-fixing. It disregarded the interest of 130,000,000 Americans as consumers. It attempted to tell every business man, large and small, how to run his business.

The NRA was the direct opposite of the American system of free competition. It was an attempt to supplant American initiative with Washington dictation. And what happened? Monopolies prospered and a little New Jersey pants-presser went to jail.

I am against private monopoly. I am against monopolistic practices. I am against the monopoly of an all-powerful central government. And while I am President I intend to see that the anti-trust laws are strengthened and enforced without fear or favor.

I intend to see that government bureaucracy never again starts choking business. I intend to see that American initiative has a chance to give jobs to American workers. And I intend to broaden the market for American products by encouraging freer interchange of goods in world trade.

And what does the President propose for industry? He pays tribute to free initiative at Chicago on a Wednesday and to planned economy at Detroit on a Thursday. One day the President's son says the NRA will be revived. The next day the President's son says it will not. When the President was asked about NRA last Tuesday in a press conference, he said "You pay your money and you take your choice." What does he mean?

The answer is: No one can be sure.

Growing out of the troubles of agriculture and industry is the intensely human problem of unemployment. What is the record on this?

In 1932 the President said that 11,000,000 Americans were looking for work. Today, according to the American Federation of Labor there are still 11,000,000 Americans looking for work. Yet the President boasts of recovery in one city in terms of a baseball game and in another city in terms of a patient he has cured.

These fellow-citizens of ours can and will be re-employed. There is no need for one-fifth of our working population to be condemned to live in an economic world apart. There is work to be done in this country more than enough to give jobs to all the unemployed. This work will start just as soon as uncertainty in government policies is replaced by confidence.

There can be no confidence when the government is proud of spending more than it takes in.

There can be no confidence when the government creates uncertainty about the value of money.

There can be no confidence when the government threatens to control every detail of our economic life.

There can be no confidence when the government proclaims that the way to have more is to produce less.

In short, there can be no confidence while this administration remains in power.

As Chief Executive I intend to follow a course that will restore confidence.

I intend to be open and above-board on the policies of my administration.

I intend in the task of reconstruction to make use of the best talent available irrespective of party.

I intend to throw out all plans based on scarcity.

I intend to put an end to this administration's policy of "try anything once." The time has come for a steady hand at the wheel.

And what does the President propose to restore confidence? Another "breathing spell"?

The answer is: No one can be sure.

Of course re-employment cannot come overnight. In the meantime those in need must have relief. Consider the administration's record here.

The Democratic platform in 1932 condemned the "improper and excessive use of money in political activities."

In defiance of this pledge we have had an outrageous use of public money for political purposes. Public funds appropriated for relief have been used in an attempt to buy the votes of our less fortunate citizens. But it will not do them any good. The votes of the American people are not for sale.

As Chief Executive I intend to see that relief is purged of politics. There is ample money in this country to take care of those in need. When I am President they will be taken care of. This is the plain will of the American people.

And what does the President propose to do about relief? How does he propose to free the victims of the depression from political exploitation?

The answer is: No one can be sure.

In a highly industrialized society we must provide for the protection of the aged.

The present administration claims it has done this through its Social Security Act. But the act does not give security. It is based upon a conception that is fundamentally wrong. It assumes that the American people are so improvident that they must be compelled to save by a paternal government.

Beginning next Jan. 1, workers, no matter how small their wages, will have their pay docked—they will have their pay docked for the purpose of building up a phantom reserve fund—a fund that any future Congress can spend any time it sees fit and for any purpose it sees fit.

I cannot understand how any administration would dare to perpetrate such a fraud upon our workers.

The Republican party proposes to replace this unworkable hodgepodge by a plan that is honest, fair and financially sound. We propose that the funds for security payments shall be provided as we go along. We propose that they shall be obtained from a direct and specific tax widely distributed. We propose that all American citizens over 65 shall receive whatever additional income is necessary to keep them from need.

I repeat: The workers will start to pay for the present plan next Jan. 1. They will pay as wage-earners through a direct deduction from their pay. They will pay both as wage-earners and consumers through the tax levied on their employers' payrolls. And don't let any one tell you otherwise. Even the Democratic Attorney General of New York admits this. Last March, before the New York Court of Appeals, he said that a tax on employers' payrolls, although levied on the employer, will be—and I quote—"shifted either to wage-earners or consumers or both."

And what does the President propose to do about these taxes? Is he going to continue a plan that takes money from workers without any assurance that they will get back what they put in?

The answer is: No one can be sure.

Since the NRA was declared unconstitutional and largely because it was declared unconstitutional—there has been some improvement in business.

But there has been no reduction in the total of government spending. In the year ended last June the Federal Government spent nearly $9,000,000,000. This is an all-time peace-time high.

We will spend this year over $900,000,000 more for the ordinary routine expenditures of government than in 1934. And we will spend $1,500,000,000 more for relief than in 1934.

Under this administration seventy-five new agencies have been created.

Two hundred and fifty thousand additional employes have been foisted on the taxpayers. The Federal payroll has reached the staggering sum of $1,500,000,000 a year.

As I said at Chicago, any one at all familiar with what has been going on could almost count on the fingers of one hand foolish experiments the government could cut out and save at least $1,000,000,000 any time it wanted to.

I pledge myself to put an end to extravagance and waste. I pledge myself to stop the policy that glorifies spending. I pledge myself to balance the budget.

And what is the President going to do? Is he going to stop his policy of spending for spending's sake?

The answer is: No one can be sure.

I come finally to the underlying and fundamental issue of this campaign. This is the question of whether our American form of government is to be preserved.

Let us turn once more to the record.

The President has been responsible for nine acts declared unconstitutional by the Supreme Court.

He has publicly urged Congress to pass a law, even though it had reasonable doubts as to its constitutionality.

He has publicly belittled the Supreme Court of the United States.

He has publicly suggested that the Constitution is an outworn document.

He has retained in high office men outspoken in their contempt for the American form of government.

He has sponsored laws which have deprived States of their constitutional rights.

Every one of these actions—and the list is by no means complete—strikes at the heart of the American form of government.

Our Constitution is not a lifeless piece of paper. It is the underlying law of the land and the charter of the liberties of our people. The people, and they alone, have the right to amend or destroy it. Until the people in their combined wisdom decide to make the change, it is the plain duty of the people's servants to keep within the Constitution. It is the plain meaning of the oath of office that they shall keep within the Constitution.

Our Federal system allows great leeway. But if changes in our civilization make amendment to the Constitution desirable it should be amended. It has been amended in the past. It can be in the future.

I have already made my position clear on this question. I am on record that, if proper working conditions cannot be regulated by the States, I shall favor a constitutional amendment giving the States the necessary powers.

And what are the intentions of the President with respect to the Constitution? Does he believe changes are required? If so, will an amendment be submitted to the people, or will he attempt to get around the Constitution by tampering with the Supreme Court?

The answer is: No one can be sure.

We want more than a material recovery in this country. We want a moral and spiritual recovery as well. We have been allowing material things to obscure the great religious and spiritual values. But life is more than bread. Character is the supreme thing. We have been weakening those very qualities upon which character is built. It would be tragedy if in our attempt to win prosperity we should lose our own souls. It would be an overwhelming disaster if we should forget that it is righteousness that exalteth a nation.

Forty-eight hours from tonight, standing where I am standing, there will be a President of the United States. He will be seeking re-election.

A little more than forty-eight hours after he has spoken, the American people will be streaming to the polls.

Here once again I ask him to speak what is in his mind. It is his duty, not only as President, but also as an American, to tell what his purposes and intentions really are. It is his duty, as it is my duty, to trust the "combined wisdom of the people."

The people of this country will not trust a man who does not trust them. If he trusts them he will answer the questions being asked from one end of the country to the other.

Does he favor reviving the principles of the National Recovery Act? Or does he favor the American system of free initiative?

Does he favor reviving the principles of the Agricultural Adjustment Act? Or does he favor allowing the farmer to be a lord on his own farm?

Does he favor concentrating more and more power in the hands of the Chief Executive? Or does he favor a return to the American form of government?

These three things are inseparable. If he wants the AAA, he must have the NRA. If he wants the NRA, he must have the AAA. And both are impossible without increased powers for the Chief Executive.

And so, in closing this meeting, I leave a challenge with the President. I say to him: Mr. President, I am willing to trust the people. I am willing to stand up and say openly that I am against economic planning by the government. I am against the concentration of power in the hands of the Chief Executive.

Tell us where you stand, Mr. President. Tell us not in generalities, but clearly, so that no one can mistake your meaning. And tell us why you have evaded the issue until the eve of the election.

I leave my gage at your feet.

My gage is the gauge of your confidence, Mr. President, your confidence in the American people.

My gage is the gauge of your duty, Mr. President, your duty to the American people.

My gage is the gauge of your faith, Mr. President, your faith in the American people.

By the words that you speak in forty-eight hours the American people will know the measure of your confidence and your duty and your faith in their wisdom.

SELECTION 33

Action Defended: FDR Speaks at Madison Square Garden, 1936

Franklin Roosevelt refused to argue "philosophy." He came to the campaign in fighting posture. Failures like the National Recovery Administration were a galling memory, but they were past. The uncertainties and confusion of 1935 had been cast aside. A new program, marked by the Wagner Act and the Social Security Act, had emerged to give point and direction to his crusade. And there stood firmly established from the early New Deal the solid progress of the agricultural programs, of the Civilian Conservation Corps, of banking reform, of the Tennessee Valley Authority, of the relief programs. His speech at Madison Square Garden was a model of political salesmanship. He pushed aside the rankling arguments over details. He cast his critics in a role of the meanest villainy. He spoke to his national radio audience in slogans of achievement and promise which made him seem, yet again, the crusader for the future against the black knights of special interest and antique inhibition. His victory was stunning, 523 electoral votes to Landon's 8. Roosevelt carried every state except Maine and Vermont. The popular vote was 27, 751, 597 to 16, 679, 583.

Roosevelt's speech of October 31, 1936 may be found in Samuel Rosenman (ed.), The Public Papers and Addresses of Franklin D. Roosevelt, Volume Five: The People Approve, 1936 *(New York: Random House, 1938), pages 566–573.*

On the eve of a national election, it is well for us to stop for a moment and analyze calmly and without prejudice the effect on our Nation of a victory by either of the major political parties.

The problem of the electorate is far deeper, far more vital than the continuance in the Presidency of any individual. For the greater issue goes beyond units of humanity—it goes to humanity itself.

In 1932 the issue was the restoration of American democracy; and the American people were in a mood to win. They did win. In 1936 the issue is the preservation of their victory. Again they are in a mood to win. Again they will win.

More than four years ago in accepting the Democratic nomination in Chicago, I said: "Give me your help not to win votes alone, but to win in this crusade to restore America to its own people."

The banners of that crusade still fly in the van of a Nation that is on the march.

It is needless to repeat the details of the program which this Administration has been hammering out on the anvils of experience. No amount of misrepresentation or statistical contortion can conceal or blur or smear that record. Neither the attacks of unscrupulous enemies nor the exaggerations of over-zealous friends will serve to mislead the American people.

What was our hope in 1932? Above all other things the American people wanted peace. They wanted peace of mind instead of gnawing fear.

First, they sought escape from the personal terror which had stalked them for three years. They wanted the peace that comes from security in their homes: safety for their savings, permanence in their jobs, a fair profit from their enterprise.

Next, they wanted peace in the community, the peace that springs from the ability to meet the needs of community life: schools, playgrounds, parks, sanitation, highways—those things which are expected of solvent local government. They sought escape from disintegration and bankruptcy in local and state affairs.

They also sought peace within the Nation: protection of their currency, fairer wages, the ending of long hours of toil, the abolition of child labor, the elimination of wild-cat speculation, the safety of their children from kidnappers.

And, finally, they sought peace with other Nations—peace in a world of unrest. The Nation knows that I hate war, and I know that the Nation hates war.

I submit to you a record of peace; and on that record a well-founded expectation for future peace—peace for the individual, peace for the community, peace for the Nation, and peace with the world.

Tonight I call the roll—the roll of honor of those who stood with us in 1932 and still stand with us today.

Written on it are the names of millions who never had a chance—men at starvation wages, women in sweatshops, children at looms.

Written on it are the names of those who despaired, young men and young women for whom opportunity had become a will-o'-the-wisp.

Written on it are the names of farmers whose acres yielded only bitterness, business men whose books were portents of disaster, home owners who were faced with eviction, frugal citizens whose savings were insecure.

Written there in large letters are the names of countless other Americans of all parties and all faiths, Americans who had eyes to see and hearts to understand, whose consciences were burdened because too many of their fellows were burdened, who looked on these things four years ago and said, "This can be changed. We will change it."

We still lead that army in 1936. They stood with us then because in 1932 they believed. They stand with us today because in 1936 they know. And with them stand millions of new recruits who have come to know.

Their hopes have become our record.

We have not come this far without a struggle and I assure you we cannot go further without a struggle.

For twelve years this Nation was afflicted with hear-nothing, see-nothing, do-nothing Government. The Nation looked to Government but the Government looked away. Nine mocking years with the golden calf and three long years of the scourge! Nine crazy years at the ticker and three long years in the breadlines! Nine mad years of mirage and three long years of despair! Powerful influences strive today to restore that kind of government with its doctrine that that Government is best which is most indifferent.

For nearly four years you have had an Administration which instead of twirling its thumbs has rolled up its sleeves. We will keep our sleeves rolled up.

We had to struggle with the old enemies of peace—business and financial monopoly, speculation, reckless banking, class antagonism, sectionalism, war profiteering.

They had begun to consider the Government of the United States as a mere appendage to their own affairs. We know now that Government by organized money is just as dangerous as Government by organized mob.

Never before in all our history have these forces been so united against one candidate as they stand today. They are unanimous in their hate for me—and I welcome their hatred.

I should like to have it said of my first Administration that in it the forces of selfishness and of lust for power met their match. I should like to have it said of my second Administration that in it these forces met their master.

The American people know from a four-year record that today there is only one entrance to the White House—by the front door. Since March 4, 1933, there has been only one pass-key to the White House. I have carried that key in my pocket. It is there tonight. So long as I am President, it will remain in my pocket.

Those who used to have pass-keys are not happy. Some of them are desperate. Only desperate men with their backs to the wall would descend so far below the level of decent citizenship as to foster the current pay-envelope campaign against America's working people. Only reckless men, heedless of consequences, would risk the disruption of the hope for a new peace between worker and employer by returning to the tactics of the labor spy.

Here is an amazing paradox! The very employers and politicians and publishers who talk most loudly of class antagonism and the destruction of the American system now undermine that system by this attempt to coerce the votes of the wage earners of this country. It is the 1936 version of the old threat to close down the factory or the office if a particular candidate does not win. It is an old strategy of tyrants to delude their victims into fighting their battles for them.

Every message in a pay envelope, even if it is the truth, is a command to vote according to the will of the employer. But this propaganda is worse—it is deceit.

They tell the worker his wage will be reduced by a contribution to some vague form of old-age insurance. They carefully conceal from him the fact that for every dollar of premium he pays for that insurance, the employer pays another dollar. That omission is deceit.

They carefully conceal from him the fact that under the federal law, he receives another insurance policy to help him if he loses his job, and that the premium of that policy is paid 100 percent by the employer and not one cent by the worker. They do not tell him that the insurance policy that is bought for him is far more favorable to him than any policy that any private insurance company could afford to issue. That omission is deceit.

They imply to him that he pays all the cost of both forms of insurance. They carefully conceal from him the fact that for every dollar put up by him his employer puts up three dollars—three for one. And that omission is deceit.

But they are guilty of more than deceit. When they imply that the reserves thus created against both these policies will be stolen by some future Congress, diverted to some wholly foreign purpose, they attack the integrity and honor of American Government itself. Those who suggest that, are already aliens to the spirit of American democracy. Let them emigrate and try their lot under some foreign flag in which they have more confidence.

The fraudulent nature of this attempt is well shown by the record of votes on the passage of the Social Security Act. In addition to an overwhelming majority of Democrats in both Houses, seventy-seven Republican Representatives voted for it and only eighteen against it and fifteen Republican Senators voted for it and only five against it. Where does this last-minute drive of the Republican leadership leave these Republican Representatives and Senators who helped enact this law?

I am sure the vast majority of law-abiding businessmen who are not parties to this propaganda fully appreciate the extent of the threat to honest business contained in this coercion.

I have expressed indignation at this form of campaigning and I am confident that the overwhelming majority of employers, workers and the general public share that indignation and will show it at the polls on Tuesday next.

Aside from this phase of it, I prefer to remember this campaign not as bitter but only as hard-fought. There should be no bitterness or hate where the sole thought is the welfare of the United States of America. No man can occupy the office of President without realizing that he is President of all the people.

It is because I have sought to think in terms of the whole Nation that I am confident that today, just as four years ago, the people want more than promises.

Our vision for the future contains more than promises.

This is our answer to those who, silent about their own plans, ask us to state our objectives.

Of course we will continue to seek to improve working conditions for the workers of America—to reduce hours over-long, to increase wages that spell starvation, to end the labor of children, to wipe out sweatshops. Of course we will continue every effort to end monopoly in business, to support collective bargaining, to stop unfair competition, to abolish dishonorable trade practices. For all these we have only just begun to fight.

Of course we will continue to work for cheaper electricity in the homes and on the farms of America, for better and cheaper transportation, for low interest rates, for sounder home financing, for better banking, for the regulation of security issues, for reciprocal trade among nations, for the wiping out of slums. For all these we have only just begun to fight.

Of course we will continue our efforts in behalf of the farmers of

America. With their continued cooperation we will do all in our power to end the piling up of huge surpluses which spelled ruinous prices for their crops. We will persist in successful action for better land use, for reforestation, for the conservation of water all the way from its source to the sea, for drought and flood control, for better marketing facilities for farm commodities, for a definite reduction of farm tenancy, for encouragement of farmer cooperatives, for crop insurance and a stable food supply. For all these we have only just begun to fight.

Of course we will provide useful work for the needy unemployed; we prefer useful work to the pauperism of a dole.

Here and now I want to make myself clear about those who disparage their fellow citizens on the relief rolls. They say that those on relief are not merely jobless—that they are worthless. Their solution for the relief problem is to end relief—to purge the rolls by starvation. To use the language of the stock broker, our needy unemployed would be cared for when, as, and if some fairy godmother should happen on the scene.

You and I will continue to refuse to accept that estimate of our unemployed fellow Americans. Your Government is still on the same side of the street with the Good Samaritan and not with those who pass by on the other side.

Again—what of our objectives?

Of course we will continue our efforts for young men and women so that they may obtain an education and an opportunity to put it to use. Of course we will continue our help for the crippled, for the blind, for the mothers, our insurance for the unemployed, our security for the aged. Of course we will continue to protect the consumer against unnecessary price spreads, against the costs that are added by monopoly and speculation. We will continue our successful efforts to increase his purchasing power and to keep it constant.

For these things, too, and for a multitude of others like them, we have only just begun to fight.

All this—all these objectives—spell peace at home. All our actions, all our ideals, spell also peace with other nations.

Today there is war and rumor of war. We want none of it. But while we guard our shores against threats of war, we will continue to remove the causes of unrest and antagonism at home which might make our people easier victims to those for whom foreign war is profitable. You know well that those who stand to profit by war are not on our side in this campaign.

"Peace on earth, good will toward men"—democracy must cling to that message. For it is my deep conviction that democracy cannot live without that true religion which gives a nation a sense of justice and of moral purpose. Above our political forums, above our market places stand the altars of our faith—altars on which burn the fires of devotion that maintain all that is best in us and all that is best in our Nation.

We have need of that devotion today. It is that which makes it possible for government to persuade those who are mentally prepared to fight each other to go on instead, to work for and to sacrifice for each other. That is why we need to say with the Prophet: "What doth the Lord require of thee—but to do justly, to love mercy and to walk humbly with thy God." That is why the recovery we seek, the recovery we are winning, is more than economic. In it are included justice and love and humility, not for ourselves as individuals alone, but for our Nation.

That is the road to peace.

SELECTION 

Consensus Established: Wendell Willkie Accepts the Accomplishments of the Decade, 1940

By 1940, the terms of American political competition had changed sharply. Roosevelt as a person dominated the politics of the nation. The New Deal crusading spirit had moderated, despite the brief flurry of hysteria in the wake of the 1938 recession. The new challenge of war had provided both an antidote to Depression and a ghastly, distracting challenge for the future. Roosevelt appealed for national unity in the name of defense. And the nation had come to accept within the national consensus much of the Roosevelt action which, in 1933 or even 1936, had still appeared open to debate. There was little talk now of repealing social security, or tearing down the Tennessee Valley Authority, or taking the Federal government out of relief.

The emergence of the new consensus was sharply traced in the speeches of Wendell L. Willkie (1892–1944), the Republican candidate for President in 1940. This was especially remarkable since Willkie had won the nomination only after a sharp struggle in the convention. He had been swept to the top not by the professionals but by the inspired amateurs of his party, and he personally had only recently been the very symbol of anti–New Deal sentiment. It had been Willkie, the officer of a southern utility company, who had led the crusade against TVA; it was now Willkie, the homely Indiana farmboy and sophisticated Wall Street lawyer, who led the Republican party into the new era. Willkie was no longer willing to take the fatal ground of 1929. He would instead seek new ground from which one could establish the failures of the Democrats to make good on the very dream they had sketched, new ground from which Republicans could run the lines of a more hopeful policy based less thoroughly on the action of government.

But Willkie's problem was grave. Roosevelt still dominated the scene. And, while Republicans could still be sharp and effective in criticism, Willkie's own dream for the future remained fatefully hazy and general. He suffered sniping from the rear by conservatives of his own party who saw him only as a rumpled Roosevelt. In the battle to meet FDR on his own ground, he was facing a master whom he could challenge but not quite outreach. And the campaign was muddied by the desperate issue of foreign policy upon which neither candidate could draw clear distinctions.

Willkie lost: he polled 22,305,198 to Roosevelt's 27,244,160. He won only 82 of the 531 electoral college votes. And he registered in the process the fact that America had arrived at a new plateau of political and social consensus. There could never again be a return to 1929.

The standard book is Donald B. Johnson, The Republican Party and Wendell Willkie *(1960). See also the previously mentioned volumes by Leuchtenburg, Gosnell, and Burns, as well as the histories of the Republican party by Malcolm Moos and George H. Mayer.*

Excerpts from Willkie's address in New York City on April 25, 1940, and from his interview on TVA on June 16, 1940, are from This Is Wendell Willkie *(New York: Dodd, Mead, 1940), pages 148–153, 218–19, 223–225, 230–233.*

Now, these are days when every man calls himself a liberal. Republicans, Democrats, New Dealers, Socialists, Communists, business men, artists, young men or old men, rich men or poor men—they all claim the label of liberalism. In my business travels around this country in the past two or three years I have met and talked with hundreds of people of very different kinds, and not one of them was a conservative.

It is, of course, impossible to define the term "liberal" so that it will include all of these groups. Somebody, somewhere, is out of line. But if we cannot arrive at an acceptable definition for liberalism, we can certainly agree upon one common quality—one fundamental characteristic—without which no man can have a shadow of a claim to the title. The liberal is a man who believes in freedom for himself and for other people.

If the results of freedom were not satisfactory in terms of human welfare, it would no longer be a wise policy for the world to follow. Economic freedom can mean very little to a man who is starving. If free economic enterprise is unable to provide jobs and products for this country, then, obviously, some other system should be tried. It seems to me that it is on this point that the liberal and the reactionary really find their issue.

The liberal believes that the purpose of government is to make men free and, thus having freedom, men will be able to build up a productive and prosperous society. The reactionary may desire, with equal sincerity, a prosperous society, but he believes it can be achieved only by the concentration of economic or political power. . . .

It is clear now that the system of 1929 could not be permitted to stand. Democracy . . . needed more social controls. These the New Deal supplied, in a vast network of regulation. The liberal cannot object to these reforms in principle. He realizes the national character of the great American corporations and of many business and financial operations; he realizes that an extension of Federal authority is necessary to establish adequate control over these matters. It is certainly a proper question for the defenders of the present government, therefore, to turn to him and say, "If you are opposed to this government, what powers would you take away?"

For example, the conscientious liberal would surely not rescind Securities and Exchange Commission acts and return that regulation to the states. He would not demand that the Federal government keep its hands off interstate utilities or utility holding companies. He would not challenge the wisdom of having the right of collective bargaining recognized by law. He would not say it was no concern of the Federal government whether or not the aged had pensions or the worker had unemployment allowances. In fact, the liberal would find himself in agreement with most of the objects of this new legislation, although he might want to modify many of its provisions and change many of its methods.

What attitude, then, does the liberal take toward the present government?

The answer is what it has always been. To the liberal the purpose of government is unchangeable. It is to leave men free. . . .

And the liberal does not see in the present Administration any will to leave men free. He sees only an attempt to increase the powers of government. For the old American principle that government is a liability to be borne by the citizens for the sake of peace, order and security, the New Deal has substituted the notion that government is an asset without which none of us can survive. The present huge Federal organization with its payroll of over a million employees, its dozens of agencies and commissions, its expenses of several billion dollars a year, represents an entirely new concept of government. It is government regarded, not as a supplementary influence, but as a dominant force in the lives of the people. Its growth becomes desirable in itself, instead of desirable only if it promotes the ease and expansion of the people's activities, the happiness and independence of their lives. Our forefathers believed that progress came from the energies of the people: the function of government was merely to prevent those energies from getting out of bounds. Today the government publicly proclaims the failure of the people's enterprises and has adopted the principle that progress comes from government itself.

This hostility toward domestic business is the more extraordinary in view of the government's friendly attitude toward foreign trade. Without entering here into technical arguments as to methods by which they are to be brought about, international trade agreements which lead to further interchange of goods between nations and the establishment of an international monetary standard are, in my opinion, indispensable to our complete recovery and future economy. America might live without international trade, but only with an economy managed either by business monopolies or government control. Likewise, despite recent pronouncements to the contrary by some opposed to the present Administration, we do have a vital interest in continuance of the English and French way of life. . . .

Two weeks ago at America's Town Meeting of the Air, the Attorney General of the United States was debating the topic "What Are the Essential Differences Between the Republican and the Democratic Parties?" Mr. Jackson struck another blow at the idea that any of the government's present powers were of an emergency nature, or were considered to be temporary. He stated: "We must complete a long-term program to take the place of short-term remedies and emergency experiments." He maintained that the government's responsibility was to provide "economic opportunity and security," and he remarked with some surprise:

"The real powers in the Republican party contend, and I think that they honestly believe, that economic opportunity and security for the great majority of our citizens are unattainable by government effort."

I cannot speak for "the real powers of the Republican party." But I hope that Mr. Jackson has defined their attitude correctly, for personally I do, indeed, contend and believe that "economic opportunity and security for the great majority of our citizens are unattainable by government effort." In fact, the free enterprise system is based on just the opposite thesis. We have believed that economic opportunity and security for the great majority of our citizens will never be attainable through the government and are only attainable through free private enterprise. In the past 150 years we have gone a long way toward proving it.

Government has never created an invention, never founded an industry and never successfully operated a business. Our quarrel with the New Deal is on exactly the issue defined by Mr. Jackson: whether the government or the people shall manage the people's enterprises.

Well, we have given the government eight years to prove its theory and it has failed to do so. One-third of the nation is still in need. Ten million men are still unemployed. The deficit continues to increase. The people, I hope, are now ready to try again the other theory: to release the enterprises of the people from the terrific weight of bureaucracy and to rededicate the government to the purpose of leaving men free. This does not mean, as Mr. Roosevelt suggested in his speech to the Young Democrats, a return to the 1929 way of life. The country's liberals are not all in Washington.

In a time of bitter argument, it is often helpful to turn to an outside expert who has no connection with either side of the controversy and whose opinion is, therefore, unemotional and unbiased. The internationally known magazine "The Economist," of London, belongs in that category. In a recent issue "The Economist" discusses the theory that the United States "is growing old" and says that "It is difficult to take this theory seriously—or to know whether its partisans themselves take it seriously." "The Economist" raises this question:

"If the United States with its vast areas, its low debt, its inexhaustible natural resources, its rising population is a mature economy, what is Great Britain? And yet our 'decadent' economy has contrived, during the decade when America was standing still, to go ahead as fast as on the average of the great Victorian era of expansion. Ten years ago the per capita national income of the United States was one-third larger than the British. Today it is probably no larger at all. . . . The American economy seems to have forgotten, for the moment, how to grow. But the probable explanation of this economic anemia is to be found not in any arrival at 'maturity' but rather in the existence of institutional obstructions to a free flow of capital."

For the development of any economic enterprise three human factors are fundamental. The first is the inventor, who has the idea for a new device or a new method or a new product; the second is the investor, who has sufficient confidence in the inventor's dream to give him the necessary capital to develop it; the third is the administrator or manager, who can organize the business and keep it going.

I believe that we have more men in these three categories in America today than ever before in our history. We have always been an inventive nation. We spend several hundred million dollars a year on industrial research. Last year we patented 43,000 inventions. And there are plenty of potential investors. Never before in the history of the country has there been so much money lying idle in the banks. In these two categories of invention and investment, the condition of abundance can be statistically proved. I have no statistical proof for the condition of the third factor of business management, but I have this personal conviction: that never before in American history have there been so many business executives who are not only skilled in the technique of running their jobs, but who have a new and far more enlightened attitude toward their social responsibilities.

These three types of men have constituted the triumphant triumvirate of our economic past. They are equally important to our future. Their activities, if released from government restrictions, can provide jobs enough and products enough to restore prosperity to America. But first we shall have to remove the political restrictions. The activities of the present Administration have drained the vitality and confidence from American industry. It is ironic that in view of these conditions the government should then turn upon industry and denounce it for its failure to recover and make wild charges concerning a "strike" of capital. Industry is being criticized for being unable to do what government prevents it from doing.

An Interview on TVA

Wendell L. Willkie today expressed an opinion "that you can't turn the clock back on TVA." Mr. Willkie, president of the Commonwealth & Southern Corporation, which locked horns spectacularly with the Tennessee Valley Authority, declared that any attempt to force TVA to "retrogress" would be futile.

"Any President of the United States who tried to turn TVA back to the private utilities would be extremely unrealistic," he asserted in an interview for the Scripps-Howard newspapers.

"To say that I have no quarrel with the way TVA was established and was operated during its period of expansion would be dishonest," Mr. Willkie said.

"I will say that its establishment in the Tennessee Valley was ruthless. But there it is; these dams have been built, distribution systems have been acquired. It is an accomplished fact. Now let's give TVA a real and honest chance to see what it can do or cannot do for the benefit of all the people."

Mr. Willkie does not believe that TVA should expand to take in more territory. But he believes that in its present territory it should not be "unfairly disturbed."

"There is one thing I do demand of TVA," he said, "I think TVA itself should demand it. That is an honest, fair, crystal-clear system of bookkeeping that will let the people know exactly what TVA is doing, and what its efficiency is in comparison with the private utilities.

"Let's not only show its cost but clearly show the differential of cost between its operation and that of a private company. Let's see it operate in this territory over a long enough period to give it a real test—say five years. Then the people will be able to decide whether it should be expanded, contracted or just what. Such procedure is the democratic process.

"I think some method should be set up to take care of expansion, if expansion ever should be voted on. Back in 1934 that was my greatest criticism of TVA.

"I went to Mr. Roosevelt in 1934, and to the TVA Board, and offered to sell the Tennessee Electric Power properties that TVA later acquired. The offer was refused. Five years of wrangling, five years of letting water which is power flow unused down the Tennessee River, followed. Then in 1939 we sold these properties to TVA for $80,000,000, not far from the figure we would have sold for in 1934.

"I think some impartial board should have been set up—I think it still should be set up, if after a real test of TVA an expansion of the system is decided on—to set a fair price on properties taken over.

"I don't think TVA should be both judge and advocate."

One phase of TVA's program which won unstinted praise from Mr. Willkie is its soil-conservation program.

"That has been a job well done," he said. "The program should be continued and, if anything, enlarged. Soil conservation is a very proper governmental function."

He believes TVA should be run in the manner of a private corporation.

"TVA should be allowed to choose its employees as does a corporation," he said. "Political patronage must be kept out. Its personnel must be chosen and advanced on a merit basis.

"I have never heard any criticism of TVA's choice of employees and I don't think political patronage has got into the system. I see no reason for changing the present set up as far as employee selection and management are concerned."

Mr. Willkie said he thought TVA should pay taxes in just the same manner and same proportion as the private utilities. "But if this isn't done, in its bookkeeping and its reports to the public this difference in tax burden should be made clear to the public."

Subject to reasonable restrictions by Congress, he believes TVA should be allowed to handle its income much as the income of a private corporation is handled.

TVA has three dams under construction, the final three of its original program of 10 dams. Mr. Willkie would not commit himself specifically as to the completion of these dams, but he did say that they should be completed if TVA's financial operation and the state of the "public purse" permitted.

"The public debt is reaching toward the staggering figure of $45,000,000,000," he said. "Then to top it off we're going to spend upwards of 10 billions for defense.

"I think we are going to enter into a period of economy outside the field of defense. That is very understandable, because the taxes are going to hit enough people so that it hurts.

"Already the base is being broadened with lower exemptions and rates are being upped in fairly low brackets. That is necessary. It can't all come from the rich, because if we took all their income it still wouldn't be enough to pay the bills.

"This tax spread is going to make all the country economy-conscious. TVA's appropriations may be affected."

However, Mr. Willkie did have this to say concerning the dams:

"Nothing is more important than defense, and there is nothing which might well mask more political log-rolling than the flag-waving variety of national defense.

"But if some impartial group, the United States Army or its engineers for instance, did say that the completion of these dams was a link in our national defense, the dams should be completed and as rapidly as those charged with our defense thought necessary and possible."

Mr. Willkie was outspoken in favor of rural electrification, which he said he considered not an economic but a social problem.

"I proposed a plan to the President a long time ago, under which a revolving fund of $100,000,000 would be set up to take care of rural electrification," he said.

"Take this power into the farm homes, and then make up—either to TVA, if in its area, or to the private power companies if in their areas—the loss that carrying power to these rural areas would entail. As the load builds up, these areas might well become profitable. When they do, let the original government expenditure be paid back out of profits and used to replenish the revolving funds."

Mr. Willkie pulled no punches in his criticism of certain TVA methods. But he did express a belief that the period of agitation over public vs. private utilities was a thing of the past until TVA's program has a chance to prove its merit or lack of merit.

PART **FIVE**

The Dynamic Constitution

The Roosevelt administration chose to work, if possible, within the Constitution, although some thought the crisis sufficient justification for extraconstitutional emergency action. The President did *imply obliquely during his Inaugural Address that he might take direct action, if Congress should fail to measure up to its "responsibilities," but his legislative draftsmen went to great ends to find support in the nation's charter for their new, untried approaches to the problem.*

Yet the action of the administration demanded a broadening of traditional definitions of the Constitution. In general, the legislation required a liberal view of Federal government power and a narrow view of the restrictions which might be implied from the Constitution to buttress state monopolies of power. The New Deal looked back to the kind of reasoning which Chief Justice John Marshall had adopted over one hundred years before to support the Federal government's action in chartering a United States Bank (McCullogh v. Maryland, *1819*)*. The acts which set up the National Recovery Administration, the Tennessee Valley Authority, and the Agricultural Adjustment Administration, and a score of others, implied that the "necessary and proper" clause must be construed liberally, as Marshall had done, to allow Federal action not specifically authorized in the Constitution, provided it was thought to be generally consistent with the objectives of the document. And they required a narrow interpretation of the Tenth Amendment, which reserved to the states those powers not given to the Federal government. To justify much of the New Deal action, it would be necessary to conceive that this amendment was simply redundant, that it took away no power from the Federal government, that it laid down no restrictions not found elsewhere in the Constitution.*

More specifically, the New Deal raised questions about four significant sections of the national charter:

1. The "commerce clause" authorized Congress to "regulate commerce" with foreign nations and "among the several States." Would it not be pos-

sible, despite extensive precedents to the contrary, for the courts to rule (a) that "commerce" was a broad process which included industry and agriculture as well as transportation and (b) that any *regulation of such commerce might be legal, so long as it did not "take life, liberty or property" without "due process of law," and so long as it was not forbidden elsewhere in the Constitution?*

2. The taxing power was not limited except that it must be used uniformly throughout the country, and for the "common Defence and general Welfare," that "direct" taxes must be apportioned among the several states according to population, and that export duties must be avoided. Would it not then be possible, the precedents being mixed, to rule that taxes might be used for regulation as well as for revenue? Or, failing this, might it not be possible merely to assume, without looking carefully, that Congress always intended revenue purposes when it laid taxes?

3. The Constitution authorized Congress to " . . . provide for . . . the general Welfare." Contrary precedents aside, would it not be possible to see this clause as a grand authorization of power to do, by spending, many things which Congress was not authorized to do by legislation? Congress might pass laws only for the purposes outlined in Article I, Section 8. Congress might spend, *it was said, for any purpose consistent with "the general Welfare."*

4. The general structure of the Constitution authorizes Congress to legislate and the President to see that the laws are faithfully executed. Would it not be possible for Congress to delegate much of its detailed legislative power in a given matter to the President, as it did in NRA, on the theory that the President was in fact merely arranging the detailed execution of the law?

There were other issues, but these were central. AAA and NRA, for example, stood irrevocably upon the broad interpretation of the commerce power. The method chosen to finance AAA depended upon a liberal understanding of the tax power. The NRA codes were worthless unless a generous concept of Congress's right to delegate its authority was undertaken. And so it went.

In the American structure of government, the final decision on matters of constitutional interpretation lies with the Federal courts, in fact with the judges of the United States Supreme Court. This fact is not stated in the Constitution. It is true simply because the Supreme Court stands at the end of the legislative process. No law can be enforced without its ap-

proval and aid. There is no appeal in our procedure from its decision. But the judicial process grinds slowly. Ordinarily a case must be brought first in a Federal district court, either by a government trying to enforce a law or a private individual or group taking an appeal from an administrative decision. The case must be heard and decided there. Then it may be appealed, usually to a circuit court, and then it may be appealed again to the United States Supreme Court. The process ordinarily takes two or three years. The Roosevelt administration, then, had for the moment whatever freedom its own judgment, Congress, and public opinion would allow it. It had this freedom for approximately two years; then it must face the courts.

The Supreme Court ordinarily exercises its powers of judicial finality with care. In fact, in 1933 it stood at the point of not having declared an act of Congress unconstitutional since the Dred Scott decision of 1857. But the moment was an extraordinary one. The administration and the Congress had challenged tradition at numerous and fundamental points. The style of the administration was dramatic enough to raise spectres of dictatorship, to make some people fear the end of the Constitution. Once the edge of crisis had been dulled by the action of 1933 and 1934, it was entirely possible for reasonable men to disagree as to the urgency of the crisis. Finally, the Court itself was made up largely of conservative men, devoted in personality and in the commitment of their prior opinions to the very landmarks of traditionalism and stability which Roosevelt was challenging.

The Court's veto power had been feared. When it came, however, the action was more sweeping and more prohibitive of the future than had been fully expected. A decision in January, 1935, suggested the trend, declaring the oil-regulation section of the NRA unconstitutional because of excessive delegation of legislative power to the President (Panama Oil Refining Co. v. Ryan). *Then late in the spring came the spate of sharp opinions which cut deeply into the whole New Deal program and which negated, among others, the Farm Mortgage Moratorium Act* (Louisville Joint Stock Land Bank v. Radford) *and the National Recovery Administration* (A. L. A. Schechter Corp. v. United States). *But the problem was not merely that existing legislation was rendered worthless. More significant by far was the fact that the restrictive constitutional interpretations indicated by the Court put into sharp issue the fundamental question of whether the Federal government could act effectively at all in promoting economic recovery.*

A Note on the Reading of Supreme Court Opinions

When reading an opinion of the United States Supreme Court, students should keep in mind the fact that the Court is doing two jobs simultaneously. It is deciding a specific issue between parties, often between the United States government and an individual or corporation. Second, it is interpreting the Constitution or the law or an administrative regulation and laying down a more or less general rule which may be followed by lesser courts in the future and heeded by lawyers seeking guidance in handling similar cases. Students should also remember that the setting of interpretation is a subtle matter, often centering upon very narrow and precise changes in meaning, and sometimes involving conflicting interpretations. It is not at all unusual to have inconsistent lines of precedent available to the two sides in a case, or to have many years, and cases, elapse before the definitive interpretation becomes clear.

Something of the mechanics of the court should also be kept in mind. First, the "opinion of the Court" is merely the official opinion of the majority. It represents the conclusion *reached by at least a majority of the judges. But the* reasoning *itself may on some occasions represent the thinking only of the judge who wrote the opinion. In such cases, other concurring opinions may be filed suggesting the differing paths by which other justices reached the common conclusion. Frequently, dissenting opinions will be filed which suggest the conclusions and reasoning of the justices who voted against the majority.*

In such complicated circumstances, the precise status of the official opinion depends upon how many justices supported its reasoning, as well as its conclusions, and also upon one's own judgment as to whether the opinion represents a line of interpretation likely to be followed in the future by the Court. Often the opinion will be significant for the issues it chooses not to raise, thereby maintaining the existing precedents on the matter.

The cases involving the New Deal display one great advantage for the student, in that they make the issues clear, face the problems almost too dramatically and precisely. A student reading a Supreme Court opinion should, then, look for several things:

1. The facts of the case.

2. The decision in the particular case. What happened to the parties involved?

3. The constitutional issues decided and the conclusions reached regarding them.

4. The line of argument, both logic and precedent, by which the judges reached their conclusions.

A useful general discussion of the constitutional history of the period may be found in Carl Swisher, American Constitutional Development, *2d ed. (1954).*

The NRA Declared Unconstitutional: The Schechter Case, 1935

A number of significant constitutional issues were raised by the National Recovery Act and by the Codes of Fair Competition drawn up and implemented under its authority. Central to the whole plan was the question whether Congress in the first instance and then, in turn, the President could delegate to committees of private industry the authority to write such codes. At stake in the larger sense was the boundary between Congress and the White House in the separation-of-powers system. In a narrower sense, what was at issue was the definition of the distinction between law and administrative ruling. In more substantive matters, the fate of the National Recovery Administration relied upon the interpretation of the commerce clause or upon the question whether emergency did not itself grant special extraconstitutional powers to government.

The case of Schecter v. United States *raised these issues directly, since the Schechter Company was in the business of local distribution of poultry, a form of limited commerce which traditionally had been thought to be* intra- *rather than* interstate *commerce. The Court's reaction to these points not only spelled the end of the experiment with NRA but also raised serious questions regarding the constitutionality of much of the central New Deal legislation. If NRA fell, under what FDR came to call the "horse and buggy" interpretation of the commerce clause, would not AAA also? In fact, the Court seemed bent upon preserving a traditional approach to the power of the Federal government, and in particular to the power of the executive, which would render ineffective much of what the administration had tried to do.*

*It soon became apparent that the Schechter case was no isolated instance but was rather the boundary marker for a whole line of cases. On the same day that it killed NRA, the Court declared unconstitutional the Frazier-Lemke Farm Mortgage Act (*Louisville Joint Stock Land Bank v. Radford*). In January, 1936, AAA was declared invalid (*United States v. Butler*). Agriculture, the Court said, was not interstate commerce. The processing tax used to finance AAA was ruled to be a misuse of the tax power for regulatory purposes, and a discriminatory one at that. In rapid order came rulings against the Municipal Bankruptcy Act of 1934 (*Ashton v. Cameron County Water Improvement District No. 1, *1936), the Guffey Coal Act (*Carter v. Carter Coal Co., *1936), a New York State Minimum Wage Statute (*Morehead v. New York ex rel. *Tipaldo, 1936). The Schechter Case had been unanimously decided. But others hung upon one- or two-vote balances, 5 to 4 or 6 to 3, for example. The bitterness of the Court's attack, the narrowness of the margins added further controversy to a dispute already difficult because it centered upon both the central legal concepts and the fundamental social issues of the age.*

On the reactions of the Supreme Court to the New Deal and the subsequent battle between Roosevelt and the Court, see, among others, Samuel Hendel, Charles Evans Hughes and the Supreme Court *(1951); Merlo J. Pusey,* Charles Evans Hughes *(1951); Alpheus T. Mason,* Harlan Fiske Stone: Pillar of the

Law *(1956), and* Brandeis: A Free Man's Life *(1946); John Frank,* Mr. Justice Black *(1949); and Eugene Gerhart,* America's Advocate: Robert H. Jackson *(1958).*

The case provided here is A. L. A. Schechter Corp. v. United States, *295 U.S. 519–551,* passim *(1935).*

Mr. Chief Justice Hughes delivered the opinion of the court.

Petitioners in No. 854 were convicted in the District Court of the United States for the Eastern District of New York on eighteen counts of an indictment charging violations of what is known as the "Live Poultry Code. . . ." By demurrer to the indictment and appropriate motions on the trial the defendants contended (1) that the code had been adopted pursuant to an unconstitutional delegation by Congress of legislative power; (2) that it attempted to regulate intrastate transactions which lay outside the authority of Congress; and (3) that in certain provisions it was repugnant to the due process clause of the Fifth Amendment. . . . Defendants ordinarily purchase their live poultry from commission men at the West Washington Market in New York City or at the railroad terminals serving the city, but occasionally they purchase from commission men in Philadelphia. They buy the poultry for slaughter and resale. After the poultry is trucked to their slaughter-house markets in Brooklyn, it is there sold, usually within twenty-four hours, to retail poultry dealers and butchers who sell directly to consumers. The poultry purchased from defendants is immediately slaughtered, prior to delivery, by schochtim in defendant's employ. Defendants do not sell poultry in interstate commerce. . . .

The "Live Poultry Code" was approved by the President on April 13, 1934. Its divisions indicate its nature and scope. The code has eight articles entitled (1) purposes, (2) definitions, (3) hours, (4) wages, (5) general labor provisions, (6) administration, (7) trade practice provisions, and (8) general. . . .

First. Two preliminary points are stressed by the government with respect to the appropriate approach to the important questions presented. We are told that the provision of the statute authorizing the adoption of codes must be viewed in the light of the grave national crisis with which Congress was confronted. Undoubtedly, the conditions to which power is addressed are always to be considered when the exercise of power is challenged. Extraordinary conditions may call for extraordinary remedies. But the argument necessarily stops short of an attempt to justify action which lies outside the sphere of constitutional authority. Extraordinary conditions do not create or enlarge constitutional power. The Constitution established a national government with powers deemed to be adequate, as they have proved to be both in war and peace, but these powers of the national government are limited by the constitutional grants. Those who act under these grants are not at liberty to transcend the imposed limits because they believe that more or different power is necessary. Such assertions of extra-constitutional authority were anticipated and precluded by the explicit terms of the Tenth Amendment, "The powers not delegated to the United States by the Constitution, nor prohibited by it to the States, are reserved to the States respectively, or to the people."

The further point is urged that the national crisis demanded a broad and intensive co-operative effort by those engaged in trade and industry, and that this necessary co-operation was sought to be fostered by permitting them to initiate the adoption of codes. But the statutory plan is not simply one for voluntary effort. It does not seek merely to endow voluntary trade or industrial associations or groups with privileges or immunities. It involves the coercive exercise of the law-making power. The codes of fair competition which the statute attempts to authorize are codes of laws. If valid, they place all persons within their reach under the obligation of positive law, binding equally those who assent and those who do not assent. Violations of the provisions of the codes are punishable as crimes.

Second. The question of the delegation of legislative power. We recently had occasion to review the pertinent decisions and the general principles which govern the determination of this question. . . . The Constitution provides that "all legislative powers herein granted shall be vested in a Congress of the United States, which shall consist of a Senate and House of Representatives." Art. 1, § 1. And the Congress is authorized "to make all laws which shall be necessary and proper for carrying into execution" its general power. Art. 1, § 8, ¶ 18. The Congress is not permitted to abdicate or to transfer to others the essential legislative functions with which it is thus vested. We have repeatedly recognized the necessity of adapting legislation to complex conditions involving a host of details with which the National Legislature cannot deal directly. We pointed out in the Panama Ref. Co. case that the Constitution has never been regarded as denying to Congress the necessary resources of flexibility and practicality, which will enable it to perform its function in laying down policies and establishing standards, while leaving to selected instrumentalities the making of subordinate rules within prescribed limits and the determination of facts to which the policy as declared by the Legislature is to apply. But we said that the constant recognition of the necessity and validity of such provisions, and the wide range of administrative authority which has been developed by means of them, cannot be allowed to obscure the limitations of the authority to delegate, if our constitutional system is to be maintained.

Accordingly, we look to the statute to see whether Congress has overstepped these limitations,—whether Congress in authorizing "Codes of Fair Competition" has itself established the standards of legal obligation, thus performing its essential legislative function, or, by the failure to enact such standards, has attempted to transfer that function to others. . . .

For a statement of the authorized objectives and content of the "codes of fair competition" we are referred repeatedly to the "declaration of policy" in § 1 of Title I of the Recovery Act. Thus, the approval of a code by the President is conditioned on his finding that it "will tend to effectuate the policy of this title." Section 3 (a). The President is authorized to impose such conditions "for the protection of consumers, competitors, employes and others, and in furtherance of the public interest, and may provide such exceptions to and exemptions from the provisions of such code as the President in his discretion deems necessary to effectuate the policy herein declared." The "policy herein declared" is manifestly that set forth in § 1. That declaration embraces a broad range of objectives. Among them we find the elimination of "unfair competitive practices." But even if this clause were to be taken to relate to practices which fall under the ban of existing law, either common law or statute, it is still only one of the authorized aims described in § 1. It is there declared to be "the policy of Congress"—

> to remove obstructions to the free flow of interstate and foreign commerce which tend to diminish the amount thereof; and to provide for the general welfare by promoting the organization of industry for the purpose of co-operative action among trade groups, to induce and maintain united action of labor and management under adequate governmental sanctions and supervision, to eliminate unfair competitive practices, to promote the fullest possible utilization of the present productive capacity of industries, to avoid undue restriction of production (except as may be temporarily required), to increase the consumption of industrial and agricultural products by increasing purchasing power, to reduce and relieve unemployment, to improve standards of labor, and otherwise to rehabilitate industry and to conserve natural resources.

Under § 3, whatever "may tend to effectuate" these general purposes may be included in the "codes of fair competition." We think the conclusion is inescapable that the authority sought to be conferred by § 3 was not merely to deal with "unfair competitive practices" which offend against existing law, and could be the subject of judicial condemnation without further legislation, or to create administrative machinery for the application of established principles of law to particular instances of violation. Rather, the purpose is clearly disclosed to authorize new and controlling prohibitions through codes of laws which would embrace what the formulators would propose, and what the President would approve, or prescribe, as wise and beneficent measures for the government of trades and industries in order to bring about their rehabilitation, correction and development, according to the general declaration of policy in § 1. Codes of laws of this sort are styled "codes of fair competition."

We find no real controversy upon this point and we must determine the validity of the code in question in this aspect. . . .

The Government urges that the codes will "consist of rules of competition deemed fair for each industry—by representative members of that industry, by the persons most vitally concerned and most familiar with its problems." Instances are cited in which Congress has availed itself of such assistance: as e. g., in the exercise of its authority over the public domain, with respect to the recognition of local customs or rules of miners as to mining claims, or in matters of a more or less technical nature, as in designating the standard height of drawbars. But would it be seriously contended that Congress could delegate its legislative authority to trade or industrial associations or groups so as to empower them to enact the laws they deem to be wise and beneficent for the rehabilitation and expansion of their trade or industries? Could trade or industrial associations or groups be constituted legislative bodies for that purpose because such associations or groups are familiar with the problems of their enterprises? And could an effort of that sort be made valid by such a preface of generalities as to permissible aims as we find in § 1 of title I? The answer is obvious. Such a delegation of legislative power is unknown to our law and is utterly inconsistent with the constitutional prerogatives and duties of Congress.

The question, then, turns upon the authority which § 3 of the Recovery Act vests in the President to approve or prescribe. If the codes have standing as penal statutes, this must be due to the effect of the executive action. But Congress cannot delegate legislative power to the President to exercise an unfettered discretion to make whatever laws he thinks may be needed or advisable for the rehabilitation and expansion of trade or industry. . . .

Accordingly we turn to the Recovery Act to ascertain what limits have been set to the exercise of the President's discretion. *First,* the President, as a condition of approval, is required to find that the trade or industrial associations or groups which propose a code "impose no inequitable restrictions on admission to membership" and are "truly representative." That condition, however, relates only to the status of the initiators of the new laws and not to the permissible scope of such laws. *Second,* the President is required to find that the code is not "designed to promote monopolies or to eliminate or oppress small enterprises and will not operate to discriminate against them." And to this is added a proviso that the code "shall not permit monopolies or monopolistic practices." But these restrictions leave virtually untouched the field of policy envisaged by § 1, and in that wide field of legislative possibilities the proponents of a code, refraining from monopolistic designs, may roam at will and the President may approve or disapprove their proposals as he may see fit. That is the precise effect of the further finding that the President is to make—that the code "will tend to effectuate the policy of this title." While this is called a finding, it is really but a statement of an opinion as to the general effect upon the promotion of trade or industry of a scheme of laws. These are the only findings which Congress has made essential in order to put into operation a legislative code having the aims described in the "Declaration of Policy."

Nor is the breadth of the President's discretion left to the necessary implications of this limited requirement as to his findings. As already noted, the President in approving a code may impose his own conditions, adding to or taking from what is proposed, as "in his discretion" he thinks necessary "to effectuate the policy" declared by the act. Of course, he has no less liberty when he prescribes a code on his own motion or on complaint, and he is free to prescribe one if a code has not been approved. The act provides for the creation by the President of administrative agencies to assist him, but the action or reports of such agencies, or of his other assistants—their recommendations and findings in relation to the making of codes—have no sanction beyond the will of the President, who may accept, modify or reject them as he pleases. Such recommendations or findings in no way limit the authority which § 3 undertakes to vest in the President with no other conditions than those there specified. And this authority relates to a host of different trades and industries, thus extending the President's discretion to all the varieties of laws which he may deem to be beneficial in dealing with the vast array of commercial and industrial activities throughout the country.

Such a sweeping delegation of legislative power finds no support in the decisions upon which the government especially relies. . . .

To summarize and conclude upon this point: § 3 of the Recovery Act is without precedent. It supplies no standards for any trade, industry or activity. It does not undertake to prescribe rules of conduct to be applied to particular states of fact determined by appropriate administrative procedure. Instead of prescribing rules of conduct, it authorizes the making of codes to prescribe them. For that legislative undertaking, § 3 sets up no standards, aside from the statement of the general aims of rehabilitation, correction and expansion described in § 1. In view of the scope of that broad declaration, and of the nature of the few restrictions that are imposed, the discretion of the President in approving or prescribing codes, and thus enacting laws for the government of trade and industry throughout the country, is virtually unfettered. We think that the code-making authority thus conferred is an unconstitutional delegation of legislative power.

Third. *The question of the application of the provisions of the Live Poultry Code to intrastate transactions.* Although the validity of the codes (apart from the question of delegation) rests upon the commerce clause of the Constitution, § 3 (a) is not in terms limited to interstate and foreign commerce. From the generality of terms, and from the argument of the Government at the bar it would appear that § 3 (a) was designed to authorize codes without that limitation. But under § 3 (f) penalties are confined to violations of a code provision "in any transaction in or affecting interstate or foreign commerce." This aspect of the case presents the question whether the particular provisions of the Live Poultry Code, which the defendants were convicted for violating and for having conspired to violate, were within the regulating power of Congress.

These provisions relate to the hours and wages of those employed by defendants in their slaughterhouses in Brooklyn and to the sales there made to retail dealers and butchers.

1. Were these transactions "*in*" interstate commerce? Much is made of the fact that almost all the poultry coming to New York is sent there from other States. But the code provisions, as here applied, do not concern the transportation of the poultry from other States to New York, or the transactions of the commission men or others to whom it is consigned, or the sales made by such consignees to defendants. When defendants had made their purchases, whether at the West Washington Market in New York City or at the railroad terminals serving the city, or elsewhere, the poultry was trucked to their slaughterhouses in Brooklyn for local disposition. The interstate transactions in relation to that poultry then ended. Defendants held the poultry at their slaughterhouse markets for slaughter and local sale to retail dealers and butchers, who in turn sold directly to consumers. Neither the slaughtering nor the sales by defendants were transactions in interstate commerce. . . .

The undisputed facts thus afford no warrant for the argument that the poultry handled by defendants at their slaughterhouse markets was in a "*current*" or "*flow*" of interstate commerce and was thus subject to congressional regulation. The mere fact that there may be a constant flow of commodities into a State does not mean that the flow continues after the property has arrived and has become commingled with the mass of property within the State and is there held solely for local disposition and use. So far as the poultry herein questioned is concerned, the flow in interstate commerce had ceased. The poultry had come to a permanent rest within the State. It was not held, used or sold by defendants in relation to any further transactions in interstate commerce and was not destined for transportation to other States. Hence, decisions which deal with a stream of interstate commerce—where goods come to rest within a State temporarily and are later to go forward in interstate commerce—and with the regulations of transactions involved in that practical continuity of movement, are not applicable here. . . .

2. Did the defendants' transactions directly "affect" interstate commerce so as to be subject to Federal regulation? The power of Congress extends not only to the regulation of transactions which are part of interstate commerce, but to the protection of that commerce from injury. It matters not that the injury may be due to the conduct of those engaged in intrastate operations. Thus, Congress may protect the safety of those employed in interstate transportation "no matter what may be the source of the dangers which threaten it. . . ."

In determining how far the Federal Government may go in controlling intrastate transactions upon the ground that they "affect" interstate commerce, there is a necessary and well-established distinction between direct and indirect effects. The precise line can be drawn only as individual cases arise, but the distinction is clear in principle. Direct effects are illustrated by the railroad cases we have cited, as, e. g., the effect of failure to use prescribed safety appliances on railroads which are the highways of both interstate and intrastate commerce, injury to an employe engaged in interstate transportation by the negligence of an employe engaged in an intrastate movement, the fixing of rates for intrastate transportation which unjustly discriminate against interstate commerce. But where the effect of intrastate transactions upon interstate commerce is merely indirect, such transactions remain within the domain of State power. If the commerce clause were construed to reach all enterprises and transactions which could be said to have an indirect effect upon interstate commerce, the Federal authority would embrace practically all the activities of the people and the authority of the State over its domestic concerns would exist only by sufferance of the Federal Government. Indeed, on such a theory, even the development of the State's commercial facilities would be subject to Federal control.

The distinction between direct and indirect effects has been clearly recognized in the application of the Antitrust Act. Where a combination or conspiracy is formed, with the intent to restrain interstate commerce or to monopolize any part of it, the violation of the statute is clear. . . . But where that intent is absent, and the objectives are limited to intrastate activities, the fact that there may be an indirect effect upon interstate commerce does not subject the parties to the Federal statute, notwithstanding its broad provisions. This principle has frequently been applied in litigation growing out of labor disputes. . . .

While these decisions related to the application of the Federal statute, and not to its constitutional validity, the distinction between direct and indirect effects of intrastate transactions upon interstate commerce must be recognized as a fundamental one, essential to the maintenance of our constitutional system. Otherwise, as we have said, there would be virtually no limit to the Federal power, and for all practical purposes we should have a completely centralized government. We must consider the provisions here in question in the light of this distinction.

The question of chief importance relates to the provisions of the Code as to the hours and wages of those employed in defendants' slaughterhouse markets. It is plain that these requirements are imposed in order to govern the details of defendants' management of their local business. The persons employed in slaughtering and selling in local trade are not employed in interstate commerce. Their hours and wages have no direct relation to interstate commerce. The question of how many hours these employes should work and what they should be paid differs in no essential respect from similar questions in other local businesses which handle commodities brought into a State and there dealt in as a part of its internal commerce. This appears from an examination of the considerations urged by the Government with respect to conditions in the poultry trade. Thus, the Government argues that hours and wages affect prices; that slaughterhouse men sell at a small margin above operating costs; that labor represents 50 to 60 per cent of these costs; that a slaughterhouse operator paying lower wages or reducing his cost by exacting long hours of work translates his saving into lower prices; that this results in demands for a cheaper grade of goods, and that the cutting of prices brings about a demoralization of the price structure. Similar conditions may be adduced in relation to other businesses. The argument of the Government proves too much. If the Federal Government may determine the wages and hours of employes in the internal commerce of a State, because of their relation to cost and prices and their indirect effect upon interstate commerce, it would seem that a similar control might be exerted over other elements of cost, also affecting prices, such as the number of employes, rents, advertising, methods of doing business, etc. All the processes of production and distribution that enter into cost could likewise be controlled. If the cost of doing an intrastate business is in itself the permitted object of Federal control, the extent of the regulation of cost would be a question of discretion and not of power.

The Government also makes the point that efforts to enact State legislation establishing high labor standards have been impeded by the belief that unless similar action is taken generally, commerce will be diverted from the States adopting such standards, and that this fear of diversion has led to demands for Federal legislation on the subject of wages and hours. The apparent implication is that the Federal authority under the commerce clause should be deemed to extend to the establishment of rules to govern wages and hours in intrastate trade and industry generally throughout the country, thus overriding the authority of the States to deal with domestic problems arising from labor conditions in their internal commerce.

It is not the province of the Court to consider the economic advantages or disadvantages of such a centralized system. It is sufficient to say that the Federal Constitution does not provide for it. Our growth and development have called for wide use of the commerce power of the Federal Government in its control over the expanded activities of interstate commerce and in protecting that commerce from burdens, interferences and conspiracies to restrain and monopolize it. But the authority of the Federal Government may not be pushed to such an extreme as to destroy the distinction, which the commerce clause itself establishes, between commerce "among the several States" and the internal concerns of a State. The same answer must be made to the contention that is based upon the serious economic situation which led to the passage of the Recovery Act—the fall in prices, the decline in wages and employment, and the curtailment of the market for commodities. Stress is laid upon the great importance of maintaining wage distributions which would provide the necessary stimulus in starting "the cumulative forces making for expanding commercial activity." Without in any way disparaging this motive, it is enough to say that the recuperative efforts of the Federal Government must be made in a manner consistent with the authority granted by the Constitution.

We are of the opinion that the attempt through the provisions of the Code to fix the hours and wages of employes of defendants in their intrastate business was not a valid exercise of Federal power. . . .

On both the grounds we have discussed, the attempted delegation of legislative power and the attempted regulation of intrastate transactions which affect interstate commerce only indirectly, we hold the code provisions here in question to be invalid and that the judgment of conviction must be reversed.

The Battle with the Court: FDR's Fireside Chat on Judicial Reform, 1937

Decisions of the Court in 1935 and 1936 had emasculated much of the New Deal. The National Recovery Administration was gone, as were the Railway Retirement Act and the Farm Mortgage Moratorium. The Agricultural Adjustment Administration had been cut down, although a substitute, the Soil Conservation and Domestic Allotment Act, was providing funds and devices for a limited continuation of its program. Portents were grave for some of the central legislation of the later New Deal. If the commerce clause were not broad enough to provide cover for code regulation of the poultry markets, would the Court see it as broad enough to provide justification for the labor regulation of the Wagner Act, for example?

Roosevelt kept his peace until after the 1936 campaign, and for several months more. But he was considering quietly a variety of propositions which advisors funneled to his desk. It seemed clear that the roadblocks thrown down by the Court must be removed if the administration were to provide action consistent with the implication of its election mandate. And it appeared clear that the roadblocks could be removed only by a change in personnel of the Supreme Court. Yet the independence of the judiciary generally and the prestige of the Supreme Court in particular were two of the most sacred propositions in the structure of American government. Roosevelt felt his own prestige to be enormous, but even so there was great danger that an attack upon the Court would rebound against its author, strong though he might be.

The stratagem Roosevelt finally adopted was carefully kept in secret until the end of February, 1937. Many of the President's own aides and intimates knew nothing of it. Roosevelt proposed an enlargement of the Court based in large part upon the propositions that the older justices were overworked and tired, that the Federal court calendars were clogged, that the machinery of justice was inexcusably slow. But it was evident to all—in fact the President made it quite clear—that the central benefit would lie in tipping the close balances of the Court toward a broader interpretation favoring the New Deal measures on which the justices must soon act.

No proposal of FDR caused such controversy as this. Eventually he lost, for Congress, while passing the part of the proposition which allowed for voluntary retirement at age 70 on full pay, and providing for certain other unobjectionable reforms, refused the President the power to make additional appointments. Roosevelt lost for many reasons; his party and his legislative leaders had not been properly prepared; the argument appeared to many people devious and conspiratorial; the Chief Justice himself successfully challenged Roosevelt's contention that the Court was laggard in its labors; a key legislative leader, Senator Joe Robinson of Arkansas, died at an important point in the maneuvering. There were others, but perhaps the crucial problem was the fact that the President was unable to sell the American people generally on a proposition which appeared to upset the basic constitutional traditions of the government. It was not, however, because he did not try. The Fireside Chat reproduced here provides the argument by which FDR sought to arouse public opinion and to direct the overwhelming support he had enjoyed in the 1936 election toward the successful resolution of his struggle with the Court.

The Fireside Chat of March 9, 1937, may be found in Samuel Rosenman (ed.), The Public Papers and Addresses of Franklin D. Roosevelt, Volume Six: The Constitution Prevails, 1937 *(New York: Macmillan, 1941), pages 122–133.*

Tonight, sitting at my desk in the White House, I make my first radio report to the people in my second term of office.

I am reminded of that evening in March, four years ago, when I made my first radio report to you. We were then in the midst of the great banking crisis.

Soon after, with the authority of the Congress, we asked the Nation to turn over all of its privately held gold, dollar for dollar, to the Government of the United States.

Today's recovery proves how right that policy was.

But when, almost two years later, it came before the Supreme Court its constitutionality was upheld only by a five-to-four vote. The change of one vote would have thrown all the affairs of this great Nation back into hopeless chaos. In effect, four Justices ruled that the right under a private contract to exact a pound of flesh was more sacred than the main objectives of the Constitution to establish an enduring Nation.

In 1933 you and I knew that we must never let our economic system get completely out of joint again—that we could not afford to take the risk of another great depression.

We also became convinced that the only way to avoid a repetition of those dark days was to have a government with power to prevent and to cure the abuses and the inequalities which had thrown that system out of joint.

We then began a program of remedying those abuses and inequalities—to give balance and stability to our economic system—to make it bomb-proof against the causes of 1929.

Today we are only part-way through that program—and recovery is speeding up to a point where the dangers of 1929 are again becoming possible, not this week or month perhaps, but within a year or two.

National laws are needed to complete that program. Individual or local or state effort alone cannot protect us in 1937 any better than ten years ago.

It will take time—and plenty of time—to work out our remedies administratively even after legislation is passed. To complete our program of protection in time, therefore, we cannot delay one moment in making certain that our National Government has power to carry through.

Four years ago action did not come until the eleventh hour. It was almost too late.

If we learned anything from the depression we will not allow ourselves to run around in new circles of futile discussion and debate, always postponing the day of decision.

The American people have learned from the depression. For in the last three national elections an overwhelming majority of them voted a mandate that the Congress and the President begin the task of providing that protection—not after long years of debate, but now.

The Courts, however, have cast doubts on the ability of the elected Congress to protect us against catastrophe by meeting squarely our modern social and economic conditions.

We are at a crisis in our ability to proceed with that protection. It is a quiet crisis. There are no lines of depositors outside closed banks. But to the far-sighted it is far-reaching in its possibilities of injury to America.

I want to talk with you very simply about the need for present action in this crisis—the need to meet the unanswered challenge of one-third of a Nation ill-nourished, ill-clad, ill-housed.

Last Thursday I described the American form of Government as a three horse team provided by the Constitution to the American people so that their field might be plowed. The three horses are of course, the three branches of government—the Congress, the Executive and the Courts. Two of the horses are pulling in unison today; the third is not. Those who have intimated that the President of the United States is trying to drive that team, overlook the simple fact that the President, as Chief Executive, is himself one of the three horses.

It is the American people themselves who are in the driver's seat.

It is the American people themselves who want the furrow plowed.

It is the American people themselves who expect the third horse to pull in unison with the other two.

I hope that you have re-read the Constitution of the United States in these past few weeks. Like the Bible, it ought to be read again and again.

It is an easy document to understand when you remember that it was called into being because the Articles of Confederation under which the original thirteen States tried to operate after the Revolution showed the need of a National Government with power enough to handle national problems. In its Preamble, the Constitution states that it was intended to form a more perfect Union and promote the general welfare; and the powers given to the Congress to carry out those purposes can be best described by saying that they were all the powers needed to meet each and every problem which then had a national character and which could not be met by merely local action.

But the framers went further. Having in mind that in succeeding generations many other problems then undreamed of would become national problems, they gave to the Congress the ample broad powers "to levy taxes . . . and provide for the common defense and general welfare of the United States."

That, my friends, is what I honestly believe to have been the clear and underlying purpose of the patriots who wrote a Federal Constitution to create a National Government with national power, intended as they said, "to form a more perfect union . . . for ourselves and our posterity."

For nearly twenty years there was no conflict between the Congress and the Court. Then Congress passed a statute which, in 1803, the Court said violated an express provision of the Constitution. The Court claimed the power to declare it unconstitutional and did so declare it. But a little later the Court itself admitted that it was an extraordinary power to exercise and through Mr. Justice Washington laid down this limitation upon it: "It is but a decent respect due to the wisdom, the integrity and the patriotism of the legislative body, by which any law is passed, to presume in favor of its validity until its violation of the Constitution is proved beyond all reasonable doubt."

But since the rise of the modern movement for social and economic progress through legislation, the Court has more and more often and more and more boldly asserted a power to veto laws passed by the Congress and State Legislatures in complete disregard of this original limitation.

In the last four years the sound rule of giving statutes the benefit of all reasonable doubt has been cast aside. The Court has been acting not as a judicial body, but as a policy-making body.

When the Congress has sought to stabilize national agriculture, to improve the conditions of labor, to safeguard business against unfair competition, to protect our national resources, and in many other ways, to serve our clearly national needs, the majority of the Court has been assuming the power to pass on the wisdom of these Acts of the Congress—and to approve or disapprove the public policy written into these laws.

That is not only my accusation. It is the accusation of most distinguished Justices of the present Supreme Court. I have not the time to quote to you all the language used by dissenting Justices in many of these cases. But in the case holding the Railroad Retirement Act unconstitutional, for instance, Chief Justice Hughes said in a dissenting opinion that the majority opinion was "a departure from sound principles," and placed "an unwarranted limitation upon the commerce clause." And three other Justices agreed with him.

In the case holding the A.A.A. unconstitutional, Justice Stone said of the majority opinion that it was a "tortured construction of the Constitution." And two other Justices agreed with him.

In the case holding the New York Minimum Wage Law unconstitutional, Justice Stone said that the majority were actually reading into the Constitution their own "personal economic predilections," and that if the legislative power is not left free to choose the methods of solving the problems of poverty, subsistence and health of large numbers in the community, then "government is to be rendered impotent." And two other Justices agreed with him.

In the face of these dissenting opinions, there is no basis for the claim made by some members of the Court that something in the Constitution has compelled them regretfully to thwart the will of the people.

In the face of such dissenting opinions, it is perfectly clear, that as Chief Justice Hughes has said: "We are under a Constitution, but the Constitution is what the Judges say it is."

The Court in addition to the proper use of its judicial functions has improperly set itself up as a third House of the Congress—a super-legislature, as one of the justices has called it—reading into the Constitution words and implications which are not there, and which were never intended to be there.

We have, therefore, reached the point as a Nation where we must take action to save the Constitution from the Court and the Court from itself. We must find a way to take an appeal from the Supreme Court to the Constitution itself. We want a Supreme Court which will do justice under the Constitution—not over it. In our Courts we want a government of laws and not of men.

I want—as all Americans want—an independent judiciary as proposed by the framers of the Constitution. That means a Supreme Court that will enforce the Constitution as written—that will refuse to amend the Constitution by the arbitrary exercise of judicial power—amendment by judicial say-so. It does not mean a judiciary so independent that it can deny the existence of facts universally recognized.

How then could we proceed to perform the mandate given us? It was said in last year's Democratic platform, "If these problems cannot be effectively solved within the Constitution, we shall seek such clarifying amendment as will assure the power to enact those laws, adequately to regulate commerce, protect public health and safety, and safeguard economic security." In other words, we said we would seek an amendment only if every other possible means by legislation were to fail.

When I commenced to review the situation with the problem squarely before me, I came by a process of elimination to the conclusion that, short of amendments, the only method which was clearly constitutional, and would at the same time carry out other much needed reforms, was to infuse new blood into all our Courts. We must have men worthy and equipped to carry out impartial justice. But, at the same time, we must have Judges who will bring to the Courts a present-day sense of the Constitution—Judges who will retain in the Courts the judicial functions of a court, and reject the legislative powers which the Courts have today assumed.

In forty-five out of the forty-eight States of the Union, Judges are chosen not for life but for a period of years. In many States Judges must retire at the age of seventy. Congress has provided financial security by offering life pensions at full pay for Federal Judges on all Courts who are willing to retire at seventy. In the case of Supreme Court Justices, that pension is $20,000 a year. But all Federal Judges, once appointed, can, if they choose, hold office for life, no matter how old they may get to be.

What is my proposal? It is simply this: whenever a Judge or Justice of any Federal Court has reached the age of seventy and does not avail himself of the opportunity to retire on a pension, a new member shall be appointed by the President then in office, with the approval, as required by the Constitution, of the Senate of the United States.

That plan has two chief purposes. By bringing into the judicial system a steady and continuing stream of new and younger blood, I hope, first, to make the administration of all Federal justice speedier and, therefore, less costly; secondly, to bring to the decision of social and economic problems younger men who have had personal experience and contact with modern facts and circumstances under which average men have to live and work. This plan will save our national Constitution from hardening of the judicial arteries.

The number of Judges to be appointed would depend wholly on the decision of present Judges now over seventy, or those who would subsequently reach the age of seventy.

If, for instance, any one of the six Justices of the Supreme Court now over the age of seventy should retire as provided under the plan, no additional place would be created. Consequently, although there never can be more than fifteen, there may be only fourteen, or thirteen, or twelve. And there may be only nine.

There is nothing novel or radical about this idea. It seeks to maintain the Federal bench in full vigor. It has been discussed and approved by many persons of high authority ever since a similar proposal passed the House of Representatives in 1869.

Why was the age fixed at seventy? Because the laws of many States, the practice of the Civil Service, the regulations of the Army and Navy, and the rules of many of our Universities and of almost every great private business enterprise, commonly fix the retirement age at seventy years or less.

The statute would apply to all the courts in the Federal system. There is general approval so far as the lower Federal courts are concerned. The plan has met opposition only so far as the Supreme Court of the United States itself is concerned. If such a plan is good for the lower courts it certainly ought to be equally good for the highest Court from which there is no appeal.

Those opposing this plan have sought to arouse prejudice and fear by crying that I am seeking to "pack" the Supreme Court and that a baneful precedent will be established.

What do they mean by the words "packing the Court"?

Let me answer this question with a bluntness that will end all *honest* misunderstanding of my purposes.

If by that phrase "packing the Court" it is charged that I wish to place on the bench spineless puppets who would disregard the law and would decide specific cases as I wished them to be decided, I make this answer: that no President fit for his office would appoint, and no Senate of honorable men fit for their office would confirm, that kind of appointees to the Supreme Court.

But if by that phrase the charge is made that I would appoint and the Senate would confirm Justices worthy to sit beside present members of the Court who understand those modern conditions, that I will appoint Justices who will not undertake to override the judgment of the Congress on legislative policy, that I will appoint Justices who will act as Justices and not as legislators—if the appointment of such Justices can be called "packing the Courts," then I say that I and with me the vast majority of the American people favor doing just that thing—now.

Is it a dangerous precedent for the Congress to change the number of the Justices? The Congress has always had, and will have, that power. The number of Justices has been changed several times before, in the Administrations of John Adams and Thomas Jefferson—both signers of the Declaration of Independence—Andrew Jackson, Abraham Lincoln and Ulysses S. Grant.

I suggest only the addition of Justices to the bench in accordance with a clearly defined principle relating to a clearly defined age limit. Fundamentally, if in the future, America cannot trust the Congress it elects to refrain from abuse of our Constitutional usages, democracy will have failed far beyond the importance to it of any kind of precedent concerning the Judiciary.

We think it so much in the public interest to maintain a vigorous judiciary that we encourage the retirement of elderly Judges by offering them a life pension at full salary. Why then should we leave the fulfillment of this public policy to chance or make it dependent upon the desire or prejudice of any individual Justice?

It is the clear intention of our public policy to provide for a constant flow of new and younger blood into the Judiciary. Normally every President appoints a large number of District and Circuit Judges and a few members of the Supreme Court. Until my first term practically every President of the United States had appointed at least one member of the Supreme Court. President Taft appointed five members and named a Chief Justice; President Wilson, three; President Harding, four, including a Chief Justice; President Coolidge, one; President Hoover, three, including a Chief Justice.

Such a succession of appointments should have provided a Court well-balanced as to age. But chance and the disinclination of individuals to leave the Supreme bench have now given us a Court in which five Justices will be over seventy-five years of age before next June and one over seventy. Thus a sound public policy has been defeated.

I now propose that we establish by law an assurance against any such ill-balanced Court in the future. I propose that hereafter, when a Judge reaches the age of seventy, a new and younger Judge shall be added to the Court automatically. In this way I propose to enforce a sound public policy by law instead of leaving the composition of our Federal Courts, including the highest, to be determined by chance or the personal decision of individuals.

If such a law as I propose is regarded as establishing a new precedent, is it not a most desirable precedent?

Like all lawyers, like all Americans, I regret the necessity of this controversy. But the welfare of the United States, and indeed of the Constitution itself, is what we all must think about first. Our difficulty with the Court today rises not from the Court as an institution but from human beings within it. But we cannot yield our constitutional destiny to the personal judgment of a few men who, being fearful of the future, would deny us the necessary means of dealing with the present.

This plan of mine is no attack on the Court; it seeks to restore the Court to its rightful and historic place in our system of Constitutional Government and to have it resume its high task of building anew on the Constitution "a system of living law." The Court itself can best undo what the Court has done.

I have thus explained to you the reasons that lie behind our efforts to secure results by legislation within the Constitution. I hope that thereby the difficult process of constitutional amendment may be rendered unnecessary. But let us examine that process.

There are many types of amendment proposed. Each one is radically different from the other. There is no substantial group within the Congress or outside it who are agreed on any single amendment.

It would take months or years to get substantial agreement upon the type and language of an amendment. It would take months and years thereafter to get a two-thirds majority in favor of that amendment in *both* Houses of the Congress.

Then would come the long course of ratification by three-fourths of all the States. No amendment which any powerful economic interests or the leaders of any powerful political party have had reason to oppose has ever been ratified within anything like a reasonable time. And thirteen States which contain only five percent of the voting population can block ratification even though the thirty-five States with ninety-five percent of the population are in favor of it.

A very large percentage of newspaper publishers, Chambers of Commerce, Bar Associations, Manufacturers' Associations, who are trying to give the impression that they really do want a constitutional amendment would be the first to exclaim as soon as an amendment was proposed. "Oh! I was for an amendment all right, but this amendment that you have proposed is not the kind of an amendment that I was thinking about. I am, therefore, going to spend my time, my efforts and my money to block that amendment, although I would be awfully glad to help get some other kind of amendment ratified."

Two groups oppose my plan on the ground that they favor a constitutional amendment. The first includes those who fundamentally object to social and economic legislation along modern lines. This is the same group who during the campaign last Fall tried to block the mandate of the people.

Now they are making a last stand. And the strategy of that last stand is to suggest the time-consuming process of amendment in order to kill off by delay the legislation demanded by the mandate.

To them I say: I do not think you will be able long to fool the American people as to your purposes.

The other group is composed of those who honestly believe the amendment process is the best and who would be willing to support a reasonable amendment if they could agree on one.

To them I say: we cannot rely on an amendment as the immediate or only answer to our present difficulties. When the time comes for action, you will find that many of those who pretend to support you will sabotage any constructive amendment which is proposed. Look at these strange bed-fellows of yours. When before have you found them really at your side in your fights for progress?

And remember one thing more. Even if an amendment were passed, and even if in the years to come it were to be ratified, its meaning would depend upon the kind of Justices who would be sitting on the Supreme Court bench. An amendment, like the rest of the Constitution, is what the Justices say it is rather than what its framers or you might hope it is.

This proposal of mine will not infringe in the slightest upon the civil or religious liberties so dear to every American.

My record as Governor and as President proves my devotion to those liberties. You who know me can have no fear that I would tolerate the destruction by any branch of government of any part of our heritage of freedom.

The present attempt by those opposed to progress to play upon the fears of danger to personal liberty brings again to mind that crude and cruel strategy tried by the same opposition to frighten the workers of America in a pay-envelope propaganda against the Social Security Law. The workers were not fooled by that propaganda then. The people of America will not be fooled by such propaganda now.

I am in favor of action through legislation:

First, because I believe that it can be passed at this session of the Congress.

Second, because it will provide a reinvigorated, liberal-minded Judiciary necessary to furnish quicker and cheaper justice from bottom to top.

Third, because it will provide a series of Federal Courts willing to enforce the Constitution as written, and unwilling to assert legislative powers by writing into it their own political and economic policies.

During the past half century the balance of power between the three great branches of the Federal Government, has been tipped out of balance by the Courts in direct contradiction of the high purposes of the framers of the Constitution. It is my purpose to restore that balance. You who know me will accept my solemn assurance that in a world in which democracy is under attack, I seek to make American democracy succeed. You and I will do our part.

The Defense of the Court: The "New York Times" Replies to Roosevelt, 1937

The responses to Roosevelt's appeal for "judicial reform" were massive and violent. The negative arguments were well summed up in the editorial in which the New York Times *explained its opposition to the so-called court-packing bill. In addition to providing relevant reasoning, this editorial, taken along with Roosevelt's Fireside Chat, presents an interesting case study in the techniques of partisan presentation. Both FDR and the* Times *start from certain implicit, but divergent, assumptions. Both stress the facts of the case most appropriate to the partisan view being argued. FDR underlines the principles involved and the future implications of the decisions; the* Times *stresses the limited, immediate impact of the decisions upon the legislation involved. But no fact is illustrated by the two pieces quite so dramatically as the fact that one's attitude toward the Court battle was likely to be shaped by one's views on the substantive legislation at stake. To some degree, the* New York Times *is really saying that the New Deal has gone quite far enough, in any case. Finally, the* Times *piece is interesting also because it makes clear how much the context by which we judge events has changed in the past thirty years. Particularly instructive in this regard is the* Times's *attitude toward the Public Utility Act of 1935 and toward the Wagner Labor Relations Act.*

One of the reasons why the Times's *view of the issues seems in retrospect unrealistic is the fact that Roosevelt won out in the long run. The "switch" of one vote on the Court soon gave the New Deal 5-to-4 majorities, on the matter of the Wagner Act, for example. After the retirement of Mr. Justice Willis Van Devanter, Roosevelt was able to tip the balance permanently by the appointment of Justice Hugo Black, in August 1937. Van Devanter's departure had been made possible by the retirement provisions of Roosevelt's bill, which had been salvaged and passed by the Congress. Other retirements soon followed. It became more and more a "Roosevelt Court," as the President was able to appoint in rapid succession, during somewhat less than three years, Stanley Reed, Felix Frankfurter, William O. Douglas, and Frank Murphy.*

But to speak of the "Roosevelt Court" is to oversimplify. Their general direction was to approve the expansion of Federal power. They were by no means unanimous, however. The "Roosevelt Justices" often disagreed. Yet, after 1937, the battles were no longer so bitter, or so central to the structure of government. A new consensus on the power of government had been established; Court, White House, and Capitol were in general harmony regarding it. Disputes were now at the level of interpretation and application, and the Court raised no significant challenges to the constitutionality of major Federal legislation.

For an appraisal of the new Court which gradually took shape after 1937, see C. Herman Pritchett, The Roosevelt Court: 1937–1947 *(1948).*

The editorial printed here is from the New York Times, *February 14, 1937, page 8E.*

THE PRESIDENT'S PLAN

Three principal arguments have been advanced in behalf of the President's plan to alter the personnel of the Supreme Court by act of Congress. First, it is said that the present court is obstructing orderly social progress by its practice of invalidating necessary measures enacted by the Administration. Second, it is claimed that in the last election the President received a virtual mandate to put an end to the situation, even though he did not propose or discuss his present method of doing it. Third, it is asserted that the President has chosen the wisest course of action available to him in the circumstances.

I

As for the first of these arguments, the argument that the court is blocking social progress, the record shows that eight laws enacted by the Roosevelt administration have been held unconstitutional. These eight laws are:

1. A measure providing for the conversion of building and loan associations to Federal charters.
2. A measure which was never on the Administration's own program, but which was forced on it through a filibuster staged by HUEY LONG, providing for a moratorium on farm mortgages.
3. A measure which the President said was "crudely drawn" and which was signed by him only after "a difficult decision" providing for the payment of railway pensions.
4. An act, known as the Municipal Bankruptcy Act, of which practically no use was ever made.
5. A "hot oil" law for the petroleum industry, which dealt with a situation which is no longer present.
6. The law creating NRA, a statute held to be flagrantly unconstitutional by a unanimous Supreme Court, including its three stanch liberals, precisely at the time when Congress was preparing to discard the measure anyway.
7. AAA, which has been both defended and denounced at length, but which

was in any case a pre-drought measure for the prevention of farm surpluses which do not exist at present.

8. The Guffey Coal Act, which established a "little NRA" for the bituminous coal industry, with provisions which included wages-and-hours regulations.

In addition to these eight measures, there are two others which may be held unconstitutional at the present session of the court. One is the Public Utility Act of 1935, a measure whose "death sentence clause" has been criticized by many reasonable people as high-handed and confiscatory. The other is the Wagner Labor Relations Act, an admittedly partisan measure, drawn solely in the interest of a single group and of so little practical value that the Government itself made no use of it in the case of the most important labor controversy to arise since the passage of the act.

It must be said, of course, that this list does not include the New York Minimum Wage Law, a measure held to be unconstitutional in a regrettable 5-to-4 decision handed down last June. But this decision involved a State law, not an enactment of the Roosevelt administration, and it is reasonable to believe that the normal process of change in the court's membership will alter its position on such State legislation at an early date. The switch of a single vote would be sufficient for this purpose.

Of the Roosevelt Administration's own program, it is fair to say that the eight measures which have been declared unconstitutional, and the two which may be held unconstitutional at the present session, are not the measures which have won the President the support of many thoughtful, middle-of-the-road progressives. Doubtless these measures have appealed to various "blocs" and factions. But it is difficult to believe that, for the nation as a whole, they really represent the best work of the Roosevelt Administration—work to be placed on a par with such statesmanlike achievements as its foreign policy, its reciprocal trade agreements, its revision of the banking laws, its reorganization of the Federal Reserve System, its regulation of the Stock Exchanges, its control of the issuance of securities, its social security legislation, its brilliant handling of the bank panic.

It is still more difficult to believe that the social progress of the country has really been obstructed by the invalidation of a particular group of eight measures, some of which were forced on the Administration against its will, some of which dealt with situations no longer in existence, some of which were seldom used, and some of which achieved in the long run the intense unpopularity and the widespread disregard which characterized the last days of NRA.

II

The President apparently having reached a different conclusion, we come to the second argument: namely, the question of his "mandate."

Those who hold that he received a mandate in the last election for his present plan do not attempt to argue that the Democratic platform embodied the proposal he now offers, or to assert that the President himself so much as mentioned this plan on a single occasion during the entire course of his campaign. Rather, they rely upon one or the other of two deductions: either they say that the country must have known that the President would change the personnel of the Supreme Court in any case, in the event of his re-election, as rapidly as its present members died, retired, or resigned, or else they say that the Republicans repeatedly charged that the President would do something of the kind that he has now done, and that they thereby made the issue for him.

So far as the first theory is concerned, the President has now shown that he is unwilling to wait for the present members of the court to die, retire or resign. As for the second theory, it must be said that a mandate achieved by the process of failing to reply to the accusation of an adversary is circuitously obtained.

One thing can be said with certainty: the President has no mandate for this plan from those who would have withheld their support from him in the last election had they known during the campaign that he would subsequently pursue this course.

III

The third argument in behalf of the President's proposal is that it represents the wisest and least dangerous course of action available to him in the present circumstances. From this opinion we dissent. The wisest course for MR. ROOSEVELT to follow was the course which this newspaper ventured on more than one occasion to hope that he would follow during his second Administration. This course, as it seemed clearly to be indicated both by the needs of the occasion and by the President's own apparent recognition of these needs, was to consolidate as effectively as possible the gains of the recovery movement; to perfect the many reforms and innovations already introduced, before risking new adventures; to rid the President's office of the vast, unhealthy "war powers" vested in it during the emergency of the depression, rather than to seek still further powers; to restore the normal processes of democratic government in this country, after the storm of 1929-to-1933, by decentralizing the heavily overcentralized authority of the government and by strengthening once more the traditional American system of checks and balances.

That course was the wisest course for the President to pursue. It is not a course from which he was swerved by influences beyond his control. For it is difficult to believe that the present Congress could force on the President a major policy objectionable to him, by a two-thirds vote overriding a Presidential veto.

If, however, MR. ROOSEVELT chose to propose a change in the Constitution or the court, a constitutional amendment giving the country an opportunity to express an opinion directly on the question would have been preferable to the plan which he has followed. There would have been certain inevitable dangers in any amendment which might have been proposed. But at least, this method would have had the merit of meeting the issue squarely, without exposing the Administration to the charge that it has sought to solve a great constitutional question by resort to political cleverness.

SELECTION 38

The New Powers of Government Accepted: The Court Approves the National Labor Relations Act, 1937

*It was the Supreme Court's decision on the constitutionality of the Wagner Act in April, 1937, which gave to the nation its first clear indication that the Court was ready to accept the basic interpretation upon which the New Deal relied. The shift was a narrow one, accomplished by the vote of one man, Mr. Justice Owen Roberts. Roberts had never been a doctrinaire or extreme traditionalist. Before the President's Court plan had been announced, Roberts had already cast his vote in favor of a minimum wage law in the state of Washington, and against a rigorous reading of the due process of law clause as a restriction on the "police power" of the states (*West Coast Hotel Co. v. Parrish*). In the Wagner Act case, he and his colleagues faced a renewed challenge to the narrow interpretation of the commerce clause on the basis of which they had knocked down both NRA and AAA. They faced the challenge at the very moment in which the President was seeking to curb the Court's authority and to bring the Court's views into line with those of the other branches.*

Roberts, along with Hughes, Brandeis, Cardozo, and Stone, cast his prestige on the side of the liberal interpretation of the clause, the view that Congress might regulate whatever affected the broad "stream of commerce" of which a factory or a market might be considered an integral part, rather than a detached and isolated sector immune from Federal regulation. The Court established limits—but they were significantly more liberal to the government than had been the previous ones. And the Court went on to make additional important points: (1) It established clearly the plenary nature of the power to regulate, and (2) it recognized as a "fundamental" right the right of laboring men to organize.

This case represents a revolution, albeit a quiet and orderly one, in the nature of the American Constitution and government. It signaled the national acceptance of a new concept of both the power and the responsibility of the Federal government, and it marked a reestablishment of the independence and authority of the Supreme Court and of its institutionalized right to final decision on the meaning of the law.

While Roosevelt won his battle for broader powers, he lost his skirmish for the realignment of the balances between Court and White House. There is little evidence that he cared much, for it was the green light to legislation and not the authority over the Court that he really wanted. Yet he had paid a high price in terms of loss of prestige, disruption of party unity, destruction of the enthusiastic support necessary for further crusading legislation.

For organized labor, the case was of inestimable importance. It registered the acceptance into the law of the basic proposition upon which it was possible for the right to organize and to strike to be guaranteed by the Federal government, and, eventually, for minimum wages and maximum hours legislation to be assured.

The most useful studies on the subject are Milton Derber and Edwin Young (eds.), Labor and the New Deal *(1957) and Irving Bernstein,* The New Deal Collective Bargaining Policy *(1950).*

The case provided here is National Labor Relations Board v. Jones and Laughlin Steel Company, *301 U.S. 22–49 (1937).*

Mr. Chief Justice Hughes delivered the opinion of the Court.

In a proceeding under the National Labor Relations Act of 1935, the National Labor Relations Board found that the respondent, Jones & Laughlin Steel Corporation, had violated the Act by engaging in unfair labor practices affecting commerce. The proceeding was instituted by the Beaver Valley Lodge No. 200, affiliated with the Amalgamated Association of Iron, Steel and Tin Workers of America, a labor organization. The unfair labor practices charged were that the corporation was discriminating against members of the union with regard to hire and tenure of employment, and was coercing and intimidating its employees in order to interfere with their self-organization. The discriminatory and coercive action alleged was the discharge of certain employees.

The National Labor Relations Board, sustaining the charge, ordered the corporation to cease and desist from such discrimination and coercion, to offer reinstatement to ten of the employees named, to make good their losses in pay, and to post for thirty days notices that the corporation would not discharge or discriminate against members, or those desiring to become members, of the labor union. As the corporation failed to comply, the Board petitioned the Circuit Court of Appeals to enforce the order. The court denied the petition, holding that the order lay beyond the range of federal power. . . . We granted *certiorari*. . . .

Contesting the ruling of the Board, the respondent argues (1) that the Act is in reality a regulation of labor relations and not of interstate commerce; (2) that the Act can have no application to the respondent's relations with its production employees because they are not subject to regulation by the federal government; and (3) that the provisions of the Act violate § 2 of Article 3 and the Fifth and Seventh Amendments of the Constitution of the United States. . . .

The record presents no ground for setting aside the order of the Board so far as the facts pertaining to the circumstances and purpose of the discharge of the employees are concerned. Upon that point it is sufficient to say that the evidence supports the findings of the Board that respondent discharged these men "because of their union activity and for the purpose of discouraging membership in the union." We turn to the questions of law which respondent urges in contesting the validity and application of the Act.

First. The scope of the Act.—The Act is challenged in its entirety as an attempt to regulate all industry, thus invading the reserved powers of the States over their local concerns. It is asserted that the references in the Act to interstate and foreign commerce are colorable at best; that the Act is not a true regulation of such commerce or of matters which directly affect it but on the contrary has the fundamental object of placing under the compulsory supervision of the Federal government all industrial labor relations within the nation. The argument seeks support in the broad words of the preamble (section one) and in the sweep of the provisions of the Act, and it is further insisted that its legislative history shows an essential universal purpose in the light of which its scope cannot be limited by either construction or by the application of the separability clause.

If this conception of terms, intent and consequent inseparability were sound, the Act would necessarily fall by reason of the limitation upon the Federal power which inheres in the constitutional grant, as well as because of the explicit reservation of the Tenth Amendment. . . . The authority of the Federal government may not be pushed to such an extreme as to destroy the distinction, which the commerce clause itself establishes, between commerce "among the several States" and the internal concerns of a State. That distinction between what is national and what is local in the activities of commerce is vital to the maintenance of our Federal system.

But we are not at liberty to deny effect to specific provisions, which Congress has constitutional power to enact, by superimposing upon them inferences from general legislative declarations of an ambiguous character, even if found in the same statute. The cardinal principle of statutory construction is to save and not to destroy. We have repeatedly held that as between two possible interpretations of a statute, by one of which it would be unconstitutional and by the other valid, our plain duty is to adopt that which will save the act. Even to avoid a serious doubt the rule is the same. . . .

We think it clear that the National Labor Relations Act may be construed so as to operate within the sphere of constitutional authority. The jurisdiction conferred upon the Board, and invoked in this instance, is found in § 10 (a), which provides:

> Sec. 10 (a). The Board is empowered, as hereinafter provided, to prevent any person from engaging in any unfair labor practice (listed in § 8) affecting commerce.

The critical words of this provision, prescribing the limits of the Board's authority in dealing with the labor practices, are "affecting commerce." The Act specifically defines the "commerce" to which it refers (§ 2 (6)):

> The term "commerce" means trade, traffic, commerce, transportation, or communication among the several States, or between the District of Columbia or any Territory of the United States and any State or other Territory, or between any foreign country and any State, Territory, or the District of Columbia, or within the District of Columbia or any Territory, or between points in the same State but through any other State or any Territory or the District of Columbia or any foreign country.

There can be no question that the commerce thus contemplated by the Act (aside from that within a Territory or the District of Columbia) is interstate and foreign commerce in the constitutional sense. The Act also defines the term "affecting commerce" (§ 2 (7)):

> The term "affecting commerce" means in commerce, or burdening or obstructing commerce or the free flow of commerce, or having led or tending to lead to a labor dispute burdening or obstructing commerce or the free flow of commerce.

This definition is one of exclusion as well as inclusion. The grant of authority to the Board does not purport to extend to the relationship between all industrial employees and employers. Its terms do not impose collective bargaining upon all industry regardless of effects upon interstate or foreign commerce. It purports to reach only what may be deemed to burden or obstruct that commerce and, thus qualified, it must be construed as contemplating the exercise of control within constitutional bounds. It is a familiar principle that acts which directly burden or obstruct interstate or foreign commerce, or its free flow, are within the reach of the congressional power. Acts having that effect are not rendered immune because they grow out of labor disputes. . . . It is the effect upon commerce, not the source of the injury, which is the criterion. Whether or not particular action does affect commerce in such a close and intimate fashion as to be subject to Federal control, and hence to lie within the authority conferred upon the Board, is left by the statute to be determined as individual cases arise. We are thus to inquire whether in the instant case the constitutional boundary has been passed.

Second. The unfair labor practices in question.—The unfair labor practices found by the Board are those defined in § 8, subdivisions (1) and (3). These provide:

> Sec. 8. It shall be an unfair labor practice for an employer—
>
> (1) To interfere with, restrain, or coerce employees in the exercise of the rights guaranteed in § 7.
>
> (3) By discrimination in regard to hire or tenure of employment or any term or condition of employment to encourage or discourage membership in any labor organization.

Section 8, subdivision (1), refers to § 7, which is as follows:

> Sec. 7. Employees shall have the right to self-organization, to form, join, or assist labor organizations, to bargain collectively through representatives of their own choosing, and to engage in concerted activities, for the purpose of collective bargaining or other mutual aid or protection.

Thus, in its present application, the statute goes no further than to safeguard the right of employees to self-organization and to select representatives of their own choosing for collective bargaining or other mutual protection without restraint or coercion by their employer.

That is a fundamental right. Employees have as clear a right to organize and select their representatives for lawful purposes as the respondent has to organize its business and select its own officers and agents. Discrimination and coercion to prevent the free exercise of the right of employees to self-organization and representation is a proper subject for condemnation by competent legislative authority. Long ago we stated the reason for labor organizations. We said that they were organized out of the necessities of the situation; that a single employee was helpless in dealing with an employer; that he was dependent ordinarily on his daily wage for the maintenance of himself and family; that if the employer refused to pay him the wages that he thought fair, he was nevertheless unable to leave the employ and resist arbitrary and unfair treatment; that union was essential to give laborers opportunity to deal on an equality with their employer. . . . We reiterated these views when we had under consideration the Railway Labor Act of 1926. Fully recognizing the legality of collective action on the part of employees in order to safeguard their proper interests, we said that Congress was not required to ignore this right but could safeguard it. Congress could seek to make appropriate collective action of employees an instrument of peace rather than of strife. We said that such collective action would be a mockery if representation were made futile by interference with freedom of choice. Hence the prohibition by Congress of interference with the selection of representatives for the purpose of negotiation and conference between employers and employees, "instead of being an invasion of the constitutional right of either, was based on the recognition of the rights of both." . . . We have reasserted the same principle in sustaining the application of the Railway Labor Act as amended in 1934.

Third. The application of the Act to employees engaged in production.—The principle involved.—Respondent says that whatever may be said of employees engaged in interstate commerce, the industrial relations and activities in the manufacturing department of respondent's enterprise are not subject to Federal regulation. The argument rests upon the proposition that manufacturing in itself is not commerce. . . .

The Government distinguishes these cases. The various parts of respondent's enterprise are described as interdependent and as thus involving "a great movement of iron ore, coal and limestone along well-defined paths to the steel mills, thence through them, and thence in the form of steel products into the consuming centers of the country—a definite and well-understood course of business." It is urged that these activities constitute a "stream" or "flow" of commerce, of which the Aliquippa manufacturing plant is the focal point, and that industrial strife at that point would cripple the entire movement. . . . Reference is made to our decision sustaining the Packers and Stockyards Act. . . .

The Court found that the stockyards were but a "throat" through which the current of commerce flowed and the transactions which there occurred could not be separated from that movement. Hence the sales at the stockyards were not regarded as merely local transactions, for while they created "a local change of title" they did not "stop the flow," but merely changed the private interests in the subject of the current. . . .

Respondent contends that the instant case presents material distinctions. Respondent says that the Aliquippa plant is extensive in size and represents a large investment in buildings, machinery and equipment. The raw materials which are brought to the plant are delayed for long periods and, after being subjected to manufacturing processes "are changed substantially as to character, utility and value." The finished products which emerge "are to a large extent manufactured without reference to pre-existing orders and contracts and are entirely different from the raw materials which enter at the other end." Hence respondent argues that "If importation and exportation in interstate commerce do not singly transfer purely local activities into the field of congressional regulation, it should follow that their combination would not alter the local situation. . . ."

We do not find it necessary to determine whether these features of defendant's business dispose of the asserted analogy to the "stream of commerce" cases. The instances in which that metaphor has been used are but particular, and not exclusive, illustrations of the protective power which the Government invokes in support of the present Act. The congressional authority to protect interstate commerce from burdens and obstructions is not limited to transactions which can be deemed to be an essential part of a "flow" of interstate or foreign commerce. Burdens and obstructions may be due to injurious action springing from other sources. The fundamental principle is that the power to regulate commerce is the power to enact "all appropriate legislation" for "its protection and advancement. . . ." to adopt measures "to promote its growth and insure its safety . . . to foster, protect, control and restrain. . . ." That power is plenary and may be exerted to protect interstate commerce "no matter what the source of the dangers which threaten it. . . ."

Although activities may be intrastate in character when separately considered, if they have such a close and substantial relation to interstate commerce that their control is essential or appropriate to protect that commerce from burdens and obstructions, Congress cannot be denied the power to exercise that control. Undoubtedly the scope of this power must be considered in the light of our dual system of government and may not be extended so as to embrace effects upon interstate commerce so indirect and remote that to embrace them, in view of our complex society, would effectually obliterate the distinction between what is national and what is local and create a completely centralized government. The question is necessarily one of degree. As the Court said in Board of Trade v. Olsen. . . .

> Whatever amounts to more or less constant practice, and threatens to obstruct or unduly to burden the freedom of interstate commerce is within the regulatory power of Congress under the commerce clause and it is primarily for Congress to consider and decide the fact of the danger and meet it.

That intrastate activities, by reason of close and intimate relations to interstate commerce, may fall within Federal control is demonstrated in the case of carriers who are engaged in both interstate and intrastate transportation. There Federal control has been found essential to secure the freedom of interstate traffic from interference or unjust discrimination and to promote the efficiency of the interstate service. . . . It is manifest that intrastate rates deal *primarily* with a local activity. But in rate-making they bear such a close relation to interstate rates that effective control of the one must embrace some control over the other. Id. Under the Transportation Act of 1920, Congress went so far as to authorize the Interstate Commerce Commission to establish a state-wide level of intrastate rates in order to prevent an unjust discrimination against interstate commerce. . . . Other illustrations are found in the broad requirements of the Safety Appliance Act and the Hours of Service Act. It is said that this exercise of Federal power has relation to the maintenance of adequate instrumentalities of interstate commerce. But the agency is not superior to the commerce which uses it. The protective power extends to the former because it exists as to the latter.

The close and intimate effect which brings the subject within the reach of Federal power may be due to activities in relation to productive industry although the industry when separately viewed is local. . . .

Upon the same principle, the Anti-Trust Act has been applied to the conduct of employees engaged in production. . . .

It is thus apparent that the fact that the employees here concerned were engaged in production is not determinative. The question remains as to the effect upon interstate commerce of the labor practice involved. . . .

Fourth. Effects of the unfair labor practice in respondent's enterprise.—Giving full weight to respondent's contention with respect to a break in the complete continuity of the "stream of commerce" by reason of respondent's manufacturing operations, the fact remains that the stoppage of those operations by industrial strife would have a most serious effect upon interstate commerce. In view of respondent's far-flung activities, it is idle to say that the effect would be indirect or remote. It is obvious that it would be immediate and might be catastrophic. We are asked to shut our eyes to the plainest facts of our national life and to deal with the question of direct and indirect effects in an intellectual vacuum. Because there may be but indirect and remote effects upon interstate commerce in connection with a host of local enterprises throughout the country, it does not follow that other industrial activities do not have such a close and intimate relation to interstate commerce as to make the presence of industrial strife a matter of the most urgent national concern. When industries organize themselves on a national scale, making their relation to interstate commerce the dominant factor in their activities, how can it be maintained that their industrial labor relations constitute a forbidden field into which Congress may not enter when it is necessary to protect interstate commerce from the paralyzing consequences of industrial war? We have often said that interstate commerce itself is a practical conception. It is equally true that interferences with that commerce must be appraised by a judgment that does not ignore actual experience.

Experience has abundantly demonstrated that the recognition of the right of employees to self-organization and to have representatives of their own choosing for the purpose of collective bargaining is often an essential condition of industrial peace. Refusal to confer and negotiate has been one of the most prolific causes of strife. This is such an outstanding fact in the history of labor disturbances that it is a proper subject of judicial notice and requires no citation of instances. . . . But with respect to the appropriateness of the recognition of self-organization and representation in the promotion of peace, the question is not essentially different in the case of employees in industries of such a character that interstate commerce is put in jeopardy from the case of employees of transportation companies. And of what avail is it to protect the facility of transportation, if interstate commerce is throttled with respect to the commodities to be transported!

These questions have frequently engaged the attention of Congress and have been the subject of many inquiries. The steel industry is one of the great basic industries of the United States, with ramifying activities affecting interstate commerce at every point. The Government aptly refers to the steel strike of 1919–1920 with its far-reaching consequences. The fact that there appears to have been no major disturbance in that industry in the more recent period did not dispose of the possibilities of future and like dangers to interstate commerce which Congress was entitled to foresee and to exercise its protective power to forestall. It is not necessary again to detail the facts as to respondent's enterprise. Instead of being beyond the pale, we think that it presents in a most striking way the close and intimate relation which a manufacturing industry may have to interstate commerce and we have no doubt that Congress had constitutional authority to safeguard the right of respondent's employees to self-organization and freedom in the choice of representatives for collective bargaining.

Fifth. The means which the Act employs.—Questions under the due process clause and other constitutional restrictions.—Respondent asserts its right to conduct its business in an orderly manner without being subjected to arbitrary restraints. What we have said points to the fallacy in the argument. Employees have their correlative right to organize for the purpose of securing the redress of grievances and to promote agreements with employers relating to rates of pay and conditions of work.... Restraint for the purpose of preventing an unjust interference with that right cannot be considered arbitrary or capricious. The provision of § 9 (a) that representatives, for the purpose of collective bargaining, of the majority of the employees in an appropriate unit shall be the exclusive representatives of all the employees in that unit, imposes upon the respondent only the duty of conferring and negotiating with the authorized representatives of its employees for the purpose of settling a labor dispute. This provision has its analogue in § 2, Ninth, of the Railway Labor Act which was under consideration in Virginia R. Co. v. System Federation, R. E. D. The decree which we affirmed in that case required the Railway Company to treat with the representative chosen by the employees and also to refrain from entering into collective labor agreements with anyone other than their true representative as ascertained in accordance with the provisions of the Act. We said that the obligation to treat with the true representative was exclusive and hence imposed the negative duty to treat with no other. We also pointed out that, as conceded by the Government, the injunction against the Company's entering into any contract concerning rules, rates of pay and working conditions except with a chosen representative was "designed only to prevent collective bargaining with anyone purporting to represent employees" other than the representative they had selected. It was taken "to prohibit the negotiation of labor contracts generally applicable to employees" in the described unit with any other representative than the one so chosen, "but not as precluding such individual contracts" as the Company might "elect to make directly with individual employees." We think this construction also applies to § 9 (a) of the National Labor Relations Act.

The Act does not compel agreements between employers and employees. It does not compel any agreement whatever. It does not prevent the employer "from refusing to make a collective contract and hiring individuals on whatever terms" the employer "may by unilateral action determine." The Act expressly provides in § 9 (a) that any individual employee or a group of employees shall have the right at any time to present grievances to their employer. The theory of the Act is that free opportunity for negotiation with accredited representatives of employees is likely to promote industrial peace and may bring about the adjustments and agreements which the Act in itself does not attempt to compel. . . .

The Act does not interfere with the normal exercise of the right of the employer to select its employees or to discharge them. The employer may not, under cover of that right, intimidate or coerce its employees with respect to their self-organization and representation, and, on the other hand, the Board is not entitled to make its authority a pretext for interference with the right of discharge when that right is exercised for other reasons than such intimidation and coercion. The true purpose is the subject of investigation with full opportunity to show the facts. It would seem that when employers freely recognize the right of their employees to their own organizations and their unrestricted right of representation there will be much less occasion for controversy in respect to the free and appropriate exercise of the right of selection and discharge.

The Act has been criticised as one-sided in its application; that it subjects the employer to supervision and restraint and leaves untouched the abuses for which employees may be responsible; that it fails to provide a more comprehensive plan,—with better assurances of fairness to both sides and with increased chances of success in bringing about, if not compelling, equitable solutions of industrial disputes affecting interstate commerce. But we are dealing with the power of Congress, not with a particular policy, or with the extent to which policy should go. We have frequently said that the legislative authority, exerted within its proper field, need not embrace all the evils within its reach. The Constitution does not forbid "cautious advance, step by step," in dealing with the evils which are exhibited in activities within the range of legislative power. . . .

The procedural provisions of the Act are assailed. But these provisions, as we construe them, do not offend against the constitutional requirements governing the creation and action of administrative bodies. . . . The Act establishes standards to which the Board must conform. There must be complaint, notice and hearing. The Board must receive evidence and make findings. The findings as to the facts are to be conclusive, but only if supported by evidence. The order of the Board is subject to review by the designated court, and only when sustained by the court may the order be enforced. Upon that review all questions of the jurisdiction of the Board and the regularity of its proceedings, all questions of constitutional right or statutory authority are open to examination by the court. We construe the procedural provisions as affording adequate opportunity to secure judicial protection against arbitrary action in accordance with the well-settled rules applicable to administrative agencies set up by Congress to aid in the enforcement of valid legislation. . . .

Our conclusion is that the order of the Board was within its competency and that the Act is valid as here applied. The judgment of the Circuit Court of Appeals is reversed and the cause is remanded for further proceedings in conformity with this opinion.

Reversed.

The Court Broadens the Rights of Citizens: The Second Flag Salute Case, 1943

Preoccupied with the titanic clash over the New Deal, Americans tended to forget in the 1930s that the most significant role of the courts had always been to provide for the rights of individuals a reliable defense against erratic, arbitrary, or unauthorized exercise of governmental power. In this process, the courts must inevitably act as arbitrators between the rights of the individual and the rights of the group. And just as inevitably it must be the courts which decide the precise definitions of those rights.

In fact, the New Deal cases themselves had turned upon the Supreme Court's definition of individual rights—economic rights. The Agricultural Adjustment Administration, the National Recovery Administration, the National Labor Relations Board, and others had been challenged by individuals and groups who claimed their property rights were being destroyed by the particular act involved. It became the task of the Court to decide where private property rights ended and public power began, but this aspect of the constitutional question had often been overlooked in the national preoccupation with the political and economic questions of larger policy at stake.

When the Court moved away from the crisis of 1937 with its prestige and power intact, there was relatively little consideration of the long-range impact of this fact, aside from the general concern that the "balance" of government and the "separation" of powers be maintained. Perhaps one of the least expected and certainly one of the most significant results was the fact that the Court was able to move firmly and without challenge to the business of readjusting the definitions of individual civil liberties under modern conditions. In general, this readjustment meant two things: (1) an enlargement of the Supreme Court's role as a defender of individual rights and (2) a broadening of the definition of those rights.

Eventually the trends which the Roosevelt Court set in matters of civil liberty would lead in the postwar world to the broadest definitions of freedom of speech yet accepted by the courts, to a considerable strengthening of both religious liberty and the ban against the use of governmental power to strengthen or support a particular religion, and to the most nearly honest interpretation yet achieved of the constitutional barrier against racial discrimination. For the moment, the progress was small. There was little challenge to freedom of speech until the war. There was relatively little activity regarding the procedural rights governing the nature of trials in criminal courts. But the concept of religious liberty was broadened significantly.

The important religious liberty cases were brought by a group usually called Jehovah's Witnesses. Imbued with both a unique missionary spirit and a special objection to acts of patriotic symbolism, they raised a series of new issues in the constant conflict between their spiritual obligations and the world about them. Under the leadership of Justice Hugo Black, the Court proved highly sympathetic. Before the end of the 1940s it had ruled that religious liberty included among other things the right to go from house to house requesting permission to come in and play a religious recording, the right to go through the streets of a city with a sound truck on a Sunday morning preaching a sermon, and, in the cases printed here, the right of children to claim, for religious reasons, exemption from a compulsory flag salute ceremony in school.

Many of the Jehovah's Witnesses' cases involved states rather than the Federal government. The First Amendment was not involved in such cases, but the Fourteenth Amendment was. Providing as it does that "no State shall take the life, liberty or property of a person without due process of law," it gave the Supreme Court great room for maneuver in defining individual rights as against state *power. "Liberty," and "property" were both open-ended words, their meaning being completely at the discretion of the Court. "Due process of law" raised even larger possibilities, for the Court had accepted for over fifty years the concept of substantive due process, as well as that of procedural due process. Procedural due process had always meant simply that appropriate rights and concepts of legislative and judicial procedure must be used.* Substantive *due process was, however, a concept that the very substance of a law, procedure aside, might be so extreme, confiscatory, unusual, or arbitrary as to be beyond all allowance. Thus, when questions of rights against the states were raised, the courts could—in fact must—decide what was appropriate to be claimed as a right, whether the proper procedure had been followed, and finally, whether the alleged violation of the right was so extreme as to be disallowed.*

In their search for a definition of the word "liberty" in the Fourteenth Amendment, the Court increasingly turned to the Federal Bill of Rights. These first ten amendments protected the individual only against the Federal government. Furthermore the Court was not willing to state flatly that the entire Bill of Rights could be applied against the states via the word "liberty" in the Fourteenth Amendment. Yet in case after case, the Court did add specific bits, particularly of the First Amendment, to the meaning of the Fourteenth.

*The Barnette case given below is one of the important milestones in this trend. It is particularly interesting because the issue raised in it was a clearly debatable one. In fact, in the Gobitis case in 1940 (*Minersville School District v. Gobitis*) the Court had ruled that every child in a classroom might be compelled to go through the flag salute. Now, in 1943, the Court was reversing itself and raising the dignity of religious conviction to a new position clearly above at least the ceremonial demands of patriotism.*

The Barnette case was sharply controversial, but it remained the law, and it forecast accurately the liberal spirit of interpretation which characterized the Court's view on matters of personal liberty for the next twenty years.

Particularly useful discussions of the problem are Osmond K. Fraenkel, The Supreme Court and Civil Liberty *(1960), and Paul G. Kauper,* Civil Liberties and the Constitution *(1962).*

The case printed below is West Virginia Board of Education v. Barnette, *319 U.S. 624–671 (1943).*

Mr. Justice Jackson delivered the opinion of the Court:

Following the decision by this Court on June 3, 1940, in Minersville School Dist. v. Gobitis the West Virginia legislature amended its statutes to require all schools therein to conduct courses of instruction in history, civics, and in the Constitutions of the United States and of the State "for the purpose of teaching, fostering and perpetuating the ideals, principles, and spirit of Americanism, and increasing the knowledge of the organization and machinery of the government." Appellant Board of Education was directed, with advice of the State Superintendent of Schools, to "prescribe the courses of study covering these subjects" for public schools. The Act made it the duty of private, parochial and denominational schools to prescribe courses of study "similar to those required for the public schools."

The Board of Education on January 9, 1942, adopted a resolution containing recitals taken largely from the Court's Gobitis opinion and ordering that the salute to the flag become "a regular part of the program of activities in the public schools," that all teachers and pupils "shall be required to participate in the salute honoring the Nation represented by the Flag; provided, however, that refusal to salute the Flag be regarded as an Act of insubordination, and shall be dealt with accordingly."

The resolution originally required the "commonly accepted salute to the Flag" which it defined. Objections to the salute as "being too much like Hitler's" were raised by the Parent and Teachers Association, the Boy and Girl Scouts, the Red Cross, and the Federation of Women's Clubs. Some modification appears to have been made in deference to these objections, but no concession was made to Jehovah's Witnesses. What is now required is the "stiff-arm" salute, the saluter to keep the right hand raised with palm turned up while the following is repeated: "I pledge allegiance to the Flag of the United States of America and to the Republic for which it stands; one Nation, indivisible, with liberty and justice for all."

Failure to conform is "insubordination" dealt with by expulsion. Readmission is denied by statute until compliance. Meanwhile the expelled child is "unlawfully absent" and may be proceeded against as a delinquent. His parents or guardians are liable to prosecution, and if convicted are subject to fine not exceeding $50 and jail term not exceeding thirty days.

Appellees, citizens of the United States and of West Virginia, brought suit in the United States District Court for themselves and others similarly situated asking its injunction to restrain enforcement of these laws and regulations against Jehovah's Witnesses. The Witnesses are an unincorporated body teaching that the obligation imposed by law of God is superior to that of laws enacted by temporal government. Their religious beliefs include a literal version of Exodus, Chapter 20, verses 4 and 5, which says: "Thou shalt not make unto thee any graven image, or any likeness of anything that is in heaven above, or that is in the earth beneath, or that is in the water under the earth; thou shalt not bow down thyself to them, nor serve them." They consider that the flag is an "image" within this command. For this reason they refuse to salute it.

Children of this faith have been expelled from school and are threatened with exclusion for no other cause. Officials threaten to send them to reformatories maintained for criminally inclined juveniles. Parents of such children have been prosecuted and are threatened with prosecutions for causing delinquency.

The Board of Education moved to dismiss the complaint setting forth these facts and alleging that the law and regulations are an unconstitutional denial of religious freedom, and of freedom of speech, and are invalid under the "due process" and "equal protection" clauses of the Fourteenth Amendment to the Federal Constitution. The cause was submitted on the pleadings to a District Court of three judges. It restrained enforcement as to the plaintiffs and those of that class. The Board of Education brought the case here by direct appeal.

This case calls upon us to reconsider a precedent decision, as the Court throughout its history often has been required to do. Before turning to the Gobitis Case, however, it is desirable to notice certain characteristics by which this controversy is distinguished.

The freedom asserted by these appellees does not bring them into collision with rights asserted by any other individual. It is such conflicts which most frequently require intervention of the State to determine where the rights of one end and those of another begin. But the refusal of these persons to participate in the ceremony does not interfere with or deny rights of others to do so. Nor is there any question in this case that their behavior is peaceable and orderly. The sole conflict is between authority and rights of the individual. The State asserts power to condition access to public education on making a prescribed sign and profession and at the same time to coerce attendance by punishing both parent and child. The latter stand on a right of self-determination in matters that touch individual opinion and personal attitude.

As the present Chief Justice said in dissent in the Gobitis Case, the State may "require teaching by instruction and study of all in our history and in the structure and organization of our government, including the guaranties of civil liberty, which tend to inspire patriotism and love of country." . . .

Here, however, we are dealing with a compulsion of students to declare a belief. They are not merely made acquainted with the flag salute so that they may be informed as to what it is or even what it means. The issue here is whether this slow and easily neglected route to arouse loyalties constitutionally may be short-cut by substituting a compulsory salute and slogan. This issue is not prejudiced by the Court's previous holding that where a State, without compelling attendance, extends college facilities to pupils who voluntarily enroll, it may prescribe military training as part of the course without offense to the Constitution. It was held that those who take advantage of its opportunities may not on ground of conscience refuse compliance with such conditions. . . . In the present case attendance is not optional. That case is also to be distinguished from the present one because, independently of college privileges or requirements, the State has power to raise militia and impose the duties of service therein upon its citizens.

There is no doubt that, in connection with the pledges, the flag salute is a form of utterance. Symbolism is a primitive but effective way of communicating ideas. The use of an emblem or flag to symbolize some system, idea, institution, or personality, is a short cut from mind to mind. Causes and nations, political parties, lodges and ecclesiastical groups seek to knit the loyalty of their followings to a flag or banner, a color or design. The State announces rank, function, and authority through crowns and maces, uniforms and black robes; the church speaks through the Cross, the Crucifix, the altar and shrine, and clerical raiment. Symbols of State often convey political ideas just as religious symbols come to convey theological ones. Associated with many of these symbols are appropriate gestures of acceptance or respects, a salute, a bowed or bared head, a bended knee. A person gets from a symbol the meaning he puts into it, and what is one man's comfort and inspiration is another's jest and scorn. . . .

It is also to be noted that the compulsory flag salute and pledge requires affirmation of a belief and an attitude of mind. It is not clear whether the regulation contemplates that pupils forego any contrary convictions of their own and become unwilling converts to the prescribed ceremony or whether it will be acceptable if they simulate assent by words without belief and by a gesture barren of meaning. It is now a commonplace that censorship or suppression of expression of opinion is tolerated by our Constitution only when the expression presents a clear and present danger of action of a kind the State is empowered to prevent and punish. It would seem that involuntary affirmation could be commanded only on even more immediate and urgent grounds than silence. But here the power of compulsion is invoked without any allegation that remaining passive during a flag salute ritual creates a clear and present danger that would justify an effort even to muffle expression. To sustain the compulsory flag salute we are required to say that a Bill of Rights which guards the individual's right to speak his own mind, left it open to public authorities to compel him to utter what is not in his mind.

Whether the First Amendment to the Constitution will permit officials to order observance of ritual of this nature does not depend upon whether as a voluntary exercise we would think it to be good, bad or merely innocuous. Any credo of nationalism is likely to include what some disapprove or to omit what others think essential, and to give off different overtones as it takes on different accents or interpretations. If official power exists to coerce acceptance of any patriotic creed, what it shall contain cannot be decided by courts, but must be largely discretionary with the ordaining authority, whose power to prescribe would no doubt include power to amend. Hence validity of the asserted power to force an American citizen publicly to profess any statement of belief or to engage in any ceremony of assent to one, presents questions of power that must be considered independently of any idea we may have as to the utility of the ceremony in question.

Nor does the issue as we see it turn on one's possession of particular religious views or the sincerity with which they are held. While religion supplies appellees' motive for enduring the discomforts of making the issue in this case, many citizens who do not share these religious views hold such a compulsory rite to infringe constitutional liberty of the individual. It is not necessary to inquire whether nonconformist beliefs will exempt from the duty to salute unless we first find power to make the salute a legal duty.

The Gobitis decision, however, *assumed,* as did the argument in that case and in this, that power exists in the State to impose the flag salute discipline upon school children in general. The Court only examined and rejected a claim based on religious beliefs of immunity from an unquestioned general rule. The question which underlies the flag salute controversy is whether such a ceremony so touching matters of opinion and political attitude may be imposed upon the individual by official authority under powers committed to any political organization under our Constitution. We examine rather than assume existence of this power and, against this broader definition of issues in this case, re-examine specific grounds assigned for the Gobitis decision.

1. It was said that the flag-salute controversy confronted the Court with "the problem which Lincoln cast in memorable dilemma: 'Must a government of necessity be too *strong* for the liberties of its people or too *weak* to maintain its own existence?' " and that the answer must be in favor of strength. . . .

We think these issues may be examined free of pressure or restraint growing out of such considerations.

It may be doubted whether Mr. Lincoln would have thought that the strength of government to maintain itself would be impressively vindicated by our confirming power of the state to expel a handful of children from school. Such oversimplification, so handy in political debate often lacks the precision necessary to postulates of judicial reasoning. If validly applied to this problem, the utterance cited would resolve every issue of power in favor of those in authority and would require us to override every liberty thought to weaken or delay execution of their policies.

Government of limited power need not be anemic government. Assurance that rights are secure tends to diminish fear and jealousy of strong government, and by making us feel safe to live under it makes for its better support. Without promise of a limiting Bill of Rights it is doubtful if our Constitution could have mustered enough strength to enable its ratification. To enforce those rights today is not to choose weak government over strong government. It is only to adhere as a means of strength to individual freedom of mind in preference to officially disciplined uniformity for which history indicates a disappointing and disastrous end.

The subject now before us exemplifies this principle. Free public education, if faithful to the ideal of secular instruction and political neutrality, will not be partisan or enemy of any class, creed, party, or faction. If it is to impose any ideological discipline, however, each party or denomination must seek to control, or failing that, to weaken the influence of the educational system. Observance of the limitations of the Constitution will not weaken government in the field appropriate for its exercise.

2. It was also considered in the Gobitis Case that functions of educa-

tional officers in states, counties and school districts were such that to interfere with their authority "would in effect make us the school board for the country."

The Fourteenth Amendment, as now applied to the States, protects the citizen against the State itself and all of its creatures—Boards of Education not excepted. These have, of course, important, delicate, and highly discretionary functions, but none that they may not perform within the limits of the Bill of Rights. That they are educating the young for citizenship is reason for scrupulous protection of Constitutional freedoms of the individual, if we are not to strangle the free mind at its source and teach youth to discount important principles of our government as mere platitudes.

Such Boards are numerous and their territorial jurisdiction often small. But small and local authority may feel less sense of responsibility to the Constitution, and agencies of publicity may be less vigilant in calling it to account. The action of Congress in making flag observance voluntary and respecting the conscience of the objector in a matter so vital as raising the Army contrasts sharply with these local regulations in matters relatively trivial to the welfare of the nation. There are village tyrants as well as village Hampdens, but none who acts under color of law is beyond reach of the Constitution.

3. The Gobitis opinion reasoned that this is a field "where courts possess no marked and certainly no controlling competence," that it is committed to the legislatures as well as the courts to guard cherished liberties and that it is constitutionally appropriate to "fight out the wise use of legislative authority in the form of public opinion and before legislative assemblies rather than to transfer such a contest to the judicial arena," since all the "effective means of inducing political changes are left free. . . ."

The very purpose of a Bill of Rights was to withdraw certain subjects from the vicissitudes of political controversy, to place them beyond the reach of majorities and officials and to establish them as legal principles to be applied by the courts. One's right to life, liberty, and property, to free speech, a free press, freedom of worship and assembly, and other fundamental rights may not be submitted to vote; they depend on the outcome of no elections.

In weighing arguments of the parties it is important to distinguish between the due process clause of the Fourteenth Amendment as an instrument for transmitting the principles of the First Amendment and those cases in which it is applied for its own sake. The test of legislation which collides with the Fourteenth Amendment, because it also collides with the principles of the First, is much more definite than the test when only the Fourteenth is involved. Much of the vagueness of the due process clause disappears when the specific prohibitions of the First become its standard. The right of a State to regulate, for example, a public utility may well include, so far as the due process test is concerned, power to impose all of the restrictions which a legislature may have a "rational basis" for adopting. But freedoms of speech and of press, of assembly, and of worship may not be infringed on such slender grounds. They are susceptible of restriction only to prevent grave and immediate danger to interests which the state may lawfully protect. It is important to note that while it is the Fourteenth Amendment which bears directly upon the State it is the more specific limiting principles of the First Amendment that finally govern this case.

Nor does our duty to apply the Bill of Rights to assertions of official authority depend upon our possession of marked competence in the field where the invasion of rights occurs. True, the task of translating the majestic generalities of the Bill of Rights, conceived as part of the pattern of liberal government in the eighteenth century, into concrete restraints on officials dealing with the problems of the twentieth century, is one to disturb self-confidence. These principles grew in soil which also produced a philosophy that the individual was the center of society, that his liberty was attainable through mere absence of governmental restraints, and that government should be entrusted with few controls and only the mildest supervision over men's affairs. We must transplant these rights to a soil in which the laissez-faire concept or principle of non-interference has withered at least as to economic affairs, and social advancements are increasingly sought through closer integration of society and through expanded and strengthened governmental controls. These changed conditions often deprive precedents of reliability and cast us more than we would choose upon our own judgment. But we act in these matters not by authority of our competence but by force of our commissions. We cannot, because of modest estimates of our competence in such specialties as public education, withhold the judgment that history authenticates as the function of this Court when liberty is infringed.

4. Lastly, and this is the very heart of the Gobitis opinion, it reasons that "national unity is the basis of national security," that the authorities have "the right to select appropriate means for its attainment," and hence reaches the conclusion that such compulsory measures toward "national unity" are constitutional. Upon the verity of this assumption depends our answer in this case.

National unity as an end which officials may foster by persuasion and example is not in question. The problem is whether under our Constitution compulsion as here employed is a permissible means for its achievement.

Struggles to coerce uniformity of sentiment in support of some end thought essential to their time and country have been waged by many good as well as by evil men. Nationalism is a relatively recent phenomenon but at other times and places the ends have been racial or territorial security, support of a dynasty or regime, and particular plans for saving souls. As first and moderate methods to attain unity have failed, those bent on its accomplishment must resort to an ever increasing severity. As governmental pressure toward unity becomes greater, so strife becomes more bitter as to whose unity it shall be. Probably no deeper division of our people could proceed from any provocation than from finding it necessary to choose what doctrine and whose program public educational officials shall compel youth to unite in embracing. Ultimate futility of such attempts to compel coherence is the lesson of every such effort from the Roman drive to stamp out Christianity as a disturber of its pagan unity, the Inquisition, as a means to religious and dynastic unity, the Siberian exiles as a means to Russian unity, down to the fast failing efforts of our present totalitarian enemies. Those who begin coercive elimination of dissent soon find themselves exterminating dissenters. Compulsory unification of opinion achieves only the unanimity of the graveyard.

It seems trite but necessary to say that the First Amendment to our Constitution was designed to avoid these ends by avoiding these beginnings. There is no mysticism in the American concept of the State or of the nature or origin of its authority. We set up government by consent of the governed, and the Bill of Rights denies those in power any legal opportunity to coerce that consent. Authority here is to be controlled by public opinion, not public opinion by authority.

The case is made difficult not because the principles of its decision are obscure but because the flag involved is our own. Nevertheless, we apply the limitations of the Constitution with no fear that freedom to be intellectually and spiritually diverse or even contrary will disintegrate the social organization. To believe that patriotism will not flourish if patriotic ceremonies are voluntary and spontaneous instead of a compulsory routine is to make an unflattering estimate of the appeal of our institutions to free minds. We can have intellectual individualism and the rich cultural diversities that we owe to exceptional minds only at the price of occasional eccentricity and abnormal attitudes. When they are so harmless to others or to the State as those we deal with here, the price is not too great. But freedom to differ is not limited to things that do not matter much. That would be a mere shadow of freedom. The test of its substance is the right to differ as to things that touch the heart of the existing order.

If there is any fixed star in our constitutional constellation, it is that no official, high or petty, can prescribe what shall be orthodox in politics, nationalism, religion, or other matters of opinion or force citizens to confess by word or act their faith therein. If there are any circumstances which permit an exception, they do not now occur to us.

We think the action of the local authorities in compelling the flag salute and pledge transcends constitutional limitations on their power and invades the sphere of intellect and spirit which it is the purpose of the First Amendment to our Constitution to reserve from all official control.

The decision of this Court in Minersville School Dist. v. Gobitis and the holdings of those few per curiam decisions which preceded and foreshadowed it are overruled, and the judgment enjoining enforcement of the West Virginia Regulation is affirmed.

A Small Step toward Racial Equality: The Mitchell Case, 1941

The same Court which rushed to the defense of religious liberty undertook gradually to explore the thorny jungle of race discrimination in the law. During the long period since 1876, two things had conspired to provide a curtain behind which the states, despite the Fourteenth Amendment, could develop an elaborate structure of official discrimination, officially sponsored inequality. One was the interpretation of the "equal protection of the laws" clause of the Fourteenth Amendment. Since Plessy v. Ferguson *[163 U.S. 537 (1896)], "equal" had meant "equal but separate," and the equality had in fact been nonexistent. The second was the sheer fact that the Federal courts had neither the machinery, the traditions, nor the desire to enter the South and make* de facto *judgments regarding "equality." The result had been an Orwellian kind of situation in which "equal" meant "unequal," and all the world except the Supreme Court had known it.*

The Mitchell case printed below was a particularly significant turning point in the Court's treatment of race discrimination. It follows the Plessy v. Ferguson *tradition in insisting that segregation per se is not illegal but that* unequal *segregation is. But it goes farther than previous cases in insisting that equal treatment by a state government is a right not to be abated simply because equality would be inconvenient, impractical, or expensive. Further, the Court insists that the equality must be real. It would be another decade before the Court would be willing to subscribe to the argument that separate facilities could never be equal. For the moment, however, the Mitchell case represented a considerable step forward in the fight to implement the Fourteenth Amendment.*

On this question and others involving Negro history, see John Hope Franklin, From Slavery to Freedom *(1947). On civil rights questions, among the more useful volumes are Robert K. Carr,* Federal Protection of Civil Rights: Quest for a Sword *(1947), and Milton R. Konvitz,* A Century of Civil Rights *(1961).*

The excerpt given here is from Mitchell v. United States, *et al., 313 U.S. 88–97 (1941).*

Mr. Chief Justice Hughes delivered the opinion of the Court: . . . Appellant, a Negro resident of Chicago, and a member of the House of Representatives of the United States, left Chicago for Hot Springs on the evening of April 20, 1937, over the lines of the Illinois Central Railroad Company to Memphis, Tennessee, and the Rock Island beyond, traveling on a round-trip ticket he had purchased at three cents per mile. He had requested a bedroom on the Chicago-Hot Springs Pullman sleeping car but none being available he was provided with a compartment as far as Memphis in the sleeper destined to New Orleans. Just before the train reached Memphis, on the morning after leaving Chicago, he had a Pullman porter transfer him to the Chicago-Hot Springs sleeper on the same train. Space was there available and the porter assigned him a particular seat in that car for which he was to pay the established fare of ninety cents. Shortly after leaving Memphis and crossing the Mississippi River into Arkansas, the train conductor took up the Memphis-Hot Springs portion of his ticket but refused to accept payment for the Pullman seat from Memphis and, in accordance with custom, compelled him over his protest and finally under threat of arrest to move into the car provided for colored passengers. This was in purported compliance with an Arkansas statute requiring segregation of colored from white persons by the use of cars or partitioned sections providing "equal, but separate and sufficient accommodations" for both races. Later the conductor returned the portion of the ticket he had taken up and advised the appellant that he could get a refund on the basis of the coach fare of two cents per mile from Memphis. That refund was not claimed from defendants and was not sought before the Commission, but it was found that the carriers stood ready to make it upon application. . . .

The Commission further found that the Pullman car contained ten sections of berths and two compartment drawing rooms; that the use of one of the drawing rooms would have amounted to segregation under the state law and ordinarily such combinations are available to colored passengers upon demand, the ninety cent fare being applicable. Occasionally they are used by colored passengers but in this instance both drawing rooms were already occupied by white passengers. The Pullman car was of modern design and had all the usual facilities and conveniences found in standard sleeping cars. It was air-conditioned, had hot and cold running water and separate flushable toilets for men and women. It was in excellent condition throughout. First-class white passengers had, in addition to the Pullman sleeper, the exclusive use of the train's only dining-car and only observation-parlor car, the latter having somewhat the same accommodations for day use as the Pullman car.

The coach for colored passengers, though of standard size and steel construction, was "an old combination affair," not air-conditioned, divided by partitions into three main parts, one for colored smokers, one for white smokers and one in the center for colored men and women, known as the women's section, in which appellant sat. There was a toilet in each section but only the one in the women's section was equipped for flushing and it was for the exclusive use of colored women. The car was without wash basins, soap, towels, or running water, except in the women's section. The Commission stated that, according to appellant, the car was "filthy and foul smelling," but that the testimony of defendants' witnesses was to the contrary.

The Commission found that in July, 1937, about three months after complainant's journey above mentioned, the old combination coach was replaced by a modern, all-steel, air-conditioned coach, which was divided by a partition into two sections, one for colored and the other for white passengers, and had comfortable seats. In each section there are wash basins, running hot and cold water, "and separate flush toilets for men and women." This coach, the Commission said, was "as fully desirable in all its appointments as the coach used entirely by white passengers traveling at second-class fares."

The Commission also found that the demand of colored passengers for Pullman accommodations over the route in question was shown to have been negligible for many years; that "only about one negro to twenty white passengers rides this train from and to points on the line between Memphis and Hot Springs," and there is hardly ever a demand from a colored passenger for Pullman accommodations. The conductor estimated that this demand did not amount to one per year. What demand there may have been at ticket offices did not appear.

The Commission's conclusion was thus stated: "The present coach properly takes care of colored second-class passengers, and the drawing rooms and compartments in the sleeper provide proper Pullman accommodations for colored first-class passengers, but there are no dining-car nor observation-parlor car accommodations for the latter, and they cannot lawfully range through the train."

The Commission, though treating the enforcement of the state law as a matter for state authorities, thought that in deciding the case on the facts presented it must recognize that the state law required the defendants to segregate colored passengers; that in these circumstances the present colored-passenger coach and the Pullman drawing rooms met the requirements of the Act; and that as there was comparatively little colored traffic and no indication that there was likely to be such demand for dining-car and observation-parlor car accommodations by colored passengers as to warrant the running of any extra cars or the construction of partitions, the discrimination and prejudice was "plainly not unjust or undue." The Commission observed that it was only differences in treatment of the latter character that were "unlawful and within the power of this Commission to condemn, remove and prevent."

From the dismissal of the complaint, five Commissioners dissented. . . . The undisputed facts showed conclusively that, having paid a first-class fare for the entire journey from Chicago to Hot Springs, and having offered to pay the proper charge for a seat which was available in the Pullman car for the trip from Memphis to Hot Springs, he was compelled, in accordance with custom, to leave that car and ride in a second-class car and was thus denied the standard conveniences and privileges afforded to first-class passengers. This was manifestly a discrimination against him in the course of his interstate journey and admittedly that discrimination was based solely upon the fact that he was a Negro. The question whether this was a discrimination forbidden by the Interstate Commerce Act is not a question of segregation but one of equality of treatment. The denial to appellant of equality of accommodations because of his race would be an invasion of a fundamental individual right which is guaranteed against state action by the Fourteenth Amendment. . . . and in view of the nature of the right and of our constitutional policy it cannot be maintained that the discrimination as it was alleged was not essentially unjust. In that aspect it could not be deemed to lie outside the purview of the sweeping prohibitions of the Interstate Commerce Act.

We have repeatedly said that it is apparent from the legislative history of the Act that not only was the evil of discrimination the principal thing aimed at, but that there is no basis for the contention that Congress intended to exempt any discriminatory action or practice of interstate carriers affecting interstate commerce which it had authority to reach. . . . We find no sound reason for the failure to apply this principle by holding the discrimination from which the appellant suffered to be unlawful and by forbidding it in the future.

That there was but a single instance was not a justification of the treatment of the appellant. Moreover, the Commission thought it plain that "the incident was mentioned as representative of an alleged practice that was expected to continue." And the Commission found that the ejection of appellant from the Pullman car and the requirement that he should continue his journey in a second-class car was "in accordance with custom," that is, as we understand it, according to the custom which obtained in similar circumstances.

Nor does the change in the carrier's practice avail. That did not alter the discrimination to which appellant had been subjected, and as to the future the change was not adequate. It appears that since July, 1937, the carrier has put in service a coach for colored passengers which is of equal quality with that used by second-class white passengers. But, as the Government well observes, the question does not end with travel on second-class tickets. It does not appear that colored passengers who have bought first-class tickets for transportation by the carrier are given accommodations which are substantially equal to those afforded to white passengers. The Government puts the matter succinctly: "When a drawing room is available, the carrier practice of allowing colored passengers to use one at Pullman seat rates avoids inequality as between the accommodations specifically assigned to the passenger. But when none is available, as on the trip which occasioned this litigation, the discrimination and inequality of accommodation become self-evident. It is no answer to say that the colored passengers, if sufficiently diligent and forehanded, can make their reservations so far in advance as to be assured of first-class accommodations. So long as white passengers can secure first-class reservations on the day of travel and the colored passengers cannot, the latter are subjected to inequality and discrimination because of their race." And the Commission has recognized that inequality persists with respect to certain other facilities such as dining-car and observation-parlor car accommodations.

We take it that the chief reason for the Commission's action was the "comparatively little colored traffic." But the comparative volume of traffic cannot justify the denial of a fundamental right of equality of treatment, a right specifically safeguarded by the provisions of the Interstate Commerce Act. We thought a similar argument with respect to volume of traffic to be untenable in the application of the Fourteenth Amendment. We said that it made the constitutional right depend upon the number of persons who may be discriminated against, whereas the essence of that right is that it is a personal one. . . . While the supply of particular facilities may be conditioned upon there being a reasonable demand therefor, if facilities are provided, substantial equality of treatment of persons traveling under like conditions cannot be refused. It is the individual, we said, who is entitled to the equal protection of the laws,—not merely a group of individuals, or a body of persons according to their numbers. . . . And the Interstate Commerce Act expressly extends its prohibitions to the subjecting of "any particular person" to unreasonable discriminations.

On the facts here presented, there is no room, as the Government properly says, for administrative or expert judgment with respect to practical difficulties. It is enough that the discrimination shown was palpably unjust and forbidden by the Act.

The decree of the District Court is reversed and the cause is remanded with directions to set aside the order of the Commission and to remand the case to the Commission for further proceedings in conformity with this opinion.

Reversed.

PART SIX

Reluctant Involvement: Foreign Policy, 1929–1938

In the winter of 1919–1920 the Senate had repudiated Woodrow Wilson's League of Nations, and with it the treaties which had ended the First World War and reconstructed the map of Europe. But there were some responsibilities the nation could *not ignore; in August, 1921, the United States signed its own separate peace treaties with Germany, Austria, and Hungary. And there were some responsibilities the nation did not* wish *to ignore. American policy makers had been particularly concerned with two broad questions. The first was the prevention of an arms race, which, it was thought, might lead to yet another world war, and which would be in any case disastrously expensive. Almost equally significant from an American point of view was the creation of arrangements in East Asia and the Pacific which would limit the increasingly vigorous, expansionist role which Japan might be expected to play in that area, now that Russia had been debilitated by revolution, France and England had been weakened by war, and Germany had been removed from the scene completely.*

That the United States was unwilling to ignore either of these problems suggests that its foreign policy cannot exactly be labeled as one of "isolationism." It was, of course, a nationalist policy, perhaps even an irresponsible one, for American diplomats undermined the very position they staked out by refusing to make arrangements for action in case the treaties be broken. But, if isolationism means a retreat from the rest of the world, a refusal to be concerned beyond one's own borders, then this was not an isolationist policy.

Under the leadership of Secretary of State Charles Evans Hughes (1862–1948) the Harding administration sponsored the Washington Conference of 1921, inviting the major powers, Great Britain, France, Italy, and Japan, as well as four "minor" powers with particular interests in East Asia, Belgium, China, the Netherlands, and Portugal. The results were (1) the so-called Four-Power Treaty to stabilize the Pacific and prevent further armament of the islands; (2) an agreement for the limitation of naval growth by certain prearranged ratios, the Five-Power Treaty; and (3) a Nine-Power Treaty, signed in February, 1922, in which all the powers with East Asian interests agreed to respect the "sovereignty, the independence and the territorial and administrative integrity of China."

At the end of December, 1927, Secretary of State Frank B. Kellogg (1856–1937) suggested the device which became both the capstone of the United States postwar foreign policy and also a major ground for the ridicule directed against American foreign policy in this period. Building upon a more limited suggestion by the French Foreign Minister, Aristide Briand, Kellogg proposed a multilateral treaty to "outlaw" war as an instrument of national policy. The treaty was signed in August, 1928. Eventually over sixty nations subscribed to it.

There was no machinery for the enforcement of any of these treaty obligations, and they would all fail. Leaders of American foreign policy proved unrealistic in their conceptions of world problems. But much more important was the fact that Americans, being reluctant to undertake obligations, were powerless to demand them of others.

The great stock market crash of 1929 and the concomitant Depression made much of American foreign policy appear either outmoded or simply irrelevant. The Hoover administration sought to continue the lines of development suggested by the Washington Conference Treaties at the London Naval Conference of 1930 and the Geneva Disarmament Conference of 1932, but with little result. Instead, it was forced to deal with the first major bankruptcy of its policy when Japan invaded Manchuria during September, 1931, in open violation of the Kellogg-Briand Pact. It was forced increasingly to face dilemmas of economic foreign policy as world markets decreased with Depression. War debts to the United States were defaulted, and the demands increased at home for even higher tariff barriers.

For the first Roosevelt administration, foreign policy was at best a peripheral matter. It was largely a holding operation, designed to keep the nation as much disengaged as possible and to preserve the largest possible amount of freedom of action for the United States in the solution of its economic problems. FDR appears to have viewed the Depression as one of essentially domestic origins. He certainly viewed the problem of recovery as a domestic challenge. In June of 1933, after considerable initial con-

fusion, he "torpedoed" the London Economic Conference, with a sharp message refusing, for the moment, American cooperation in the stabilization of international exchange rates. He had sent delegates with ambiguous instructions, reflecting his own uncertainties regarding foreign policy during his first months in the White House. Now, when forced to choose, he cast his vote against international agreement and in favor of the freedom he wanted in order to maneuver prices at home. The continuing naval disarmament discussions he could treat with ease. It was all but ordained that they should fail and Roosevelt could make the gesture of participating without any real commitment. He continued to press fruitlessly for Senate approval of the World Court, but American participation in the League of Nations he had long since abandoned as impossible.

FDR could virtually ignore Europe and make impotent gestures against Japanese aggression in Asia, but with the Latin American nations he could do neither. They were too close. The United States was too intimately involved. And there already were precedents, stretching all the way back into the Wilson administration, for a more liberal and permissive policy, for a moderation of the old imperialism of Dogface and Dollar. In handling the nation's relationships with Europe and Asia before 1937, Roosevelt would work haphazardly and reluctantly, merely responding to the pressures of occasional events. But in the affairs of the Western Hemisphere he would lead vigorously in the development of a consistent policy.

Foster R. Dulles, America's Rise to World Power: 1898–1955 *(1955), and Jean Baptiste Duroselle,* From Wilson to Roosevelt: The Foreign Policy of the United States, 1913–1945 *(1963) are particularly recommended as surveys of the foreign policy of this era. For a brief treatment, see Allan Nevins,* The New Deal and World Affairs *(1950). See also, for the Hoover administration's policies, Robert Ferrell,* American Diplomacy and the Great Depression *(1957). Especially valuable among the memoirs are Cordell Hull,* The Memoirs of Cordell Hull *(1948), two volumes, and Henry L. Stimson and McGeorge Bundy,* On Active Service in Peace and War *(1948).*

Transition to the "Good Neighbor": Cordell Hull Redefines the Monroe Doctrine, 1933

In December, 1933, the administration faced a major inter-American conference at Montevideo, Uruguay. Latin American nations were eager to test the temper and direction of this new leadership in Washington. Yet Roosevelt was prepared to be no more specific than necessary, to incur no more commitments than essential. There was a danger that the other nations, under Argentina's leadership, would insist upon a sharper repudiation of United States intervention than Washington wished.

Under the circumstances, Roosevelt sent Secretary of State Cordell Hull (1871–1955) to Montevideo with careful instructions to avoid such fundamental issues as mutual defense and repudiation of intervention and to emphasize harmless matters like the plan for an inter-American highway or the blueprinting of a network of airfields. Hull was unable to hold the line all the way. He was compelled to approve gracefully a strong Argentine-supported resolution against intervention by any American nation in the affairs of another.

Hull's instructions to his delegation regarding their handling of the "Monroe Doctrine" at the conference is very revealing. It includes the President's golden phrases about the "good neighbor." But it also contains an unusually frank statement of the selfish and unilateral nature of the Monroe Doctrine and of the administration's intention to keep it that way.

It is perhaps significant that Hull chose to quote from a famous State Department memorandum on the Monroe Doctrine by Reuben Clark (1928) only those parts which underline the unilateral nature of the policy, and to leave aside that section of it which suggested that the Monroe Doctrine could not provide legal cover for United States intervention in the internal affairs of another nation.

Regarding American policy in the Western Hemisphere generally, the essential book is Dexter Perkins, A History of the Monroe Doctrine *(1955). Also useful are Samuel Flagg Bemis,* The Latin-American Policy of the United States *(1943); Alexander De Conde,* Herbert Hoover's Latin-American Policy *(1951); Edward Guerrant,* Roosevelt's Good Neighbor Policy *(1950); and Bryce Wood,* The Making of the Good Neighbor Policy *(1961).*

The document here is from U.S. Department of State, Foreign Relations of the United States: 1933 *(Washington: Government Printing Office, 1949), volume 4, pages 137–139.*

It is not the desire of this Government that the Monroe Doctrine should be discussed at the Conference.

In the view of this Government, that Doctrine has no place in the discussions of the Conference as it is essentially a national policy of the United States. It is not a part of international law nor is it a "regional understanding," to refer to the inaccurate phrase used in the Covenant of the League of Nations. While conditions have changed, and the attitude of the non-American Powers does not at this time give rise to apprehension with respect to aggression on their part as against at least the stronger Latin American Republics, still the Monroe Doctrine, however infrequent or limited may be the necessity of its application, should be maintained in its integrity and no action should be countenanced by this Government which would in the slightest degree impair its efficacy.

Note may be taken of the content of this Doctrine. Properly understood, it is opposed (*a*) to any non-American action encroaching upon the political independence of American States under any guise, and (*b*) to any acquisition by any non-American Power of any territorial control over American soil by any process whatever. It may be observed that the United States is uninfluenced even by the willingness or desire of an American State to yield any transfer of its territory or to submit to any form of political control or influence of a non-American State. In maintaining its position, the United States has been governed primarily by its own interests, involving its conception of what was essential to its security and its distinctive position in this hemisphere. Its unselfish and friendly regard for its American neighbors has had a potent influence and should never fail of recognition in an estimate of our traditional policy, but the controlling consideration has been one of national interest.

Mr. J. Reuben Clark, in his memorandum to the Secretary of State of December 17, 1928, pertinently stated:

> The Doctrine does not concern itself with purely inter-American relations; it has nothing to do with the relationship between the United States and other American nations, except where other American nations shall become involved with European governments in arrangements which threaten the security of the United States, and even in such cases, the Doctrine runs against the European country, not the American nation, and the United States would primarily deal thereunder with the European country and not with the American nation concerned. The Doctrine states a case of the United States *vs.* Europe, and not of the United States *vs.* Latin America. Furthermore, the fact should never be lost to view that in applying this Doctrine during the period of one hundred years since it was announced, our Government has over and over again driven it in as a shield between Europe and the Americas to protect Latin America from the political and territorial thrusts of Europe; and this was done at times when the American nations were weak and struggling for the establishment of stable, permanent governments; when the political morality of Europe sanctioned, indeed encouraged, the acquisition of territory by force; and when many of the great powers of Europe looked with eager, covetous eyes to the rich, undeveloped areas of the American hemisphere.

In maintaining and applying the Monroe Doctrine the United States has commonly avoided concerted action with other States, especially European States. Nor has the Government of the United States been disposed to enter into an arrangement with States of this hemisphere for the purpose of safeguarding them against conduct which would be regarded by this Government as in violation of the Monroe Doctrine. The essential character of the Doctrine itself has led to the taking of this attitude which it is believed should be maintained. The nature of the Doctrine should not be altered, its strength weakened or its effect diminished by any concert.

On the other hand, it should always be remembered that the Monroe Doctrine thus fully maintained as a national policy of the United States, carries with it no suggestion which threatens in any sense the just independence, or the political integrity of the American States; much less does it involve any thought of action inimical to their security or interest. On the contrary, it has received a constantly widening recognition on the part of thoughtful Latin Americans, as a bulwark of their independence, safety and progress. The United States has not, and does not intend to use, this national policy for the purpose of conserving any other national interest than its own essential security. The United States seeks no territory; it does not seek to establish any state of tutelage with respect to any American Republic; it has no desire to aggrandize itself at the expense of its Latin American neighbors or to promote selfish interests in diminution of their own. It earnestly desires a common prosperity.

There is thus nothing in the Monroe Doctrine which is opposed to Pan American cooperation. It establishes the necessary and most hopeful bases of that cooperation. As stated by President Roosevelt before the Special Session of the Governing Board of the Pan American Union on the occasion of the celebration of Pan American Day, April 12, 1933:

> The essential qualities of a true Pan Americanism must be the same as those which constitute a good neighbor, namely, mutual understanding, and, through such understanding, a sympathetic appreciation of the other's point of view. It is only in this manner that we can hope to build up a system of which confidence, friendship and good-will are the cornerstones.
>
> In this spirit the people of every Republic on our continent are coming to a deep understanding of the fact that the Monroe Doctrine, of which so much has been written and spoken for more than a century, was and is directed at the maintenance of independence by the peoples of the continent. It was aimed and is aimed against the acquisition in any manner of the control of additional territory in this hemisphere by any non-American power.

No arrangement should be entered into, or resolution agreed to, which could possibly be interpreted as curtailing in any way the application by the United States of the Monroe Doctrine. There should be no opening for the limitation of its action in that application through acquiescence in any arrangement whereby an American State could accept non-American control of its territory or political action. No opportunity should be given to a non-American state through any Pan American agreement to seek to impair the position which the United States has won through its assertion of its national policy.

This Government, however, has no objection to the adoption of resolutions, if this course is desired by the Latin American Republics, asserting their opposition to all attempts at aggression or invasion of their rights by non-American Powers. . . .

A Step toward Latin-American Cooperation: The Declaration of Lima, 1938

Throughout the five years after the Montevideo Conference, the policy of the United States gradually moved toward the development of institutions for inter-American cooperation and defense. Frequent hemispheric conferences were supported by the United States to provide a milieu for the resolution of differences and an atmosphere in which the old charge of Yankee imperialism might be dampened. As the Eighth Conference met at Lima, in December, 1938, the Western Hemisphere nations were already concerned over the increasing tensions in Europe and the evident build-up of German and Italian influence in South America. This was the year of Munich.

The two sets of principles adopted at Lima clearly indicate the direction being taken by international relations in the Western Hemisphere. But they indicate also that the United States and its neighbors were still thinking in terms of general cooperation, rather than the specific institutions for mutual defense which would be worked out later in the conference at Havana (1940).

The Lima Declarations are taken from U.S. Department of State, Peace and War: United States Foreign Policy, 1931–1941 *(Washington: Government Printing Office, 1943), pages 439–441. This volume will be cited hereafter simply as* Peace and War.

The Eighth International Conference of American States,

Considering:

That the peoples of America have achieved spiritual unity through the similarity of their republican institutions, their unshakable will for peace, their profound sentiment of humanity and tolerance, and through their absolute adherence to the principles of international law, of the equal sovereignty of states and of individual liberty without religious or racial prejudices;

That on the basis of such principles and will, they seek and defend the peace of the continent and work together in the cause of universal concord;

That respect for the personality, sovereignty, and independence of each American state, constitutes the essence of international order sustained by continental solidarity, which historically has found expression in declarations of various states, or in agreements which were applied, and sustained by new declarations and by treaties in force; that the Inter-American Conference for the Maintenance of Peace, held at Buenos Aires, approved on December 21, 1936, the declaration of the principles of inter-American solidarity and cooperation, and approved, on December 23, 1936, the protocol of nonintervention; the Governments of the American States

Declare:

First. That they reaffirm their continental solidarity and their purpose to collaborate in the maintenance of the principles upon which the said solidarity is based;

Second. That faithful to the above-mentioned principles and to their absolute sovereignty, they reaffirm their decision to maintain them and to defend against all foreign intervention or activity that may threaten them;

Third. And in case the peace, security or territorial integrity of any American republic is thus threatened by acts of any nature that may impair them, they proclaim their common concern and their determination to make effective their solidarity, coordinating their respective sovereign wills by means of the procedure of consultation, established by conventions in force and by declarations of the inter-American conferences, using the measures which in each case the circumstances may make advisable. It is understood that the Governments of the American Republics will act independently in their individual capacity, recognizing fully their juridical equality as sovereign states;

Fourth. That in order to facilitate the consultations established in this and other American peace instruments, the Ministers for Foreign Affairs of the American Republics, when deemed desirable and at the initiative of anyone of them, will meet in their several capitals by rotation and without protocolary character. Each government may, under special circumstances or for special reasons, designate a representative as a substitute for its Minister for Foreign Affairs;

Fifth. This declaration shall be known as the "Declaration of Lima."

Declaration of American Principles by the Eighth International Conference of American States, December 24, 1938

Declaration of American Principles:

Whereas

The need for keeping alive the fundamental principles of relations among nations was never greater than today; and

Each state is interested in the preservation of world order under law, in peace with justice, and in the social and economic welfare of mankind.

The Governments of the American Republics resolve

To proclaim, support and recommend, once again, the following principles, as essential to the achievement of the aforesaid objectives:

1. The intervention of any state in the internal or external affairs of another is inadmissible;
2. All differences of international character should be settled by peaceful means;
3. The use of force as an instrument of national or international policy is proscribed;
4. Relations between states should be governed by the precepts of international law;
5. Respect for and the faithful observance of treaties constitute the indispensable rule for the development of peaceful relations between states, and treaties can only be revised by agreement of the contracting parties;
6. Peaceful collaboration between representatives of the various states and the development of intellectual interchange among their peoples is conducive to an understanding by each of the problems of the other as well as of problems common to all, and makes more readily possible the peaceful adjustment of international controversies;
7. Economic reconstruction contributes to national and international well-being, as well as to peace among nations; and
8. International cooperation is a necessary condition to the maintenance of the aforementioned principles.

SELECTION 43

Japanese Aggression and Impotent Protest: The Stimson Doctrine, 1931

Although the location was distant, events in Manchuria in the late 1920s and early 1930s represented a far greater threat to American security than anything likely to take place in Latin America. Few Americans recognized this at first. But, by the autumn of 1931, Japanese armed expansion in Manchuria had become a matter of deep concern not only to Britain and France in the League of Nations but also to President Hoover and Secretary of State Henry L. Stimson. It was a complicated problem for American diplomacy. The Chinese were weak. Russian intervention was also a possibility. The United States was clearly unwilling, perhaps unable, to commit any considerable military force in the area. And the whole was further complicated by the question of whether the United States should cooperate with the League of Nations, which it had refused to join.

Hoover and Stimson finally decided to launch a line of protest parallel to that of the League of Nations but to avoid actual joint action. Hoover was set against any policy which might lead to war. He viewed economic sanctions as carrying such a danger. Under the circumstances, the Stimson protests carried little weight. His note of October 20, 1931, printed below, reminding Japan of her obligations under the Kellogg-Briand Pact to outlaw war, is a pitiful case in point. His final position, made clear to Japan and China on January 7, 1932, was little, if any, more influential. It refused United States recognition to conquests made in violation of the Kellogg-Briand Pact. Yet Stimson's diplomacy recognized the realities of the situation in East Asia more concretely than they would be recognized again in public policy until the Second World War had begun.

United States Far Eastern foreign policy is usefully discussed in T. A. Bisson, American Policy in the Far East: 1931–1941 *(1941); Joseph C. Grew,* Ten Years in Japan *(1944) and* Turbulent Era: A Diplomatic Record of Forty Years, 1904–1945 *(1952), two volumes; Herbert Feis,* The Road to Pearl Harbor *(1950); and the recent biography of Stimson by Elting Morison,* Turmoil and Tradition *(1960). Especially useful on the subject of the roles of the President and the Secretary of State in the development of the policy toward Japan is Richard N. Current, "The Stimson Doctrine and the Hoover Doctrine,"* American Historical Review, *volume 59, April, 1954, pages 513–542.*

The note published below is from Peace and War, *pages 158–159.*

The Government and people of the United States have observed with concern the events of the last month in Manchuria. When the difference between Japan and China came to a head on September 19th one of the parties to the dispute referred the matter to the League of Nations and since that time the American Government by representations through diplomatic channels, has steadily cooperated with the League in its efforts to secure a peaceful settlement. A threat of war, wherever it may arise, is of profound concern to the whole world and for this reason the American Government, like other Governments, was constrained to call to the attention of both disputants the serious dangers involved in the present situation.

This Government now desires, as do other signatories of the Treaty for the Renunciation of War, particularly to call to the attention of the Japanese and the Chinese Governments the obligations which they voluntarily assumed when they became parties to that Treaty, especially the obligations of Article II, which reads:

> The High Contracting Parties agree that the settlement or solution of all disputes or conflicts of whatever nature or of whatever origin they may be, which may arise among them, shall never be sought except by pacific means.

The American Government takes this occasion again to express its earnest hope that Japan and China will refrain from any measures which might lead to war and that they will find it possible in the near future to agree upon a method for resolving by peaceful means, in accordance with their promises and in keeping with the confident expectations of public opinion throughout the world, the issues over which they are at present in controversy.

SELECTION 44

A Warning from Tokyo: Ambassador Grew Reports and Prophesies, 1934

The threat posed to the stability of Eastern Asia by the Japanese expansion remained one of the facts of international life throughout the whole decade. The gestures of reprimand made by the League of Nations, President Hoover, and Secretary Stimson proved of little effect, at first. The conquest of Manchuria was complete by January, 1932. In September, the puppet state of Manchukuo was set up. Meanwhile, the undeclared war had raged into North China, and Shanghai had been occupied by the Japanese. Late in May, 1933, the invaders withdrew from Shanghai, reluctantly responding to an aroused world opinion. But they had accomplished for the moment their major objective. Manchuria was an economic and political satellite and was firmly established as a military buffer against the Soviet Union.

American policy was indecisive after the spring of 1932. Both Hoover and Roosevelt were preoccupied with the nation's economic problems. Neither was anxious to face a crisis in Asia. At the end of December, 1934, Japan created a new dimension to the issue by announcing that it would no longer be bound by the Washington Naval Treaty of 1922. In the negotiations leading to the Second London Naval Conference she sought parity with the United States and Great Britain. The United States refused, and Japan finally withdrew from the conference on January 15, 1936.

Although the United States was unwilling to press its policy in Asia, it was equally unwilling to support, even by gesture, the development of a Japanese navy which could challenge American security in the Pacific. The alternatives available and the considerations upon which American policy was based were analyzed clearly in a number of comprehensive reports to the State Department and the President by Joseph Clark Grew (1880–1965), the United States Ambassador to Tokyo. Grew was both a professional diplomat and a friend of President Roosevelt. He frequently wrote to the President personally. But none of his communications was more clear, forceful, and timely than this letter to the Secretary of State on December 27, 1934, when it had become clear that Japan would renounce naval disarmament.

The most revealing recent study is Dorothy Borg, The United States and the Far Eastern Crisis of 1933–1938 *(1964). The document published here is a letter from Ambassador Joseph C. Grew to the Secretary of State, December 27, 1934,* Peace and War, *pages 236–244.*

Sir:

Now that the London Naval Conversations have terminated, I should like to convey to the Department various thoughts in this general connection to which the Department may desire to give consideration if and when the conversations are renewed or a naval conference convoked. I shall be contributing little that is new, for most of the facts and opinions set forth herein have already been brought to the Department's attention in previous reports. Furthermore the attitude, policy and action of our delegation in London, as directed by the Government and as revealed in the various summaries of developments telegraphed to this Embassy on October 25 and 31, November 22 and December 10, and in certain press reports, have indicated a sound comprehension of the situation in the Far East as it exists today. The firm stand of our Government and delegation to maintain the present naval ratios intact in the face of Japanese intransigence, as well as their decision that the action of the Japanese Government in denouncing the Washington Naval Treaty automatically created a new situation in which the conversations must be suspended *sine die*, leaving the Japanese to return home empty handed, were especially gratifying to those of us who have watched the developments in London from this angle. The purpose of this despatch is therefore mainly to summarize and to place my views in concise form on record for the future.

The thought which is uppermost in my mind is that the United States is faced, and will be faced in future, with two main alternatives. One is to be prepared to withdraw from the Far East, gracefully and gradually perhaps, but not the less effectively in the long run, permitting our treaty rights to be nullified, the Open Door to be closed, our vested economic interests to be dissolved and our commerce to operate unprotected. There are those who advocate this course, and who have advocated it to me personally, on the ground that any other policy will entail the risk of eventual war with Japan. . . . In their opinion, "the game is not worth the candle" because the United States can continue to subsist comfortably even after relinquishing its varied interests in the Far East, thereby eliminating the risk of future war.

The other main alternative is to insist, and to continue to insist, not aggressively yet not the less firmly, on the maintenance of our legitimate rights and interests in this part of the world and, so far as practicable, to support the normal development of those interests constructively and progressively.

There has already been abundant indication that the present Administration in Washington proposes to follow the second of these alternatives. For purposes of discussion we may therefore, I assume, discard the hypothesis of withdrawal and examine the future outlook with the assurance that our Government has not the slightest intention of relinquishing the legitimate rights, vested interests, non-discriminatory privileges for equal opportunity and healthful commercial development of the United States in the Far East.

In following this second and logical course, there should be and need be nothing inconsistent, so far as our own attitude is concerned, with the policy of the good neighbor. The determination to support and protect our legitimate interests in the Far East can and should be carried out in a way which, while sacrificing no point of principle, will aim to restrict to a minimum the friction between the United States and Japan inevitably arising from time to time as a result of that determination.

The administration of that policy from day to day becomes a matter of diplomacy, sometimes delicate, always important, for much depends on the method and manner of approach to the various problems with which we have been, are, and will continue to be faced. With the ultra-sensitiveness of the Japanese, arising out of a marked inferiority complex which manifests itself in the garb of an equally marked superiority complex, with all its attendant bluster, chauvinism, xenophobia and organized national propaganda, the method and manner of dealing with current controversies assumes a significance and importance often out of all proportion to the nature of the controversy. That the Department fully appreciates this fact has been amply demonstrated by the instructions issued to this Embassy since the present Administration took office, and it has been our endeavor to carry out those instructions, or to act on our own initiative when such action was called for, with the foregoing considerations constantly in view.

But behind our day to day diplomacy lies a factor of prime importance, namely national support, demonstrated and reinforced by national preparedness. I believe that a fundamental element of that preparedness should be the maintenance of the present naval ratios in principle and the eventual achievement and maintenance of those ratios, so far as they apply to Japan, in fact. With such a background, and only with such a background, can we pursue our diplomacy with any confidence that our representations will be listened to or that they will lead to favorable results. General Douglas MacArthur, Chief of Staff of the United States Army, was recently reported in the press as saying: "Armies and navies, in being efficient, give weight to the peaceful words of statesmen, but a feverish effort to create them when once a crisis is imminent simply provokes attack." We need thorough preparedness not in the interests of war but of peace.

It is difficult for those who do not live in Japan to appraise the present temper of the country. An American Senator, according to reports, has recently recommended that we should accord parity to Japan in order to avoid future war. Whatever the Senator's views may be concerning the general policy that we should follow in the Far East, he probably does not realize what harm that sort of public statement does in strengthening the Japanese stand and in reinforcing the aggressive ambitions of the expansionists. The Japanese press of course picks out such statements by prominent Americans and publishes them far and wide, thus confirming the general belief in Japan that the pacifist element in the United States is preponderantly strong and in the last analysis will control the policy and action of our Government. Under such circumstances there is a general tendency to characterize our diplomatic representations as bluff and to believe that they can safely be disregarded without fear of implementation. It would be helpful if those who share the Senator's views could hear and read some of the things that are constantly being said and written in Japan, to the effect that Japan's destiny is to subjugate and rule the world (*sic*), and could realize the expansionist ambitions which lie not far from the surface in the minds of certain elements in the Army and Navy, the patriotic societies and the intense nationalists throughout the country. Their aim is to obtain trade control and eventually predominant political influence in China, the Philippines, the Straits Settlements, Siam and the Dutch East Indies, the Maritime Provinces and Vladivostok, one step at a time, as in Korea and Manchuria, pausing intermittently to consolidate and then continuing as soon as the intervening obstacles can be overcome by diplomacy or force. With such dreams of empire cherished by many, and with an army and navy capable of taking the bit in their own teeth and running away with it regardless of the restraining influence of the saner heads of the Government in Tokyo (a risk which unquestionably exists and of which we have already had ample evidence in the Manchurian affair), we would be reprehensibly somnolent if we were to trust to the security of treaty restraints or international comity to safeguard our own interests or, indeed, our own property.

I may refer here to my despatch No. 608 of December 12, 1933, a re-reading of which is respectfully invited because it applies directly to the present situation. That despatch reported a confidential conversation with the Netherlands Minister, General Pabst, a shrewd and rational colleague with long experience in Japan, in which the Minister said that in his opinion the Japanese Navy, imbued as it is with patriotic and chauvinistic fervor and with a desire to emulate the deeds of the Army in order not to lose caste with the public, would be perfectly capable of descending upon and occupying Guam at a moment of crisis or, indeed, at any other moment, regardless of the ulterior consequences. I do not think that such an insane step is likely, yet the action of the Army in Manchuria, judged from the point of view of treaty rights and international comity, might also have been judged as insensate. The important fact is that under present circumstances, and indeed under circumstances which may continue in future (although the pendulum of chauvinism throughout Japanese history has swung to and fro in periodic cycles of intensity and temporary relaxation) the armed forces of the country are perfectly capable of over-riding the restraining control of the Government and of committing what might well amount to national "hara-kiri" in a mistaken conception of patriotism.

When Japanese speak of Japan's being the "stabilizing factor" and the "guardian of peace" of East Asia, what they have in mind is a Pax Japonica with eventual complete commercial control, and, in the minds of some, eventual complete political control of East Asia. While Ambassador Saito may have been misquoted in a recent issue of the Philadelphia Bulletin as saying that Japan will be prepared to fight to maintain that conception of peace, nevertheless that is precisely what is in the minds of many Japanese today. There is a swashbuckling temper in the country, largely developed by military propaganda, which can lead Japan during the next few years, or in the next few generations, to any extremes unless the saner minds in the Government prove able to cope with it and to restrain the country from national suicide.

The efficacy of such restraint is always problematical. Plots against the Government are constantly being hatched. We hear, for instance, that a number of young officers of the 3rd Infantry Regiment and students from the Military Academy in Tokyo were found on November 22 to have planned to assassinate various high members of the Government, including Count Makino, and that students of the Military Academy were confined to the school area for a few days after the discovery of that plot, which had for its object the placing in effect at once of the provisions of the now celebrated "Army pamphlet" (see despatch No. 1031 of November 1, 1934). A similar alleged plot to attack the politicians at the opening of the extraordinary session of the Diet—another May 15th incident—is also said to have been discovered and nipped in the bud. Such plots aim to form a military dictatorship. It is of course impossible to substantiate these rumors, but they are much talked about and it is unlikely that so much smoke would materialize without some fire. I wish that more Americans could come out here and live here and gradually come to sense the real potential risks and dangers of the situation instead of speaking and writing academically on a subject which they know nothing whatever about, thereby contributing ammunition to the Japanese military and extremists who are stronger than they have been for many a day. The idea that a great body of liberal thought lying just beneath the surface since 1931 would be sufficiently strong to emerge and assume control with a little foreign encouragement is thoroughly mistaken. The liberal thought is there, but it is inarticulate and largely impotent, and in all probability will remain so for some time to come.

At this point I should like to make the following observation. From reading this despatch, and perhaps from other reports periodically submitted by the Embassy, one might readily get the impression that we are developing something of an "anti-Japanese" complex. This is not the case. One can dislike and disagree with certain members of a family without necessarily feeling hostility to the family itself. For me there are no finer people in the world than the type of Japanese exemplified by such men as . . . and a host of others. I am rather inclined to place . . . in the same general category; if he could have his way unhampered by the military I believe that he would steer the country into safer and saner channels. One of these friends once sadly remarked to us: "We Japanese are always putting our worst foot foremost, and we are too proud to explain ourselves." This is profoundly true. Theirs has been and is a "bungling diplomacy." They habitually play their cards badly. Amau's statement of April 17 was a case in point. The declaration of the oil monopoly in Manchuria at this particular juncture, thereby tending to drive Great Britain into the other camp at a moment when closer Anglo-Japanese cooperation was very much in view, was another. While it is true that the military and the extremists are primarily responsible for the "bungling diplomacy" of Japan, the Japanese as a race tend to be inarticulate, more at home in action than with words. The recent negotiations in Batavia amply illustrated the fact that Japanese diplomats, well removed from home influences and at liberty to choose their own method and manner of approach, are peculiarly insensitive to the unhappy effects of arbitrary pronouncements. They have learned little from the sad experience of Hanihara. But the military and the extremists know little and care little about Japan's relations with other countries, and it is the desire of people like Shiratori, Amau and other Government officials to enhance their own prestige at home and to safeguard their future careers by standing in well with the military that brings about much of the trouble. Perhaps we should be grateful that they so often give their hand away in advance.

But all this does not make us less sympathetic to the better elements in Japanese life or in any sense "anti-Japanese." Japan is a country of paradoxes and extremes, of great wisdom and of great stupidity, an apt illustration of which may be found in connection with the naval conversations; while the naval authorities and the press have been stoutly maintaining that Japan cannot adequately defend her shores with less than parity, the press and the public, in articles, speeches and interviews, have at the same time been valiantly boasting that the Japanese Navy is today stronger than the American Navy and could easily defeat us in case of war. In such an atmosphere it is difficult, very difficult, for a foreigner to keep a detached and balanced point of view. We in the Embassy are making that effort, I hope with success, and in the meantime about all we can do is to keep the boat from rocking dangerously. Constructive work is at present impossible. Our efforts are concentrated on the thwarting of destructive influences.

Having placed the foregoing considerations on record, I have less hesitation in reiterating and emphasizing with all conviction the potential dangers of the situation and the prime importance of American national preparedness to meet it. As a nation we have taken the lead in international efforts towards the restriction and reduction of armaments. We have had hopes that the movement would be progressive, but the condition of world affairs as they have developed during the past twelve years since the Washington Conference has not afforded fruitful ground for such progress. Unless we are prepared to subscribe to a "Pax Japonica" in the Far East, with all that this movement, as conceived and interpreted by Japan, is bound to entail, we should rapidly build up our navy to treaty strength, and if and when the Washington Naval Treaty expires we should continue to maintain the present ratio with Japan regardless of cost, a peace-time insurance both to cover and to reduce the risk of war. In the meantime every proper step should be taken to avoid or to offset the belligerent utterances of jingoes no less than the defeatist statements of pacifists in the United States, many of which find their way into the Japanese press, because the utterances of the former tend to enflame public sentiment against our country, while the statements of the latter convey an impression of American weakness, irresolution and bluff.

My own opinion, although it can be but guesswork, is that Japan will under no circumstances invite a race in naval armaments, and that having found our position on the ratios to be adamant, further propositions will be forthcoming within the next two years before the Washington Treaty expires, or before our present building program is fully completed. When the United States has actually completed its naval building program to treaty limits, then, it is believed, and probably not before then, Japan will realize that we are in earnest and will seek a compromise. We believe that Japan's naval policy has been formulated on the premise that the United States would never build up to treaty strength, a premise which has been strengthened in the past by the naval policy of the past two Administrations, by the apparent strength of the pacifist element in the United States, and more recently by the effects of the depression.

While it is true that Japan, by sedulously forming and stimulating public opinion to demand parity with the United States in principle if not in fact, has burned her bridges behind her, nevertheless the Japanese leaders are past-masters at remoulding public opinion in the country by skillful propaganda to suit new conditions. Once convinced that parity is impossible, it is difficult to believe that she will allow matters to come to a point where competitive building becomes unavoidable. With a national budget for 1935–1936 totaling 2,193,414,289 yen, of which about 47% is for the Army and Navy, and with an estimated national debt in 1936 of 9,880,000,000 yen, nearly equal to the Cabinet Bureau of Statistics estimate of the national income for 1930, namely 10,635,000,000 yen; with her vast outlay in Manchuria, her already heavily taxed population and the crying need of large sections of her people for relief funds, it is difficult to see how Japan could afford to embark upon a program of maintaining naval parity with the United States and Great Britain.

Having registered our position firmly and unequivocally, we can now afford to await the next move on the part of Japan. I believe that it will come.

So far as we can evaluate here the proceedings of the recent preliminary naval conversations in London, I am of the opinion that the most important and the most valuable result issuing therefrom has been the apparent tendency towards closer Anglo-American cooperation in the Far East. If we can count in future—again as a direct result of Japan's "bungling diplomacy"—on a solid and united front between the United States and Great Britain in meeting Japan's flaunting of treaty rights and her unrestrained ambitions to control East Asia, the future may well assume a brighter aspect for all of us.

Theodore Roosevelt enunciated the policy "Speak softly but carry a big stick." If our diplomacy in the Far East is to achieve favorable results, and if we are to reduce the risk of an eventual war with Japan to a minimum, that is the only way to proceed. Such a war may be unthinkable, and so it is, but the spectre of it is always present and will be present for some time to come. It would be criminally short-sighted to discard it from our calculations, and the best possible way to avoid it is to be adequately prepared, for preparedness is a cold fact which even the chauvinists, the military, the patriots and the ultra-nationalists in Japan, for all their bluster concerning "provocative measures" in the United States, can grasp and understand. The Soviet Ambassador recently told me that a prominent Japanese had said to him that the most important factor in avoiding a Japanese attack on the Maritime Provinces was the intensive Soviet military preparations in Siberia and Vladivostok. I believe this to be true, and again, and yet again, I urge that our own country be adequately prepared to meet all eventualities in the Far East.

The Counselor, the Naval Attaché and the Military Attaché of this Embassy, having separately read this despatch, have expressed to me their full concurrence with its contents both in essence and detail.

Respectfully yours,
JOSEPH C. GREW

SELECTION 45

An Early Appraisal of Hitler: An American Diplomat Reports on "The Main Purpose of the Nazis," 1934

If Americans were only mildly disturbed in 1934 by the mounting threat in Asia, they were virtually immune to the incipient dangers of European totalitarianism. Neither Hitler nor Mussolini had yet marched as an aggressor upon a neighbor. To the extent that they were interested at all in European affairs, Americans were concerned with passing judgments upon nations which had defaulted on their war debt payments to the United States. The Johnson Act of April, 1934, prohibited further loans to such nations. From the spring of 1934 through 1936, the nation's discussion of foreign policy was warped by the testimony and pronouncements developed by the Senate Munitions Investigating Committee. Under the leadership of Senator Gerald P. Nye, it concentrated upon demonstrating a conspiracy theory of war, and it fed the propaganda campaign to convince Americans that they had been tricked into the First World War by munitions magnates and bankers, that they must avoid another involvement at any cost. When Mussolini gave the signal for a new age of total expansion with the attack on Ethiopia, the nation's reaction was the Neutrality Act of 1935, which sought to insulate the United States by requiring an arms embargo against all belligerents, once the President had recognized the existence of a state of war. Roosevelt had asked for authority to use such embargoes selectively against belligerents. He signed the bill reluctantly, and, in general, supported the policy of neutrality throughout the next four years. He continued to press for legislation which would give the White House more power of choice in discriminating among assailants and defenders, but he did so without vigor.

Long before congressmen and Americans generally were aware of the deep dangers inherent in fascism and Nazism, the State Department was both informed and concerned. Symptomatic of the hard-headed reports it had from its people on the scene was the keen appraisal of Nazi aims provided in April, 1934, by Douglas Miller, then Acting Commercial Attaché in Vienna. It was in fact so perceptive that it reads, in retrospect, like a summary of what actually happened after 1937.

One of the best modern studies of Roosevelt's foreign policy regarding Europe is Robert A. Divine, The Illusion of Neutrality *(1962). Denna F. Fleming records the story of* The United States and the World Court *(1945). An interesting and revealing contemporary document is William E. Dodd,* Ambassador Dodd's Diary: 1933–1938 *(1941)*

The document given below is from Douglas Miller, "Memorandum to the Embassy, April 17, 1934," Peace and War, *pages 211–214.*

The fundamental purpose is to secure a greater share of the world's future for the Germans, the expansion of German territory and growth of the German race until it constitutes the largest and most powerful nation in the world, and ultimately, according to some Nazi leaders, until it dominates the entire globe.

The German people suffering from a traditional inferiority complex, smarting from their defeat in the war and the indignities of the post-war period, disillusioned in their hopes of a speedy return to prosperity along traditional lines, inflamed by irresponsible demagogic slogans and flattered by the statement that their German racial inheritance gives them inherent superior rights over other peoples, have to a large measure adopted the National Socialist point of view for the time being.

Economic Aims

There are two other purposes subsidiary to the main purpose. Germany is to be made the economic center of a self-sustaining territorial block whose dependent nations in Central and Eastern Europe will look to Berlin for leadership. This block is to be so constituted that it can defy wartime blockade and be large enough to give the peoples in it the benefits of free trade now enjoyed by the 48 American States. In accordance with this purpose, an agricultural self-sufficiency program has been adopted, foreign foodstuffs are being rigorously excluded or the imported supply secured in increasing quantities from Central and Southeastern Europe. A hereditary peasantry has been set up, firmly attached to the soil through the prohibition of the sale or mortgaging of the peasants' land or crops. An increasing number of commodities have been placed under Government monopolies with fixed prices to consumers and producers, the principle of the numerus clausus or fixed number of persons engaged in any occupation has been increasingly adopted. The National Socialist conception of the correct or Government-fixed price instead of the price fixed by supply and demand has been introduced.

Social Aims

The second subsidiary purpose is the welding of all individuals in the present and future Greater Germany into a homogeneous racial family, gladly obedient to the will of its leader, with class and cultural differences inside the country eliminated, but a sharp line drawn between Germans and the foreign world outside. In carrying out this purpose, the Jews are to be entirely eliminated, the Slavic or eastern elements in the population to be minimized and eventually bred out of the race. A national religion is in process of organization; trade unions, political parties and all social, political, cultural, trade or other organizations not affiliated with the National Socialist party, have been abolished, the individual's rights have been largely taken away. In the future the nation is to count for everything, the individual for nothing. Germany is to engage in a gigantic struggle with the rest of the world to grow at the expense of its neighbors. The German population owes the nation the patriotic duty of supporting it and bringing forward all necessary sacrifices to reach the common goal.

Retention of Power

To these long-distance objectives must be added the fourth and most important purpose of all, namely to retain control at all costs. The National Socialist party may compromise on distant objectives, if necessary, but cannot compromise on a question of retaining its absolute hold on the German people. This control had been gained by making most irresponsible and extravagant promises; by the studied use of the press, the radio, public meetings, parades, flags, uniforms, and all methods of working on popular psychology and finally by the use of force. This control once lost, could never be regained. It is absolutely necessary for the party to continue to make a show of success and to keep popular enthusiasm and fanaticism alive. There must be no open criticism or grumbling, even discussion of the future form of the State, the form in which industry is to be organized, or the laws regarding the hereditary peasantry is prohibited. Since the German public is politically inept and unusually docile, the Nazi movement has been able to dominate the situation for the past year, but the hard facts of the economic situation are beginning to be felt by the more intelligent Germans, particularly bankers, business men, professional men and persons who have touch with the outside world.

Danger of War

The Nazis are not satisfied with the existing map of Europe. They are at heart belligerent and aggressive. True, they desire nothing more than a period of peace for several years in which they can gradually re-arm and discipline their people. This period may be 5 years, 10 years, or longer, but the more completely their experiments succeed the more certain is a large-scale war in Europe some day.

Nazis Want to Wipe Out 1918

In estimating the aims and purposes of the National Socialist movement, we must not make the mistake of putting too much reliance on public statements designed for consumption abroad which breathe the spirit of good peace and will and assert the intention of the Government to promote the welfare of the German people and good relations with their neighbors. Nor should we imagine that the present Government leaders will feel and act as we would in their circumstances, namely think only of Germany's welfare. The real emotional drive behind the Nazi program is not so much love of their own country as dislike of other countries. The Nazis will never be content in merely promoting the welfare of the German people.

They desire to be feared and envied by foreigners and to wipe out the memory of 1918 by inflicting humiliations in particular upon the French, the Poles, the Czechs and anybody else they can get their hands on.

A careful examination of Hitler's book and his public speeches reveals the fact that he cannot be considered as absolutely sane and normal on this subject. The same is true of many other Nazi leaders. They have capitalized the wounded inferiority complex of the German people, and magnified their own bitter feelings into a cult of dislike against the foreign world which is past the bounds of ordinary good sense and reason. Let us repeat this fact and let it sink in, the National Socialist movement is building a tremendous military machine, physically very poorly armed, but morally aggressive and belligerent. The control of this machine lies in the hands of narrow, ignorant and unscrupulous adventurers who have been slightly touched with madness from brooding over Germany's real or imagined wrongs, as well as the slights and indignities thrown in their own individual way as they attempted to organize the movement. Power of this kind concentrated in hands like these is dangerous. The Nazis are determined to secure more power and more territory in Europe. If this is voluntarily given to them by peaceful means, well and good, but if not, they will certainly use force. That is the only meaning behind the manifold activities of the movement in Germany today.

Warnings from the Past: A Poet Regrets the Futility of an Earlier War, 1933

Public opinion is beaten together from many words, spun from myriad themes, a blending of vision, fear, and fantasy. So it was with American attitudes toward the mounting tensions in Europe and Asia. It all depended upon who was doing the talking, and—more important—upon the particular facet of his life he was, for the moment, reflecting. Most Americans felt fear when Hitler's half-armed troops swept into the Rhineland in 1936. And most Americans perhaps indulged on occasion the fantasy of complete detachment which transfixed a large group of their so-called isolationist fellow citizens. There was also recklessness and avoidance, disgust and greed in the web of notions which passed for a public opinion. But as strong as any mood was the bitter pall of frustration and regret which hung over discussions of the First World War. As they looked back upon the death, disease, and heartbreak, it was easy for Americans to see merely futility and to swear that never again would American lives be wasted with such ghastly frivolity in a conflict so far from home. The disillusionment was general and deep. Antiwar plays and novels were popular. History was rewritten to cut the romance and glory from war.

Poets and artists were keenly attuned to this frustration. Many of them had themselves seen, heard, and smelled the obscene filth of war. They would be particularly sensitive now that it all seemed to have been a mistake. Archibald MacLeish (1892–   ), who would later be Librarian of Congress, Assistant Secretary of State, and then Harvard professor, was one of these. MacLeish caught with sad precision the moods that made the rumors of new wars particularly ghastly. But his "Lines for an Interment" were published in 1933. Like the great majority of his countrymen, MacLeish would swing gradually throughout the next seven years toward deeper and deeper concern with the brutality and amorality of the new imperialism. By 1942, this eloquent "nay-sayer" of the twenties had become the passionate poet of the new crusade against totalitarian terror.

The lines quoted here are from Archibald MacLeish, "Lines for an Interment," in The Collected Poems of Archibald MacLeish *(Boston: Houghton Mifflin, 1962), pages 86–87.*

Now it is fifteen years you have lain in the meadow:
The boards at your face have gone through: the earth is
Packed down and the sound of the rain is fainter:
The roots of the first grass are dead.

It's a long time to lie in the earth with your honor:
The world, Soldier, the world has been moving on.

The girls wouldn't look at you twice in the cloth cap:
Six years old they were when it happened:

It bores them even in books: "Soissons besieged!"
As for the gents they have joined the American Legion:

Belts and a brass band and the ladies' auxiliaries:
The Californians march in the OD silk.

We are all acting again like civilized beings:
People mention it at tea . . .

The Facts of Life we have learned are Economic:
You were deceived by the detonations of bombs:

You thought of courage and death when you thought of warfare.
Hadn't they taught you the fine words were unfortunate?

Now that we understand we judge without bias:
We feel of course for those who had to die:

Women have written us novels of great passion
Proving the useless death of the dead was a tragedy.

Nevertheless it is foolish to chew gall:
The foremost writers on both sides have apologized:

The Germans are back in the Midi with cropped hair:
The English are drinking the better beer in Bavaria.

You can rest now in the rain in the Belgian meadow—
Now that it's all explained away and forgotten:
Now that the earth is hard and the wood rots:

Now you are dead . . .

Restating American Foreign Policy: FDR's Chautauqua Speech, 1936

By 1936 it had become clear that the foreign policy of the 1920s was, at least in its specific measures, bankrupt. Japanese activities in China and the Pacific had made a grim joke of the Nine-Power Treaty to stabilize China and the Five-Power Treaty to neutralize the Pacific. The Kellogg-Briand Pact now appeared shabby and phony as only thoughtless idealism can when its naiveté is exposed. What remained, unhappily, was not a determination to fill the power vacuum which the United States had helped create and which had so tempted Japan, but rather merely a deadly bitterness and fatigue. Having fought for peace and then left the conference table, Americans now regretted that they had fought at all. Having ventured in the twenties to seek peace through balance and then failed to hold its side of the balance, the United States appeared to reject now the search for peace itself.

And there was Depression. Economic disaster created its own priorities, and Roosevelt set them along nationalistic lines. He eschewed international currency stabilization, shelved the reciprocal trade agreements program until 1934 and then moved only slowly with it, and espoused a series of measures which treated recovery as if it were something to be sought only between Nantucket Island and San Francisco Bay. Nothing in foreign affairs would be allowed to impede the recovery plan, and domestic legislation took so much time that little effort or attention could be salvaged for international relations. One exception was necessarily Latin America. Yet, even here, the general trend was disengagement, rather than increased responsibility.

In fact, Roosevelt chose not to lead actively in foreign affairs. Keeping only a light hand upon the tiller, he allowed the increasingly isolationist strong-

men of the Senate, Gerald P. Nye, Burton K. Wheeler, Hiram Johnson, William E. Borah, to fix the nation's course with increasing rigidity. This remained the case even after the tragedy in Europe had begun to deepen. Mussolini attacked Ethiopia in October, 1935; Hitler discredited the Versailles Treaty when he marched into the "demilitarized" Rhine Valley in March, 1936. In 1936, the Spanish Civil War erupted. But when Roosevelt finally spoke out in a major foreign policy speech at Chautauqua, New York, it was with mild words of frustration and a firm statement of withdrawal. There was talk of the "good neighbor," but the stress lay upon the nation's hatred of war.

American popular views of foreign policy as recorded in the opinion polls are summarized in Hadley Cantril et al., Public Opinion: 1935–1946 *(1951). The most thorough scholarship on the situation is that of William L. Langer and S. Everett Gleason,* The Challenge to Isolation: 1937–1940 *(1952).*

Roosevelt's Chautauqua Address of August 14, 1936, may be found in Samuel Rosenman (ed.), The Public Papers and Addresses of Franklin D. Roosevelt, Volume Five: The People Approve, 1936 *(New York: Random House, 1938), pages 286–292.*

Long before I returned to Washington as President of the United States, I had made up my mind that pending what might be called a more opportune moment on other continents, the United States could best serve the cause of a peaceful humanity by setting an example. That was why on the 4th of March, 1933, I made the following declaration:

> In the field of world policy I would dedicate this Nation to the policy of the good neighbor—the neighbor who resolutely respects himself and, because he does so, respects the rights of others—the neighbor who respects his obligations and respects the sanctity of his agreements in and with a world of neighbors.

This declaration represents my purpose; but it represents more than a purpose, for it stands for a practice. To a measurable degree it has succeeded; the whole world now knows that the United States cherishes no predatory ambitions. We are strong; but less powerful Nations know that they need not fear our strength. We seek no conquest; we stand for peace.

In the whole of the Western Hemisphere our good-neighbor policy has produced results that are especially heartening.

The noblest monument to peace and to neighborly economic and social friendship in all the world is not a monument in bronze or stone, but the boundary which unites the United States and Canada—3,000 miles of friendship with no barbed wire, no gun or soldier, and no passport on the whole frontier.

Mutual trust made that frontier. To extend the same sort of mutual trust throughout the Americas was our aim.

The American Republics to the south of us have been ready always to cooperate with the United States on a basis of equality and mutual respect, but before we inaugurated the good-neighbor policy there were among them resentment and fear, because certain Administrations in Washington had slighted their national pride and their sovereign rights.

In pursuance of the good-neighbor policy, and because in my younger days I had learned many lessons in the hard school of experience, I stated that the United States was opposed definitely to armed intervention.

We have negotiated a Pan-American convention embodying the principle of non-intervention. We have abandoned the Platt Amendment which gave us the right to intervene in the internal affairs of the Republic of Cuba. We have withdrawn American marines from Haiti. We have signed a new treaty which places our relations with Panama on a mutually satisfactory basis. We have undertaken a series of trade agreements with other American countries to our mutual commercial profit. At the request of two neighboring Republics, I hope to give assistance in the final settlement of the last serious boundary dispute between any of the American Nations.

Throughout the Americas the spirit of the good neighbor is a practical and living fact. The twenty-one American Republics are not only living together in friendship and in peace; they are united in the determination so to remain.

To give substance to this determination a conference will meet on December 1, 1936, at the capital of our great Southern neighbor, Argentina, and it is, I know, the hope of all Chiefs of State of the Americas that this will result in measures which will banish wars forever from this vast portion of the earth.

Peace, like charity, begins at home; that is why we have begun at home. But peace in the Western world is not all that we seek.

It is our hope that knowledge of the practical application of the good-neighbor policy in this hemisphere will be borne home to our neighbors across the seas.

For ourselves we are on good terms with them—terms in most cases of straightforward friendship, of peaceful understanding.

But, of necessity, we are deeply concerned about tendencies of recent years among many of the Nations of other continents. It is a bitter experience to us when the spirit of agreements to which we are a party is not lived up to. It is an even more bitter experience for the whole company of Nations to witness not only the spirit but the letter of international agreements violated with impunity and without regard to the simple principles of honor. Permanent friendships between Nations as between men can be sustained only by scrupulous respect for the pledged word.

In spite of all this we have sought steadfastly to assist international movements to prevent war. We cooperated to the bitter end—and it was a bitter end—in the work of the General Disarmament Conference. When it failed we sought a separate treaty to deal with the manufacture of arms and the international traffic in arms. That proposal also came to nothing. We participated—again to the bitter end—in a conference to continue naval limitations, and when it became evident that no general treaty could be signed because of the objections of other Nations, we concluded with Great Britain and France a conditional treaty of qualitative limitation which, much to my regret, already shows signs of ineffectiveness.

We shun political commitments which might entangle us in foreign wars; we avoid connection with the political activities of the League of Nations; but I am glad to say that we have cooperated whole-heartedly in the social and humanitarian work at Geneva. Thus we are a part of the world effort to control traffic in narcotics, to improve international health, to help child welfare, to eliminate double taxation and to better working conditions and laboring hours throughout the world.

We are not isolationists except in so far as we seek to isolate ourselves completely from war. Yet we must remember that so long as war exists on earth there will be some danger that even the Nation which most ardently desires peace may be drawn into war.

I have seen war. I have seen war on land and sea. I have seen blood running from the wounded. I have seen men coughing out their gassed lungs. I have seen the dead in the mud. I have seen cities destroyed. I have seen two hundred limping, exhausted men come out of line—the survivors of a regiment of one thousand that went forward forty-eight hours before. I have seen children starving. I have seen the agony of mothers and wives. I hate war.

I have passed unnumbered hours, I shall pass unnumbered hours, thinking and planning how war may be kept from this Nation.

I wish I could keep war from all Nations; but that is beyond my power. I can at least make certain that no act of the United States helps to produce or to promote war. I can at least make clear that the conscience of America revolts against war and that any Nation which provokes war forfeits the sympathy of the people of the United States.

Many causes produce war. There are ancient hatreds, turbulent frontiers, the "legacy of old forgotten, far-off things, and battles long ago." There are new-born fanaticisms, convictions on the part of certain peoples that they have become the unique depositories of ultimate truth and right.

A dark old world was devastated by wars between conflicting religions. A dark modern world faces wars between conflicting economic and political fanaticisms in which are intertwined race hatreds. To bring it home, it is as if within the territorial limits of the United States, forty-eight Nations with forty-eight forms of government, forty-eight customs barriers, forty-eight languages, and forty-eight eternal and different verities, were spending their time and their substance in a frenzy of effort to make themselves strong enough to conquer their neighbors or strong enough to defend themselves against their neighbors.

In one field, that of economic barriers, the American policy may be, I hope, of some assistance in discouraging the economic source of war and therefore a contribution toward the peace of the world. The trade agreements which we are making are not only finding outlets for the products of American fields and American factories but are also pointing the way to the elimination of embargoes, quotas and other devices which place such pressure on Nations not possessing great natural resources that to them the price of peace seems less terrible than the price of war.

We do not maintain that a more liberal international trade will stop war; but we fear that without a more liberal international trade, war is a natural sequence.

The Congress of the United States has given me certain authority to provide safeguards of American neutrality in case of war.

The President of the United States, who, under our Constitution, is vested with primary authority to conduct our international relations, thus has been given new weapons with which to maintain our neutrality.

Nevertheless—and I speak from a long experience—the effective maintenance of American neutrality depends today, as in the past, on the wisdom and determination of whoever at the moment occupy the offices of President and Secretary of State.

It is clear that our present policy and the measures passed by the Congress would, in the event of a war on some other continent, reduce war profits which would otherwise accrue to American citizens. Industrial and agricultural production for a war market may give immense fortunes to a few men; for the Nation as a whole it produces disaster. It was the prospect of war profits that made our farmers in the West plow up prairie land that should never have been plowed, but should have been left for grazing cattle. Today we are reaping the harvest of those war profits in the dust storms which have devastated those war-plowed areas.

It was the prospect of war profits that caused the extension of monopoly and unjustified expansion of industry and a price level so high that the normal relationship between debtor and creditor was destroyed.

Nevertheless, if war should break out again in another continent, let us not blink the fact that we would find in this country thousands of Americans who, seeking immediate riches—fools' gold—would attempt to break down or evade our neutrality.

They would tell you—and, unfortunately, their views would get wide publicity—that if they could produce and ship this and that and the other article to belligerent Nations, the unemployed of America would all find work. They would tell you that if they could extend credit to warring Nations that credit would be used in the United States to build homes and factories and pay our debts. They would tell you that America once more would capture the trade of the world.

It would be hard to resist that clamor; it would be hard for many Americans, I fear, to look beyond—to realize the inevitable penalties, the inevitable day of reckoning, that come from a false prosperity. To resist the clamor of that greed, if war should come, would require the unswerving support of all Americans who love peace.

If we face the choice of profits or peace, the Nation will answer—must answer—"We choose peace." It is the duty of all of us to encourage such a body of public opinion in this country that the answer will be clear and for all practical purposes unanimous.

With that wise and experienced man who is our Secretary of State, whose statesmanship has met with such wide approval, I have thought and worked long and hard on the problem of keeping the United States at peace. But all the wisdom of America is not to be found in the White House or in the Department of State; we need the meditation, the prayer, and the positive support of the people of America who go along with us in seeking peace.

No matter how well we are supported by neutrality legislation, we must remember that no laws can be provided to cover every contingency, for it is impossible to imagine how every future event may shape itself. In spite of every possible forethought, international relations involve of necessity a vast uncharted area. In that area safe sailing will depend on the knowledge and the experience and the wisdom of those who direct our foreign policy. Peace will depend on their day-to-day decisions.

At this late date, with the wisdom which is so easy after the event and so difficult before the event, we find it possible to trace the tragic series of small decisions which led Europe into the Great War in 1914 and eventually engulfed us and many other Nations.

We can keep out of war if those who watch and decide have a sufficiently detailed understanding of international affairs to make certain that the small decisions of each day do not lead toward war and if, at the same time, they possess the courage to say "no" to those who selfishly or unwisely would let us go to war.

Of all the Nations of the world today we are in many ways most singularly blessed. Our closest neighbors are good neighbors. If there are remoter Nations that wish us not good but ill, they know that we are strong; they know that we can and will defend ourselves and defend our neighborhood.

We seek to dominate no other Nation. We ask no territorial expansion. We oppose imperialism. We desire reduction in world armaments.

We believe in democracy; we believe in freedom; we believe in peace. We offer to every Nation of the world the handclasp of the good neighbor. Let those who wish our friendship look us in the eye and take our hand.

Blueprint for Disengagement: The Neutrality Act, 1937

The policy remained neutrality. Its major inspiration lay in Congress. Franklin Roosevelt would have preferred a discretionary law under which the President could withhold support from an "aggressor" without hurting the defendant. But Congress preferred to avoid nice moral distinctions which might bring retaliation from an aggressor, and the President went along. The first, "temporary" act of August 1, 1935, banned, whenever the President officially recognized the existence of a state of war, the sale, export, or transportation of arms to belligerents, and made it clear that travel by Americans on belligerent ships was to be at their own risk. The Second Neutrality Act of 1936 made loans to belligerents illegal. Reprinted below is the Third Neutrality Act, the so-called permanent one. It reenacted the terms of the earlier measures and added two major provisions: American travel on belligerent ships was banned completely, and the President was authorized to prohibit the trade with belligerents of certain raw materials, except on cash-and-carry terms. Here was a step toward isolation, but without the loss of economic activity, wages, and profits which a total embargo would have brought. "Freedom of the seas" had been completely abandoned for the dual goals of profits and peace. Yet it could hardly be overlooked that, in the nature of things, the cash-and-carry provisions might immensely aid the Western Allies, England and France—and also Japan—but could help Germany, Italy, and China very little indeed. Despite its "amoral" and essentially unrealistic nature, the Neutrality Act of 1937 was probably one of the most popular actions in foreign policy in the nation's history. It was passed by a vote of 376 to 13 in the House, 63 to 6 in the Senate.

Among the more useful studies are Walter Johnson, The Battle against Isolation *(1944) and William L. Langer and S. Everett Gleason,* The Challenge to Isolation: 1937–1940 *(1952).*

The Neutrality Act of May 1, 1937, is in U.S. Statutes at Large, *volume 50, pages 121–128.*

R*esolved by the Senate and House of Representatives of the United States of America in Congress assembled,* That the joint resolution entitled "Joint resolution providing for the prohibition of the export of arms, ammunition, and implements of war to belligerent countries; the prohibition of the transportation of arms, ammunition, and implements of war by vessels of the United States for the use of belligerent states; for the registration and licensing of persons engaged in the business of manufacturing, exporting, or importing arms, ammunition, or implements of war; and restricting travel by American citizens on belligerent ships during war," approved August 31, 1935, as amended, is amended to read as follows:

Export of Arms, Ammunition, and Implements of War

Section 1. (a) Whenever the President shall find that there exists a state of war between, or among, two or more foreign states, the President shall proclaim such fact, and it shall thereafter be unlawful to export, or attempt to export, or cause to be exported, arms, ammunition, or implements of war from any place in the United States to any belligerent state named in such proclamation, or to any neutral state for transshipment to, or for the use of, any such belligerent state.

(b) The President shall, from time to time, by proclamation, extend such embargo upon the export of arms, ammunition, or implements of war to other states as and when they may become involved in such war.

(c) Whenever the President shall find that a state of civil strife exists in a foreign state and that such civil strife is of a magnitude or is being conducted under such conditions that the export of arms, ammunition, or implements of war from the United States to such foreign state would threaten or endanger the peace of the United States, the President shall proclaim such fact, and it shall thereafter be unlawful to export, or attempt to export, or cause to be exported, arms, ammunition, or implements of war from any place in the United States to such foreign state, or to any neutral state for transshipment to, or for the use of, such foreign state.

(d) The President shall, from time to time by proclamation, definitely enumerate the arms, ammunition, and implements of war, the export of which is prohibited by this section. The arms, ammunition, and implements of war so enumerated shall include those enumerated in the President's proclamation Numbered 2163, of April 10, 1936, but shall not include raw materials or any other articles or materials not of the same general character as those enumerated in the said proclamation, and in the Convention for the Supervision of the International Trade in Arms and Ammunition and in Implements of War, signed at Geneva June 17, 1925.

(e) Whoever, in violation of any of the provisions of this Act, shall export, or attempt to export, or cause to be exported, arms, ammunition, or implements of war from the United States shall be fined not more than $10,000, or imprisoned not more than five years, or both. . . .

(f) In the case of the forfeiture of any arms, ammunition, or implements of war by reason of a violation of this Act, no public or private sale shall be required; but such arms, ammunition, or implements of war shall be delivered to the Secretary of War for such use or disposal thereof as shall be approved by the President of the United States.

(g) Whenever, in the judgment of the President, the conditions which have caused him to issue any proclamation under the authority of this section have ceased to exist, he shall revoke the same, and the provisions of this section shall thereupon cease to apply with respect to the state or states named in such proclamation, except with respect to offenses committed, or forfeitures incurred, prior to such revocation.

Export of Other Articles and Materials

Sec. 2. (a) Whenever the President shall have issued a proclamation under the authority of section 1 of this Act and he shall thereafter find that the placing of restrictions on the shipment of certain articles or materials in addition to arms, ammunition, and implements of war from the United States to belligerent states, or to a state wherein civil strife exists, is necessary to promote the security or preserve the peace of the United States or to protect the lives of citizens of the United States, he shall so proclaim, and it shall thereafter be unlawful, except under such limitations and exceptions as the President may prescribe as to lakes, rivers, and inland waters bordering on the United States, and as to transportation on or over lands bordering on the United States, for any American vessel to carry such articles or materials to any belligerent state, or to any state wherein civil strife exists, named in such proclamation issued under the authority of section 1 of this Act, or to any neutral state for transshipment to, or for the use of, any such belligerent state or any such state wherein civil strife exists. The President shall by proclamation from time to time definitely enumerate the articles and materials which it shall be unlawful for American vessels to so transport. . . .

(c) The President shall from time to time by proclamation extend such restrictions as are imposed under the authority of this section to other states as and when they may be declared to become belligerent states under proclamations issued under the authority of section 1 of this Act.

(d) The President may from time to time change, modify, or revoke in whole or in part any proclamations issued by him under the authority of this section.

(e) Except with respect to offenses committed, or forfeitures incurred, prior to May 1, 1939, this section and all proclamations issued thereunder shall not be effective after May 1, 1939.

Financial Transactions

Sec. 3. (a) Whenever the President shall have issued a proclamation under the authority of section 1 of this Act, it shall thereafter be unlawful for any person within the United States to purchase, sell, or exchange bonds, securities, or other obligations of the government of any belligerent state or of any state wherein civil strife exists, named in such proclamation, or of any political subdivision of any such state, or of any person acting for or on behalf of the government of any such state, or of any faction or asserted government within any such state wherein civil strife exists, or of any person acting for or on behalf of any faction or asserted government within any such state wherein civil strife exists, issued after the date of such proclamation, or to make any loan or extend any credit to any such government, political subdivision, faction, asserted government, or person, or to solicit or receive any contribution for any such government, political subdivision, faction, asserted government, or person: *Provided,* That if the President shall find that such action will serve to protect the commercial or other interests of the United States or its citizens, he may, in his discretion, and to such extent and under such regulations as he may prescribe, except from the operation of this section ordinary commercial credits and short-time obligations in aid of legal transactions and of a character customarily used in normal peacetime commercial transactions. Nothing in this subsection shall be construed to prohibit the solicitation or collection of funds to be used for medical aid and assistance, or for food and clothing to relieve human suffering, when such solicitation or collection of funds is made on behalf of and for use by any person or organization which is not acting for or on behalf of any such government, political subdivision, faction, or asserted government, but all such solicitations and collections of funds shall be subject to the approval of the President and shall be made under such rules and regulations as he shall prescribe. . . .

(c) Whoever shall violate the provisions of this section or of any regulations issued hereunder shall, upon conviction thereof, be fined not more than $50,000 or imprisoned for not more than five years, or both. Should the violation be by a corporation, organization, or association, each officer or agent thereof participating in the violation may be liable to the penalty herein prescribed. . . .

Exceptions—American Republics

Sec. 4. This Act shall not apply to an American republic or republics engaged in war against a non-American state or states, provided the American republic is not cooperating with a non-American state or states in such war.

National Munitions Control Board

Sec. 5. (a) There is hereby established a National Munitions Control Board (hereinafter referred to as the 'Board') to carry out the provisions of this Act. The Board shall consist of the Secretary of State, who shall be chairman and executive officer of the Board, the Secretary of the Treasury, the Secretary of War, the Secretary of the Navy, and the Secretary of Commerce. Except as otherwise provided in this Act or by other law, the administration of this Act is vested in the Department of State. The Secretary of State shall promulgate such rules and regulations with regard to the enforcement of this section as he may deem necessary to carry out its provisions. The Board shall be convened by the chairman and shall hold at least one meeting a year.

(b) Every person who engages in the business of manufacturing, exporting, or importing any of the arms, ammunition, or implements of war referred to in this Act, whether as an exporter, importer, manufacturer, or dealer, shall register with the Secretary of State his name, or business name, principal place of business, and places of business in the United States, and a list of the arms, ammunition, and implements of war which he manufactures, imports, or exports.

(c) Every person required to register under this section shall notify the Secretary of State of any change in the arms, ammunition, or implements of war which he exports, imports, or manufactures. . . .

(d) It shall be unlawful for any person to export, or attempt to export, from the United States to any other state, any of the arms, ammunition, or implements of war referred to in this Act, or to import, or attempt to import, to the United States from any other state, any of the arms, ammunition, or implements of war referred to in this Act, without first having obtained a license therefor. . . .

(k) The President is hereby authorized to proclaim upon recommendation of the Board from time to time a list of articles which shall be considered arms, ammunition, and implements of war for the purposes of this section.

American Vessels Prohibited from Carrying Arms to Belligerent States

Sec. 6. (a) Whenever the President shall have issued a proclamation under the authority of section 1 of this Act, it shall thereafter be unlawful, until such proclamation is revoked, for any American vessel to carry any arms, ammunition, or implements of war to any belligerent state, or to any state wherein civil strife exists, named in such proclamation, or to any neutral state for transshipment to, or for the use of, any such belligerent state or any such state wherein civil strife exists.

(b) Whoever, in violation of the provisions of this section, shall take, or attempt to take, or shall authorize, hire, or solicit another to take, any American vessel carrying such cargo out of port or from the jurisdiction of the United States shall be fined not more than $10,000, or imprisoned not more than five years, or both; and, in addition, such vessel, and her tackle, apparel, furniture, and equipment, and the arms, ammunition, and implements of war on board, shall be forfeited to the United States.

Use of American Ports as Base of Supply

Sec. 7. (a) Whenever, during any war in which the United States is neutral, the President, or any person thereunto authorized by him, shall have cause to believe that any vessel, domestic or foreign, whether requiring clearance or not, is about to carry out of a port of the United States, fuel, men, arms, ammunition, implements of war, or other supplies to any warship, tender, or supply ship of a belligerent state, but the evidence is not deemed sufficient to justify forbidding the departure of the vessel . . . and if, in the President's judgment, such action will serve to maintain peace between the United States and foreign states, or to protect the commercial interests of the United States and its citizens, or to promote the security or neutrality of the United States, he shall have the power and it shall be his duty to require the owner, master, or person in command thereof, before departing from a port of the United States, to give a bond to the United States, with sufficient sureties, in such amount as he shall deem proper, conditioned that the vessel will not deliver the men, or any part of the cargo, to any warship, tender, or supply ship of a belligerent state.

(b) If the President, or any person thereunto authorized by him, shall find that a vessel, domestic or foreign, in a port of the United States, has previously cleared from a port of the United States during such war and delivered its cargo or any part thereof to a warship, tender, or supply ship of a belligerent state, he may prohibit the departure of such vessel during the duration of the war.

Submarines and Armed Merchant Vessels

Sec. 8. Whenever, during any war in which the United States is neutral, the President shall find that special restrictions placed on the use of the ports and territorial waters of the United States by the submarines or armed merchant vessels of a foreign state, will serve to maintain peace between the United States and foreign states, or to protect the commercial interests of the United States and its citizens, or to promote the security of the United States, and shall make proclamation thereof, it shall thereafter be unlawful for any such submarine or armed merchant vessel to enter a port or the territorial waters of the United States or to depart therefrom, except under such conditions and subject to such limitations as the President may prescribe. Whenever, in his judgment, the conditions which have caused him to issue his proclamation have ceased to exist, he shall revoke his proclamation and the provisions of this section shall thereupon cease to apply.

Travel on Vessels of Belligerent States

Sec. 9. Whenever the President shall have issued a proclamation under the authority of section 1 of this Act it shall thereafter be unlawful for any citizen of the United States to travel on any vessel of the state or states named in such proclamation, except in accordance with such rules and regulations as the President shall prescribe. . . .

Arming of American Merchant Vessels Prohibited

Sec. 10. Whenever the President shall have issued a proclamation under the authority of section 1, it shall thereafter be unlawful, until such proclamation is revoked, for any American vessel engaged in commerce with any belligerent state, or any state wherein civil strife exists, named in such proclamation, to be armed or to carry any armament, arms, ammunition, or implements of war, except small arms and ammunition therefor which the President may deem necessary and shall publicly designate for the preservation of discipline aboard such vessels.

Regulations

Sec. 11. The President may, from time to time, promulgate such rules and regulations, not inconsistent with law, as may be necessary and proper to carry out any of the provisions of this Act; and he may exercise any power or authority conferred on him by this Act through such officer or officers, or agency or agencies, as he shall direct. . . .

A Tentative Trial Balloon: The "Quarantine Speech" at Chicago, 1937

The year 1937 marked the beginning of Roosevelt's recognition that the new dangers to world security were both extreme and pressing. Japan had reactivated her lagging campaign for expansion; China and Japan were now at open, although undeclared, war. The Ethiopians had been crushed. Hitler was already posturing boldly after the huge success of his massive bluff in the Rhineland. And there was more time for Roosevelt to worry. The New Deal domestic program was well on the way, perhaps even lagging a bit, and the 1936 election was over.

Roosevelt determined upon a harder line and drew it sharply for the American people in a speech at Chicago in October, 1937. Here was to be heard more of a note of concern and horror than of the self-righteous frustration which had set the key for his Chautauqua speech a year earlier. There were other sharp changes of outlook. The secret of peace, he now insisted, must be "active." War must be treated like disease; war makers must be "quarantined" like the typhoid carriers. But the central implication was one which has sometimes been overlooked. The world, he now insisted, was indivisible; there was no longer any place to hide. War could be avoided only by "concerted" action against it.

The reaction to the quarantine speech was at best mixed, perhaps tending to the negative. Under pressure from Hull and other Democratic politicians, Roosevelt hastily retreated from the new position; it was now referred to sadly as having been merely a trial balloon. Hull later insisted that Roosevelt's quarantine speech had been a premature move which set back by six months the process of educating the people. But it may well be that the six months was lost precisely because he abandoned the campaign hastily when only a few early flurries of reaction were in.

Roosevelt had stated his position clearly, as the text of the speech makes evident. But, for the moment, he failed to lead.

Dorothy Borg comments usefully on this incident in "Notes on Roosevelt's Quarantine Speech," Political Science Quarterly, *volume 72, September, 1957, pages 405–433.*

The "Quarantine Speech" of October 5, 1937, is from a U.S. State Department Press Release of October 5, 1937, and may also be found in Whitney Shepardson and William O. Scroggs, The United States in World Affairs: 1937 *(New York: Harper & Row, 1938), pages 278–282.*

I am glad to come once again to Chicago and especially to have the opportunity of taking part in the dedication of this important project of civic betterment.

On my trip across the continent and back I have been shown many evidences of the result of common sense coöperation between municipalities and the Federal government, and I have been greeted by tens of thousands of Americans who have told me in every look and word that their material and spiritual well-being has made great strides forward in the past few years.

And yet, as I have seen with my own eyes, the prosperous farms, the thriving factories and the busy railroads—as I have seen the happiness and security and peace which covers our wide land—almost inevitably I have been compelled to contrast our peace with very different scenes being enacted in other parts of the world.

It is because the people of the United States under modern conditions must, for the sake of their own future, give thought to the rest of the world, that I, as the responsible executive head of the nation, have chosen this great inland city and this gala occasion to speak to you on a subject of definite national importance.

The political situation in the world, which of late has been growing progressively worse, is such as to cause grave concern and anxiety to all the peoples and nations who wish to live in peace and amity with their neighbors.

Some nine years ago the hopes of mankind for a continuing era of international peace were raised to great heights when more than sixty nations solemnly pledged themselves not to resort to arms in furtherance of their national aims and policies. The high aspirations expressed in the Briand-Kellogg Peace Pact and the hopes for peace thus raised have of late given way to a haunting fear of calamity. The present reign of terror and international lawlessness began a few years ago.

It began through unjustified interference in the internal affairs of other nations or the invasion of alien territory in violation of treaties, and has now reached a stage where the very foundations of civilization are seriously threatened. The landmarks and traditions which have marked the progress of civilization toward a condition of law, order and justice are being wiped away.

Without a declaration of war and without warning or justification of any kind civilians, including women and children, are being ruthlessly murdered with bombs from the air. In time of so-called peace ships are being attacked and sunk by submarines without cause or notice. Nations are fomenting and taking sides in civil warfare in nations that have never done them any harm. Nations claiming freedom for themselves deny it to others.

Innocent peoples and nations are being cruelly sacrificed to a greed for power and supremacy which is devoid of all sense of justice and humane consideration.

To paraphrase a recent author, "perhaps we foresee a time when men, exultant in the technique of homicide, will rage so hotly over the world that every precious thing will be in danger, every book and picture and harmony, every treasure garnered through two millenniums, the small, the delicate, the defenseless—all will be lost or wrecked or utterly destroyed."

If those things come to pass in other parts of the world, let no one imagine that America will escape, that it may expect mercy, that this Western Hemisphere will not be attacked and that it will continue tranquilly and peacefully to carry on the ethics and the arts of civilization.

If those days come "there will be no safety by arms, no help from authority, no answer in science. The storm will rage till every flower of culture is trampled and all human beings are leveled in a vast chaos."

If those days are not to come to pass—if we are to have a world in which we can breathe freely and live in amity without fear—the peace-loving nations must make a concerted effort to uphold laws and principles on which alone peace can rest secure.

The peace-loving nations must make a concerted effort in opposition to those violations of treaties and those ignorings of humane instincts which today are creating a state of international anarchy and instability from which there is no escape through mere isolation or neutrality.

Those who cherish their freedom and recognize and respect the equal right of their neighbors to be free and live in peace must work together for the triumph of law and moral principles in order that peace, justice and confidence may prevail in the world. There must be a return to a belief in the pledged word, in the value of a signed treaty. There must be recognition of the fact that national morality is as vital as private morality.

A bishop wrote me the other day: "It seems to me that something greatly needs to be said in behalf of ordinary humanity against the present practice of carrying the horrors of war to helpless civilians, especially women and children. It may be that such a protest might be regarded by many, who claim to be realists, as futile, but may it not be that the heart of mankind is so filled with horror at the present needless suffering that that force could be mobilized in sufficient volume to lessen such cruelty in the days ahead? Even though it may take twenty years, which God forbid, for civilization to make effective its corporate protest against this barbarism, surely strong voices may hasten the day."

There is a solidarity and interdependence about the modern world, both technically and morally, which makes it impossible for any nation completely to isolate itself from economic and political upheavals in the rest of the world, especially when such upheavals appear to be spreading and not declining. There can be no stability or peace either within nations or between nations except under laws and moral standards adhered to by all. International anarchy destroys every foundation for peace. It jeopardizes either the immediate or the future security of every nation, large or small. It is, therefore, a matter of vital interest and concern to the people of the United States that the sanctity of international treaties and the maintenance of international morality be restored.

The overwhelming majority of the peoples and nations of the world today want to live in peace. They seek the removal of barriers against trade. They want to exert themselves in industry, in agriculture and in business, that they may increase their wealth through the production of wealth-producing goods rather than striving to produce military planes and bombs and machine guns and cannon for the destruction of human lives and useful property.

In those nations of the world which seem to be piling armament on armament for purposes of aggression, and those other nations which fear acts of aggression against them and their security, a very high proportion of the national income is being spent directly for armaments. It runs from 30 to as high as 50 per cent.

The proportion that we in the United States spend is far less—11 or 12 per cent.

How happy we are that the circumstances of the moment permit us to put our money into bridges and boulevards, dams and reforestation, the conservation of our soil and many other kinds of useful works rather than into huge standing armies and vast supplies of implements of war.

I am compelled and you are compelled, nevertheless, to look ahead. The peace, the freedom and the security of 90 per cent of the population of the world is being jeopardized by the remaining 10 per cent who are threatening a breakdown of all international order and law. Surely the 90 per cent who want to live in peace under law and in accordance with moral standards that have received almost universal acceptance through the centuries, can and must find some way to make their will prevail.

The situation is definitely of universal concern. The questions involved relate not merely to violations of specific provisions of particular treaties; they are questions of war and of peace, of international law and especially of principles of humanity. It is true that they involve definite violations of agreements, and especially of the covenant of the League of Nations, the Briand-Kellogg Pact and the Nine Power Treaty. But they also involve problems of world economy, world security and world humanity.

It is true that the moral consciousness of the world must recognize the importance of removing injustices and well-founded grievances; but at the same time it must be aroused to the cardinal necessity of honoring sanctity of treaties, of respecting the rights and liberties of others and of putting an end to acts of international aggression.

It seems to be unfortunately true that the epidemic of world lawlessness is spreading.

When an epidemic of physical disease starts to spread, the community approves and joins in a quarantine of the patients in order to protect the health of the community against the spread of the disease.

It is my determination to pursue a policy of peace and to adopt every practicable measure to avoid involvement in war. It ought to be inconceivable that in this modern era, and in the face of experience, any nation could be so foolish and ruthless as to run the risk of plunging the whole world into war by invading and violating in contravention of solemn treaties, the territory of other nations that have done them no real harm and which are too weak to protect themselves adequately. Yet the peace of the world and the welfare and security of every nation is today being threatened by that very thing.

No nation which refuses to exercise forbearance and to respect the freedom and rights of others can long remain strong and retain the confidence and respect of other nations. No nation ever loses its dignity or good standing by conciliating its differences, and by exercising great patience with, and consideration for, the rights of other nations.

War is a contagion, whether it be declared or undeclared. It can engulf states and peoples remote from the original scene of hostilities. We are determined to keep out of war, yet we cannot insure ourselves against the disastrous effects of war and the dangers of involvement. We are adopting such measures as will minimize our risk of involvement, but we cannot have complete protection in a world of disorder in which confidence and security have broken down.

If civilization is to survive, the principles of the Prince of Peace must be restored. Shattered trust between nations must be revived.

Most important of all, the will for peace on the part of peace-loving nations must express itself to the end that nations that may be tempted to violate their agreements and the rights of others will desist from such a cause. There must be positive endeavors to preserve peace.

America hates war. America hopes for peace. Therefore, America actively engages in the search for peace.

PART **SEVEN**

Shattered Illusions: Foreign Policy, 1938–1941

The Threat of War

Decision in Disaster

Few periods in American history have been more important for the future of the Republic than the four years before December 7, 1941. These were the years in which the illusions were shattered, years during which it became clear that there was no escape from the world, that there was no happy dreamland where profits, peace, and security could be made to exist alongside war and insecurity.

The lesson was learned only slowly—and at last only by violence. The controversy until that point of violence was both enormous and bitter, and at first it ran under the guidance of the isolationists. Roosevelt felt the undertow of public opinion and drifted with the tide throughout the winter of 1937–1938. But in the spring, Hitler did with his renewed activity what Roosevelt had been completely unable to manage; more than anyone else it was the German dictator who first tipped the balance away from isolationism. In March, 1938, his troops violated Austria; in the summer they threatened Czechoslovakia; at the end of September Hitler forced from the British and French at a Munich Conference a deal which dismembered Czechoslovakia, discredited and disheartened the Western alliance and unnerved the small powers of central Europe. Tied by neutrality legislation, by uncertain public opinion, and by his own lack of leadership in the past, Roosevelt could do little more than to send formal pleas for peace to European chiefs of state.

But by the end of 1938 his position was beginning to strengthen. From that point until Pearl Harbor Day, American foreign policy can be charted as an increasingly tough series of pronouncements and action based upon three persistent and consistent goals, firmly held in sight by the administration: (1) Hitler must not be allowed to destroy Britain and control the Atlantic; (2) Japan must not be given a green light in Asia and the Western Pacific; and (3) these objectives must be gained, if possible, without the involvement of the American troops in a foreign war.

The classic studies of this period are William L. Langer and S. Everett Gleason, The Challenge to Isolation: 1937–1940 *(1952), and* The Undeclared War: 1940–1941 *(1953); also important are Walter Johnson.* The Battle against Isolation *(1944), and Wayne S. Cole,* America First: The Battleground against Intervention, 1940–1941 *(1953).*

Shattered Illusions: Foreign Policy, 1938–1941—The Threat of War

SELECTION 50

The New Line against Japan: United States Note to Tokyo, 1938

The Roosevelt administration's first major move after Manchuria came with its strong note to the Japanese government on December 30. It protested the discrimination against American interests in China implicit in the Japanese military occupation of those areas of China which they had overrun. It was a vigorous note, making the position and the protest of the United States clear. But its architects had stopped cautiously short of creating a crisis. They suggested negotiations; the fact, as the Japanese well knew, was that Americans were not prepared to show force in East Asia or in the Pacific. And the note departed only in tone from the established neutralist policy. It dealt only with the narrow interests of the United States, not with the major issues of aggression in China. It was not surprising that the Japanese took no serious notice of the protest.

The note published here is from Grew to the Japanese Minister of Foreign Affairs (Arita), December 30, 1938, in Peace and War, *pages 441–447.*

Tokyo, December 30, 1938.

Excellency: Acting under the instructions of my Government I have the honor to address to Your Excellency the following note:

The Government of the United States has received and has given full consideration to the reply of the Japanese Government of November 18 to this Government's note of October 6 on the subject of American rights and interests in China.

In the light of facts and experience the Government of the United States is impelled to reaffirm its previously expressed opinion that imposition of restrictions upon the movements and activities of American nationals who are engaged in philanthropic, educational and commercial endeavors in China has placed and will, if continued, increasingly place Japanese interests in a preferred position and is, therefore, unquestionably discriminatory in its effect against legitimate American interests. Further, with reference to such matters as exchange control, compulsory currency circulation, tariff revision, and monopolistic promotion in certain areas of China the plans and practices of the Japanese authorities imply an assumption on the part of those authorities that the Japanese Government or the regimes established and maintained in China by Japanese armed forces are entitled to act in China in a capacity such as flows from rights of sovereignty and further in so acting to disregard and even to declare nonexistent or abrogated the established rights and interests of other countries including the United States.

The Government of the United States expresses its conviction that the restrictions and measures under reference not only are unjust and unwarranted but are counter to the provisions of several binding international agreements, voluntarily entered into, to which both Japan and the United States, and in some cases other countries, are parties.

In the concluding portion of its note under reference, the Japanese Government states that it is firmly convinced that "in the face of the new situation, fast developing in Asia, any attempt to apply to the conditions of today and tomorrow inapplicable ideas and principles of the past neither would contribute toward the establishment of a real peace in East Asia nor solve the immediate issues" and that "as long as these points are understood Japan has not the slightest inclination to oppose the participation of the United States and other Powers in the great work of reconstructing East Asia along all lines of industry and trade."

The Government of the United States in its note of October 6 requested, in view of the oft reiterated assurances proffered by the Government of Japan of its intention to observe the principles of equality of opportunity in its relations with China and in view of Japan's treaty obligations so to do, that the Government of Japan abide by these obligations and carry out these assurances in practice. The Japanese Government in its reply appears to affirm that it is its intention to make its observance of that principle conditional upon an understanding by the American Government and by other governments of a "new situation" and a "new order" in the Far East as envisaged and fostered by Japanese authorities.

Treaties which bear upon the situation in the Far East have within them provisions relating to a number of subjects. In the making of those treaties, there was a process among the parties to them to give and take. Toward making possible the carrying out of some of their provisions, others among their provisions were formulated and agreed upon: toward gaining for itself the advantage of security in regard to certain matters, each of the parties committed itself to pledges of self-denial in regard to certain other matters. The various provisions agreed upon may be said to have constituted collectively an arrangement for safeguarding, for the benefit of all, the correlated principles on the one hand of national integrity and on the other hand of equality of economic opportunity. Experience has shown that impairment of the former of these principles is followed almost invariably by disregard of the latter. Whenever any government begins to exercise political authority in areas beyond the limits of its lawful jurisdiction there develops inevitably a situation in which the nationals of that government demand and are accorded, at the hands of their government, preferred treatment, whereupon equality of opportunity ceases to exist and discriminatory practices, productive of friction, prevail.

The admonition that enjoyment by the nationals of the United States of non-discriminatory treatment in China—a general and well established right—is henceforth to be contingent upon an admission by the Government of the United States of the validity of the conception of Japanese authorities of a "new situation" and a "new order" in East Asia, is, in the opinion of this Government, highly paradoxical.

This country's adherence to and its advocacy of the principle of equality of opportunity do not flow solely from a desire to obtain the commercial benefits which naturally result from the provisions of that principle. They flow from a firm conviction that observance of that principle leads to economic and political stability, which are conducive both to the internal well-being of nations and to mutually beneficial and peaceful relationships between and among nations; from a firm conviction that failure to observe that principle breeds international friction and ill-will, with consequences injurious to all countries, including in particular those countries which fail to observe it; and from an equally firm conviction that observance of that principle promotes the opening of trade channels thereby making available the markets, the raw materials and the manufactured products of the community of nations on a mutually and reciprocally beneficial basis.

The principle of equality of economic opportunity is, moreover, one to which over a long period and on many occasions the Japanese Government has given definite approval. It is one to the observance of which the Japanese Government has committed itself in various international agreements and understandings. It is one upon observance of which by other nations the Japanese Government has of its own accord and upon its own initiative frequently insisted. It is one to which the Japanese Government has repeatedly during recent months declared itself committed.

The people and the Government of the United States could not assent to the establishment at the instance of and for the special purposes of any third country of a regime which would arbitrarily deprive them of the long established rights of equal opportunity and fair treatment which are legally and justly theirs along with those of other nationals.

Fundamental principles such as the principle of equality of opportunity which have long been regarded as inherently wise and just which have been widely adopted and adhered to, and which are general in their application are not subject to nullification by a unilateral affirmation.

With regard to the implication in the Japanese Government's note that the "conditions of today and tomorrow" in the Far East call for a revision of the ideas and principles of the past, this Government desires to recall to the Japanese Government its position on the subject of revision of agreements.

This Government had occasion in the course of a communication delivered to the Japanese Government on April 29, 1934, to express its opinion that "treaties can lawfully be modified or be terminated,—but only by processes prescribed or recognized or agreed upon by the parties to them."

In the same communication this Government also said, "In the opinion of the American people and the American Government, no nation can, without the assent of the other nations concerned, rightfully endeavor to make conclusive its will in situations where there are involved the rights, the obligations and the legitimate interests of other sovereign states." In an official and public statement on July 16, 1937, the Secretary of State of the United States declared that this Government advocates "adjustment of problems in international relations by processes of peaceful negotiation and agreement."

At various times during recent decades various powers, among which have been Japan and the United States, have had occasion to communicate and to confer with regard to situations and problems in the Far East. In the conducting of correspondence and of conferences relating to these matters, the parties involved have invariably taken into consideration past and present facts and they have not failed to perceive the possibility and the desirability of changes in the situation. In the making of treaties they have drawn up and have agreed upon provisions intended to facilitate advantageous developments and at the same time to obviate and avert the arising of friction between and among the various powers which, having interests in the region or regions under reference, were and would be concerned.

In the light of these facts, and with reference especially to the purpose and the character of the treaty provisions from time to time solemnly agreed upon for the very definite purposes indicated, the Government of the United States deprecates the fact that one of the parties to these agreements has chosen to embark—as indicated both by action of its agents and by official statements of its authorities—upon a course directed toward the arbitrary creation by that power by methods of its own selection, regardless of treaty pledges and the established rights of other powers concerned, of a "new order" in the Far East. Whatever may be the changes which have taken place in the situation in the Far East and whatever may be the situation now, these matters are of no less interest and concern to the American Government than have been the situations which have prevailed there in the past, and such changes as may henceforth take place there, changes which may enter into the producing of a "new situation" and a "new order," are and will be of like concern to this Government. This Government is well aware that the situation has changed. This Government is also well aware that many of the changes have been brought about by the action of Japan. This Government does not admit, however, that there is need or warrant for any one Power to take upon itself to prescribe what shall be the terms and conditions of a "new order" in areas not under its sovereignty and to constitute itself the repository of authority and the agent of destiny in regard thereto.

It is known to all the world that various of the parties to treaties concluded for the purpose of regulating contacts in the Far East and avoiding friction therein and therefrom—which treaties contained, for those purposes, various restrictive provisions—have from time to time and by processes of negotiation and agreement contributed in the light of changed situations toward the removal of restrictions and toward the bringing about of further developments which would warrant in the light of further changes in the situation, further removals of restrictions. By such methods and processes, early restrictions upon the tariff autonomy of all countries in the Far East were removed. By such methods and processes the rights of extraterritorial jurisdiction once enjoyed by Occidental countries in relations with countries in the Far East have been given up in relations with all of those countries except China; and in the years immediately preceding and including the year 1931, countries which still possessed those rights in China including the United States were actively engaged in negotiations—far advanced—looking toward surrender of those rights. All discerning and impartial observers have realized that the United States and others of the "treaty powers" have not during recent decades clung tenaciously to their so-called "special" rights and privileges in countries of the Far East but on the contrary have steadily encouraged the development in those countries of institutions and practices in the presence of which such rights and privileges may safely and readily be given up; and all observers have seen those rights and privileges gradually being surrendered voluntarily through agreement by the Powers which have possessed them. On one point only has the Government of the United States, along with several other governments, insisted: namely, that new situations must have developed to a point warranting the removal of "special" safeguarding restrictions and that the removals be effected by orderly processes.

The Government of the United States has at all times regarded agreements as susceptible of alteration, but it has always insisted that alterations can rightfully be made only by orderly processes of negotiation and agreement among the parties thereto.

The Japanese Government has upon numerous occasions expressed itself as holding similar views.

The United States has in its international relations rights and obligations which derive from international law and rights and obligations which rest upon treaty provisions. Of those which rest on treaty provisions, its rights and obligations in and with regard to China rest in part upon provisions in treaties between the United States and China and in part on provisions in treaties between the United States and several other powers including both China and Japan. These treaties were concluded in good faith for the purpose of safeguarding and promoting the interests not of one only but of all of their signatories. The people and the Government of the United States cannot assent to the abrogation of any of this country's rights or obligations by the arbitrary action of agents or authorities of any other country.

The Government of the United States has, however, always been prepared and is now prepared to give due and ample consideration to any proposals based on justice and reason which envisage the resolving of problems in a manner duly considerate of the rights and obligations of all parties directly concerned by processes of free negotiation and new commitment by and among all of the parties so concerned. There has been and there continues to be opportunity for the Japanese Government to put forward such proposals. This Government has been and it continues to be willing to discuss such proposals, if and when put forward, with representatives of the other powers, including Japan and China, whose rights and interests are involved, at whatever time and in whatever place may be commonly agreed upon.

Meanwhile, this Government reserves all rights of the United States as they exist and does not give assent to any impairment of any of those rights.

I avail myself [etc.]
JOSEPH C. GREW

SELECTION 51

War in Europe: The President Addresses the People, 1939

In his Annual Message of January, 1939, FDR warned clearly, although in quite general terms, that neutrality legislation had proved mistaken and that a new approach must be found which would restrict aggressors and not, perchance, punish those who defended themselves. For the moment, he could only push weakly and without result. He asked for a repeal of the arms embargo, for a revised neutrality law with a presidential option in enforcement, for a cash-and-carry law on armaments as well as raw materials. In a long, bitter debate which stretched out through the summer, the isolationist leadership of Congress held its mark and cut to pieces or fought off the new proposals. American public opinion was already shifting toward the "cash-and-carry" sale of finished arms, but its trend had not yet been felt in Congress.

Then on September 3, 1939, Hitler's armies rolled across Poland. It was clear at once that both Britain and France must fight. Roosevelt spoke to the American people in the radio address printed below. His position was clearly neutralist, his aim to maintain United States security. But that his position was also pro-Allied there could be no doubt. Public opinion appears to have been with him in both cases. Two and a half weeks later the President called a special session of Congress to revise the neutrality legislation. In October, the Congress approved cash-and-carry sales of munitions as well as raw materials to belligerents.

On public opinion in this era, see Hadley Cantril (ed.), Public Opinion: 1938–1946 *(1951).*

Roosevelt's radio address of September 3, 1939 is to be found in Peace and War, *pages 483–486.*

Tonight my single duty is to speak to the whole of America.

Until 4:30 this morning I had hoped against hope that some miracle would prevent a devastating war in Europe and bring to an end the invasion of Poland by Germany.

For 4 long years a succession of actual wars and constant crises have shaken the entire world and have threatened in each case to bring on the gigantic conflict which is today unhappily a fact.

It is right that I should recall to your minds the consistent and at times successful efforts of your Government in these crises to throw the full weight of the United States into the cause of peace. In spite of spreading wars I think that we have every right and every reason to maintain as a national policy the fundamental moralities, the teachings of religion, and the continuation of efforts to restore peace—for some day, though the time may be distant, we can be of even greater help to a crippled humanity.

It is right, too, to point out that the unfortunate events of these recent years have been based on the use of force or the threat of force. And it seems to me clear, even at the outbreak of this great war, that the influence of America should be consistent in seeking for humanity a final peace which will eliminate, as far as it is possible to do so, the continued use of force between nations.

It is, of course, impossible to predict the future. I have my constant stream of information from American representatives and other sources throughout the world. You, the people of this country, are receiving news through your radios and your newspapers at every hour of the day.

You are, I believe, the most enlightened and the best informed people in all the world at this moment. You are subjected to no censorship of news; and I want to add that your Government has no information which it has any thought of withholding from you.

At the same time, as I told my press conference on Friday, it is of the highest importance that the press and the radio use the utmost caution to discriminate between actual verified fact on the one hand and mere rumor on the other.

I can add to that by saying that I hope the people of this country will also discriminate most carefully between news and rumor. Do not believe of necessity everything you hear or read. Check up on it first.

You must master at the outset a simple but unalterable fact in modern foreign relations. When peace has been broken anywhere, peace of all countries everywhere is in danger.

It is easy for you and me to shrug our shoulders and say that conflicts taking place thousands of miles from the continental United States, and, indeed, the whole American hemisphere, do not seriously affect the Americas—and that all the United States has to do is to ignore them and go about our own business. Passionately though we may desire detachment, we are forced to realize that every word that comes through the air, every ship that sails the sea, every battle that is fought does affect the American future.

Let no man or woman thoughtlessly or falsely talk of America sending its armies to European fields. At this moment there is being prepared a proclamation of American neutrality. This would have been done even if there had been no neutrality statute on the books, for this proclamation is in accordance with international law and with American policy.

This will be followed by a proclamation required by the existing Neutrality Act. I trust that in the days to come our neutrality can be made a true neutrality.

It is of the utmost importance that the people of this country, with the best information in the world, think things through. The most dangerous enemies of American peace are those who, without well-rounded information on the whole broad subject of the past, the present, and the future, undertake to speak with authority, to talk in terms of glittering generalities, to give to the Nation assurances or prophecies which are of little present or future value.

I myself cannot and do not prophesy the course of events abroad—and the reason is that because I have of necessity such a complete picture of what is going on in every part of the world, I do not dare to do so. And the other reason is that I think it is honest for me to be honest with the people of the United States.

I cannot prophesy the immediate economic effect of this new war on our Nation, but I do say that no American has the moral right to profiteer at the expense either of his fellow citizens or of the men, women, and children who are living and dying in the midst of war in Europe.

Some things we do know. Most of us in the United States believe in spiritual values. Most of us, regardless of what church we belong to, believe in the spirit of the New Testament—a great teaching which opposes itself to the use of force, of armed force, of marching armies, and falling bombs. The overwhelming masses of our people seek peace—peace at home, and the kind of peace in other lands which will not jeopardize peace at home.

We have certain ideas and ideals of national safety, and we must act to preserve that safety today and to preserve the safety of our children in future years.

That safety is and will be bound up with the safety of the Western Hemisphere and of the seas adjacent thereto. We seek to keep war from our firesides by keeping war from coming to the Americas. For that we have historic precedent that goes back to the days of the administration of President George Washington. It is serious enough and tragic enough to every American family in every State in the Union to live in a world that is torn by wars on other continents. Today they affect every American home. It is our national duty to use every effort to keep them out of the Americas.

And at this time let me make the simple plea that partisanship and selfishness be adjourned, and that national unity be the thought that underlies all others.

This Nation will remain a neutral nation, but I cannot ask that every American remain neutral in thought as well. Even a neutral has a right to take account of facts. Even a neutral cannot be asked to close his mind or his conscience.

I have said not once but many times that I have seen war and that I hate war. I say that again and again.

I hope the United States will keep out of this war. I believe that it will. And I give you assurances that every effort of your Government will be directed toward that end.

As long as it remains within my power to prevent, there will be no blackout of peace in the United States.

SELECTION 52

Halfway between Peace and War: Roosevelt Requests Lend-Lease, 1941

The winter of 1939–1940 saw six months of so-called phony war. Hitler regrouped his forces for his all but inevitable push to the West in the spring. The British and the French worked feverishly to cut through the torpor of tradition and refurbish their antique military establishments. Few recognized how very antique they were, what a dangerous delusion the Maginot Line frame of mind would prove to have been. But even within the limits of their vision, the challenge in time and money proved impossible. Planes, for example, could not be obtained to fight off the Stuka or the Messerschmitt without first building the plants in Europe or America. Under American cash-and-carry legislation, much valuable purchasing power was used up constructing facilities for American arms and aircraft factories. And soon British and French governments would face complete exhaustion of their scarce supplies of gold and dollars.

By the spring of 1940, the plight of Western Europe seemed desperate. In April, Hitler crushed Norway and Denmark; in May, he smashed the Dutch and Belgians and rolled his armies forward toward Paris. The British were pushed back against the bloody beachhead at Dunkirk. By mid-June, France had fallen. There had been hysterical cries for planes from the beleaguered French. There had been none to send. Britain, now beseiged and perhaps fated to disaster, pressed for aid. There was little to send; only slight chance of delivering it with the U-boat warfare in the Atlantic; and no way to send it, in any case, unless Britain could pay.

The Roosevelt administration pressed its own defense program with speed and popular support: over 17 billion dollars for a two-ocean navy and a conscript army. Agreements were arranged at Havana in July for joint guarantees of Western Hemisphere stability by the American republics. Transfers of European colonies were to be particularly prevented, and an agreement for joint Canadian-American defense was also reached. But, until the summer of 1940, nothing substantive was done to aid Britain. Then, on September 2, the dramatic announcement of the destroyer–airbase deal was made. The President had "sold" "overage" destroyers to Britain; the price had been a lease on land for U.S. air bases in Newfoundland and in the West Indies. Inspired by necessity and made possible by the discovery of an obscure legal device authorizing the President to "sell" obsolete armaments, this was at best a temporary expedient to deal with one aspect of the problem, the submarine menace.

During the fall and early winter the administration, and particularly the Treasury Department, worked on the lend-lease proposal which promised a substantial and systematic support for the Allies. It was presented to Congress in the State of the Union Message of January 6, 1941, which is printed below.

The message placed lend-lease in a broad and appealing context. It was not a matter simply of aid to Britain; it was a defense of freedom. The United States was not merely defending herself; she was about to become the "arsenal of democracy." And Roosevelt sought to give meaning to the fight for freedom by spelling out the major objectives of democracy at home and by giving voice to the "Four Freedoms," a statement of goals which would serve well throughout the whole war.

The general problem of the nation's transition from neutrality to involvement is discussed in Robert A. Divine, The Illusion of Neutrality *(1962). Regarding the economic and military aid itself, see Robert E. Sherwood,* Roosevelt and Hopkins *(1948) and Edward R. Stettinius,* Lend-Lease: Weapon for Victory *(1944).*

FDR's Message of January 6, 1941, is taken from the Congressional Record, *Seventy-seventh Congress, first session, volume 87, part 1, pages 44–47.*

Mr. President, Mr. Speaker, Members of the Seventy-seventh Congress, I address you, the Members of the Seventy-seventh Congress, at a moment unprecedented in the history of the Union. I use the word "unprecedented," because at no previous time has American security been as seriously threatened from without as it is today.

Since the permanent formation of our Government under the Constitution, in 1789, most of the periods of crises in our history have related to our domestic affairs. Fortunately, only one of these—the 4-year War between the States—ever threatened our national unity. Today, thank God, 130,000,000 Americans, in 48 States, have forgotten points of the compass in our national unity.

It is true that prior to 1914 the United States often had been disturbed by events in other continents. We had even engaged in two wars with European nations and in a number of undeclared wars in the West Indies, in the Mediterranean, and in the Pacific for the maintenance of American rights and for the principles of peaceful commerce. In no case, however, had a serious threat been raised against our national safety or our independence.

What I seek to convey is the historic truth that the United States, as a nation, has at all times maintained opposition to any attempt to lock us in behind an ancient Chinese wall while the procession of civilization went past. Today, thinking of our children and their children, we oppose enforced isolation for ourselves or for any part of the Americas.

That determination of ours was proved, for example, during the quarter century of wars following the French Revolution.

While the Napoleanic struggles did threaten interests of the United States because of the French foothold in the West Indies and in Louisiana, and while we engaged in the War of 1812 to vindicate our right to peaceful trade, it is, nevertheless, clear that neither France nor Great Britain nor any other nation was aiming at domination of the whole world.

In like fashion, from 1815 to 1914—99 years—no single war in Europe or in Asia constituted a real threat against our future or against the future of any other American nation.

Except in the Maximilian interlude in Mexico, no foreign power sought to establish itself in this hemisphere, and the strength of the British Fleet in the Atlantic has been a friendly strength. It is still a friendly strength.

Even when the World War broke out in 1914 it seemed to contain only small threat of danger to our own American future. But as time went on the American people began to visualize what the downfall of democratic nations might mean to our own democracy.

We need not overemphasize imperfections in the peace of Versailles. We need not harp on failure of the democracies to deal with problems of world reconstruction. We should remember that the peace of 1919 was far less unjust than the kind of "pacification" which began even before Munich and which is being carried on under the new order of tyranny that seeks to spread over every continent today. The American people have unalterably set their faces against that tyranny.

Every realist knows that the democratic way of life is at this moment being directly assailed in every part of the world—assailed either by arms or by secret spreading of poisonous propaganda by those who seek to destroy unity and promote discord in nations still at peace.

During 16 months this assault has blotted out the whole pattern of democratic life in an appalling number of independent nations, great and small. The assailants are still on the march, threatening other nations, great and small.

Therefore, as your President, performing my constitutional duty to "give to the Congress information of the state of the Union," I find it necessary to report that the future and the safety of our country and of our democracy are overwhelmingly involved in events far beyond our borders.

Armed defense of democratic existence is now being gallantly waged in four continents. If that defense fails, all the population and all the resources of Europe, Asia, Africa, and Australasia will be dominated by the conquerors. The total of those populations and their resources greatly exceeds the sum total of the population and resources of the whole of the Western Hemisphere—many times over.

In times like these it is immature—and incidentally untrue—for anybody to brag that an unprepared America, single-handed, and with one hand tied behind its back, can hold off the whole world.

No realistic American can expect from a dictator's peace international generosity, or return of true independence, or world disarmament, or freedom of expression, or freedom of religion—or even good business.

Such a peace would bring no security for us or for our neighbors. "Those who would give up essential liberty to purchase a little temporary safety deserve neither liberty nor safety."

As a Nation we may take pride in the fact that we are soft-hearted; but we cannot afford to be soft-headed.

We must always be wary of those who, with sounding brass and a tinkling cymbal, preach the "ism" of appeasement.

We must especially beware of that small group of selfish men who would clip the wings of the American eagle in order to feather their own nests.

I have recently pointed out how quickly the tempo of modern warfare could bring into our very midst the physical attack which we must expect if the dictator nations win this war.

There is much loose talk of our immunity from immediate and direct invasion from across the seas. Obviously, as long as the British Navy retains its power, no such danger exists. Even if there were no British Navy, it is not probable that any enemy would be stupid enough to attack us by landing troops in the United States from across thousands of miles of ocean, until it had acquired strategic bases from which to operate.

But we learn much from the lessons of the past years in Europe—particularly the lesson of Norway, whose essential seaports were captured by treachery and surprise built up over a series of years.

The first phase of the invasion of this hemisphere would not be the landing of regular troops. The necessary strategic points would be occupied by secret agents and their dupes, and great numbers of them are already here, and in Latin America.

As long as the aggressor nations maintain the offsensive, they, not we, will choose the time and the place and the method of their attack.

That is why the future of all American republics is today in serious danger.

That is why this annual message to the Congress is unique in our history.

That is why every member of the executive branch of the Government and every Member of the Congress face great responsibility—and great accountability.

The need of the moment is that our actions and our policy should be devoted primarily—almost exclusively—to meeting this foreign peril. For all our domestic problems are now a part of the great emergency.

Just as our national policy in internal affairs has been based upon a decent respect for the rights and dignity of all our fellow-men within our gates, so our national policy in foreign affairs has been based on a decent respect for the rights and dignity of all nations, large and small. And the justice of morality must and will win in the end.

Our national policy is this:

First, by an impressive expression of the public will and without regard to partisanship, we are committed to all-inclusive national defense.

Second, by an impressive expression of the public will and without regard to partisanship, we are committed to full support of all those resolute peoples, everywhere, who are resisting aggression and are thereby keeping war away from our hemisphere. By this support, we express our determination that the democratic cause shall prevail, and we strengthen the defense and security of our own Nation.

Third, by an impressive expression of the public will and without regard to partisanship, we are committed to the proposition that principles of morality and considerations for our own security will never permit us to acquiesce in a peace dictated by aggressors and sponsored by appeasers. We know that enduring peace cannot be bought at the cost of other people's freedom.

In the recent national election there was no substantial difference between the two great parties in respect to that national policy. No issue was fought out on this line before the American electorate. Today it is abundantly evident that American citizens everywhere are demanding and supporting speedy and complete action in recognition of obvious danger.

Therefore, the immediate need is a swift and driving increase in our armament production.

Leaders of industry and labor have responded to our summons. Goals of speed have been set. In some cases these goals are being reached ahead of time; in some cases we are on schedule; in other cases there are slight but not serious delays; and in some cases—and I am sorry to say very important cases—we are all concerned by the slowness of the accomplishment of our plans.

The Army and Navy, however, have made substantial progress during the past year. Actual experience is improving and speeding up our methods of production with every passing day. And todays' best is not good enough for tomorrow.

I am not satisfied with the progress thus far made. The men in charge of the program represent the best in training, ability, and patriotism. They are not satisfied with the progress thus far made. None of us will be satisfied until the job is done.

No matter whether the original goal was set too high or too low, our objective is quicker and better results.

To give two illustrations:

We are behind schedule in turning out finished airplanes; we are working day and night to solve the innumerable problems and to catch up.

We are ahead of schedule in building warships; but we are working to get even further ahead of schedule.

To change a whole nation from a basis of peacetime production of implements of peace to a basis of wartime production of implements of war is no small task. And the greatest difficulty comes at the beginning of the program, when new tools and plant facilities and new assembly lines and shipways must first be constructed before the actual matériel begins to flow steadily and speedily from them.

The Congress, of course, must rightly keep itself informed at all times of the progress of the program. However, there is certain information, as the Congress itself will readily recognize, which, in the interests of our own security and those of the nations we are supporting must of needs be kept in confidence.

New circumstances are constantly begetting new needs for our safety. I shall ask this Congress for greatly increased new appropriations and authorizations to carry on what we have begun.

I also ask this Congress for authority and for funds sufficient to manufacture additional munitions and war supplies of many kinds, to be turned over to those nations which are now in actual war with aggressor nations.

Our most useful and immediate role is to act as an arsenal for them as well as for ourselves. They do not need manpower. They do need billions of dollars' worth of the weapons of defense.

The time is near when they will not be able to pay for them in ready cash. We cannot, and will not, tell them they must surrender merely because of present inability to pay for the weapons which we know they must have.

I do not recommend that we make them a loan of dollars with which to pay for these weapons—a loan to be repaid in dollars.

I recommend that we make it possible for those nations to continue to obtain war materials in the United States, fitting their orders into our own program. Nearly all of their matériel would, if the time ever came, be useful for our own defense.

Taking counsel of expert military and naval authorities, considering what is best for our own security, we are free to decide how much should be kept here and how much should be sent abroad to our friends who, by their determined and heroic resistance, are giving us time in which to make ready our own defense.

For what we send abroad we shall be repaid, within a reasonable time following the close of hostilities, in similar materials or, at our option, in other goods of many kinds which they can produce and which we need.

Let us say to the democracies, "We Americans are vitally concerned in your defense of freedom. We are putting forth our energies, our resources, and our organizing powers to give you the strength to regain and maintain a free world. We shall send you, in ever-increasing numbers, ships, planes, tanks, guns. This is our purpose and our pledge."

In fulfillment of this purpose we will not be intimidated by the threats of dictators that they will regard as a breach of international law and as an act of war our aid to the democracies which dare to resist their aggression. Such aid is not an act of war, even if a dictator should unilaterally proclaim it so to be.

When the dictators are ready to make war upon us, they will not wait for an act of war on our part. They did not wait for Norway or Belgium or the Netherlands to commit an act of war.

Their only interest is in a new one-way international law, which lacks mutuality in its observance and, therefore, becomes an instrument of oppression.

The happiness of future generations of Americans may well depend upon how effective and how immediate we can make our aid felt. No one can tell the exact character of the emergency situations that we may be called upon to meet. The Nation's hands must not be tied when the Nation's life is in danger.

We must all prepare to make the sacrifices that the emergency—as serious as war itself—demands. Whatever stands in the way of speed and efficiency in defense preparations must give way to the national need.

A free nation has the right to expect full cooperation from all groups. A free nation has the right to look to the leaders of business, of labor, and of agriculture to take the lead in stimulating effort, not among other groups but within their own groups.

The best way of dealing with the few slackers or trouble makers in our midst is, first, to shame them by patriotic example; and if that fails, to use the sovereignty of government to save government.

As men do not live by bread alone, they do not fight by armaments alone. Those who man our defenses, and those behind them who build our defenses, must have the stamina and courage which come from an unshakable belief in the manner of life which they are defending. The mighty action which we are calling for cannot be based on a disregard of all things worth fighting for.

The Nation takes great satisfaction and much strength from the things which have been done to make its people conscious of their individual stake in the preservation of democratic life in America. Those things have toughened the fiber of our people, have renewed their faith and strengthened their devotion to the institutions we make ready to protect.

Certainly this is no time to stop thinking about the social and economic problems which are the root cause of the social revolution which is today a supreme factor in the world.

There is nothing mysterious about the foundations of a healthy and strong democracy. The basic things expected by our people of their political and economic systems are simple. They are:

Equality of opportunity for youth and for others.

Jobs for those who can work.

Security for those who need it.

The ending of special privilege for the few.

The preservation of civil liberties for all.

The enjoyment of the fruits of scientific progress in a wider and constantly rising standard of living.

These are the simple and basic things that must never be lost sight of in the turmoil and unbelievable complexity of our modern world. The inner and abiding strength of our economic and political systems is dependent upon the degree to which they fulfill these expectations.

Many subjects connected with our social economy call for immediate improvement.

As examples:

We should bring more citizens under the coverage of old-age pensions and unemployment insurance.

We should widen the opportunities for adequate medical care.

We should plan a better system by which persons deserving or needing gainful employment may obtain it.

I have called for personal sacrifice. I am assured of the willingness of almost all Americans to respond to that call.

A part of the sacrifice means the payment of more money in taxes. In my Budget message I recommend that a greater portion of this great defense program be paid for from taxation than we are paying today. No person should try, or be allowed, to get rich out of this program; and the principle of tax payments in accordance with ability to pay should be constantly before our eyes to guide our legislation.

If the Congress maintains these principles, the voters, putting patriotism ahead of pocketbooks, will give you their applause.

In the future days, which we seek to make secure, we look forward to a world founded upon four essential human freedoms.

The first is freedom of speech and expression everywhere in the world.

The second is freedom of every person to worship God in his own way everywhere in the world.

The third is freedom from want, which, translated into world terms, means economic understandings which will secure to every nation a healthy peacetime life for its inhabitants everywhere in the world.

The fourth is freedom from fear—which, translated into world terms, means a world-wide reduction of armaments to such a point and in such a thorough fashion that no nation will be in a position to commit an act of physical aggression against any neighbor—anywhere in the world.

That is no vision of a distant millenium. It is a definite basis for a kind of world attainable in our own time and generation. That kind of world is the very antithesis of the so-called new order of tyranny which the dictators seek to create with the crash of a bomb.

To that new order we oppose the greater conception—the moral order. A good society is able to face schemes of world domination and foreign revolutions alike without fear.

Since the beginning of our American history we have been engaged in change—in a perpetual peaceful revolution—a revolution which goes on steadily, quietly adjusting itself to changing conditions—without the concentration camp or the quicklime in the ditch. The world order which we seek is the cooperation of free countries, working together in a friendly, civilized society.

This Nation has placed its destiny in the hands and heads and hearts of its millions of free men and women; and its faith in freedom under the guidance of God. Freedom means the supremacy of human rights everywhere. Our support goes to those who struggle to gain those rights or keep them. Our strength is in our unity of purpose.

To that high concept there can be no end save victory.

Commitment in Matériel: Lend-Lease Act, 1941

Lend-lease itself was authorized by a simple, straightforward piece of legislation which became law in March, 1941. While Congress maintained a considerable amount of authority in the matter of making appropriations, it provided a simple structure of administration and set the whole operation clearly within the war and defense power of the Federal government, for the purposes of constitutional justification. An initial appropriation of 7 billion dollars grew eventually to a total of 50,226,845,387 dollars. Originally limited chiefly to the British, it was expanded to cover the Soviet Union after Hitler's invasion of June 22, 1941. Eventually aid went to most of the powers which fought against the German-Italian-Japanese "Axis." Conceived as a step short of war, designed to bolster the British and thereby perhaps stave off American involvement, it became after December 7, 1941, a device by which American matériel could be efficiently distributed among the Allies in terms of need and effectiveness.

The Lend-Lease Act of March 11, 1941, is in U.S. Statutes at Large, *volume 55, part 1, pages 31–33, and is also available in* Peace and War, *pages 627–630.*

Be *it enacted by the Senate and House of Representatives of the United States of America in Congress assembled,* That this Act may be cited as "An Act to Promote the Defense of the United States".

Sec. 2. As used in this Act—

(a) The term "defense article" means—

(1) Any weapon, munition, aircraft, vessel, or boat;

(2) Any machinery, facility, tool, material, or supply necessary for the manufacture, production, processing, repair, servicing, or operation of any article described in this subsection;

(3) Any component material or part of or equipment for any article described in this subsection;

(4) Any agricultural, industrial or other commodity or article for defense.

Such term "defense article" includes any article described in this subsection: Manufactured or procured pursuant to section 3, or to which the United States or any foreign government has or hereafter acquires title, possession, or control.

(b) The term "defense information" means any plan, specification, design, prototype, or information pertaining to any defense article.

Sec. 3. (a) Notwithstanding the provisions of any other law, the President may, from time to time, when he deems it in the interest of national defense, authorize the Secretary of War, the Secretary of the Navy, or the head of any other department or agency of the Government—

(1) To manufacture in arsenals, factories, and shipyards under their jurisdiction, or otherwise procure, to the extent to which funds are made available therefor, or contracts are authorized from time to time by the Congress, or both, any defense article for the government of any country whose defense the President deems vital to the defense of the United States.

(2) To sell, transfer title to, exchange, lease, lend, or otherwise dispose of, to any such government any defense article, but no defense article not manufactured or procured under paragraph (1) shall in any way be disposed of under this paragraph, except after consultation with the Chief of Staff of the Army or the Chief of Naval Operations of the Navy, or both. The value of defense articles disposed of in any way under authority of this paragraph, and procured from funds heretofore appropriated, shall not exceed $1,300,000,000. The value of such defense articles shall be determined by the head of the department or agency concerned or such other department, agency or officer as shall be designated in the manner provided in the rules and regulations issued hereunder. Defense articles procured from funds hereafter appropriated to any department or agency of the Government, other than from funds authorized to be appropriated under this Act, shall not be disposed of in any way under authority of this paragraph except to the extent hereafter authorized by the Congress in the Acts appropriating such funds or otherwise.

(3) To test, inspect, prove, repair, outfit, recondition, or otherwise to place in good working order, to the extent to which funds are made

available therefor, or contracts are authorized from time to time by the Congress, or both, any defense article for any such government, or to procure any or all such services by private contract.

(4) To communicate to any such government any defense information, pertaining to any defense article furnished to such government under paragraph (2) of this subsection.

(5) To release for export any defense article disposed of in any way under this subsection to any such government.

(b) The terms and conditions upon which any such foreign government receives any aid authorized under subsection (a) shall be those which the President deems satisfactory, and the benefit to the United States may be payment or repayment in kind or property, or any other direct or indirect benefit which the President deems satisfactory.

(c) After June 30, 1943, or after the passage of a concurrent resolution by the two Houses before June 30, 1943, which declares that the powers conferred by or pursuant to subsection (a) are no longer necessary to promote the defense of the United States, neither the President nor the head of any department or agency shall exercise any of the powers conferred by or pursuant to subsection (a); except that until July 1, 1946, any of such powers may be exercised to the extent necessary to carry out a contract or agreement with such a foreign government made before July 1, 1943, or before the passage of such concurrent resolution, whichever is the earlier.

(d) Nothing in this Act shall be construed to authorize or to permit the authorization of convoying vessels by naval vessels of the United States.

(e) Nothing in this Act shall be construed to authorize or to permit the authorization of the entry of any American vessel into a combat area in violation of section 3 of the Neutrality Act of 1939.

Sec. 4. All contracts or agreements made for the disposition of any defense article or defense information pursuant to section 3 shall contain a clause by which the foreign government undertakes that it will not, without the consent of the President, transfer title to or possession of such defense article or defense information by gift, sale, or otherwise, or permit its use by anyone not an officer, employee, or agent of such foreign government. . . .

Sec. 5. . . . (b) The President from time to time, but not less frequently than once every ninety days, shall transmit to the Congress a report of operations under this Act except such information as he deems incompatible with the public interest to disclose. . . .

Sec. 6. (a) There is hereby authorized to be appropriated from time to time, out of any money in the Treasury not otherwise appropriated, such amounts as may be necessary to carry out the provisions and accomplish the purposes of this Act. . . .

Sec. 8. The Secretaries of War and of the Navy are hereby authorized to purchase or otherwise acquire arms, ammunition, and implements of war produced within the jurisdiction of any country to which section 3 is applicable, whenever the President deems such purchase or acquisition to be necessary in the interests of the defense of the United States.

Sec. 9 The President may, from time to time, promulgate such rules and regulations as may be necessary and proper to carry out any of the provisions of this Act; and he may exercise any power or authority conferred on him by this Act through such department, agency, or officer as he shall direct.

Sec. 10. Nothing in this Act shall be construed to change existing law relating to the use of the land and naval forces of the United States, except insofar as such use relates to the manufacture, procurement, and repair of defense articles, the communication of information and other noncombatant purposes enumerated in this Act. . . .

Approved, March 11, 1941.

Commitment in Principle: The Atlantic Charter, 1941

By the summer of 1941, both the extent of American commitment and the nature of the world struggle had become quite clear. In March and April, as lend-lease was being formally approved, Germany threw the British onto the defensive with a deep lunge toward the Middle East. While General Erwin Rommel pushed the British in North Africa back upon Tobruk, other German forces swept efficiently and ruthlessly through the mountain passes of Yugoslavia and Greece. The invasion began on March 24. By June 1 it was over, with Yugoslavia, Greece, and Crete in German hands, the Balkans outflanked and Hitler firmly established with a staging area for an assault on Suez and the East. On April 13 Japan, Italy, and Germany signed a nonaggression treaty. On June 22 Russia was invaded. On July 24 Japan occupied a part of French Indochina, and the President made it clear that the United States could not tolerate further unchecked Japanese expansion. Japan and the United States each froze the assets of the other. The military forces of the Philippines were nationalized and mobilized. Sensitive and desperate talks began between Japan and the United States.

The American response to the accelerating pace and expanding scope of the war had been clear. On April 9 the United States accepted the defense of Greenland as its responsibility. On April 21–27 United States planning officers met quietly with British and French officers at Singapore and worked out combined strategy to be employed if Japan attacked United States possessions or forces. In late May and early June, Roosevelt declared a national emergency, closed German and Italian consulates in the United States. On July 7 United States forces landed in Iceland by arrangement with the Icelandic government.

In early August, FDR disappeared from Washington, making his way aboard the cruiser Augusta *to Argentia Bay, Newfoundland, where he met Prime Minister Winston Churchill for secret strategy meetings. It was partly that Churchill and Roosevelt simply wanted to discuss the allocation of resources and the strategy of large-scale war in which they were jointly caught. But the most significant result of the conference was the brief, eloquent statement of goals which they worked out together and issued as a public communiqué. It pitched the objective high and on a moral plane. It was a remarkable piece of propaganda; it was an effective rallying device for popular support; it was a basic charter upon which would be built the world opinion by which the Allies might be disciplined in the postwar arrangements. By the end of September, fifteen of the Allies, including the Soviet Union, had signed the "Atlantic Charter."*

Churchill's views of this and later conferences with Roosevelt are to be found in his memoirs of the war, The Second World War *(1948–1953), six volumes.*

The Atlantic Charter of August 14, 1941, has been taken from Peace and War, *pages 718–719.*

Joint declaration of the President of the United States of America and the Prime Minister, Mr. Churchill, representing His Majesty's Government in the United Kingdom, being met together, deem it right to make known certain common principles in the national policies of their respective countries on which they base their hopes for a better future for the world.

First, their countries seek no aggrandizement, territorial or other;

Second, they desire to see no territorial changes that do not accord with the freely expressed wishes of the peoples concerned;

Third, they respect the right of all peoples to choose the form of government under which they will live; and they wish to see sovereign rights and self-government restored to those who have been forcibly deprived of them;

Fourth, they will endeavor, with due respect for their existing obligations, to further the enjoyment by all States, great or small, victor or vanquished, of access, on equal terms, to the trade and to the raw materials of the world which are needed for their economic prosperity;

Fifth, they desire to bring about the fullest collaboration between all nations in the economic field with the object of securing, for all, improved labor standards, economic advancement and social security;

Sixth, after the final destruction of the Nazi tyranny, they hope to see established a peace which will afford to all nations the means of dwelling in safety within their own boundaries, and which will afford assurance that all the men in all the lands may live out their lives in freedom from fear and want;

Seventh, such a peace should enable all men to traverse the high seas and oceans without hindrance;

Eighth, they believe that all of the nations of the world, for realistic as well as spiritual reasons must come to the abandonment of the use of force. Since no future peace can be maintained if land, sea or air armaments continue to be employed by nations which threaten, or may threaten, aggression outside of their frontiers, they believe, pending the establishment of a wider and permanent system of general security, that the disarmament of such nations is essential. They will likewise aid and encourage all other practicable measures which will lighten for peace-loving peoples the crushing burden of armaments.

The Dissident View: Charles Lindbergh Argues against Intervention, 1941

The increasing American commitments of 1941 were made only with great controversy and against strong resistance. Most of them could be made at all only because there was no need to ask the approval of the Congress. The destroyer–air base deal, the occupation of Greenland and of Iceland, the strategy session at Singapore were all undertaken under the executive power. Congress still spoke largely with "isolationist" sentiments, and when it moved along with FDR, as it did on lend-lease legislation, it did so at least in part as a device for staving off war. And congressional opinion placed serious limits upon the President's range of maneuver. For example, as late as August 12, the House of Representatives developed so much resistance to selective service that the extension of the act was passed by only a one-vote margin.

But American isolationism was not all of one piece. There were pacifists who abhorred war on moral grounds and slackers who merely wanted to avoid being shot. There was much of the old fear of Europe, as well as some specific prejudice against Britain. There were anti-Semites and there were Germanophiles, and there were people who were isolationist simply because FDR was not. There were many who were not isolationists at all, but rather nationalists or imperialists. Some who eschewed all entanglement in Europe favored a headlong involvement in Asia. And there were many who simply did not see that the United States had anything at stake in this particular war, or that it could win the war. One of these was Colonel Charles A. Lindbergh, who spoke widely during 1940 and 1941 under the auspices of the America First Committee. America First had been organized to focus, direct, and support the propaganda and pressure against Roosevelt's "interventionist" policies and to match the challenge set up by William Allen White's Committee to Defend America by Aiding the Allies. Lindbergh was one of America First's favorite spokesmen. He was hugely popular as the bashful, charming national hero who had flown the Atlantic solo for the first time. He and his wife, Anne Morrow, the daughter of a popular Republican Ambassador to Mexico, had increased in popularity with their books about their adventures, and with their genuinely modest behavior. By the end of the 1930s the Lindberghs had become one of those folk-families to whom the American people automatically responded with sympathy.

Charles A. Lindbergh's sincerity and concern seemed beyond all question. Further, he was presumed to be an expert on aircraft and he was presumed to have the necessary information. Before the war, he had toured Europe, watched maneuvers in Germany as well as in Britain and France, and had come away convinced of the Reich's insuperable air power. Lindbergh might make the most evident errors—implying, for example, that Poland had gone to war to support England, whereas the reverse was actually true. But Americans listened when Charles Lindbergh talked. One of his most significant speeches, reprinted here, was delivered at Madison Square Garden in Manhattan on April 24, 1941.

Wayne S. Cole, America First *(1953) is an important study of the movement. Arthur S. Vandenburg,* Private Papers *(1952) is the revealing record of one of the isolationist leaders. See also Selig Adler,* The Isolationist Impulse *(1957).*

Lindbergh's speech is taken from the New York Times, *April 24, 1941, page 12.*

There are many viewpoints from which the issues of this war can be argued. Some are primarily idealistic. Some are primarily practical. One should, I believe, strive for a balance of both. But, since the issues that can be covered in a single address are limited, tonight I shall discuss the war from a viewpoint which is primarily practical. It is not that I believe ideals are unimportant, even among the realities of war; but if a nation is to survive in a hostile world, its ideals must be backed by the hard logic of military practicability. If the outcome of war depended upon ideals alone, this would be a different world than it is today.

I know I will be severely criticized by the interventionists in America when I say we should not enter a war unless we have a reasonable chance of winning. That, they will claim, is far too materialistic a standpoint. They will advance again the same arguments that were used to persuade France to declare war against Germany in 1939. But I do not believe that our American ideals, and our way of life, will gain through an unsuccessful war. And I know that the United States is not prepared to wage war in Europe successfully at this time. We are no better prepared today than France was when the interventionists in Europe persuaded her to attack the Siegfried Line.

I have said before, and I will say again, that I believe it will be a tragedy to the entire world if the British Empire collapses. That is one of the main reasons why I opposed this war before it was declared, and why I have constantly advocated a negotiated peace. I did not feel that England and France had a reasonable chance of winning. France has now been defeated; and, despite the propaganda and confusion of recent months, it is now obvious that England is losing the war. I believe this is realized even by the British Government. But they have one last desperate plan remaining. They hope that they may be able to persuade us to send another American Expeditionary Force to Europe and to share with England militarily, as well as financially, the fiasco of this war.

I do not blame England for this hope, or for asking for our assistance. But we now know that she declared a war under circumstances which led to the defeat of every nation that sided with her from Poland to Greece. We know that in the desperation of war England promised to all these nations armed assistance that she could not send. We know that she misinformed them, as she has misinformed us, concerning her state of preparation, her military strength, and the progress of the war.

In time of war, truth is always replaced by propaganda. I do not believe we should be too quick to criticize the actions of a belligerent nation. There is always the question whether we, ourselves, would do better under similar circumstances. But we in this country have a right to think of the welfare of America first, just as the people in England thought first of their own country when they encouraged the smaller nations of Europe to fight against hopeless odds. When England asks us to enter this war, she is considering her own future, and that of her empire. In making our reply, I believe we should consider the future of the United States and that of the Western Hemisphere.

It is not only our right, but it is our obligation as American citizens to look at this war objectively and to weigh our chances for success if we should enter it. I have attempted to do this, especially from the standpoint of aviation; and I have been forced to the conclusion that we cannot win this war for England, regardless of how much assistance we send.

I ask you to look at the map of Europe today and see if you can suggest any way in which we could win this war if we entered it. Suppose we had a large army in America, trained and equipped. Where would we send it to fight? The campaigns of the war show only too clearly how difficult it is to force a landing, or to maintain an army, on a hostile coast.

Suppose we took our Navy from the Pacific, and used it to convoy British shipping. That would not win the war for England. It would, at best, permit her to exist under the constant bombing of the German Air fleet. Suppose we had an air force that we could send to Europe. Where could it operate? Some of our squadrons might be based in the British Isles; but it is physically impossible to base enough aircraft in the British Isles alone to equal in strength the aircraft that can be based on the Continent of Europe.

I have asked these questions on the supposition that we had in existence an Army and an air force large enough and well enough equipped to send to Europe; and that we would dare to remove our Navy from the Pacific. Even on this basis, I do not see how we could invade the Continent of Europe successfully as long as all of that Continent and most of Asia is under Axis domination. But the fact is that none of these suppositions are correct. We have only a one-ocean Navy. Our Army is still untrained and inadequately equipped for foreign war. Our air force is deplorably lacking in modern fighting planes because most of them have already been sent to Europe.

When these facts are cited, the interventionists shout that we are defeatists, that we are undermining the principles of democracy, and that we are giving comfort to Germany by talking about our military weakness. But everything I mention here has been published in our newspapers, and in the reports of congressional hearings in Washington. Our military position is well known to the governments of Europe and Asia. Why, then, should it not be brought to the attention of our own people?

I say it is the interventionist in America, as it was in England and in France, who gives comfort to the enemy. I say it is they who are undermining the principles of democracy when they demand that we take a course to which more than 80 per cent of our citizens are opposed. I charge them with being the real defeatists, for their policy has led to the defeat of every country that followed their advice since this war began. There is no better way to give comfort to an enemy than to divide the people of a nation over the issue of foreign war. There is no shorter road to defeat than by entering a war with inadequate preparation. Every nation that has adopted the interventionist policy of depending on some one else for its own defense has met with nothing but defeat and failure.

When history is written, the responsibility for the downfall of the democracies of Europe will rest squarely upon the shoulders of the interventionists who led their nations into war uninformed and unprepared. With their shouts of defeatism, and their disdain of reality, they have already sent countless thousands of young men to death in Europe. From the campaign of Poland to that of Greece, their prophesies have been false and their policies have failed. Yet these are the people who are calling us defeatists in America today. And they have led this country, too, to the verge of war.

There are many such interventionists in America, but there are more people among us of a different type. That is why you and I are assembled here tonight. There is a policy open to this nation that will lead to success—a policy that leaves us free to follow our own way of life, and to develop our own civilization. It is not a new and untried idea. It was advocated by Washington. It was incorporated in the Monroe Doctrine. Under its guidance, the United States has become the greatest nation in the world.

It is based upon the belief that the security of a nation lies in the strength and character of its own people. It recommends the maintenance of armed forces sufficient to defend this hemisphere from attack by any combination of foreign powers. It demands faith in an independent American destiny. This is the policy of the America First Committee today. It is a policy not of isolation, but of independence; not of defeat, but of courage. It is a policy that led this nation to success during the most trying years of our history, and it is a policy that will lead us to success again.

We have weakened ourselves for many months, and still worse, we have divided our own people by this dabbling in Europe's wars. While we should have been concentrating on American defense we have been forced to argue over foreign quarrels. We must turn our eyes and our faith back to our own country before it is too late. And when we do this, a different vista opens before us. Practically every difficulty we would face in invading Europe becomes an asset to us in defending America. Our enemy, and not we, would then have the problem of transporting millions of troops across the ocean and landing them on a hostile shore. They, and not we, would have to furnish the convoys to transport guns and trucks and munitions and fuel across three thousand miles of water. Our battleships and . . . submarines would then be fighting close to their home bases. We would then do the bombing from the air and the torpedoing at sea. And if any part of an enemy convoy should ever pass our navy and our air force, they would still be faced with the guns of our coast artillery and behind them the divisions of our Army.

The United States is better situated from a military standpoint than any other nation in the world. Even in our present condition of unpreparedness no foreign power is in a position to invade us today. If we concentrate on our own defenses and build the strength that this nation should maintain, no foreign army will ever attempt to land on American shores.

War is not inevitable for this country. Such a claim is defeatism in the true sense. No one can make us fight abroad unless we ourselves are willing to do so. No one will attempt to fight us here if we arm ourselves as a great nation should be armed. Over a hundred million people in this nation are opposed to entering the war. If the principles of democracy mean anything at all, that is reason enough for us to stay out. If we are forced into a war against the wishes of an overwhelming majority of our people, we will have proved democracy such a failure at home that there will be little use fighting for it abroad.

The time has come when those of us who believe in an independent American destiny must band together and organize for strength. We have been led toward war by a minority of our people. This minority has power. It has influence. It has a loud voice. But it does not represent the American people. During the last several years I have traveled over this country from one end to the other. I have talked to many hundreds of men and women, and I have letters from tens of thousands more, who feel the same way as you and I.

Most of these people have no influence or power. Most of them have no means of expressing their convictions, except by their vote which has always been against this war. They are the citizens who have had to work too hard at their daily jobs to organize political meetings. Hitherto, they have relied upon their vote to express their feelings; but now they find that it is hardly remembered except in the oratory of a political campaign. These people—the majority of hard-working American citizens, are with us. They are the true strength of our country. And they are beginning to realize, as you and I, that there are times when we must sacrifice our normal interests in life in order to insure the safety and the welfare of our nation.

Such a time has come. Such a crisis is here. That is why the America First Committee has been formed—to give voice to the people who have no newspaper, or newsreel, or radio station at their command to give voice to the people who must do the paying, and the fighting, and the dying if this country enters the war.

Whether or not we do enter the war rests upon the shoulders of you in this audience, upon us here on this platform, upon meetings of this kind that are being held by Americans in every section of the United States today. It depends upon the action we take, and the courage we show at this time. If you believe in an independent destiny for America, if you believe that this country should not enter the war in Europe, we ask you to join the America First Committee in its stand. We ask you to share our faith in the ability of this nation to defend itself, to develop its own civilization, and to contribute to the progress of mankind in a more constructive and intelligent way than has yet been found by the warring nations of Europe. We need your support, and we need it now. The time to act is here. I thank you.

Defense of Policy: The "New York Times" Replies to "America First," 1941

The battle for control of America's mind and policy was waged bitterly in the spring and summer of 1941. That the "interventionists" were winning became increasingly evident. The press of facts, the odds of the gamble were on their side, as well as the weight of Presidential leadership and executive authority. The New York Times's *response to Charles Lindbergh's speech was symptomatic of the substantial newspaper and magazine support the administration received. But the editorial also suggests the peculiar irony of the moment: the battle of opinion was fought out largely over concern with Hitler. But yet the supreme, decisive challenge, unsuspected yet, was shaping up in the Pacific.*

The editorial printed here is from the New York Times, *April 30, 1941, page 18.*

I

In New York Harbor, on an island close to the steamship lanes, stands the most famous statue in the world. It is not the most beautiful statue, but to many millions of passengers coming up the bay it has seemed to be. It stands for one of the dearest dreams in human history—Liberty.

The millions who pursued that dream began to come before there was a statue to greet them. They came first when the shores were lined with solemn woods. They came in sailing ships when the voyage required two months or more. They came in crowded steamship steerage under hardships not much less. They came to Plymouth Rock and to Ellis Island.

They came for one reason, escape: escape from religious or political persecution, from caste systems, from overcrowding and from lack of opportunity. But the hope of leaving all of the Old World behind could not be realized. Their hearts and heads forbade it. Their roots in its culture ran too deep. And the sea itself grew ever narrower. Express steamers began to cross it long ago in less than a week. Airplanes can span it now in less than a day. The wireless leaps it in less than a second. Emotion, ideas, even physical force can now move around the world more effectively than they could cross the tiniest country a century and a half ago.

There is no isolation. There are only lines of defense. Distance is vanishing. Strategy is everything. And strategy in this year of grace has become the art and science of survival: survival in the personal sense, survival of ideas, survival of culture and tradition, survival of a way of life.

II

Those who tell us now that the sea is still our certain bulwark, and that the tremendous forces sweeping the Old World threaten no danger to the New, give the lie to their own words in the precautions they would have us take.

To a man they favor an enormous strengthening of our defenses. Why? Against what danger would they have us arm if none exists? To what purpose would they have us spend these almost incredible billions upon billions for ships and planes, for tanks and guns, if there is no immediate threat to the security of the United States? Why are we training the youth of the country to bear arms? Under pressure of what fear are we racing against time to double and quadruple our industrial production?

No man in his senses will say that we are arming against Canada or our Latin-American neighbors to the south, against Britain or the captive states of Europe. We are arming solely for one reason. We are arming against Hitler's Germany—a great predatory Power in alliance with Japan.

It has been said, times without number, that if Hitler cannot cross the English Channel he cannot cross three thousand miles of sea. But there is only one reason why he has not crossed the English Channel. That is because forty-five million determined Britons in a heroic resistance have converted their island into an armed base from which proceeds a steady stream of sea and air power. As Secretary Hull has said: "It is not the water that bars the way. It is the resolute determination of British arms. Were the control of the seas by Britain lost, the Atlantic would no longer be an obstacle—rather, it would become a broad highway for a conqueror moving westward."

That conqueror does not need to attempt at once an invasion of continental United States in order to place this country in deadly danger. We shall be in deadly danger the moment British sea power fails; the moment the eastern gates of the Atlantic are open to the aggressor; the moment we are compelled to divide our one-ocean Navy between two oceans simultaneously.

The combined Axis fleets outmatch our own; they are superior in numbers to our fleet in every category of vessel, from warships and aircraft-carriers to destroyers and submarines. The combined Axis air strength will be much greater than our own if Hitler strikes in time—and when has he failed to strike in time? The master of Europe will have at his command shipways that can outbuild us, the resources of twenty conquered nations to furnish his materials, the oil of the Middle East to stoke his engines, the slave labor of a continent—bound by no union rules, and not working on a forty-hour week—to turn out his production.

Grant Hitler the gigantic prestige of a victory over Britain, and who can doubt that the first result, on our side of the ocean, would be the prompt appearance of imitation Nazi regimes in a half-dozen Latin-American nations, forced to be on the winning side, begging favors, clamoring for admission to the Axis? What shall we do then? Make war upon these neighbors; send armies to fight in the jungles of Central or South America; run the risk of outraging native sentiment and turning the whole continent against us? Or shall we sit tight while the area of Nazi influence draws ever closer to the Panama Canal and a spreading checkerboard of Nazi airfields provides ports of call for German planes that may choose to bomb our cities?

III

But even if Hitler gave us time, what kind of "time" would we have at our disposal?

There are moral and spiritual dangers for this country as well as physical dangers in a Hitler victory. There are dangers to the mind and heart as well as to the body and the land.

Victorious in Europe, dominating Africa and Asia through his Axis partners, Hitler could not afford to permit the United States to live an untroubled and successful life, even if he wished to. We are the arch-enemy of all he stands for: the very citadel of that "pluto-democracy" which he hates and scorns. As long as liberty and freedom prevailed in the United States there would be a constant risk for Hitler that our ideas and our example might infect the conquered countries which he was bending to his will. In his own interest he would be forced to harry us at every turn.

Who can doubt that our lives would be poisoned every day by challenges and insults from Nazi politicians; that Nazi agents would stir up anti-American feeling in every country they controlled; that Nazi spies would overrun us here; that Hitler would produce a continual series of lightning diplomatic strokes—alliances and "non-aggression pacts" to break our will; in short, that a continuous war of nerves, if nothing worse, would be waged against us?

And who can doubt that, in response, we should have to turn our own nation into an armed camp, with all our traditional values of culture, education, social reform, democracy and liberty subordinated to the single, all-embracing aim of self-preservation? In this case we should indeed experience "regimentation." Every item of foreign trade, every transaction in domestic commerce, every present prerogative of labor, every civil liberty we cherish, would necessarily be regulated in the interest of defense.

But the most tragic aspect of this attempt to survive, alone on our continent, is that it would amount at best merely to sustaining life in a charnel house. With Britain gone, with the bright lamp of English liberty extinguished, with all hope of resurrection denied to the little democracies that have contributed so generously to our civilization and our culture, with the hobnailed boots of an ignorant and obscene barbarism echoing in every capital from London to Athens, we should live in a new world, changed beyond all recognition.

In this downfall of democracy outside the United States there would come, for many of our own people, a loss of faith in our own democratic system. Our confidence would be undermined, our vision dimmed, our ranks divided. In a dark, uncertain world we should stand alone, deriving from no other country the sustaining strength of a common faith in our democratic institutions.

What would it profit us to achieve, at last, this perfect isolation?

IV

The Statue of Liberty in New York Harbor has looked down across the bay at many men who have crossed the ocean to find freedom. It stands now as a silent witness to the fact that we are already locked in mortal combat with the German system.

American courage and American idealism, together with the sound common sense of the American people, summon us to the defense both of our physical security and of those moral and spiritual values which alone make life worth living. This defense means many things. It means, in the first instance, a clear recognition that the most dangerous of all courses we could follow in this hour of decision is a policy of drift: of do-nothing while there is still time to act effectively; of letting hesitancy ripen into disagreement, and disagreement curdle into factions which will split the country.

It means strong leadership in Washington: a willingness to forego the methods of indirection and surprise and veiled hints and innuendo, and to state the plain facts of the situation boldly. It means leadership which is as generous as it is strong: leadership which is willing to forget old quarrels, ready to bring into positions of high power and into the innermost confidence of the Government the accredited spokesmen of the opposition party; leadership which is at last prepared to delegate all necessary authority to the engineers of American production.

It means a genuinely firm insistence that strikes or lockouts in defense industries will no longer be tolerated by public opinion. It means more immediate aid to the brave people who are now fighting in the front line of our defense. It means encouragement to American aviators who are ready to fly our own planes in the battle over Britain. It means a determination to see that our vital supplies reach England, under the protection of our own guns. Above all else it means a decision to avoid the same mistake that the democracies have made over and over again—the mistake of "too little and too late."

There is no escape in isolation. We have only two alternatives. We can surrender or we can do our part in holding the line. We can defend, with all the means in our power, the rights that are morally and legally ours. If we decide for the American tradition, for the preservation of all that we hold dear in the years that lie ahead, we shall take our place in the line and play our part in the defense of freedom.

Against the "Drift to War": An Appeal from Landon, Hoover, and Fourteen Other Republicans, 1941

While the argument increased in intensity, the circumstances sometimes changed its nature. Early in August, 1941, a statement by Alfred N. Landon, Herbert Hoover, and other Republican leaders betrayed both the partisan possibilities of the debate and the new question raised by Russian participation in the war and by the broadening of American naval commitments to "deliver" the lend-lease goods.

Success of the anti-interventionists' campaign is a matter of some dispute. It did not, perhaps, change the minds of many people. The fact is, Americans' minds were quite generally divided between conflicting commitments to the broad values of Western civilization and to the narrow demands of momentary peace. But certainly, the anti-interventionist campaign moderated the administration's actions, slowed it down, made clear above all else that Congress would not join the shooting war short of some great catastrophe.

The statement quoted below is from the New York Times, *August 6, 1941, page 6.*

The American people should insistently demand that Congress put a stop to step-by-step projection of the United States into undeclared war. Congress has not only the sole power to declare war but also the power and responsibility to keep the country out of war unless and until both Houses have otherwise decided.

Exceeding its expressed purpose, the lease-lend bill has been followed by naval action, by military occupation of bases outside the Western Hemisphere, by promise of unauthorized aid to Russia and by other belligerent moves.

Such warlike steps, in no case sanctioned by Congress, undermine its constitutional powers and the fundamental principles of democratic government. The representatives of the people in passing the lease-lend bill, expressed the national conviction that preservation of the British Empire and China is desirable for us and for civilization.

We hold that view but the intent of Congress was that lease-lend material should be transferred to belligerent ownership in the United States and utilized only to protect the independence of democracies.

We hold that in giving generous aid to these democracies at our seaboard we have gone as far as is consistent either with law, with sentiment or with security. Recent events raise doubts that this war is a clear-cut issue of liberty and democracy. It is not purely a world conflict between tyranny and freedom. The Anglo-Russian alliance has dissipated that illusion.

In so far as this is a war of power-politics, the American people want no part in it. American participation is far more likely to destroy democracy in this country and thus in the Western Hemisphere than to establish it in Europe. The hope of civilization now rests primarily upon the preservation of freedom and democracy in the United States.

That will be lost for a generation if we join in this war. We maintain that American lives should be sacrificed only for American independence or to prevent the invasion of the Western Hemisphere.

Few people honestly believe that the Axis is now, or will in the future be in a position to threaten the independence of any part of this hemisphere if our defenses are properly prepared.

Energies of this country should be concentrated on the defense of our own liberties. Freedom in America does not depend on the outcome of struggles for material power between other nations.

Shattered Illusions: Foreign Policy, 1938–1941—Decision in Disaster

SELECTION **58**

The President Charts the Relationships between Europe and Asia: Letter from FDR to Ambassador Grew, 1941

The President himself saw some close relationships between the war in Europe and the threat in Asia. He sketched out certain of these in a private letter to his old friend, Joseph C. Grew, the Ambassador to Tokyo. Written at the very beginning of 1941, this letter suggests that Roosevelt was approaching the crisis of the year with a clear understanding that the United States was faced with one massive threat to its security, rather than with a series of isolated and petty dangers, as some isolationists thought.

This letter of January 21, 1941, is to be found in U.S. Department of State, Foreign Relations of the United States, 1941, *(Washington: Government Printing office, 1956), volume 4, pages 6–8.*

Washington, January 21, 1941.

Dear Joe: I have given careful consideration to your letter of December 14.

First, I want to say how helpful it is to have your over-all estimates and reflections—based as they are upon a rare combination of first-hand observation, long experience with our Japanese relations, and masterly judgment. I find myself in decided agreement with your conclusions.

I also want you to know how much I appreciate your kind words of congratulation on my re-election and your expression of confidence in my conduct of our foreign affairs.

As to your very natural request for an indication of my views as to certain aspects of our future attitude toward developments in the Far East, I believe that the fundamental proposition is that we must recognize that the hostilities in Europe, in Africa, and in Asia are all parts of a single world conflict. We must, consequently, recognize that our interests are menaced both in Europe and in the Far East. We are engaged in the task of defending our way of life and our vital national interests wherever they are seriously endangered. Our strategy of self-defense must be a global strategy which takes account of every front and takes advantage of every opportunity to contribute to our total security.

You suggest as one of the chief factors in the problem of our attitude toward Japan the question whether our getting into war with Japan would so handicap our help to Britain in Europe as to make the difference to Britain between victory and defeat. In this connection it seems to me that we must consider whether, if Japan should gain possession of the region of the Netherlands East Indies and the Malay Peninsula, the chances of England's winning in her struggle with Germany would not be decreased thereby. The British Isles, the British in those Isles, have been able to exist and to defend themselves not only because they have prepared strong local defenses but also because as the heart and the nerve center of the British Empire they have been able to draw upon vast resources for their sustenance and to bring into operation against their enemies economic, military and naval pressures on a world-wide scale. They live by importing goods from all parts of the world and by utilizing large overseas financial resources. They are defended not only by measures of defense carried out locally but also by distant and widespread economic, military, and naval activities which both contribute to the maintenance of their supplies, deny certain sources of supply to their enemies, and prevent those enemies from concentrating the full force of their armed power against the heart and the nerve center of the Empire. The British need assistance along the lines of our generally established policies at many points, assistance which in the case of the Far East is certainly well within the realm of "possibility" so far as the capacity of the United States is concerned. Their defense strategy must in the nature of things be global. Our strategy of giving them assistance toward ensuring our own security must envisage both sending of supplies to England and helping to prevent a closing of channels of communication to and from various parts of the world, so that other important sources of supply will not be denied to the British and be added to the assets of the other side.

You also suggest as chief factors in the problem the questions whether and when Britain is likely to win the European war. As I have indicated above, the conflict is world-wide, not merely a European war. I firmly believe, as I have recently declared publicly, that the British, with our help, will be victorious in this conflict. The conflict may well be long and we must bear in mind that when England is victorious she may not have left the strength that would be needed to bring about a rearrangement of such territorial changes in the western and southern Pacific as might occur during the course of the conflict if Japan is not kept within bounds. I judge from the remarks which appear at the bottom of page 4 and at the top of page 5 of your letter that you, too, attach due importance to this aspect of the problem.

I am giving you my thoughts at this length because the problems which we face are so vast and so interrelated that any attempt even to state them compels one to think in terms of five continents and seven seas. In conclusion, I must emphasize that, our problem being one of defense, we can not lay down hard and fast plans. As each new development occurs we must, in the light of the circumstances then existing, decide when and where and how we can most effectively marshal and make use of our resources.

With warmest regards,
[FRANKLIN D. ROOSEVELT]

Basis for War

Throughout the summer of 1941, tensions between Japan and the United States mounted. Japan rejected all demands for withdrawal of her troops in China or French Indochina. The United States, by freezing Japanese assets, laid down what amounted to an embargo on exports to Japan. A Japanese-proposed meeting with Premier Prince Fumimaro Konoye was turned aside by Roosevelt because there was insufficient agreement on basic principles to make such a meeting appear hopeful. In mid-October the relatively "liberal" Konoye cabinet was replaced by a military regime guided by Premier General Hideki Tojo, formerly Minister of War. Meanwhile, Japanese Ambassador Kichsaburo Nomura and special envoy Saburo Kurusu negotiated almost continuously with the State Department throughout the summer and fall of 1941. It seems clear that the United States might have been able to gain at least an uneasy temporary peace with Japan, had she been willing to pay the price: approval of Japanese expansion in China and a guaranty of the necessary raw materials. Whatever the moral issues, the price seemed too high for merely strategic reasons. Peace would come at the cost of unchecked Japanese control of East Asia and the Western Pacific. There exists a welter of diplomatic notes from the negotiations of 1941. The two published here make clear both the firm, rock-bottom positions of the two nations finally reached in the bargaining, and the deep chasm which lay between them.

The rich and controversial literature on the backgrounds of American involvement in the war might best be approached through Herbert Feis, The Road to Pearl Harbor *(1950). The events of the day are generally described in Walter Millis,* This Is Pearl *(1947) and thoroughly examined in the report of the Joint Committee on the Pearl Harbor Attack,* Senate Document *No. 244, Seventy-ninth Congress, second session.*

The documents provided here are "Draft Proposal Handed by the Japanese Ambassador (Nomura) to the Secretary of State on November 20, 1941," and "Document Handed by the Secretary of State to the Japanese Ambassador (Nomura), November 26, 1941," drawn respectively from pages 801–802 and 810–812 of Peace and War.

JAPANESE PROPOSALS OF NOVEMBER 20, 1941

1. Both the Governments of Japan and the United States undertake not to make any armed advancement into any of the regions in the South-eastern Asia and the Southern Pacific area excepting the part of French Indo-China where the Japanese troops are stationed at present.
2. The Japanese Government undertakes to withdraw its troops now stationed in French Indo-China upon either the restoration of peace between Japan and China or the establishment of an equitable peace in the Pacific area.

In the meantime the Government of Japan declares that it is prepared to remove its troops now stationed in the southern part of French Indo-China to the northern part of the said territory upon the conclusion of the present arrangement which shall later be embodied in the final agreement.

3. The Government of Japan and the United States shall cooperate with a view to securing the acquisition of those goods and commodities which the two countries need in Netherlands East Indies.
4. The Governments of Japan and the United States mutually undertake to restore their commercial relations to those prevailing prior to the freezing of the assets.

The Government of the United States shall supply Japan a required quantity of oil.

5. The Government of the United States undertakes to refrain from such measures and actions as will be prejudicial to the endeavors for the restoration of general peace between Japan and China.

UNITED STATES PROPOSALS OF NOVEMBER 26, 1941

Outline of Proposed Basis for Agreement between the United States and Japan

Section I

Draft Mutual Declaration of Policy. The Government of the United States and the Government of Japan both being solicitous for the peace of the Pacific affirm that their national policies are directed toward lasting and extensive peace throughout the Pacific area, that they have no territorial designs in that area, that they have no intention of threatening other countries or of using military force aggressively against any neighboring nation, and that, accordingly, in their national policies they will actively support and give practical application to the following fundamental principles upon which their relations with each other and with all other governments are based:

1. The principle of inviolability of territorial integrity and sovereignty of each and all nations.
2. The principle of non-interference in the internal affairs of other countries.
3. The principle of equality, including equality of commercial opportunity and treatment.
4. The principle of reliance upon international cooperation and conciliation for the prevention and pacific settlement of controversies and for improvement of international conditions by peaceful methods and processes.

The Government of Japan and the Government of the United States have agreed that toward eliminating chronic political instability, preventing recurrent economic collapse, and providing a basis for peace, they will actively support and practically apply the following principles in their economic relations with each other and with other nations and peoples:

1. The principle of non-discrimination in international commercial relations.
2. The principle of international economic cooperation and abolition of extreme nationalism as expressed in excessive trade restrictions.
3. The principle of non-discriminatory access by all nations to raw material supplies.
4. The principle of full protection of the interests of consuming countries and populations as regards the operation of international commodity agreements.
5. The principle of establishment of such institutions and arrangements of international finance as may lend aid to the essential enterprises and the continuous development of all countries and may permit payments through processes of trade consonant with the welfare of all countries.

Section II

Steps to Be Taken by the Government of the United States and by the Government of Japan. The Government of the United States and the Government of Japan propose to take steps as follows:

1. The Government of the United States and the Government of Japan will endeavor to conclude a multilateral non-aggression pact among the British Empire, China, Japan, the Netherlands, the Soviet Union, Thailand and the United States.

2. Both Governments will endeavor to conclude among the American, British, Chinese, Japanese, the Netherlands and Thai Governments an agreement whereunder each of the Governments would pledge itself to respect the territorial integrity of French Indochina and, in the event that there should develop a threat to the territorial integrity of Indochina, to enter into immediate consultation with a view to taking such measures as may be deemed necessary and advisable to meet the threat in question. Such agreement would provide also that each of the Governments party to the agreement would not seek or accept preferential treatment in its trade or economic relations with Indochina and would use its influence to obtain for each of the signatories equality of treatment in trade and commerce with French Indochina.

3. The Government of Japan will withdraw all military, naval, air and police forces from China and from Indochina.

4. The Government of the United States and the Government of Japan will not support—militarily, politically, economically—any government or regime in China other than the National Government of the Republic of China with capital temporarily at Chungking.

5. Both Governments will give up all extraterritorial rights in China, including rights and interests in and with regard to international settlements and concessions, and rights under the Boxer Protocol of 1901.

Both Governments will endeavor to obtain the agreement of the British and other governments to give up extraterritorial rights in China, including rights in international settlements and in concessions and under the Boxer Protocol of 1901.

6. The Government of the United States and the Government of Japan will enter into negotiations for the conclusion between the United States and Japan of a trade agreement, based upon reciprocal most-favored-nation treatment and reduction of trade barriers by both countries, including an undertaking by the United States to bind raw silk on the free list.

7. The Government of the United States and the Government of Japan will, respectively, remove the freezing restrictions on Japanese funds in the United States and on American funds in Japan.

8. Both Governments will agree upon a plan for the stabilization of the dollar-yen rate, with the allocation of funds adequate for this purpose, half to be supplied by Japan and half by the United States.

9. Both Governments will agree that no agreement which either has concluded with any third power or powers shall be interpreted by it in such a way as to conflict with the fundamental purpose of this agreement, the establishment and preservation of peace throughout the Pacific area.

10. Both Governments will use their influence to cause other governments to adhere to and to give practical application to the basic political and economic principles set forth in this agreement.

Casting the Die: FDR Requests a Declaration of War against Japan, 1941

The Japanese answer to the diplomatic dilemma of 1941 was the assault on Pearl Harbor. The attack of December 7, 1941 was a military masterpiece. Surprise was so great that it seemed indecently effective. No one in American command expected an attack that day—or at that place. Pearl Harbor and

Hickam Field were ready for sabotage—sadly vulnerable to the kind of air assault which came. The havoc was monstrous. Japan accomplished precisely what she had set out to do: neutralize the United States as a naval power in the Pacific for a period long enough to assure control of Southeast Asia.

But, on December 7, 1941, Japan accomplished some things she perhaps did not intend to do, and in the long run they were more significant. She introduced the United States to modern warfare, cutting by sheer destruction through the lag in American military and naval technology. By destroying the battleships she forced the United States to build at once a light, fast carrier fleet, the only kind of power which could destroy Japanese air power. More important, Japan unified the American people as neither FDR nor the nagging piecemeal crises of the Atlantic could do. When the President went before the Congress to request a Declaration of War, he could build upon the injured pride, the anger and fear, and the deep sorrow of the American people.

Roosevelt's war message is here taken from the Congressional Record, *Seventy-seventh Congress, first session, volume 87, part 9, pages 9519–9520.*

Yesterday, December 7, 1941—a date which will live in infamy—the United States of America was suddenly and deliberately attacked by naval and air forces of the Empire of Japan.

The United States was at peace with that Nation and, at the solicitation of Japan, was still in conversation with its Government and its Emperor looking toward the maintenance of peace in the Pacific. Indeed, one hour after Japanese air squadrons had commenced bombing in Oahu, the Japanese Ambassador to the United States and his colleague delivered to the Secretary of State a formal reply to a recent American message. While this reply stated that it seemed useless to continue the existing diplomatic negotiations, it contained no threat or hint of war or armed attack.

It will be recorded that the distance of Hawaii from Japan makes it obvious that the attack was deliberately planned many days or even weeks ago. During the intervening time the Japanese Government has deliberately sought to deceive the United States by false statements and expressions of hope for continued peace.

The attack yesterday on the Hawaiian Islands has caused severe damage to American naval and military forces. Very many American lives have been lost. In addition American ships have been reported torpedoed on the high seas between San Francisco and Honolulu.

Yesterday the Japanese Government also launched an attack against Malaya.

Last night Japanese forces attacked Hong Kong.

Last night Japanese forces attacked Guam.

Last night Japanese forces attacked the Philippine Islands.

Last night the Japanese attacked Wake Island.

This morning the Japanese attacked Midway Island.

Japan has, therefore, undertaken a surprise offensive extending throughout the Pacific area. The facts of yesterday speak for themselves. The people of the United States have already formed their opinions and well understand the implications to the very life and safety of our Nation.

As Commander in Chief of the Army and Navy I have directed that all measures be taken for our defense.

Always will we remember the character of the onslaught against us.

No matter how long it may take us to overcome this premeditated invasion, the American people in their righteous might will win through to absolute victory.

I believe I interpret the will of the Congress and of the people when I assert that we will not only defend ourselves to the uttermost but will make very certain that this form of treachery shall never endanger us again.

Hostilities exist. There is no blinking at the fact that our people, our territory, and our interests are in grave danger.

With confidence in our armed forces—with the unbounded determination of our people—we will gain the inevitable triumph—so help us God.

I ask that the Congress declare that since the unprovoked and dastardly attack by Japan on Sunday, December 7, a state of war has existed between the United States and the Japanese Empire.

PART **EIGHT**

War for the World

When the United States was driven into the war in December, 1941, the struggle had already been going on for ten years in Asia and for over two years in Europe. By now it was genuinely a world war, with hardly any area of the globe untouched. Only two types of nations could remain neutral, those which combined weakness with remoteness from strategic location, and those, like Sweden and Switzerland, whose neutrality was generally convenient for the various belligerents. In December, 1941, the war seemed to be running favorably for the aggressors. With the United States for the moment badly wounded, her capital fleet disabled, her preparations for air and naval war inadequate, Japan would move efficiently to the South and East for six months—through the Malay Peninsula, the Philippines, the Dutch East Indies to the very doorway of Australia. Islands assigned to her as mandates from the League of Nations, particularly the Marshalls and the Marianas, would provide a defensive screen against ocean attack, as well as the staging facilities for forward action. In May and June, hastily gathered American carrier forces stemmed the Japanese wave at the battles of Coral Sea and Midway. In August, American marines launched their first assault upon Japan's island bastions. But 1942 was largely, for the United States, a year of massive preparation.

While the Japanese plunged south in their drive to control the Pacific, Hitler's forces kept the British in the Eastern Mediterranean on a constant, uneasy defensive and rolled deep into Russia. Only in the late summer of 1942 did the German offensive begin to waver. Early in November the assault on Egypt buckled, and General Erwin Rommel's Afrika Corps began a slow retreat. On November 7–8 a limited Anglo-American invasion of North Africa began. Eventually it would move across the Straits to Sicily and Italy and make the Mediterranean a second major front throughout the remainder of the war. But the principal effort would be a cross-channel invasion of northern France, to defeat Hitler in his own heartland. This gigantic undertaking could be launched only on June 6, 1944, and the major commitment of America's manpower, technical effort, and raw materials had to be husbanded for that effort. But, in addition, American supplies went steadily forward to support the Italian campaign, the British efforts in Egypt, Greece, and the Middle East, the massive Russian campaign, which rolled back the German armies on a formidable front running from the Baltic to the Balkans. American supplies buttressed the defense of Chiang Kai-shek's China, of Burma and of India. Almost singlehandedly American troops, the Air Force and the Navy, fought the dirty, slow, bloody battle to regain the Philippines, to destroy Japanese sea power, to blast the Asian enemy from their island positions.

1944 became the year of Allied advances all over the world. In October, the invasion of the Philippines began. By the end of the year Superfortresses were raiding Japan from bases on Saipan in the Marianas. The Russians were pushing into Poland and Hungary; American troops had crossed the German frontiers in September. At the end of the year, American and British troops were fighting against Germany's last, desperate tactical assault at the Battle of the Bulge. But by February, 1945, the relentless Allied offensive in Germany had begun. On April 29, the German armies in Italy surrendered. The next day, Hitler committed suicide. On May 7, German forces surrendered unconditionally. On August 6, with invasion forces ready to move, the United States dropped the first atomic bomb on Hiroshima. Three days later, Nagasaki was similarly blasted. On August 14, Japan surrendered.

A. Russell Buchanan, The United States and World War II *(1964), two volumes, is a good general history of the war from the American point of view. Also useful, albeit brief, is Fletcher Pratt,* War for the World *(1950). World War II is already the most heavily reported and studied war in human history. Official histories abound, but one which is classic as both history and literature is Samuel E. Morison,* History of United States Naval Operations in World War II *(1947–1960), fifteen volumes. Its companion, the multivolume* United States Army in World War II, *is published by the Office of the Chief of Military History, Department of the Army, under the general editorship of Kent Roberts Greenfield. Among the military memoirs, one of the most important is Dwight D. Eisenhower,* Crusade in Europe *(1948).*

Shock: E. E. Cummings Records the Nation's Rendezvous with Hell, 1944

Shock was one of the qualities of American experience once war came. For a generation born of World War I, raised with violence and schooled by Hitler headlines, Americans were astonishingly naive about war. The nation soon learned from Bataan, and from the U-boat hunting grounds off Nantucket and Fire Island and Miami Beach, what war was really like. E. E. Cummings, with his tight economy of words and his instinct for the visceral meaning, put the matter precisely.

The verse quoted here is from E. E. Cummings, Poems: 1923–1954 *(New York: Harcourt, Brace & World, 1954), page 396.*

plato told

him:he couldn't
believe it(jesus

told him;he
wouldn't believe
it)lao

tsze
certainly told
him,and general
(yes

mam)
sherman;
and even
(believe it
or

not)you
told him:i told
him;we told him
(he didn't believe it,no

sir)it took
a nipponized bit of
the old sixth

avenue
el;in the top of his head:to tell

him

SELECTION 62

Pride: The Bureau of the Budget Explains Some of the Difficulties

War was a source of pride as well as of shock. The industrial and logistic challenge was for that time unprecedented, almost unthinkable. Yet, within a period of only three years, the nation met and surpassed the challenge, with the production, among other things, of over 11,000 ships, almost 300,000 aircraft, 2½ million machine guns. Among the most formidable problems were those of coordination. In the selection reprinted below from an official description of the economic war effort, the Bureau of the Budget describes some of these challenges.

An interesting contemporary account of the problems of production and management is Donald M. Nelson, Arsenal of Democracy: The Story of American War Production *(1946). Joel Seidman,* American Labor from Defense to Reconversion *(1953) is a scholarly and reliable study.*

The excerpt given here is a small part of the document, U.S. Bureau of the Budget, The United States at War: Development and Administration of the War Program by the Federal Government *(Washington: Government Printing Office, 1946), pages 112–115.*

The Impact of Unlimited Procurement

Under the traditional American system, industry does not produce war munitions until there are Government orders; Government orders are not placed until there are appropriations; and appropriations are not made until requests based on estimates and supporting information are submitted to Congress for action. In fact, in peacetime, the control over the whole process centers in the appropriation by Congress. It was natural, therefore, for procurement officers not to take vigorous action to raise war production before appropriations were available. Not only was this against the whole tradition of the past, but it would, if carried far enough, have been a criminal offense. But any restriction, real or imagined, imposed by appropriations, disappeared after the declaration of war. Appropriations were made in lump sums, so that appropriation language no longer limited the military agencies in their war activities.

While Congress had slowed up the building of training camps only a few months earlier, it now acted with great dispatch. Within 6 months, almost $100,000,000,000 was appropriated, and in the next 4 months another $60,000,000,000 was added (chart 1). Of these stupendous authorizations, the Army received $95 billion, the Navy $50 billion, lend-lease $5 billion, and the Maritime Commission $3.5 billion. Never before or since, have such immense financial authorizations been given in so short a period.

By spring the floodgates were open. Equipped with virtually unlimited financial authorizations, the procurement agencies went to work to place their contracts with the industries of America. This was not too difficult.

Industry was now eager to get into war work, especially as the WPB materials orders and limitation orders began to interfere with normal production of civilian items. The services were equipped with high priorities, which gave the contractors confidence that they would be able to get the materials and components they required, price arrangements were generous and elastic, and the manufacturers were not unwilling, under pressure, to sign additional contracts even when their plants were already full, hoping to expand, or find some other method of discharging their inflated obligations. With this combination of circumstances, over $100 billion of contracts were placed in the first 6 months of 1942. In other words, industry signed up to deliver for war more than the total production of the American economy in the Nation's most prosperous and productive prior year. At the time there were also some $20 billion of orders outstanding, mostly for munitions. The new orders included $68 billion for munitions, $12.6 billions for industrial expansion, and $6.9 billions for military construction.

Under this flood of war orders, a number of things were bound to happen, and did happen.

First, it became utterly impossible to produce everything ordered at any time in any near future. It was an industrial impossibility. The total called for was in excess of our industrial capacity.

Second, there was a resulting collision between the various production programs and between the men who were responsible for them. Merchant ships took steel from the Navy, and the landing craft cut into both. The Navy took aluminum from aircraft. Rubber took valves from escort vessels, from petroleum, and from the Navy. The pipe lines took steel from ships, new tools, and the railroads. And at every turn there were foreign demands to be met as well as requirements for new plants.

Third, all semblance of balance in the production program disappeared because of the different rates of contracting and of production that resulted from the scramble to place orders. If there ever had been a planned

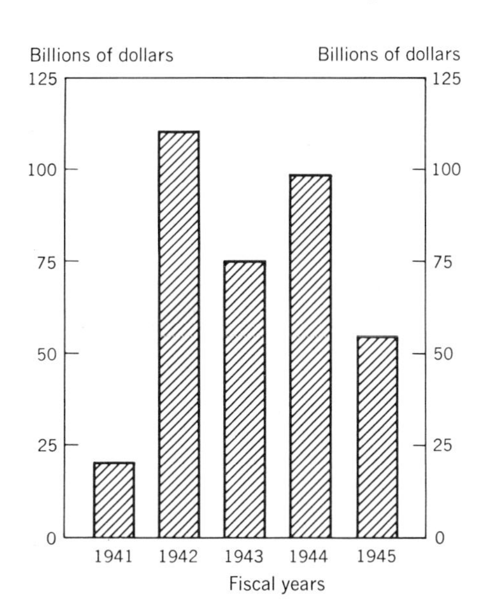

CHART 1. *Federal Appropriations for War.* (Source: Treasury Department.)

balance between men, ships, tanks, planes, supplies, weapons, ammunition, and new facilities, and there is no evidence that there was, that balance disappeared in the differential time required to develop the orders, the differential energies of the various procurement officers, and the differential difficulties of getting production out.

Fourth, there was terrific waste in conversion. After a tragically slow start, many a plant was changed over to war production when its normal product was more needed than its new product. Locomotive plants went into tank production, when locomotives were more necessary—but the Tank Division did not know this. Truck plants began to produce airplanes, a change that caused shortages of trucks later on. In some cases, plants were converted at great cost of steel and copper, when a fraction of the precious metals involved would have brought a greater return at some other place in the economy. The scramble for a production we could not attain, brought us waste instead.

Fifth, we built many new factories, and expanded many others, which we could not use and did not need. Many of these factories we could not supply with labor or with raw materials, or if we had, we would not have been able to fly the planes or shoot the ammunition that would have come out of them. But in the process we used up critical materials and man-

CHART 2. *Productive Facility Expansion by Source of Funds.* [Source: Civilian Production Administration (formerly War Production Board).]

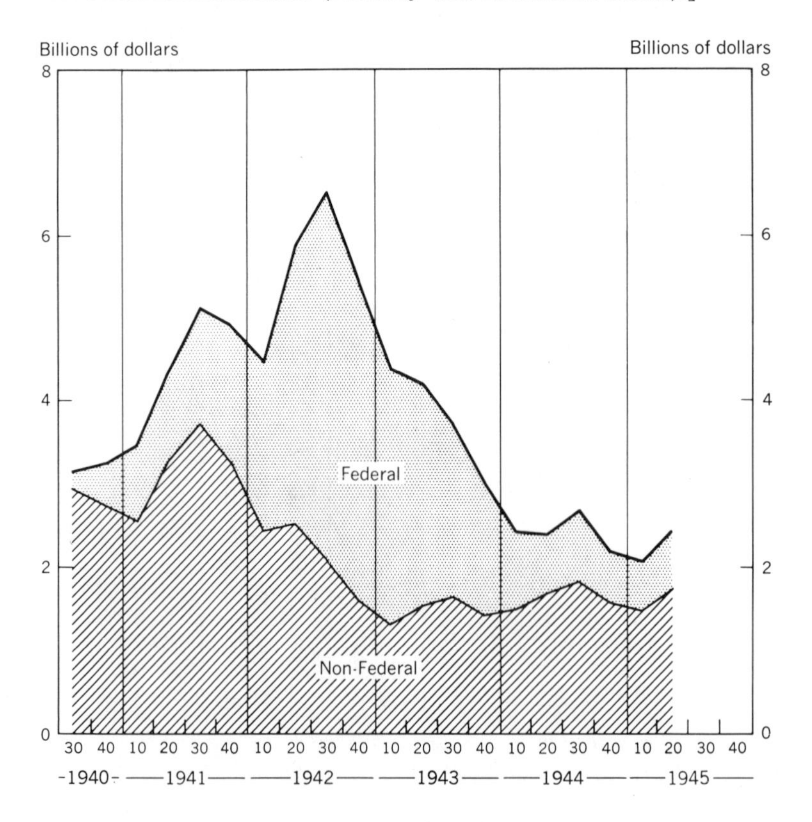

power which might better have gone into something else. In the light of the tremendous contracts outstanding especially in the early part of 1942, however, these plants seemed necessary to some people, and under the system they were given high priorities. In most cases they were also financed by the Government. The result was, however, an overconcentration of contracts in the larger corporations and a failure to fully utilize the facilities of many small manufacturers whose plants could have produced "bits and pieces." It did not escape the attention of Congress that better utilization of small plants could have reduced the necessary expansion of facilities.

Finally, the priority system broke down because of "priority inflation." People with military contracts had the right to take more scarce materials and components than there were, so that a priority or an allocation became nothing more than a "hunting license." In other words, those who were issuing priorities did not limit their high-ranking authorizations within the allocations given them by the Requirements Committee. In fact, there was very little connection between the two, partly because the allocations were based on a quarterly time schedule, while the priorities carried no terminal date and were good at any time.

Whether it would have been possible, within the time available, by better planning of procurement to prevent the consequence of indiscriminate placement of contracts without delaying the advance of production is a complex question. The determination of the construction program for ordnance plants, for example, required not only that we know in what quantities and at what times a particular ordnance item would be needed, but also that the output rate of plants producing by new methods and on unprecedented scales be predicted. Control over other types of procurement would have required types of data, such as the usage of materials in the manufacture of particular items, and administrative techniques not yet developed. Whatever the hypothetical possibilities might have been, the general policy in the first few months of the war was to permit the placement of contracts until difficulties developed. Then the War Production Board proceeded to deal with the problems born of experience.

Fear and Hysteria: The Japanese Relocation, "Hirabayashi v. United States," 1943

Even though Americans proved to be relatively secure behind their ocean barriers, uncertainties early in the war created much fear and some hysteria. Blackouts were enforced to cut the bright glare of the coastal cities, which silhouetted—for submarines to attack—the freighters off American coasts. Rumors of sabotage kept the nation uneasy. A single shell-lobbing exploit by a lone Japanese submarine off a California beach set the West Coast in a panic. But nothing was quite so disturbing for many Americans as the existence of large numbers of Japanese-Americans, particularly in the West Coast cities. There seemed a constant danger of espionage and sabotage—perhaps, at first, even the danger of armed uprising. Americans' lack of preparedness on December 7 made them even more hysterical in the weeks which followed. If Pearl Harbor could happen, was any possibility beyond reason?

In the first few weeks after Pearl Harbor, these hysterical fears combined with envy and race prejudice to produce one of the most extensive violations of civil liberties and due process in the nation's history. Japanese-Americans, citizens as well as aliens, were registered, watched, and controlled by military curfew in the West Coast states. In February, 1942, President Roosevelt authorized the War Department to restrict them from military areas. Between February 19 and March 29, over 100,000 Japanese-Americans were forcibly removed from their homes and businesses on the Coast and herded into "relocation" camps in the interior. Many citizens, many with sons fighting in the armed services, were forcibly held in these detention camps throughout the war. Only in January, 1945, was the mass exclusion from the West Coast ended.

This policy of exclusion, fanatically conceived and ruthlessly carried out, produced a number of Federal court cases, for it challenged constitutional rights as well as concepts of ethics and justice. The particular case in which the Supreme Court's opinion is printed here grew from the violation of military curfew by a United States citizen and his subsequent arrest and conviction. The opinion describes the facts of the case and some of the relevant considerations, then disposes of the constitutional issues raised. The case does not raise the question whether a curfew is appropriate or legal. Hirabayashi challenged, instead, the right of Congress to delegate to the military the authority to impose such a curfew and the right of the Federal government in general to discriminate against citizens of Japanese ancestry. The Court's opinion approving the action laid the groundwork for later cases in which the arrests and relocation were approved. More important, they laid stress upon the war power, placing it above the rest of the Constitution.

On the impact of World War II upon civil liberties and constitutional interpretation generally, one should read Edward S. Corwin, Total War and the Constitution *(1947). The treatment of the Japanese is discussed in Morton Grodzins,* Americans Betrayed: Politics and the Japanese Evacuation *(1949), and in Jacobus ten Broek, Edward N. Barnhart, and Floyd W. Matson,* Prejudice, War and the Constitution: Japanese-American Evacuation and Resettlement *(1954).*

The case given here is Hirabayashi v. United States, *320 U.S. 83–105 (1943).*

Mr. Chief Justice Stone delivered the opinion of the Court:

Appellant, an American citizen of Japanese ancestry, was convicted in the district court of violating the Act of Congress of March 21, 1942 . . . which makes it a misdemeanor knowingly to disregard restrictions made applicable by a military commander to persons in a military area prescribed by him as such, all as authorized by an Executive Order of the President.

The questions for our decision are whether the particular restriction violated, namely that all persons of Japanese ancestry residing in such an area be within their place of residence daily between the hours of 8:00 p. m. and 6:00 a. m., was adopted by the military commander in the exercise of an unconstitutional delegation by Congress of its legislative power, and whether the restriction unconstitutionally discriminated between citizens of Japanese ancestry and those of other ancestries in violation of the Fifth Amendment.

The indictment is in two counts. The second charges that appellant, being a person of Japanese ancestry, had on a specified date, contrary to a restriction promulgated by the military commander of the Western Defense Command, Fourth Army, failed to remain in his place of residence in the designated military area between the hours of 8:00 o'clock p. m. and 6:00 a. m. The first count charges that appellant, on May 11 and 12, 1942, had, contrary to a Civilian Exclusion Order issued by the military commander, failed to report to the Civil Control Station within the designated area, it appearing that appellant's required presence there was a preliminary step to the exclusion from that area of persons of Japanese ancestry.

By demurrer and plea in abatement, which the court overruled, appellant asserted that the indictment should be dismissed because he was an American citizen who had never been a subject of and had never borne allegiance to the Empire of Japan, and also because the Act of March 21, 1942, was an unconstitutional delegation of Congressional power. On the trial to a jury it appeared that appellant was born in Seattle in 1918, of Japanese parents who had come from Japan to the United States, and who had never afterward returned to Japan; that he was educated in the Washington public schools and at the time of his arrest was a senior in the University of Washington; that he had never been in Japan or had any association with Japanese residing there.

The evidence showed that appellant had failed to report to the Civil Control Station on May 11 or May 12, 1942, as directed, to register for evacuation from the military area. He admitted failure to do so, and stated it had at all times been his belief that he would be waiving his rights as an American citizen by so doing. The evidence also showed that for like reason he was away from his place of residence after 8:00 p. m. on May 9, 1942. The jury returned a verdict of guilty on both counts and appellant was sentenced to imprisonment for a term of three months on each, the sentences to run concurrently. . . .

On December 8, 1941, one day after the bombing of Pearl Harbor by a Japanese air force, Congress declared war against Japan. . . . The President promulgated Executive Order No. 9066. . . . The Order recited that "the successful prosecution of the war requires every possible protection against espionage and against sabotage to national-defense material, national-defense premises, and national-defense utilities. . . . By virtue of the authority vested in him as President and as Commander in Chief of the Army and Navy, the President purported to "authorize and direct the Secretary of War, and the Military Commanders whom he may from time to time designate, whenever he or any designated Commander deems such action necessary or desirable, to proscribe military areas in such places and of such extent as he or the appropriate Military Commander may determine, from which any or all persons may be excluded, and with respect to which, the right of any person to enter, remain in, or leave shall be subject to whatever restrictions the Secretary of War or the appropriate Military Commander may impose in his discretion."

On February 20, 1942, the Secretary of War designated Lt. General J. L. DeWitt as Military Commander of the Western Defense Command, comprising the Pacific Coast states and some others, to carry out there the duties prescribed by Executive Order No. 9066. On March 2, 1942, General DeWitt promulgated Public Proclamation No. 1. The proclamation recited that the entire Pacific Coast "by the geographical location is particularly subject to attack, to attempted invasion by the armed forces of nations with which the United States is now at war, and, in connection therewith, is subject to espionage and acts of sabotage, thereby requiring the adoption of military measures necessary to establish safeguards against such enemy operations." It stated that "the present situation requires as a matter of military necessity the establishment in the territory embraced by the Western Defense Command of Military Areas and Zones thereof;" it specified and designated as military areas certain areas within the Western Defense Command; and it declared that "such persons or classes of persons as the situation may require" would, by subsequent proclamation, be excluded from certain of these areas, but might be permitted to enter or remain in certain others, under regulations and restrictions to be later prescribed. Among the military areas so designated by Public Proclamation No. 1 was Military Area No. 1, which embraced, besides the southern part of Arizona, all the coastal region of the three Pacific Coast states, including the City of Seattle, Washington, where appellant resided. Military Area No. 2, designated by the same proclamation, included those parts of the coastal states and of Arizona not placed within Military Area No. 1.

Public Proclamation No. 2 of March 16, 1942, issued by General DeWitt, made like recitals and designated further military areas and zones. It contained like provisions concerning the exclusion, by subsequent proclamation, of certain persons or classes of persons from these areas, and the future promulgation of regulations and restrictions applicable to persons remaining within them.

An Executive Order of the President, No. 9102, of March 18, 1942, established the War Relocation Authority, in the Office for Emergency Management of the Executive Office of the President; it authorized the Director of War Relocation Authority to formulate and effectuate a program for the removal, relocation, maintenance and supervision of persons designated under Executive Order No. 9066, already referred to, and it conferred on the Director authority to prescribe regulations necessary or desirable to promote the effective execution of the program.

Congress, by the Act of March 21, 1942, provided: "That whoever shall enter, remain in, leave, or commit any act in any military area or military zone prescribed, under the authority of an Executive Order of the President, by the Secretary of War, or by any military commander designated by the Secretary of War, contrary to the restrictions applicable to any such area or zone or contrary to the order of the Secretary of War or any such military commander, shall, if it appears that he knew or should have known of the existence and extent of the restrictions or order and that his act was in violation thereof, be guilty of a misdemeanor and upon conviction shall be liable" to fine or imprisonment, or both.

Three days later, on March 24, 1942, General DeWitt issued Public Proclamation No. 3. After referring to the previous designation of military areas by Public Proclamations Nos. 1 and 2, it recited that ". . . the present situation within these Military Areas and Zones requires as a matter of military necessity the establishment of certain regulations pertaining to all enemy aliens and all persons of Japanese ancestry within said Military Areas and Zones. . . ." It accordingly declared and established that from and after March 27, 1942, "all alien Japanese, all alien Germans, all alien Italians, and all persons of Japanese ancestry residing or being within the geographical limits of Military Area No. 1 . . . shall be within their place of residence between the hours of 8:00 p. m. and 6:00 a. m., which period is hereinafter referred to as the hours of curfew." It also imposed certain other restrictions on persons of Japanese ancestry, and provided that any person violating the regulations would be subject to the criminal penalties provided by the Act of Congress of March 21, 1942.

Beginning on March 24, 1942, the military commander issued a series of Civilian Exclusion Orders pursuant to the provisions of Public Proclamation No. 1. Each such order related to a specified area within the territory of his command. The order applicable to appellant was Civilian Exclusion Order No. 57 of May 10, 1942. It directed that from and after 12:00 noon, May 16, 1942, all persons of Japanese ancestry, both alien and non-alien, be excluded from a specified portion of Military Area No. 1 in Seattle, including appellant's place of residence, and it required a member of each family, and each individual living alone, affected by the order to report on May 11 or May 12 to a designated Civil Control Station in Seattle. Meanwhile the military commander had issued Public Proclamation No. 4 of March 27, 1942, which recited the necessity of providing for the orderly evacuation and resettlement of Japanese within the area, and prohibited all alien Japanese and all persons of Japanese ancestry from leaving the military area until future orders should permit.

Appellant does not deny that he knowingly failed to obey the curfew order as charged in the second count of the indictment, or that the order was authorized by the terms of Executive Order No. 9066, or that the challenged Act of Congress purports to punish with criminal penalties disobedience of such an order. His contentions are only that Congress unconstitutionally delegated its legislative power to the military commander by authorizing him to impose the challenged regulation, and that, even if the regulation were in other respects lawfully authorized, the Fifth Amendment prohibits the discrimination made between citizens of Japanese descent and those of other ancestry.

It will be evident from the legislative history that the Act of March 21, 1942, contemplated and authorized the curfew order which we have before us. The bill which became the Act of March 21, 1942, was introduced in the Senate on March 9th and in the House on March 10th at the request of the Secretary of War who, in letters to the Chairman of the Senate Committee on Military Affairs and to the Speaker of the House, stated explicitly that its purpose was to provide means for the enforcement of orders issued under Executive Order No. 9066. This appears in the committee reports on the bill, which set out in full the Executive Order and the Secretary's letter. . . . And each of the committee reports expressly mentions curfew orders as one of the types of restrictions which it was deemed desirable to enforce by criminal sanctions.

When the bill was under consideration, General DeWitt had published his Proclamation No. 1 of March 2, 1942, establishing Military Areas Nos. 1 and 2, and that Proclamation was before Congress. . . . A letter of the Secretary to the Chairman of the House Military Affairs Committee, of March 14, 1942, informed Congress that "General DeWitt is strongly of the opinion that the bill, when enacted, should be broad enough to enable the Secretary of War or the appropriate military commander to enforce curfews and other restrictions within military areas and zones;" and that General DeWitt had "indicated that he was prepared to enforce certain restrictions at once for the purpose of protecting certain vital national defense interests but did not desire to proceed until enforcement machinery had been set up. . . ."

The Chairman of the Senate Military Affairs Committee explained on the floor of the Senate that the purpose of the proposed legislation was to provide means of enforcement of curfew orders and other military orders made pursuant to Executive Order No. 9066. He read General DeWitt's Public Proclamation No. 1, and statements from newspaper reports that "evacuation of the first Japanese aliens and American-born Japanese" was about to begin. He also stated to the Senate that "reasons for suspected widespread fifth-column activity among Japanese" were to be found in the system of dual citizenship which Japan deemed applicable to American-born Japanese, and in the propaganda disseminated by Japanese consuls, Buddhist priests and other leaders, among American-born children of Japanese. Such was stated to be the explanation of the contemplated evacuation from the Pacific Coast area of persons of Japanese ancestry, citizens as well as aliens. Congress also had before it the Preliminary Report of a House Committee investigating national defense migration, of March 19, 1942, which approved the provisions of Executive Order No. 9066, and which recommended the evacuation, from military areas established under the order, of all persons of Japanese ancestry, including citizens. The proposed legislation provided criminal sanctions for violation of orders, in terms broad enough to include the curfew order now before us, and the legislative history demonstrates that Congress was advised that curfew orders were among those intended, and was advised also that regulation of citizen and alien Japanese alike was contemplated.

The conclusion is inescapable that Congress, by the Act of March 21, 1942, ratified and confirmed Executive Order No. 9066. . . . And so far as it lawfully could, Congress authorized and implemented such curfew orders as the commanding officer should promulgate pursuant to the Executive Order of the President. The question then is not one of congressional power to delegate to the President the promulgation of the Executive Order, but whether, acting in co-operation, Congress and the Executive have constitutional authority to impose the curfew restriction here complained of. We must consider also whether, acting together, Congress and the Executive could leave it to the designated military commander to appraise the relevant conditions and on the basis of that appraisal to say whether, under the circumstances, the time and place were appropriate for the promulgation of the curfew order and whether the order itself was an appropriate means of carrying out the Executive Order for the "protection against espionage and against sabotage" to national defense materials, premises and utilities. For reasons presently to be stated, we conclude that it was within the constitutional power of Congress and the executive arm of the Government to prescribe this curfew order for the period under consideration and that its promulgation by the military commander involved no unlawful delegation of legislative power.

Executive Order No. 9066, promulgated in time of war for the declared purpose of prosecuting the war by protecting national defense resources from sabotage and espionage, and the Act of March 21, 1942, ratifying and confirming the Executive Order, were each an exercise of the power to wage war conferred on the Congress and on the President, as Commander in Chief of the armed forces, by Articles 1 and 2 of the Constitution. . . .

We have no occasion to consider whether the President, acting alone, could lawfully have made the curfew order in question, or have authorized others to make it. For the President's action has the support of the Act of Congress, and we are immediately concerned with the question whether it is within the constitutional power of the national government, through the joint action of Congress and the Executive, to impose this restriction as an emergency war measure. The exercise of that power here involves no question of martial law or trial by military tribunal. . . .

Appellant has been tried and convicted in the civil courts and has been subjected to penalties prescribed by Congress for the acts committed.

The war power of the national government is "the power to wage war successfully." It extends to every matter and activity so related to war as substantially to affect its conduct and progress. The power is not restricted to the winning of victories in the field and the repulse of enemy forces. It embraces every phase of the national defense, including the protection of war materials and the members of the armed forces from injury and from the dangers which attend the rise, prosecution and progress of war. . . .

Since the Constitution commits to the Executive and to Congress the exercise of the war power in all the vicissitudes and conditions of warfare, it has necessarily given them wide scope for the exercise of judgment and discretion in determining the nature and extent of the threatened injury or danger and in the selection of the means for resisting it. . . .

Where, as they did here, the conditions call for the exercise of judgment and discretion and for the choice of means by those branches of the Government on which the Constitution has placed the responsibility of war-making, it is not for any court to sit in review of the wisdom of their action or substitute its judgment for theirs.

The actions taken must be appraised in the light of the conditions with which the President and Congress were confronted in the early months of 1942, many of which, since disclosed, were then peculiarly within the knowledge of the military authorities. . . .

That reasonably prudent men charged with the responsibility of our national defense had ample ground for concluding that they must face the danger of invasion, take measures against it, and in making the choice of measures consider our internal situation, cannot be doubted.

The challenged orders were defense measures for the avowed purpose of safeguarding the military area in question, at a time of threatened air raids and invasion by the Japanese forces, from the danger of sabotage and espionage. As the curfew was made applicable to citizens residing in the area only if they were of Japanese ancestry, our inquiry must be whether in the light of all the facts and circumstances there was any substantial basis for the conclusion, in which Congress and the military commander united, that the curfew as applied was a protective measure necessary to meet the threat of sabotage and espionage which would substantially affect the war effort and which might reasonably be expected to aid a threatened enemy invasion. The alternative which appellant insists must be accepted is for the military authorities to impose the curfew on all citizens within the military area, or on none. In a case of threatened danger requiring prompt action, it is a choice between inflicting obviously needless hardship on the many, or sitting passive and unresisting in the presence of the threat. We think that constitutional government, in time of war, is not so powerless and does not compel so hard a choice if those charged with the responsibility of our national defense have reasonable ground for believing that the threat is real. . . . At a time of threatened Japanese attack upon this country, the nature of our inhabitants' attachments to the Japanese enemy was consequently a matter of grave concern. Of the 126,000 persons of Japanese descent in the United States, citizens and noncitizens, approximately 112,000 resided in California, Oregon and Washington at the time of the adoption of the military regulations. Of these approximately two-thirds are citizens because born in the United States. Not only did the great majority of such persons reside within the Pacific Coast states but they were concentrated in or near three of the large cities, Seattle, Portland and Los Angeles, all in Military Area No. 1.

There is support for the view that social, economic and political conditions which have prevailed since the close of the last century, when the Japanese began to come to this country in substantial numbers, have intensified their solidarity and have in large measure prevented their assimilation as an integral part of the white population. In addition, large numbers of children of Japanese parentage are sent to Japanese language schools outside the regular hours of public schools in the locality. Some of these schools are generally believed to be sources of Japanese nationalistic propaganda, cultivating allegiance to Japan. Considerable numbers, estimated to be approximately 10,000, of American-born children of Japanese parentage have been sent to Japan for all or a part of their education.

Congress and the Executive, including the military commander, could have attributed special significance, in its bearing on the loyalties of persons of Japanese descent, to the maintenance by Japan of its system of dual citizenship. Children born in the United States of Japanese alien parents, and especially those children born before December 1, 1924, are under many circumstances deemed, by Japanese law, to be citizens of Japan. No official census of those whom Japan regards as having thus retained Japanese citizenship is available, but there is ground for the belief that the number is large.

The large number of resident alien Japanese, approximately one-third of all Japanese inhabitants of the country, are of mature years and occupy positions of influence in Japanese communities. The association of influential Japanese residents with Japanese Consulates has been deemed a ready means for the dissemination of propaganda and for the maintenance of the influence of the Japanese Government with the Japanese population in this country.

As a result of all these conditions affecting the life of the Japanese, both aliens and citizens, in the Pacific Coast area, there has been relatively little social intercourse between them and the white population. The restrictions, both practical and legal, affecting the privileges and opportunities afforded to persons of Japanese extraction residing in the United States, have been sources of irritation and may well have tended to increase their isolation, and in many instances their attachments to Japan and its institutions.

Viewing these data in all their aspects, Congress and the Executive could reasonably have concluded that these conditions have encouraged the continued attachment of members of this group to Japan and Japanese institutions. These are only some of the many considerations which those charged with the responsibility for the national defense could take into account in determining the nature and extent of the danger of espionage and sabotage, in the event of invasion or air raid attack. The extent of that danger could be definitely known only after the event and after it was too late to meet it. Whatever views we may entertain regarding the loyalty to this country of the citizens of Japanese ancestry, we cannot reject as unfounded the judgment of the military authorities and of Congress that there were disloyal members of that population, whose number and strength could not be precisely and quickly ascertained. We cannot say that the war-making branches of the Government did not have ground for believing that in a critical hour such persons could not readily be isolated and separately dealt with, and constituted a menace to the national defense and safety, which demanded that prompt and adequate measures be taken to guard against it.

Appellant does not deny that, given the danger, a curfew was an appropriate measure against sabotage. It is an obvious protection against the perpetration of sabotage most readily committed during the hours of darkness. If it was an appropriate exercise of the war power its validity is not impaired because it has restricted the citizen's liberty. Like every military control of the population of a dangerous zone in wartime, it necessarily involves some infringement of individual liberty, just as does the police establishment of fire lines during a fire, or the confinement of people to their houses during an air raid alarm—neither of which could be thought to be an infringement of constitutional right. Like them, the validity of the restraints of the curfew order depends on all the conditions which obtain at the time the curfew is imposed and which support the order imposing it.

But appellant insists that the exercise of the power is inappropriate and unconstitutional because it discriminates against citizens of Japanese ancestry, in violation of the Fifth Amendment. The Fifth Amendment contains no equal protection clause and it restrains only such discriminatory legislation by Congress as amounts to a denial of due process. . . .

Congress may hit at a particular danger where it is seen, without providing for others which are not so evident or so urgent. . . . Distinctions between citizens solely because of their ancestry are by their very nature odious to a free people whose institutions are founded upon the doctrine of equality. For that reason, legislative classification or discrimination based on race alone has often been held to be a denial of equal protection. . . . We may assume that these considerations would be controlling here were it not for the fact that the danger of espionage and sabotage, in time of war and of threatened invasion, calls upon the military authorities to scrutinize every relevant fact bearing on the loyalty of populations in the danger areas. Because racial discriminations are in most circumstances irrelevant and therefore prohibited, it by no means follows that, in dealing with the perils of war, Congress and the Executive are wholly precluded from taking into account those facts and circumstances which are relevant to measures for our national defense and for the successful prosecution of the war, and which may in fact place citizens of one ancestry in a different category from others. "We must never forget, that it is *a constitution* we are expounding," "a constitution intended to endure for ages to come, and, consequently, to be adapted to the various *crises* of human affairs." . . . The adoption by Government, in the crisis of war and of threatened invasion, of measures for the public safety, based upon the recognition of facts and circumstances which indicate that a group of one national extraction may menace that safety more than others, is not wholly beyond the limits of the Constitution and is not to be condemned merely because in other and in most circumstances racial distinctions are irrelevant. . . .

Here the aim of Congress and the Executive was the protection against sabotage of war materials and utilities in areas thought to be in danger of Japanese invasion and air attack. We have stated in detail facts and circumstances with respect to the American citizens of Japanese ancestry residing on the Pacific Coast which support the judgment of the war-waging branches of the Government that some restrictive measure was urgent. We cannot say that these facts and circumstances, considered in the particular war setting, could afford no ground for differentiating citizens of Japanese ancestry from other groups in the United States. The fact alone that attack on our shores was threatened by Japan rather than another enemy power set these citizens apart from others who have no particular associations with Japan. . . .

The Constitution as a continuously operating charter of government does not demand the impossible or the impractical. The essentials of the legislative function are preserved when Congress authorizes a statutory command to become operative, upon ascertainment of a basic conclusion of fact by a designated representative of the Government. . . . The present statute, which authorized curfew orders to be made pursuant to Executive Order No. 9066 for the protection of war resources from espionage and sabotage, satisfies those requirements. Under the Executive Order the basic facts, determined by the military commander in the light of knowledge then available, were whether that danger existed and whether a curfew order was an appropriate means of minimizing the danger. Since his findings to that effect were, as we have said, not without adequate support, the legislative function was performed and the sanction of the statute attached to violations of the curfew order. It is unnecessary to consider whether or to what extent such findings would support orders differing from the curfew order.

The conviction under the second count is without constitutional infirmity. Hence we have no occasion to review the conviction on the first count since, as already stated, the sentences on the two counts are to run concurrently and conviction on the second is sufficient to sustain the sentence. For this reason also it is unnecessary to consider the Government's argument that compliance with the order to report at the Civilian Control Station did not necessarily entail confinement in a relocation center.

Affirmed.

Courage: Ernie Pyle Reports on "The Road to Berlin," 1943

Without doubt, the quality most admired and most found when it was needed was raw courage. And the national appetite for heroes was voracious. This was the stuff from which loyalty was woven. War correspondents, treated with wise hospitality by the military services, roamed the war from the Aleutians to the Azores, from Normandy to Mindanao, collecting the stories on which the public courage thrived. At great danger to themselves, the correspondents relayed to the folk back home the romance and bluster, the toughness, and a little of the sadness of the war. Operating under self-imposed codes of censorship, the newshawks allowed little of the inefficiency, and practically none of the brutality, cowardice, or irresponsibility of the war, to creep into their stories. Theirs was the business of finding heroes.

There was generally conceded to be no war correspondent greater than Ernie Pyle (1900–1945). He despised stuffy commanders. He went where the blood, mud, and steel were. He liked GIs. In the end he died of a sniper's bullet. But perhaps the thing which most made him loved was the fact that he spoke more bluntly, with more simple language, that he played less with romance and described more directly than did most of his peers what it really was like.

Among Ernie Pyle's books are included Here Is Your War *(1943) and* Last Chapter *(1946). For another example of notable war reporting, see John Hersey,* Into the Valley *(1945).*

The chapter reproduced here is from Ernie Pyle, Brave Men *(Grosset & Dunlap, 1943), pages 246–253.*

Owing to a last-minute alteration in the arrangements, I didn't arrive on the beachhead until the morning after D-day, after our first wave of assault troops had hit the shore.

By the time we got there the beaches had been taken and the fighting had moved a couple of miles inland. All that remained on the beach was some sniping and artillery fire, and the occasional startling blast of a mine geysering brown sand into the air. That plus a gigantic and pitiful litter of wreckage along miles of shore line.

Submerged tanks and overturned boats and burned trucks and shell-shattered jeeps and sad little personal belongings were strewn all over those bitter sands. That plus the bodies of soldiers lying in rows covered with blankets, the toes of their shoes sticking up in a line as though on drill. And other bodies, uncollected, still sprawling grotesquely in the sand or half hidden by the high grass beyond the beach. That plus an intense, grim determination of work-weary men to get that chaotic beach organized and get all the vital supplies and the reinforcements moving more rapidly over it from the stacked-up ships standing in droves out to sea.

After it was over it seemed to me a pure miracle that we ever took the beach at all. For some of our units it was easy, but in the special sector where I landed our troops faced such odds that our getting ashore was like my whipping Joe Louis down to a pulp. The men who did it on that beach were men of the First and Twenty-ninth Divisions.

I want to tell you what the opening of the second front in that one sector entailed, so that you can know and appreciate and forever be humbly grateful to those both dead and alive who did it for you.

Ashore, facing us, were more enemy troops than we had in our assault waves. The advantages were all theirs, the disadvantages all ours. The Germans were dug into positions they had been working on for months, although they were not entirely complete. A 100-foot bluff a couple of hundred yards back from the beach had great concrete gun emplacements built right into the hilltop. These opened to the sides instead of to the front, thus making it hard for naval fire from the sea to reach them. They could shoot parallel with the shore and cover every foot of it for miles with artillery fire.

Then they had hidden machine-gun nests on the forward slopes, with crossfire taking in every inch of the beach. These nests were connected by networks of trenches, so that the German gunners could move about without exposing themselves.

Throughout the length of the beach, running zigzag a couple of hundred yards back from the shore line, was an immense V-shaped ditch fifteen feet deep. Nothing could cross it, not even men on foot, until fills had been made. And in other places at the far end of the beach, where the ground was flatter, they had great concrete walls. These were blasted by our naval gunfire or by explosives set by hand after we got ashore.

Our only exits from the beach were several swales or valleys, each about a hundred yards wide. The Germans made the most of those funnellike traps, sowing them with buried mines. They also contained barbed-wire entanglements with mines attached, hidden ditches, and machine guns firing from the slopes.

All this was on the shore. But our men had to go through a maze nearly as deadly before they even got ashore. Underwater obstacles were terrific.

Under the water the Germans had whole fields of evil devices to catch our boats. Several days after the landing we had cleared only channels through them and still could not approach the whole length of the beach with our ships. Even then some ship or boat would hit one of those mines and be knocked out of commission.

The Germans had masses of great six-pronged spiders—made of railroad iron and standing shoulder-high—just beneath the surface of the water, for our landing craft to run into. They had huge logs buried in the sand, pointing upward and outward, their tops just below the water. Attached to the logs were mines.

In addition to these obstacles they had floating mines offshore, land mines buried in the sand of the beach, and more mines in checkerboard rows in the tall grass beyond the sand. And the enemy had four men on shore for every three men we had approaching the shore.

And yet we got on.

Beach landings are always planned to a schedule that is set far ahead of time. They all have to be timed, in order for everything to mesh and for the following waves of troops to be standing off the beach and ready to land at the right moment. Some elements of the assault force are to break through quickly, push on inland, and attack the most obvious enemy strong points. It is usually the plan for units to be inland, attacking gun positions from behind, within a matter of minutes after the first men hit the beach.

I have always been amazed at the speed called for in these plans. Schedules will call for engineers to land at H-hour plus 2 minutes, and service troops at H-hour plus 30 minutes, and even for press censors to land at H-hour plus 75 minutes. But in the attack on my special portion of the beach—the toughest spot of all, incidentally—the schedule didn't hold.

Our men simply could not get past the beach. They were pinned down right on the water's edge by an inhuman wall of fire from the bluff. Our first waves were on that beach for hours, instead of a few minutes, before they could begin working inland.

The foxholes were still there—dug at the very edge of the water, in the sand and the small jumbled rocks that formed parts of the beach.

Medical corpsmen attended the wounded as best they could. Men were killed as they stepped out of landing craft. An officer whom I knew got a bullet through the head just as the door of his landing craft was let down. Some men were drowned.

The first crack in the beach defenses was finally accomplished by terrific and wonderful naval gunfire, which knocked out the big emplacements. Epic stories have been told of destroyers that ran right up into shallow water and had it out point-blank with the big guns in those concrete emplacements ashore.

When the heavy fire stopped, our men were organized by their officers and pushed on inland, circling machine-gun nests and taking them from the rear.

As one officer said, the only way to take a beach is to face it and keep going. It is costly at first, but it's the only way. If the men are pinned down on the beach, dug in and out of action, they might as well not be there at all. They hold up the waves behind them, and nothing is being gained.

Our men were pinned down for a while, but finally they stood up and went through, and so we took that beach and accomplished our landing. In the light of a couple of days of retrospection, we sat and talked and called it a miracle that our men ever got on at all or were able to stay on.

They suffered casualties. And yet considering the entire beachhead assault, including other units that had a much easier time, our total casualties in driving that wedge into the Continent of Europe were remarkably low—only a fraction, in fact, of what our commanders had been prepared to accept.

And those units that were so battered and went through such hell pushed on inland without rest, their spirits high, their egotism in victory almost reaching the smart-alecky stage.

Their tails were up. "We've done it again," they said. They figured that the rest of the Army wasn't needed at all. Which proves that, while their judgment in this respect was bad, they certainly had the spirit that wins battles, and eventually wars.

When I went ashore on the soil of France the first thing I wanted to do was hunt up the other correspondents I had said good-bye to a few days previously in England, and see how they had fared. Before the day of invasion we had accepted it as a fact that not everybody would come through alive.

Correspondents sort of gang together. They know the ins and outs of war, and they all work at it in much the same manner. So I knew about where to look, and I didn't have much trouble finding them.

It was early in the morning, before the boys had started out on their day's round of covering the war. I found them in foxholes dug into the rear slope of a grassy hill about a half mile from the beach. I picked them out from a distance, because I could spot Jack Thompson's beard. He was sitting on the edge of a foxhole lacing his paratrooper boots. About a dozen correspondents were there, among them three especially good friends of mine—Thompson, Don Whitehead and Tex O'Reilly.

First of all we checked with each other on what we had heard about other correspondents. Most of them were O.K. One had been killed, and one was supposed to have been lost on a sunken ship, but we didn't know who. One or two had been wounded. Three of our best friends had not been heard from at all, and it looked bad. They subsequently turned up safe.

The boys were unshaved, and their eyes were red. Their muscles were stiff and their bodies ached. They had carried ashore only their typewriters and some K rations. They had gone two days without sleep, and then had slept on the ground without blankets, in wet clothes.

But none of that mattered too much after what they had been through. They were in a sort of daze from the exhaustion and mental turmoil of battle. When anyone asked a question it would take them a few seconds to focus their thoughts and give an answer.

Two of them in particular had been through all the frightful nightmare that the assault troops had experienced—because they had gone ashore with them.

Don Whitehead hit the beach with one regiment just an hour after H-hour, Thompson at the same time with another regiment. They were on the beaches for more than four hours under that hideous cloudburst of shells and bullets.

Jack Thompson said, "You've never seen a beach like it before. Dead and wounded men were lying so thick you could hardly take a step. One officer was killed only two feet away from me."

Whitehead was still asleep when I went to his foxhole. I said, "Get up, you lazy so-and-so." He started grinning without even opening his eyes, for he knew who it was.

It was hard for him to wake up. He had been unable to sleep, from sheer exhaustion, and had taken a sleeping tablet.

Don had managed to steal one blanket on the beach and had that wrapped around him. He had taken off his shoes. His feet were so sore from walking in wet shoes and socks that he had to give them some air.

Finally he began to get himself up. "I don't know why I'm alive at all," he said. "It was really awful. For hours there on the beach the shells were so close they were throwing mud and rocks all over you. It was so bad that after a while you didn't care whether you got hit or not."

Don fished in a cardboard ration box for some cigarettes. He pulled out an envelope and threw it into the bushes. "They ain't worth a damn," he said. The envelope contained his antiseasickness tablets.

"I was sicker than hell while we were circling around in our landing craft waiting to come ashore," he said. "Everybody was sick. Soldiers were lying on the floor of the LCVP, sick as dogs."

Tex O'Reilly rode around in a boat for six hours waiting to get ashore. Everybody was wet and cold and seasick and scared. War is so romantic—if you're far away from it.

Whitehead had probably been in more amphibious landings than any other correspondent over there. I know of six he made, four of them murderously tough. And he said, "I think I have gone on one too many of these things. Not because of what might happen to me personally, but I've lost my perspective. It's like dreaming the same nightmare over and over again, and when you try to write you feel that you have written it all before. You can't think of any new or different words to say it with."

I knew only too well what he meant.

It is an ironic thing about correspondents who go in on the first few days of an invasion story. They are the only correspondents capable of telling the full and intimate drama and horror of the thing. And yet they are the ones who can't get their copy out to the world. By the time they do get it out, events have swirled on and the world doesn't care any more.

There that morning in their foxholes on the slope of the hill those correspondents were mainly worried about the communications situation. Although they had landed with the first wave, they felt sure that none of their copy had ever reached America. And even I, a day behind them, felt no assurance that my feeble reports would ever see the light of day. But in philosophical moments I can think of greater catastrophes than that.

I took a walk along the historic coast of Normandy in the country of France. It was a lovely day for strolling along the seashore. Men were sleeping on the sand, some of them sleeping forever. Men were floating in the water, but they didn't know they were in the water, for they were dead.

The water was full of squishy little jellyfish about the size of a man's hand. Millions of them. In the center of each of them was a green design exactly like a four-leafed clover. The good-luck emblem. Sure. Hell, yes.

I walked for a mile and a half along the water's edge of our many-miled invasion beach. I walked slowly, for the detail on that beach was infinite.

The wreckage was vast and startling. The awful waste and destruction of war, even aside from the loss of human life, has always been one of its outstanding features to those who are in it. Anything and everything is expendable. And we did expend on our beachhead in Normandy during those first few hours.

For a mile out from the beach there were scores of tanks and trucks and boats that were not visible, for they were at the bottom of the water—swamped by overloading, or hit by shells, or sunk by mines. Most of their crews were lost.

There were trucks tipped half over and swamped, partly sunken barges, and the angled-up corners of jeeps, and small landing craft half submerged. And at low tide you could still see those vicious six-pronged iron snares that helped snag and wreck them.

On the beach itself, high and dry, were all kinds of wrecked vehicles. There were tanks that had only just made the beach before being knocked out. There were jeeps that had burned to a dull gray. There were big derricks on caterpillar treads that didn't quite make it. There were half-tracks carrying office equipment that had been made into a shambles by a single shell hit, their interiors still holding the useless equipage of smashed typewriters, telephones, office files.

There were LCTs turned completely upside down, and lying on their backs, and how they got that way I don't know. There were boats stacked on top of each other, their sides caved in, their suspension doors knocked off.

In this shore-line museum of carnage there were abandoned rolls of barbed wire and smashed bulldozers and big stacks of thrown-away life belts and piles of shells still waiting to be moved. In the water floated empty life rafts and soldiers' packs and ration boxes, and mysterious oranges. On the beach lay snarled rolls of telephone wire and big rolls of steel matting and stacks of broken, rusting rifles.

On the beach lay, expended, sufficient men and mechanism for a small war. They were gone forever now. And yet we could afford it.

We could afford it because we were on, we had our toe hold, and behind us there were such enormous replacements for this wreckage on the beach that you could hardly conceive of the sum total. Men and equipment were flowing from England in such a gigantic stream that it made the waste on the beachhead seem like nothing at all, really nothing at all.

But there was another and more human litter. It extended in a thin little line, just like a high-water mark, for miles along the beach. This was the strewn personal gear, gear that would never be needed again by those who fought and died to give us our entrance into Europe.

There in a jumbled row for mile on mile were soldiers' packs. There were socks and shoe polish, sewing kits, diaries, Bibles, hand grenades. There were the latest letters from home, with the address on each one neatly razored out—one of the security precautions enforced before the boys embarked.

There were toothbrushes and razors, and snapshots of families back home staring up at you from the sand. There were pocketbooks, metal mirrors, extra trousers, and bloody, abandoned shoes. There were broken-handled shovels, and portable radios smashed almost beyond recognition, and mine detectors twisted and ruined.

There were torn pistol belts and canvas water buckets, first-aid kits, and jumbled heaps of life belts. I picked up a pocket Bible with a soldier's name in it, and put it in my jacket. I carried it half a mile or so and then put it back down on the beach. I don't know why I picked it up, or why I put it down again.

Soldiers carry strange things ashore with them. In every invasion there is at least one soldier hitting the beach at H-hour with a banjo slung over his shoulder. The most ironic piece of equipment marking our beach—this beach first of despair, then of victory—was a tennis racket that some soldier had brought along. It lay lonesomely on the sand, clamped in its press, not a string broken.

Two of the most dominant items in the beach refuse were cigarettes and writing paper. Each soldier was issued a carton of cigarettes just before he started. That day those cartons by the thousand, water-soaked and spilled out, marked the line of our first savage blow.

Writing paper and air-mail envelopes came second. The boys had intended to do a lot of writing in France. The letters—now forever incapable of being written—that might have filled those blank abandoned pages!

Always there are dogs in every invasion. There was a dog still on the beach, still pitifully looking for his masters.

He stayed at the water's edge, near a boat that lay twisted and half sunk at the waterline. He barked appealingly to every soldier who approached, trotted eagerly along with him for a few feet, and then, sensing himself unwanted in all the haste, he would run back to wait in vain for his own people at his own empty boat.

Over and around this long thin line of personal anguish, fresh men were rushing vast supplies to keep our armies pushing on into France. Other squads of men picked amidst the wreckage to salvage ammunition and equipment that was still usable.

Men worked and slept on the beach for days before the last D-day victim was taken away for burial.

I stepped over the form of one youngster whom I thought dead. But when I looked down I saw he was only sleeping. He was very young, and very tired. He lay on one elbow, his hand suspended in the air about six inches from the ground. And in the palm of his hand he held a large, smooth rock.

I stood and looked at him a long time. He seemed in his sleep to hold that rock lovingly, as though it were his last link with a vanishing world. I have no idea at all why he went to sleep with the rock in his hand, or what kept him from dropping it once he was asleep. It was just one of those little things without explanation that a person remembers for a long time.

The strong, swirling tides of the Normandy coast line shifted the contours of the sandy beach as they moved in and out. They carried soldiers' bodies out to sea, and later they returned them. They covered the corpses of heroes with sand, and then in their whims they uncovered them.

As I plowed out over the wet sand, I walked around what seemed to be a couple of pieces of driftwood sticking out of the sand. But they weren't driftwood. They were a soldier's two feet. He was completely covered except for his feet; the toes of his GI shoes pointed toward the land he had come so far to see, and which he saw so briefly.

A few hundred yards back on the beach was a high bluff. Up there we had a tent hospital, and a barbed-wire enclosure for prisoners of war. From up there you could see far up and down the beach, in a spectacular crow's-nest view, and far out to sea.

And standing out there on the water beyond all this wreckage was the greatest armada man has ever seen. You simply could not believe the gigantic collection of ships that lay out there waiting to unload. Looking from the bluff, it lay thick and clear to the far horizon of the sea and on beyond, and it spread out to the sides and was miles wide.

As I stood up there I noticed a group of freshly taken German prisoners standing nearby. They had not yet been put in the prison cage. They were just standing there, a couple of doughboys leisurely guarding them with tommy guns.

The prisoners too were looking out to sea—the same bit of sea that for months and years had been so safely empty before their gaze. Now they stood staring almost as if in a trance. They didn't say a word to each other. They didn't need to. The expression on their faces was something forever unforgettable. In it was the final, horrified acceptance of their doom.

The Debate about the Future, 1944

Wartime discipline and esprit de corps *moderated much political discussion, but politics could not be adjourned completely, since the Constitution fixed 1944 as a national election year, no matter what Germany or Japan might be doing.*

Under the circumstances, FDR as wartime President had immeasurable advantages. The Republican candidate, Thomas E. Dewey, labored under severe restrictions. It might be disastrous to attack too vigorously the popular President. It might seem even unpatriotic to assail the administration's conduct of the war. But Dewey, formerly a crusading district attorney in New York, now Governor of that state, undertook the risk. He flailed at inefficiency, confusion, and authoritarianism; he sought to associate the President with both bungling and radicalism, and raised the specter of postwar socialism and communism. But Dewey represented the so-called liberal wing of the Republican party. Despite vigorous rhetoric, he was no isolationist, no Coolidge conservative. He sought to stake out for his party and for himself a position in domestic politics no more conservative but on the other hand no more liberal than that of the Democrats. He would accept the New Deal, so far as it had been popular. He would, he promised, manage it more "honestly" and efficiently. Yet Dewey suggested the GOP furnish a substantial alternative. His alternative was never made completely clear; many of Dewey's own statements were fuzzy.

The speech at Charleston, West Virginia, printed below, sought to suggest that the GOP had preempted the ground of the New Deal, while the Democratic party itself had been taken over by radicals.

To some extent it was Roosevelt who had already set this tone for the campaign. Unwilling either as President or as campaigner simply to stand upon the war issues, he had gone to the people in his Annual Message of 1944 with his "economic bill of rights," a forecast of a postwar New Deal. At the same time he had argued for immediate wartime enactment of a national service law. This program suggested a larger scope of government operation in American life than had ever before been experienced. The lines between an expanded New Deal and a new "middle of the road" had thus been charted out by Thomas E. Dewey and FDR long before the latter's death, and long before the administration of Harry S. Truman, which was to give the expanded Roosevelt program a new name—the Fair Deal.

Dewey and his vice-presidential candidate, conservative Senator John Bricker of Ohio, were roundly defeated. But they were building at least in part for 1948 and beginning the exploration of new ground upon which a more successful Republican party might hope to stand.

Dewey's speech of October 7, 1944, provided here, is quoted from Vital Speeches, *volume 11, Oct. 15, 1944, pages 13–15. Roosevelt's message of January 11, 1944, has been quoted from the* Congressional Record, *Seventy-eighth Congress, second session, volume 90, part 1, pages 55–57.*

"Corporate State Not an American System": Thomas E. Dewey, 1944

Even as this terrible war moves toward our inevitable victory, we are preparing to decide the whole future of our country at the polls. If every American who believes in freedom for his country will register and vote, free America will win an overwhelming victory here at home on Nov. 7th.

That victory at the polls will mean an end to a very, very tired administration in Washington. It will mean the beginning of a new, a competent and an honest Government in Washington.

This victory at the polls will also serve to speed the defeat of Germany and Japan because it will bring an end to bungling, fumbling and incompetence in Washington.

I have already made it clear that a change in administration will mean no change in the military leadership of the war. It should be equally clear that with a change in administration the work of international organization for peace will proceed with only increased competence and zeal. I have taken unprecedented steps to put that work upon a nonpartisan basis. I intend to see that it remains a nonpartisan effort with the help of the ablest Americans of both parties in command.

Beyond victory, what kind of a country will our American men and women come home to? This election will decide that question.

We have a fateful decision to make, but that decision must be made not on vague and irresponsible political discussion but on the facts. On Thursday night of this week my opponent repeated his charge that "there are politicians and others who quite openly worked to restrict the use of the ballot in this election." Now I do not know whom Mr. Roosevelt means, because he seems to lack the courage to name names and say what he means. So let's look at the facts.

He sadly complained that not enough people vote. But he pointed with pride to the fact that in 1940 62½ per cent of the eligible voters of this nation went to the polls. Well, in the State of New York not 62½ per cent but 77 per cent of the eligible soldiers and sailors of our State have had ballots mailed to them already. Despite my opponent's attempt to play politics with the soldier vote every evidence indicates that as a nation we will have an even larger percentage of soldier votes than we will of civilians.

Let's have no more of this political pretense on a matter of importance to us all. Now we know where the truth is. And let me point out my opponent is relying for his main support upon a solid block of votes in States where millions of American citizens are deprived of their right to vote by the poll tax and by intimidation. Not once in twelve years has my opponent lifted a finger to correct this and his platform is cynically silent on the subject.

In his speech of Thursday night my opponent softly denies that he welcomes "the support of any person or group committed to communism or fascism."

Now, that is news. But doesn't this soft disclaimer come a trifle late? Only last week in Madison Square Garden Earl Browder, the head of the Communist party in America, proclaimed to 15,000 cheering adherents that the election of my opponent was essential to his aims. This is the same Earl Browder, now such a patriot, who was convicted as a draft dodger in the last war, convicted again as a perjurer and pardoned by Franklin Roosevelt in time to organize the campaign for his fourth term. The soft disclaimer does come a little late.

Now, why is my opponent's election so essential to the aims of the Communists? The answer is right in the record of this Administration. The aims of the New Dealers were stated on May 23, 1939, by Adolf Berle in a carefully written memorandum submitted to the Temporary National Economic Committee, an official agency set up to decide upon our future for us. There he said: "Over a period of years the Government will gradually come to own most of the productive plants in the United States."

Now, who is this Adolf Berle? He is one of the original brain trusters and today he holds the office of Assistant Secretary of State.

What does he mean by the Government owning "most of the productive plants in the United States." That means, of course, a system where Government would tell each of us where we could work, at what, and for how much.

Now, I do not know whether my opponent calls that system communism or national socialism, or fascism. He can take it any way he likes it. It's his program, not mine. But I do know it is not an American system and it's not a free system.

Let's just see how far we have traveled down that New Deal road. A report just released by a Congressional committee headed by a Democratic

United States Senator shows there are fifty-five Government corporations and credit agencies with net assets of twenty-seven billions. The Federal Government now owns or operates one-fifth of the manufacturing plants in the country.

Little by little, the New Deal is developing its own form of corporate State. It becomes clear why the twice convicted Comrade Browder and his friends are so eager for the re-election of my opponent. There is another reason. They love to fish in troubled waters. Their aims can best be served by unemployment and discontent. They remember that the New Deal in all its seven peace-time years never cured unemployment. They remember that in the spring of 1940 we still had 10,000,000 unemployed. They remember that under the New Deal we had to have a war to get jobs. That's why they want a fourth term and sixteen years of the New Deal. That is one of the very good reasons why it's time for a change.

Just for a moment let's look at the way this tired Administration bungled its way into conversion for war production. Then we will know how well they can convert for peace and for jobs. In August, 1939, more than six years after Hitler came to power, Mr. Roosevelt finally created a War Resources Board under Edward R. Stettinius. It worked for three months and brought in a report, but the report was buried and the board quietly died. The report is still a secret after five years. Like so many other things, we will never know about it until a new Administration opens the record of these past twelve years.

With Poland conquered, Hitler took Norway and invaded the Lowlands. At last, in response to public pressure on May 25, 1940, Mr. Roosevelt acted. He created the Office for Emergency Management under Executive Order No. 8,248.

But just four days later he piled on top of this one a seven-man advisory commission. In doing this he was repeating with exact fidelity the most notorious blunder of the first World War. Of course it failed.

So next we are handed the prize monstrosity of all, the Office of Production Management under two different heads, William Knudsen and Sidney Hillman.

It was Sidney Hillman's performance in this job that led the chairman of a Senate investigating committee to say, "If Mr. Hillman cannot or will not protect the interests of the United States, I am in favor of replacing him with some one who can and will."

The Senator who said that is now my opponent's handpicked running mate, Harry Truman. In spite of his unkind remarks the Democratic National convention was allowed to nominate Mr. Truman because he was "cleared with Sidney."

Of course that agency was a failure, too. So Mr. Roosevelt piled on still another one, the Supply Priorities and Allocations Board. That was on Aug. 28, 1941, and of course that failed too. It was not until five weeks after Pearl Harbor that Mr. Roosevelt did what should have been done at the beginning. At last we got a War Production Board with a single responsible administrator at the head of it.

But that was not the end. By way of coordinating all this confusion, and, as he said, "to resolve and determine controversies," my opponent created a sixth agency, the Office of War Mobilization. That was on May 27, 1943, eighteen months after Pearl Harbor. Still conflicting orders, overlapping responsibilities, backbiting and character assassination handicapped the war effort.

So the inevitable happened again, a little over a month ago. The War Production Board itself, fell apart. One official after another resigned in a torrent of recrimination and the head of the board was given a ticket to China.

Now, during all these months that the war effort was being hampered by open warfare in Washington, the responsible head of our Government was doing nothing about it. For weeks our daily papers carried stories of internal dissensions within the board. After it finally blew up, Mr. Roosevelt's only comment was that he had, of course, been aware of dissension but he had "hoped it would disappear." Judging by the words of my opponent it has become dreadfully clear that his Administration is too tired even to do the job at hand. It is obviously too tired for the job ahead.

We need a house cleaning in Washington. We need clear lines of authority with competent men to carry out their jobs. We need team work in our Government. That's why it's time for a change.

The American people have succeeded in the face of every difficulty in sending overwhelming supplies to our armed forces. Within a new administration we can speed victory and also be ready for reconversion to peacetime jobs.

Is there any chance the New Deal can ever do this job ahead? Not according to its own best friend. Even Henry Wallace last year described the whole picture as bureaucracy at its worst, and he added, "it is utterly inexcusable in a nation at war."

Now listen to Richard T. Frankensteen, vice president of the CIO Auto Workers Union and delegate to the national convention in which the great Democratic party was taken over by Earl Browder and Sidney Hillman. Here's what he said:

"The trouble is that no adequate over-all planning is being done to insure orderly reconversion which will lead into a post war period of full employment."

How in the name of the future of our country can such an administration be trusted with the vital task of creating peacetime jobs? How can we move ahead to peacetime jobs and opportunity under an administration that has no cure for dissension within its own ranks except for the feeble hope that "it would disappear?" How can we trust our future to an administration which talks out of one side of its mouth about Government ownership of all factories, while out of the other side of its mouth it softly disavows its Communist supporters?

On Jan. 20 of next year we shall restore honesty to our Government so that its spoken word can be trusted. We shall proceed to put into effect a program to recover those things we have lost and to make them secure.

This program I have already outlined in part.

To labor we are pledged to restore the Department of Labor with an able and experienced man from the ranks of labor at its head. We are pledged to abolish or transfer to the Department of Labor the almost countless bureaus with which the working men and women of our country now have to struggle. We are pledged to full support of the guarantees of free, collective bargaining through the National Labor Relations Act and to restore freedom from Government dictation to labor in this country.

We are pledged to work with all our hearts and souls to bring about a lasting peace through international organization with adequate force to back it up. And I may add, I have stated such a program at Louisville in detail, something my opponent has never yet done.

We are pledged to an expanding Social Security for the people of this country. Twenty million Americans have been forgotten by this Administration in the nine long years the old-age pension laws have been on the books. We propose to bring security to them as well as to make our Social Security system sound and supportable by an expanding economy. For there can be no security without a strong, free society to support it.

We are pledged that our Government shall not again use its power to set race against race, creed against creed, or class against class. We are pledged to a Government which has equal respect for the rights of agriculture, labor and business, and for every race, creed and color.

We are pledged to a future of freedom and abundance for agriculture with assurance by Government that the former will never again suffer ruinous prices. We are pledged to a scientific and expanding soil conservation program so that the soil of our country may be preserved and built up.

We are pledged to a specific program of tax relief, which will permit our job-making machinery to go to work. We are pledged to bring an end to the tired defeatism of this Administration, which talks glibly of opportunity and did nothing about it for seven peacetime years.

And what has been the answer of the New Deal to the specific proposals of our platform and the detailed statements of policy I have made on the radio in these recent weeks? We have heard nothing but glittering generalities, ghosts of the dead past and wisecracks. We have heard no answer because my opponent has no answer. We have had no answer because, in truth, as the New Deal itself has said, it wants a Government-owned America. It has no other solution.

I say there is a better way. I have outlined much of that way in detail. Ten million returning heroes will demand that better way under the freedom they have fought to win. Under divine guidance they will have here a land of security with freedom and opportunity for all.

"An Economic Bill of Rights": FDR's Annual Message, 1944

This Nation in the past 2 years has become an active partner in the world's greatest war against human slavery.

We have joined with like-minded people in order to defend ourselves in a world that has been gravely threatened with gangster rule.

But I do not think that any of us Americans can be content with mere survival. Sacrifices that we and our allies are making impose upon us all a sacred obligation to see to it that out of this war we and our children will gain something better than mere survival.

We are united in determination that this war shall not be followed by another interim which leads to new disaster—that we shall not repeat the tragic errors of ostrich isolationism—that we shall not repeat the excesses of the wild twenties when this Nation went for a joyride on a roller coaster which ended in a tragic crash.

When Mr. Hull went to Moscow in October, and when I went to Cairo and Teheran in November, we knew that we were in agreement with our allies in our common determination to fight and win this war. But there were many vital questions concerning the future peace, and they were discussed in an atmosphere of complete candor and harmony.

In the last war such discussions, such meetings, did not even begin until the shooting had stopped and the delegates began to assemble at the peace table. There had been no previous opportunities for man-to-man discussions which lead to meetings of minds. The result was a peace which was not a peace.

That was a mistake which we are not repeating in this war.

And right here I want to address a word or two to some suspicious souls who are fearful that Mr. Hull or I have made "commitments" for the future which might pledge this Nation to secret treaties or to enacting the role of Santa Claus.

To such suspicious souls—using a polite terminology—I wish to say that Mr. Churchill, and Marshal Stalin, and Generalissimo Chiang Kai-shek are all thoroughly conversant with the provisions of our Constitution. And so is Mr. Hull. And so am I.

Of course we made some commitments. We most certainly committed ourselves to very large and very specific military plans which require the use of all Allied forces to bring about the defeat of our enemies at the earliest possible time.

But there were no secret treaties or political or financial commitments.

The one supreme objective for the future, which we discussed for each nation individually, and for all the United Nations, can be summed up in one word: Security.

And that means not only physical security which provides safety from attacks by aggressors. It means also economic security, social security, moral security—in a family of nations.

In the plain down-to-earth talks that I had with the Generalissimo and Marshal Stalin and Prime Minister Churchill, it was abundantly clear that they are all most deeply interested in the resumption of peaceful progress by their own peoples—progress toward a better life. All our allies want freedom to develop their lands and resources, to build up industry, to increase education and individual opportunity, and to raise standards of living.

All our allies have learned by bitter experience that real development will not be possible if they are to be diverted from their purpose by repeated wars—or even threats of war.

China and Russia are truly united with Britain and America in recognition of this essential fact:

The best interests of each nation, large and small, demand that all freedom-loving nations shall join together in a just and durable system of peace. In the present world situation, evidenced by the actions of Germany, Italy, and Japan, unquestioned military control over disturbers of the peace is as necessary among nations as it is among citizens in a community. And an equally basic essential to peace is a decent standard of living for all individual men and women and children in all nations. Freedom from fear is eternally linked with freedom from want.

There are people who burrow through our Nation like unseeing moles, and attempt to spread the suspicion that if other nations are encouraged to raise their standards of living, our own American standard of living must of necessity be depressed.

The fact is the very contrary. It has been shown time and again that if the standard of living of any country goes up, so does its purchasing power—and that such a rise encourages a better standard of living in neighboring countries with whom it trades. That is just plain common sense—and it is the kind of plain common sense that provided the basis for our discussions at Moscow, Cairo, and Teheran.

Returning from my journeyings, I must confess to a sense of "let-down" when I found many evidences of faulty perspectives here in Washington. The faulty perspective consists in overemphasizing lesser problems and thereby underemphasizing the first and greatest problem.

The overwhelming majority of our people have met the demands of this war with magnificent courage and understanding. They have accepted inconveniences; they have accepted hardships; they have accepted tragic sacrifices. And they are ready and eager to make whatever further contributions are needed to win the war as quickly as possible—if only they are given the chance to know what is required of them.

However, while the majority goes on about its great work without complaint, a noisy minority maintains an uproar of demands for special favors for special groups. There are pests who swarm through the lobbies of the Congress and the cocktail bars of Washington, representing these special groups as opposed to the basic interests of the Nation as a whole. They have come to look upon the war primarily as a chance to make profits for themselves at the expense of their neighbors—profits in money or in terms of political or social preferment.

Such selfish agitation can be highly dangerous in wartime. It creates confusion. It damages morale. It hampers our national effort. It muddies the waters and therefore prolongs the war.

If we analyze American history impartially, we cannot escape the fact that in our past we have not always forgotten individual and selfish and partisan interests in time of war—we have not always been united in purpose and direction. We cannot overlook the serious dissensions and the lack of unity in our War of the Revolution, in our War of 1812, or in our War between the States, when the survival of the Union itself was at stake.

In the First World War we came closer to national unity than in any previous war. But that war lasted only a year and a half, and increasing signs of disunity began to appear during the final months of the conflict.

In this war we have been compelled to learn how interdependent upon each other are all groups and sections of the population of America.

Increased food costs, for example, will bring new demands for wage increases from all war workers, which will in turn raise all prices of all things including those things which the farmers themselves have to buy. Increased wages or prices will each in turn produce the same results. They all have a particularly disastrous result on all fixed income groups.

And I hope you will remember that all of us in this Government represent the fixed-income group just as much as we represent business owners, workers, and farmers. This group of fixed-income people include teachers, clergy, policemen, firemen, widows, and minors on fixed incomes, wives and dependents of our soldiers and sailors, and old-age pensioners. They and their families add up to one-quarter of our 130,000,000 people. They have few or no high-pressure representatives at the Capitol. In a period of gross inflation they would be the worst sufferers.

If ever there was a time to subordinate individual or group selfishness to the national good, that time is now. Disunity at home—bickerings, self-seeking partisanship, stoppages of work, inflation, business as usual, politics as usual, luxury as usual—these are the influences which can undermine the morale of the brave men ready to die at the front for us here.

Those who are doing most of the complaining are not deliberately striving to sabotage the national war effort. They are laboring under the delusion that the time is past when we must make prodigious sacrifices—that the war is already won and we can begin to slacken off. But the dangerous folly of that point of view can be measured by the distance that separates our troops from their ultimate objectives in Berlin and Tokyo—and by the sum of all the perils that lie along the way.

Overconfidence and complacency are among our deadliest enemies. Last spring—after notable victories at Stalingrad and in Tunisia and against the U-boats on the high seas—overconfidence became so pronounced that war production fell off. In 2 months, June and July, 1943, more than a thousand airplanes that could have been made and should have been made were not made. Those who failed to make them were not on strike. They were merely saying, "The war's in the bag—so let's relax."

That attitude on the part of anyone—Government or management or labor—can lengthen this war. It can kill American boys.

Let us remember the lessons of 1918. In the summer of that year the tide turned in favor of the Allies. But this Government did not relax. In fact, our national effort was stepped up. In August 1918, the draft-age limits were broadened from 21–31 to 18–45. The President called for "force to the utmost," and his call was heeded. And in November, only 3 months later, Germany surrendered.

That is the way to fight and win a war—all-out—and not with half-an-eye on the battle fronts abroad and the other eye-and-a-half on personal, selfish, or political interests here at home.

Therefore, in order to concentrate all our energies and resources on winning the war, and to maintain a fair and stable economy at home, I recommend that the Congress adopt:

1. A realistic tax law—which will tax all unreasonable profits, both individual and corporate, and reduce the ultimate cost of the war to our sons and daughters. The tax bill now under consideration by the Congress does not begin to meet this test.

2. A continuation of the law for the renegotiation of war contracts—which will prevent exorbitant profits and assure fair prices to the Government. For 2 long years I have pleaded with the Congress to take undue profits out of war.

3. A cost-of-food law—which will enable the Government (a) to place a reasonable floor under the prices the farmer may expect for his production; and (b) to place a ceiling on the prices a consumer will have to pay for the food he buys. This should apply to necessities only; and will require public funds to carry out. It will cost in appropriations about 1 percent of the present annual cost of the war.

4. Early reenactment of the stabilization statute of October 1942. This expires June 30th, 1944, and if it is not extended well in advance, the country might just as well expect price chaos by summer.

We cannot have stabilization by wishful thinking. We must take positive action to maintain the integrity of the American dollar.

5. A national service law—which, for the duration of the war, will prevent strikes, and, with certain appropriate exceptions, will make available for war production or for any other essential services every able-bodied adult in this Nation.

These five measures together form a just and equitable whole. I would not recommend a national service law unless the other laws were passed to keep down the cost of living, to share equitably the burdens of taxation, to hold the stabilization line, and to prevent undue profits.

The Federal Government already has the basic power to draft capital and property of all kinds for war purposes on a basis of just compensation.

As you know, I have for 3 years hesitated to recommend a national service act. Today, however, I am convinced of its necessity. Although I believe that we and our allies can win the war without such a measure, I am certain that nothing less than total mobilization of all our resources of manpower and capital will guarantee an earlier victory, and reduce the toll of suffering and sorrow and blood.

I have received a joint recommendation for this law from the heads of the War Department, the Navy Department, and the Maritime Commission. These are the men who bear responsibility for the procurement of the necessary arms and equipment, and for the successful prosecution of the war in the field. They say:

> When the very life of the Nation is in peril the responsibility for service is common to all men and women. In such a time there can be no discrimination between the men and women who are assigned by the Government to its defense at the battle front and the men and women assigned to producing the vital materials essential to successful military operations. A prompt enactment of a national service law would be merely an expression of the universality of this responsibility.

I believe the country will agree that those statements are the solemn truth.

National service is the most democratic way to wage a war. Like selective service for the armed forces, it rests on the obligation of each citizen to serve his Nation to his utmost where he is best qualified.

It does not mean reduction in wages. It does not mean loss of retirement and seniority rights and benefits. It does not mean that any substantial numbers of war workers will be disturbed in their present jobs. Let these facts be wholly clear.

Experience in other democratic nations at war—Britain, Canada, Australia, and New Zealand—has shown that the very existence of national service makes unnecessary the widespread use of compulsory power. National service has proven to be a unifying moral force—based on an equal and comprehensive legal obligation of all people in a nation at war.

There are millions of American men and women who are not in this war at all. It is not because they do not want to be in it. But they want to know where they can best do their share. National service provides that direction. It will be a means by which every man and woman can find that inner satisfaction which comes from making the fullest possible contribution to victory.

I know that all civilian war workers will be glad to be able to say many years hence to their grandchildren: "Yes, I, too, was in service in the great war. I was on duty in an airplane factory, and I helped make hundreds of fighting planes. The Government told me that in doing that I was performing my most useful work in the service of my country."

It is argued that we have passed the stage in the war where national service is necessary. But our soldiers and sailors know that this is not true. We are going forward on a long, rough road—and, in all journeys, the last miles are the hardest. And it is for that final effort—for the total defeat of our enemies—that we must mobilize our total resources. The national war program calls for the employment of more people in 1944 than in 1943.

It is my conviction that the American people will welcome this win-the-war measure which is based on the eternally just principle of "fair for one, fair for all."

It will give our people at home the assurance that they are standing four-square behind our soldiers and sailors. And it will give our enemies demoralizing assurance that we mean business—that we, 130,000,000 Americans, are on the march to Rome, Berlin, and Tokyo.

I hope that the Congress will recognize that, although this is a political year, national service is an issue which transcends politics. Great power must be used for great purposes.

As to the machinery for this measure, the Congress itself should determine its nature—but it should be wholly nonpartisan in its make-up.

Our armed forces are valiantly fulfilling their responsibilities to our country and our people. Now the Congress faces the responsibility for taking those measures which are essential to national security in this the most decisive phase of the Nation's greatest war.

Several alleged reasons have prevented the enactment of legislation which would preserve for our soldiers and sailors and marines the fundamental prerogative of citizenship—the right to vote. No amount of legalistic argument can becloud this issue in the eyes of these 10,000,000 American citizens. Surely the signers of the Constitution did not intend a document which, even in wartime, would be construed to take away the franchise of any of those who are fighting to preserve the Constitution itself.

Our soldiers and sailors and marines know that the overwhelming majority of them will be deprived of the opportunity to vote, if the voting machinery is left exclusively to the States under existing State laws—and that there is no likelihood of these laws being changed in time to enable them to vote at the next election. The Army and Navy have reported that it will be impossible effectively to administer 48 different soldier-voting laws. It is the duty of the Congress to remove this unjustifiable discrimination against the men and women in our armed forces—and to do it as quickly as possible.

It is our duty now to begin to lay the plans and determine the strategy for the winning of a lasting peace and the establishment of an American standard of living higher than ever before known. We cannot be content, no matter how high that general standard of living may be, if some fraction of our people—whether it be one-third or one-fifth or one-tenth—is ill-fed, ill-clothed, ill-housed, and insecure.

This Republic had its beginning, and grew to its present strength, under the protection of certain inalienable political rights—among them the right of free speech, free press, free worship, trial by jury, freedom from unreasonable searches and seizures. They were our rights to life and liberty.

As our Nation has grown in size and stature, however—as our industrial economy expanded—these political rights proved inadequate to assure us equality in the pursuit of happiness.

We have come to a clear realization of the fact that true individual freedom cannot exist without economic security and independence. "Necessitous men are not freemen." People who are hungry and out of a job are the stuff of which dictatorships are made.

In our day these economic truths have become accepted as self-evident. We have accepted, so to speak, a second Bill of Rights under which a new basis of security and prosperity can be established for all—regardless of station, race, or creed.

Among these are:

The right to a useful and remunerative job in the industries, or shops or farms or mines of the Nation;

The right to earn enough to provide adequate food and clothing and recreation;

The right of every farmer to raise and sell his products at a return which will give him and his family a decent living;

The right of every businessman, large and small, to trade in an atmosphere of freedom from unfair competition and domination by monopolies at home or abroad;

The right of every family to a decent home;

The right to adequate medical care and the opportunity to achieve and enjoy good health;

The right to adequate protection from the economic fears of old age, sickness, accident, and unemployment;

The right to a good education.

All of these rights spell security. And after this war is won, we must be prepared to move forward, in the implementation of these rights, to new goals of human happiness and well-being.

America's own rightful place in the world depends in large part upon how fully these and similar rights have been carried into practice for our citizens. For unless there is security here at home there cannot be lasting peace in the world.

One of the great American industrialists of our day—a man who has rendered yeoman service to his country in this crisis—recently emphasized the grave dangers of rightist reaction in this Nation. All clear-thinking businessmen share his concern. Indeed, if such reaction should develop—if history were to repeat itself and we were to return to the so-called normalcy of the 1920's—then it is certain that, even though we shall have conquered our enemies on the battlefields abroad, we shall have yielded to the spirit of fascism here at home.

I ask the Congress to explore the means for implementing this economic bill of rights—for it is definitely the responsibility of the Congress so to do. Many of these problems are already before committees of the Congress in the form of proposed legislation. I shall from time to time communicate with the Congress with respect to these and further proposals. In the event that no adequate program of progress is evolved, I am certain that the Nation will be conscious of the fact.

Our fighting men abroad—and their families at home—expect such a program and have the right to insist upon it. It is to their demands that this Government should pay heed rather than to the whining demands of selfish pressure groups who seek to feather their nests while young Americans are dying.

The foreign policy that we have been following—the policy that guided us at Moscow, Cairo, and Teheran—is based on the common-sense principle which was best expressed by Benjamin Franklin on July 4, 1776:

> We must all hang together, or assuredly we shall all hang separately.

I have often said that there are no two fronts for America in this war. There is only one front. There is one line of unity which extends from the hearts of the people at home to the men of our attacking forces in our farthest outposts. When we speak of our total effort we speak of the factory and the field and the mine as well as of the battleground—we speak of the soldier and the civilian, the citizen and his Government.

Each and every one of us has a solemn obligation under God to serve this Nation in its most critical hour—to keep this Nation great—to make this Nation greater in a better world.

From Bitterness, a Proposal: The Morgenthau Plan, 1943

Planning the postwar domestic program could be made to wait, if necessary. But Roosevelt was preeminently aware, as he indicated in his Annual Message of 1944, that postwar planning for peace must begin at once and be persistently maintained. Contacts must be made, problems examined, differences plumbed, agreements gauged and defined, if a repetition of the Versailles catastrophe were to be avoided. Modern transportation made it possible for the leaders to meet, even in wartime. The necessities of coordinating the immediate military efforts made such conferences doubly important. Roosevelt found himself moved about constantly, to Casablanca and Quebec, Cairo and Tehran in 1943, to Quebec again in 1944, to Malta and Yalta in 1945—to meet not only Churchill and Stalin, but also peripheral figures like Charles de Gaulle, Maxim Weygand, Chiang Kai-shek, the Shah of Iran, Ibn Saud, and the Pasha of Marrakesh. These were multistage conferences, with military staff commanders,

State Department people, special advisers meeting with their opposite numbers from the other allied nations. And when Roosevelt was at home in the White House, Churchill was also frequently there. No great war has ever been fought with such intimate coordination among Allied leaders. It was one of the special ironies of the situation that Churchill and Roosevelt, whose rapport was so effective in fighting the war, were fated not to wage the peace.

Wartime peace planning must necessarily concern itself with five different issues: the completion of the war and the terms of surrender; the disposition of the enemy states; the reconstruction of occupied Europe and Asia; the postwar balance of power; and the development of a United Nations for moderating these balances. Among the most immediate and most bitter of the problems was the disposition of postwar Germany. The spirit of revenge was almost insuperable during 1943 and 1944 when Allied troops were dying by the hundreds of thousands, when the full force of the Nazi mass murders was first being felt. Jews, in viewing Nazi Germany, saw nothing which could be forgiven. Russians could only fear the butchers of the Ukraine. The French could only hate the alien masters of Paris.

Under the circumstances, the plan for dealing with Germany conceived by Henry Morgenthau, Jr., Roosevelt's Secretary of the Treasury, seemed appealing. It was a fearful, hate-ridden program to dismember and deindustrialize Germany so as to assure above all else that she could never again be a military threat. Morgenthau and some of his staff developed the plan during 1943. It was presented in September, 1944, to the second Quebec Conference of Churchill and Roosevelt and was tentatively approved. Within a month, however, Roosevelt had rejected it. Apparently he had simply not, at first, understood its full implications. The plan would have created a political vacuum inviting meddling; it would have been so extreme and general in its punishment of Germany as to require the existence of a permanent police force. It would have made Germany an economic dependency upon its captors.

The plan continued to be a part of the controversy, since various aspects of it appealed to many groups. Russians, for example, liked its plans for demilitarization, the transportation of German industry to allied countries, the slave labor. France liked the restoration of the Saar, the neutralization of the Rhine. Many Americans liked the proposed early withdrawal of American troops from Europe.

One of the most significant books on the wartime diplomacy is Robert Sherwood, Roosevelt and Hopkins: An Intimate History *(1948), which draws heavily upon the papers of Harry Hopkins, one of the President's closest advisers during the war. Herbert Feis,* Churchill, Roosevelt, Stalin: The War They Waged and the Peace They Sought *(1957) is a significant, scholarly study. On the plan printed here, see John L. Chase, "The Development of the Morgenthau Plan through the Quebec Conference,"* Journal of Politics, *volume 16 (1954), pages 324–359.*

The document printed here is Henry Morgenthau, Jr., "Program to Prevent Germany from Starting a World War III," in U.S. Department of State, Historical Office, American Foreign Policy: Current Documents, 1941–49 *(Washington: Government Printing Office, 1950), or in* A Decade of American Foreign Policy: Basic Documents, 1941–1949, *Eighty-first Congress, first session, Senate Document 123, pages 502–505. This source is hereafter cited as* Decade of Foreign Policy.

1. Demilitarization of Germany

It should be the aim of the Allied Forces to accomplish the complete demilitarization of Germany in the shortest possible period of time after surrender. This means completely disarming the German Army and people (including the removal or destruction of all war material), the total destruction of the whole German armament industry, and the removal or destruction of other key industries which are basic to military strength.

2. New Boundaries of Germany

a. Poland should get that part of East Prussia which doesn't go to the U.S.S.R. and the southern portion of Silesia.

b. France should get the Saar and the adjacent territories bounded by the Rhine and the Moselle Rivers.

c. As indicated in 4 below an International Zone should be created containing the Ruhr and the surrounding industrial areas.

3. Partitioning of New Germany

The remaining portion of Germany should be divided into two autonomous, independent states, (1) a South German state comprising Bavaria, Wuerttemberg, Baden and some smaller areas and (2) a North German state comprising a large part of the old state of Prussia, Saxony, Thuringia and several smaller states.

There shall be a custom union between the new South German state and Austria, which will be restored to her pre-1938 political borders.

4. The Ruhr Area

(The Ruhr, surrounding industrial areas, as shown on the map, including the Rhineland, the Keil Canal, and all German territory north of the Keil Canal.)

Here lies the heart of German industrial power. This area should not only be stripped of all presently existing industries but so weakened and controlled that it cannot in the foreseeable future become an industrial area. The following steps will accomplish this:

a. Within a short period, if possible not longer than 6 months after the cessation of hostilities, all industrial plants and equipment not destroyed by military action shall be completely dismantled and transported to Allied Nations as restitution. All equipment shall be removed from the mines and the mines closed.

b. The area should be made an international zone to be governed by an international security organization to be established by the United Nations. In governing the area the international organization should be guided by policies designed to further the above stated objective.

5. Restitution and Reparation

Reparations, in the form of future payments and deliveries, should not be demanded. Restitution and reparation shall be effected by the transfer of existing German resources and territories, e. g.,

a. by restitution of property looted by the Germans in territories occupied by them;
b. by transfer of German territory and German private rights in industrial property situated in such territory to invaded countries and the international organization under the program of partition;
c. by the removal and distribution among devastated countries of industrial plants and equipment situated within the International Zone and the North and South German states delimited in the section on partition;
d. by forced German labor outside Germany; and
e. by confiscation of all German assets of any character whatsoever outside of Germany.

6. Education and Propaganda

a. All schools and universities will be closed until an Allied Commission of Education has formulated an effective reorganization program. It is contemplated that it may require a considerable period of time before any institutions of higher education are reopened. Meanwhile the education of German students in foreign universities will not be prohibited. Elementary schools will be reopened as quickly as appropriate teachers and text books are available.
b. All German radio stations and newspapers, magazines, weeklies, etc. shall be discontinued until adequate controls are established and an appropriate program formulated.

7. Political Decentralization

The military administration in Germany in the initial period should be carried out with a view toward the eventual partitioning of Germany. To facilitate partitioning and to assure its permanence the military authorities should be guided by the following principles:

a. Dismiss all policy-making officials of the Reich government and deal primarily with local governments.
b. Encourage the reestablishment of state governments in each of the states (Lander) corresponding to 18 states into which Germany is presently divided and in addition make the Prussian provinces separate states.
c. Upon the partition of Germany, the various state governments should be encouraged to organize a federal government for each of the newly partitioned areas. Such new governments should be in the form of a confederation of states, with emphasis on states' rights and a large degree of local autonomy.

8. Responsibility of Military for Local German Economy

The sole purpose of the military in control of the German economy shall be to facilitate military operations and military occupation. The Allied Military Government shall not assume responsibility for such economic problems as price controls, rationing, unemployment, production, reconstruction, distribution, consumption, housing, or transportation, or take any measures designed to maintain or strengthen the German economy, except those which are essential to military operations. The responsibility for sustaining the German economy and people rests with the German people with such facilities as may be available under the circumstances.

9. Controls over Development of German Economy

During a period of at least twenty years after surrender adequate controls, including controls over foreign trade and tight restrictions on capital imports, shall be maintained by the United Nations designed to prevent in the newly-established states the establishment or expansion of key industries basic to the German military potential and to control other key industries.

10. Agrarian Program

All large estates should be broken up and divided among the peasants and the system of primogeniture and entail should be abolished.

11. Punishment of War Crimes and Treatment of Special Groups

A program for the punishment of certain war crimes and for the treatment of Nazi organizations and other special groups is contained in section 11.

12. Uniforms and Parades

a. No German shall be permitted to wear, after an appropriate period of time following the cessation of hostilities, any military uniform or any uniform of any quasi military organizations.

b. No military parades shall be permitted anywhere in Germany and all military bands shall be disbanded.

13. Aircraft

All aircraft (including gliders), whether military or commercial, will be confiscated for later disposition. No German shall be permitted to operate or to help operate any aircraft, including those owned by foreign interests.

14. United States Responsibility

Although the United States would have full military and civilian representation on whatever international commission or commissions may be established for the execution of the whole German program, the primary responsibility for the policing of Germany and for civil administration in Germany should be assumed by the military forces of Germany's continental neighbors. Specifically, these should include Russian, French, Polish, Czech, Greek, Yugoslav, Norwegian, Dutch, and Belgian soldiers.

Under this program United States troops could be withdrawn within a relatively short time.

SELECTION 67

Cooperation and Planning, First Steps: Communiqués and Agreements of the Moscow Conference of Foreign Ministers, 1943

Churchill and Roosevelt met in Washington for military talks immediately after Pearl Harbor. Molotov, Churchill, and Roosevelt met there in June, 1942. In August, W. Averell Harriman and Churchill conferred with Stalin in Moscow to warn him that a second front against Germany was impossible in 1942. In January, 1943, Roosevelt and Churchill traveled to Casablanca to reach agreement on the general concept of a second front, on unconditional surrender, and on the Italian campaign. In May, 1943, at Washington, and in August at Quebec, Churchill and Roosevelt reached the central decisions regarding the cross-channel invasions and the operations in southern France and in Southeast Asia. But it was only on October 19–30, 1943, that the first formal three-power Allied conference met—the Moscow Conference of Foreign Ministers. In addition to the decisions and ambiguities recorded in the documents presented here, the conference brought Stalin's first promise to participate in the war against Japan.

The Moscow Conference paved the way for the later meetings of chiefs of state at Teheran and Yalta.

Russo-American relations have been reexamined imaginatively in William Appleman Williams, American-Russian Relations: 1781–1947 *(1952). See also John R. Deane,* The Strange Alliance: The Story of Our Efforts at Wartime Cooperation with Russia *(1947); Thomas A. Bailey,* America Faces Russia *(1950); David J. Dallin,* The Big Three: The United States, Britain and Russia *(1945). The most nearly definitive study is Herbert Feis,* Churchill, Roosevelt, Stalin: The War They Waged and the Peace They Sought *(1957).*

The documents given here are taken from Decade of Foreign Policy, *pages 9–14.*

(a) Anglo-Soviet-American Communiqué, November 1, 1943

The Conference of Foreign Secretaries of the United States of America, Mr. Cordell Hull, of the United Kingdom, Mr. Anthony Eden, and of the Soviet Union, Mr. V. M. Molotov, took place at Moscow from the 19th to the 30th of October 1943. There were twelve meetings. . . .

In the first place there were frank and exhaustive discussions of measures to be taken to shorten the war against Germany and her satellites in Europe. Advantage was taken of the presence of military advisers, representing the respective Chiefs of Staff, in order to discuss definite military operations, with regard to which decisions had been taken and which are already being prepared, and in order to create a basis for the closest military cooperation in the future between the three countries.

Second only to the importance of hastening the end of the war was the unanimous recognition by the three Governments that it was essential in their own national interests and in the interest of all peace-loving nations to continue the present close collaboration and cooperation in the conduct of the war into the period following the end of hostilities, and that only in this way could peace be maintained and the political, economic and social welfare of their peoples fully promoted.

This conviction is expressed in a declaration in which the Chinese Government joined during the Conference and which was signed by the three Foreign Secretaries and the Chinese Ambassador at Moscow on behalf of their governments. This declaration, published today, provides for even closer collaboration in the prosecution of the war and in all matters pertaining to the surrender and disarmament of the enemies with which the four countries are respectively at war. It sets forth the principles upon which the four governments agree that a broad system of international cooperation and security should be based. Provision is made for the inclusion of all other peace-loving nations, great and small, in this system.

The Conference agreed to set up machinery for ensuring the closest cooperation between the three Governments in the examination of European questions arising as the war develops. For this purpose the Conference decided to establish in London a European Advisory Commission to study these questions and to make joint recommendations to the three Governments.

Provision was made for continuing, when necessary, tripartite consultations of representatives of the three Governments in the respective capitals through the existing diplomatic channels.

The Conference also agreed to establish an Advisory Council for matters relating to Italy, to be composed in the first instance of representatives of their three governments and of the French Committee of National Liberation. Provision is made for the addition to this council of representatives of Greece and Yugoslavia in view of their special interests arising out of the aggressions of Fascist Italy upon their territory during the present war. This Council will deal with day-to-day questions, other than military operations, and will make recommendations designed to coordinate Allied policy with regard to Italy.

The three Foreign Secretaries considered it appropriate to reaffirm, by a declaration published today, the attitude of their Governments in favor of restoration of democracy in Italy.

The three Foreign Secretaries declared it to be the purpose of their Governments to restore the independence of Austria. At the same time they reminded Austria that in the final settlement account will be taken of efforts that Austria may make towards its own liberation. The declaration on Austria is published today.

The Foreign Secretaries issued at the Conference a declaration by President Roosevelt, Prime Minister Churchill and Premier Stalin containing a solemn warning that at the time of granting any armistice to any German Government those German officers and men and members of the Nazi party who have had any connection with atrocities and executions in countries overrun by German forces will be taken back to the countries in which their abominable crimes were committed to be charged and punished according to the laws of those countries.

In the atmosphere of mutual confidence and understanding which characterized all the work of the Conference, consideration was also given to other important questions. These included not only questions of a current nature, but also questions concerning the treatment of Hitlerite Germany and its satellites, economic cooperation and the assurance of general peace.

(b) Declaration on Austria, November 1, 1943

The Governments of the United Kingdom, the Soviet Union and the United States of America are agreed that Austria, the first free country to fall a victim to Hitlerite aggression, shall be liberated from German domination.

They regard the annexation imposed upon Austria by Germany on March 15th, 1938, as null and void. They consider themselves as in no way bound by any changes effected in Austria since that date. They declare that they wish to see reestablished a free and independent Austria, and thereby to open the way for the Austrian people themselves, as well as those neighboring states which will be faced with similar problems, to find that political and economic security which is the only basis for lasting peace.

Austria is reminded, however, that she has a responsibility which she cannot evade for participation in the war on the side of Hitlerite Germany, and that in the final settlement account will inevitably be taken of her own contribution to her liberation.

(c) Declaration of Four Nations on General Security, November 1, 1943

The Governments of the United States of America, the United Kingdom, the Soviet Union and China:

united in their determination, in accordance with the Declaration by the United Nations of January 1, 1942, and subsequent declarations, to continue hostilities against those Axis powers with which they respectively are at war until such powers have laid down their arms on the basis of unconditional surrender;

conscious of their responsibility to secure the liberation of themselves and the peoples allied with them from the menace of aggression;

recognizing the necessity of ensuring a rapid and orderly transition from war to peace and of establishing and maintaining international peace and security with the least diversion of the world's human and economic resources for armaments;

jointly declare:

1. That their united action, pledged for the prosecution of the war against their respective enemies, will be continued for the organization and maintenance of peace and security.
2. That those of them at war with a common enemy will act together in all matters relating to the surrender and disarmament of that enemy.
3. That they will take all measures deemed by them to be necessary to provide against any violation of the terms imposed upon the enemy.
4. That they recognise the necessity of establishing at the earliest practicable date a general international organization, based on the principle of the sovereign equality of all peace-loving states, and open to membership by all such states, large and small, for the maintenance of international peace and security.
5. That for the purpose of maintaining international peace and security pending the re-establishment of law and order and the inauguration of a system of general security, they will consult with one another and as occasion requires with other members of the United Nations with a view to joint action on behalf of the community of nations.
6. That after the termination of hostilities they will not employ their military forces within the territories of other states except for the purposes envisaged in this declaration and after joint consultation.
7. That they will confer and co-operate with one another and with other members of the United Nations to bring about a practicable general agreement with respect to the regulation of armaments in the post-war period.

V. MOLOTOV
ANTHONY EDEN
CORDELL HULL
FOO PING-SHEUNG

Moscow, 30th October, 1943.

(d) Declaration regarding Italy, November 1, 1943

The Foreign Secretaries of the United States of America, the United Kingdom and the Soviet Union have established that their three Governments are in complete agreement that Allied policy towards Italy must be based upon the fundamental principle that Fascism and all its evil influences and emanations shall be utterly destroyed and that the Italian people shall be given every opportunity to establish governmental and other institutions based upon democratic principles.

The Foreign Secretaries of the United States of America and the United Kingdom declare that the action of their Governments from the inception of the invasion of Italian territory, in so far as paramount military requirements have permitted, has been based upon this policy.

In the furtherance of this policy in the future the Foreign Secretaries of the three Governments are agreed that the following measures are important and should be put into effect:

1. It is essential that the Italian Government should be made more democratic by the introduction of representatives of those sections of the Italian people who have always opposed Fascism.
2. Freedom of speech, of religious worship, of political belief, of the press and of public meeting shall be restored in full measure to the Italian people, who shall also be entitled to form anti-Fascist political groups.
3. All institutions and organisations created by the Fascist regime shall be suppressed.
4. All Fascist or pro-Fascist elements shall be removed from the administration and from the institutions and organizations of a public character.
5. All political prisoners of the Fascist regime shall be released and accorded a full amnesty.
6. Democratic organs of local government shall be created.
7. Fascist chiefs and other persons known or suspected to be war criminals shall be arrested and handed over to justice.

In making this declaration the three Foreign Secretaries recognize that so long as active military operations continue in Italy the time at which it is possible to give full effect to the principles set out above will be determined by the Commander-in-Chief on the basis of instructions received through the Combined Chiefs of Staff. The three Governments parties to this declaration will at the request of any one of them consult on this matter.

It is further understood that nothing in this resolution is to operate against the right of the Italian people ultimately to choose their own form of government.

(e) Declaration of German Atrocities, November 1, 1943

The United Kingdom, the United States and the Soviet Union have received from many quarters evidence of atrocities, massacres and cold-blooded mass executions which are being perpetrated by the Hitlerite forces in the many countries they have overrun and from which they are now being steadily expelled. The brutalities of Hitlerite domination are no new thing and all the peoples or territories in their grip have suffered from the worst form of government by terror. What is new is that many of these territories are now being redeemed by the advancing armies of the liberating Powers and that in their desperation, the recoiling Hitlerite Huns are redoubling their ruthless cruelties. This is now evidenced with particular clearness by monstrous crimes of the Hitlerites on the territory of the Soviet Union which is being liberated from the Hitlerites, and on French and Italian territory.

Accordingly, the aforesaid three allied Powers, speaking in the interests of the thirty-two [thirty-three] United Nations, hereby solemnly declare and give full warning of their declaration as follows:

At the time of the granting of any armistice to any government which may be set up in Germany, those German officers and men and members of the Nazi party who have been responsible for, or have taken a consenting part in the above atrocities, massacres and executions, will be sent back to the countries in which their abominable deeds were done in order that they may be judged and punished according to the laws of these liberated countries and of the free governments which will be created therein. Lists will be compiled in all possible detail from all these countries having regard especially to the invaded parts of the Soviet Union, to Poland and Czechoslovakia, to Yugoslavia and Greece, including Crete and other islands, to Norway, Denmark, the Netherlands, Belgium, Luxemburg, France and Italy.

Thus, the Germans who take part in wholesale shootings of Italian officers or in the execution of French, Dutch, Belgian or Norwegian hostages or of Cretan peasants, or who have shared in the slaughters inflicted on the people of Poland or in territories of the Soviet Union which are now being swept clear of the enemy, will know that they will be brought back to the scene of their crimes and judged on the spot by the peoples whom they have outraged. Let those who have hitherto not imbrued their hands with innocent blood beware lest they join the ranks of the guilty, for most assuredly the three allied Powers will pursue them to the uttermost ends of the earth and will deliver them to their accusers in order that justice may be done.

The above declaration is without prejudice to the case of the major criminals, whose offences have no particular geographical localisation and who will be punished by the joint decision of the Governments of the Allies.

ROOSEVELT
CHURCHILL
STALIN

The Hopeful Dimension: The Connally-Fulbright Resolution, 1943

From the beginning of the discussion of postwar peace, one of the principal impediments had been fear that Congress would refuse again to implement its President's commitments. The experience of Versailles was still fresh, but the temper of both the American people and the Congress had changed sharply. Early in 1943, Senators Joseph Ball and Harold Burton, Republicans, and Carl Hatch and Lister Hill, Democrats, had moved to arouse support for postwar planning and for an international peace-keeping organization. Their B_2 H_2 *resolution made clear the bipartisan nature of this movement. But the Congress chose to speak formally through resolutions sponsored by Representa-*

tive J. W. Fulbright and by Senator Tom Connally, Chairmen of the Foreign Relations Committees. The latter resolution is provided here. It made clear to the world that Roosevelt had overwhelming congressional support in working toward what eventually became the United Nations. But it also made clear to Roosevelt that he must consult the prerogatives and preferences of the United States Senate.

The resolution given below is in the Congressional Record, *Seventy-eighth Congress, first session (Resolution 192, Nov. 5, 1943), volume 89, part 7, page 9222.*

R*esolved,* That the war against all enemies be waged until complete victory is achieved.

That the United States cooperate with its comrades-in-arms in securing a just and honorable peace.

That the United States, acting through its constitutional processes, join with free and sovereign nations in the establishment and maintenance of international authority with power to prevent aggression and to preserve the peace of the world.

That the Senate recognizes the necessity of there being established at the earliest practicable date a general international organization, based on the principle of the sovereign equality of all peace-loving states, and open to membership by all such states, large and small, for the maintenance of international peace and security.

That, pursuant to the Constitution of the United States, any treaty made to effect the purposes of this resolution, on behalf of the Government of the United States with any other nation or any association of nations, shall be made only by and with the advice and consent of the Senate of the United States, provided two-thirds of the Senators present concur.

The Power Struggle and the Postwar World: The Yalta Agreements, 1945

In a sense, all wartime roads led to Yalta, for it was there that Churchill, Roosevelt, and Stalin were forced to come firmly to grips with postwar problems and commitments. But the agreements reached there would be limited and guided by what had already been done. One thing of importance was the existing lines of geographic control. At the time of the conference, on February 4–11, 1945, Britain and the United States were firmly in control of France, Southern Italy, and Greece. It was clear that the Western Allies would control, at the war's end, Germany west of the Elbe and all of Italy. On the other hand, Russian troops were already firmly established in Poland, Rumania, Bulgaria, and Hungary. They would penetrate eastern Germany, Austria, and also Czechoslovakia by the end of hostilities. A second fact was the predominance of American military opinion that Russia must be brought to an early intervention in the war against Japan, in order to save American lives. The potential of the A-bomb was not yet firmly known; casualties were expected to be massive in the assault upon Japan's home islands. Russian aid was thought to be highly desirable, if not even crucial. A third fact was the imminence of peace in Europe. Already the prospects of postwar problems were looming above the military crisis of the moment. Tensions of the time had to be balanced against the alternate prospects of resolving issues later with the aid of a viable United Nations organization. And the advantages of bargaining at the moment had sometimes to be tempered by the desire to maintain Allied unity for the sake of postwar reconstruction and peace. From Franklin Roosevelt's point of view, Yalta presented four challenges: (1) the need to work out a solution to the German problem with which all the powers could live, but one which would not commit the United States to the unpopular policy of maintaining American troops in Europe; (2) the need to moderate and check as much as possible Russian activities in areas where the Red Army actually had control, i.e., Poland and Rumania, without inviting strong Russian interference in Allied areas such as Greece and Italy; (3) the problem of ensuring timely Russian aid against Japan; and (4) the development of agreements regarding the United Nations which would make possible unanimous Russian, British, and American support for the organization at the start.

Roosevelt did not live to see the implementation of the Yalta agreements. Some of the most significant commitments were shortly violated by the Soviet Union. The use of the A-bomb and the sudden collapse of the war with Japan brought hasty entry by the Russians into the Pacific war. This seemed all too obviously a last-minute move, designed to collect the booty. In retrospect, the Asian agreements at Yalta appeared a rude, unnecessary, and grim joke upon the United States. But the Yalta agreements must be evaluated in the context of that time, not this.

The most useful single analysis of the conference is John Snell et al., The Meaning of Yalta *(1956). Pertinent memoirs are Edward R. Stettinius,* Roosevelt and the Russians: The Yalta Conference *(1949) and James F. Byrnes,* Speaking Frankly *(1947). On Asian questions in general, see Herbert Feis,* The China Tangle: The American Effort in China from Pearl Harbor to the Marshall Mission *(1953).*

The documents printed here are of three types: preliminary correspondence, descriptive public communiqués, and specific agreements. They are from the basic source collection on the matter, U.S. Department of State, Foreign Relations of the United States, Diplomatic Papers: The Conferences at Malta and Yalta *(Washington: Government Printing Office, 1955), pages 966–984.*

President Roosevelt to Marshal Stalin

TOP SECRET [Yalta,] February 10, 1945.

My Dear Marshal Stalin: I have been thinking, as I must, of possible political difficulties which I might encounter in the United States in connection with the number of votes which the Big Powers will enjoy in the Assembly of the World Organization. We have agreed, and I shall certainly carry out that agreement, to support at the forthcoming United Nations Conference the admission of the Ukrainian and White Russian Republics as members of the Assembly of the World Organization. I am somewhat concerned lest it be pointed out that the United States will have only one vote in the Assembly. It may be necessary for me, therefore, if I am to insure whole hearted acceptance by the Congress and people of the United States of our participation in the World Organization, to ask for additional votes in the Assembly in order to give parity to the United States.

I would like to know, before I face this problem, that you would perceive no objection and would support a proposal along this line if it is necessary for me to make it at the forthcoming conference. I would greatly appreciate your letting me have your views in reply to this letter.

Most sincerely yours,
FRANKLIN D. ROOSEVELT

President Roosevelt to Prime Minister Churchill

TOP SECRET [Yalta,] February 10, 1945.

Dear Winston: As I said the other day, I am somewhat concerned over the political difficulties I am apt to encounter in the United States in connection with the ratification by the Senate of the Dumbarton Oaks agreement because of the fact that the United States alone among the three great powers will have only a single vote in the Assembly. I understand from our conversation that you would have no objection if I found it necessary to work out some way of giving the United States additional votes in order to insure parity. I am writing you this letter since I know you understand so well our political situation in the United States and I hope in reply to this letter you can give me your agreement to this suggestion if I find it necessary for our public opinion to make some proposal along those lines at the forthcoming United Nations Conference.

I am enclosing a copy of the letter which I have written to Marshal Stalin on the same subject.

Most sincerely yours,
FRANKLIN D. ROOSEVELT

Prime Minister Churchill to President Roosevelt

[Yalta,] February 11, 1945.

My Dear Franklin, I have given consideration to your letter of February 10 about the political difficulties which might arise in the United States in connection with the ratification by the Senate of the Dumbarton Oaks Agreement because of the fact that the United States alone among the three Great Powers will have only one vote in the Assembly.

Our position is that we maintained the long-established representation of the British Empire and Commonwealth; that the Soviet Government are represented by its chief member, and the two republics of the Ukraine and White Russia; and that the United States should propose the form in which their undisputed equality with every other Member State should be expressed.

I need hardly assure you that I should do everything possible to assist you in this matter.

Yours very sincerely,
WINSTON CHURCHILL

Marshal Stalin to President Roosevelt

[Translation]

Koreis, February 11, 1945.

Dear Mr. Roosevelt: I have received your letter of February 10. I entirely agree with you that, since the number of votes for the Soviet Union is increased to three in connection with the inclusion of the Soviet Ukraine and Soviet White Russia among the members of the assembly, the number of votes for the USA should also be increased.

I think that the number of votes for the USA might be increased to three as in the case of the Soviet Union and its two basic Republics. If it is necessary I am prepared officially to support this proposal.

With sincere respects
I. STALIN

TRILATERAL DOCUMENTS

Communiqué Issued at the End of the Conference

Report of the Crimea Conference

For the past eight days, Winston S. Churchill, Prime Minister of Great Britain, Franklin D. Roosevelt, President of the United States of America, and Marshal J. V. Stalin, Chairman of the Council of Peoples' Commissars of the Union of Soviet Socialist Republics have met with the Foreign Secretaries, Chiefs of Staff and other advisors in the Crimea. . . .

The following statement is made by the Prime Minister of Great Britain, the President of the United States of America, and the Chairman of the Council of Peoples' Commissars of the Union of Soviet Socialist Republics on the results of the Crimean Conference:

I. The Defeat of Germany

We have considered and determined the military plans of the three allied powers for the final defeat of the common enemy. The military staffs of the three allied nations have met in daily meetings throughout the Conference. These meetings have been most satisfactory from every point of view and have resulted in closer coordination of the military effort of the three Allies than ever before. The fullest information has been interchanged. The timing, scope and coordination of new and even more powerful blows to be launched by our armies and air forces into the heart of Germany from the East, West, North and South have been fully agreed and planned in detail.

Our combined military plans will be made known only as we execute them, but we believe that the very close working partnership among the three staffs attained at this Conference will result in shortening the war. Meetings of the three staffs will be continued in the future whenever the need arises.

Nazi Germany is doomed. The German people will only make the cost of their defeat heavier to themselves by attempting to continue a hopeless resistance.

II. The Occupation and Control of Germany

We have agreed on common policies and plans for enforcing the unconditional surrender terms which we shall impose together on Nazi Germany after German armed resistance has been finally crushed. These terms will not be made known until the final defeat of Germany has been accomplished. Under the agreed plan, the forces of the Three Powers will each occupy a separate zone of Germany. Coordinated administration and control has been provided for under the plan through a central Control Commission consisting of the Supreme Commanders of the Three Powers with headquarters in Berlin. It has been agreed that France should be invited by the Three Powers, if she should so desire, to take over a zone of occupation, and to participate as a fourth member of the Control Commission. The limits of the French zone will be agreed by the four governments concerned through their representatives on the European Advisory Commission.

It is our inflexible purpose to destroy German militarism and Nazism and to ensure that Germany will never again be able to disturb the peace of the world. We are determined to disarm and disband all German armed forces; break up for all time the German General Staff that has repeatedly contrived the resurgence of German militarism; remove or destroy all German military equipment; eliminate or control all German industry that could be used for military production; bring all war criminals to just and swift punishment and exact reparation in kind for the destruction wrought by the Germans; wipe out the Nazi party, Nazi laws, organizations and institutions, remove all Nazi and militarist influences from public office and from the cultural and economic life of the German people; and take in harmony such other measures in Germany as may be necessary to the future peace and safety of the world. It is not our purpose to destroy the people of Germany, but only when Nazism and Militarism have been extirpated will there be hope for a decent life for Germans, and a place for them in the comity of nations.

III. Reparation by Germany

We have considered the question of the damage caused by Germany to the Allied Nations in this war and recognized it as just that Germany be obliged to make compensation for this damage in kind to the greatest extent possible. A Commission for the Compensation of Damage will be established. The Commission will be instructed to consider the question of the extent and methods for compensating damage caused by Germany to the Allied Countries. The Commission will work in Moscow.

IV. United Nations Conference

We are resolved upon the earliest possible establishment with our allies of a general international organization to maintain peace and security. We believe that this is essential, both to prevent aggression and to remove the political, economic and social causes of war through the close and continuing collaboration of all peace-loving peoples.

The foundations were laid at Dumbarton Oaks. On the important question of voting procedure, however, agreement was not there reached. The present conference has been able to resolve this difficulty.

We have agreed that a Conference of United Nations should be called to meet at San Francisco in the United States on April 25th, 1945, to prepare the charter of such an organization, along the lines proposed in the informal conversations at Dumbarton Oaks.

The Government of China and the Provisional Government of France will be immediately consulted and invited to sponsor invitations to the Conference jointly with the Governments of the United States, Great Britain and the Union of Soviet Socialist Republics. As soon as the consultation with China and France has been completed, the text of the proposals on voting procedure will be made public.

V. Declaration on Liberated Europe

We have drawn up and subscribed to a Declaration on liberated Europe. This Declaration provides for concerting the policies of the three Powers and for joint action by them in meeting the political and economic problems of liberated Europe in accordance with democratic principles. The text of the Declaration is as follows:

The Premier of the Union of Soviet Socialist Republics, the Prime Minister of the United Kingdom, and the President of the United States of America have consulted with each other in the common interests of the peoples of their countries and those of liberated Europe. They jointly declare their mutual agreement to concert during the temporary period of instability in liberated Europe the policies of their three governments in assisting the peoples liberated from the domination of Nazi Germany and the peoples of the former Axis satellite states of Europe to solve by democratic means their pressing political and economic problems.

The establishment of order in Europe and the rebuilding of national economic life must be achieved by processes which will enable the liberated peoples to destroy the last vestiges of Nazism and Fascism and to creat[e] democratic institutions of their own choice. This is a principle of the Atlantic Charter—the right of all peoples to choose the form of government under which they will live—the restoration of sovereign rights and self-government to those peoples who have been forcibly deprived of them by the aggressor nations.

To foster the conditions in which the liberated peoples may exercise these rights, the three governments will jointly assist the people in any European liberated state or former Axis satellite state in Europe where in their judgment conditions require (*a*) to establish conditions of internal peace; (*b*) to carry out emergency measures for the relief of distressed people; (*c*) to form interim governmental authorities broadly representative of all democratic elements in the population and pledged to the earliest possible establishment through free elections of governments responsive to the will of the people; and (*d*) to facilitate where necessary the holding of such elections.

The three governments will consult the other United Nations and provisional authorities or other governments in Europe when matters of direct interest to them are under consideration.

When, in the opinion of the three governments, conditions in any European, liberated state or any former Axis satellite state in Europe make such action necessary, they will immediately consult together on the measures necessary to discharge the joint responsibilities set forth in this declaration.

By this declaration we reaffirm our faith in the principles of the Atlantic Charter, our pledge in the Declaration by the United Nations, and our determination to build in cooperation with other peace-loving nations a world order under law, dedicated to peace, security, freedom and the general well-being of all mankind.

In issuing this declaration, the Three Powers express the hope that the Provisional Government of the French Republic may be associated with them in the procedure suggested.

VI. Poland

We came to the Crimea Conference resolved to settle our differences about Poland. We discussed fully all aspects of the question. We reaffirm our common desire to see established a strong, free, independent and democratic Poland. As a result of our discussions we have agreed on the conditions in which a new Polish Provisional Government of National Unity may be formed in such a manner as to command recognition by the three major powers.

The agreement reached is as follows:

A new situation has been created in Poland as a result of her complete liberation by the Red Army. This calls for the establishment of a Polish Provisional Government which can be more broadly based than was possible before the recent liberation of western Poland. The Provisional Government which is now functioning in Poland should therefore be reorganized on a broader democratic basis with the inclusion of democratic leaders from Poland itself and from Poles abroad. This new Government should then be called the Polish Provisional Government of National Unity.

M. Molotov, Mr. Harriman and Sir A. Clark Kerr are authorized as a Commission to consult in the first instance in Moscow with members of the present Provisional Government and with other Polish democratic leaders from within Poland and from abroad, with a view to the reorganization of the present Government along the above lines. This Polish Provisional Government of National Unity shall be pledged to the holding of free and unfettered elections as soon as possible on the basis of universal suffrage and secret ballot. In these elections all democratic and anti-Nazi parties shall have the right to take part and to put forward candidates.

When a Polish Provisional Government of National Unity has been properly formed in conformity with the above, the Government of the U. S. S. R., which now maintains diplomatic relations with the present Provisional Government of Poland, and the Government of the United Kingdom and the Government of the United States will establish diplomatic relations with the new Polish Provisional Government of National Unity, and will exchange Ambassadors by whose reports the respective Governments will be kept informed about the situation in Poland.

The three Heads of Government consider that the eastern frontier of Poland should follow the Curzon Line with digressions from it in some regions of five to eight kilometres in favor of Poland. They recognize that Poland must receive substantial accessions of territory in the north and west. They feel that the opinion of the new Polish Provisional Government of National Unity should be sought in due course on the extent of these accessions and that the final delimitation of the western frontier of Poland should thereafter await the Peace Conference.

VII. Yugoslavia

We have agreed to recommend to Marshal Tito and Dr. Subasic that the Agreement between them should be put into effect immediately, and that a new Government should be formed on the basis of that Agreement.

We also recommend that as soon as the new Government has been formed, it should declare that:

(i) The Anti-fascist Assembly of National Liberation (Avnoj) should be extended to include members of the last Yugoslav Parliament (Skupschina) who have not compromised themselves by collaboration with the enemy, thus forming a body to be known as a temporary Parliament; and

(ii) legislative acts passed by the Anti-Fascist Assembly of National Liberation (AUNOJ) will be subject to subsequent ratification by a Constituent Assembly.

There was also a general review of other Balkan question[s].

VIII. Meetings of Foreign Secretaries

Throughout the Conference, besides the daily meetings of the Heads of Governments and the Foreign Secretaries, separate meetings of the three Foreign Secretaries, and their advisers have also been held daily.

These meetings have proved of the utmost value and the Conference agreed that permanent machinery should be set up for regular consultation between the three Foreign Secretaries. They will, therefore, meet as often as may be necessary, probably about every three or four months. These meetings will be held in rotation in the three Capitals, the first meeting being held in London, after the United Nations Conference on world organization.

IX. Unity for Peace as for War

Our meeting here in the Crimea has reaffirmed our common determination to maintain and strengthen in the peace to come that unity of purpose and of action which has made victory possible and certain for the United Nations in this war. We believe that this is a sacred obligation which our Governments owe to our peoples and to all the peoples of the world.

Only with continuing and growing co-operation and understanding among our three countries and among all the peace-loving nations can the highest aspiration of humanity be realized—a secure and lasting peace which will, in the words of the Atlantic Charter, "afford assurance that all the men in all the lands may live out their lives in freedom from fear and want."

Victory in this war and establishment of the proposed international organization will provide the greatest opportunity in all history to create in the years to come the essential conditions of such a peace.

WINSTON S. CHURCHILL
FRANKLIN D ROOSEVELT
[I. STALIN]

February 11, 1945

PROTOCOL OF THE PROCEEDINGS OF THE CRIMEA CONFERENCE

The Crimea Conference of the Heads of the Governments of the United States of America, the United Kingdom, and the Union of Soviet Socialist Republics which took place from February 4th to 11th came to the following conclusions.

I. World Organisation

It was decided:

1. that a United Nations Conference on the proposed world organisation

should be summoned for Wednesday, 25th April, 1945, and should be held in the United States of America.

2. the Nations to be invited to this Conference should be:

a. the United Nations as they existed on the 8th February, 1945 and

b. such of the Associated Nations as have declared war on the common enemy by 1st March, 1945. (For this purpose by the term "Associated Nation" was meant the eight Associated Nations and Turkey). When the Conference on World Organization is held, the delegates of the United Kingdom and United States of America will support a proposal to admit to original membership two Soviet Socialist Republics, i. e. the Ukraine and White Russia.

3. that the United States Government on behalf of the Three Powers should consult the Government of China and the French Provisional Government in regard to the decisions taken at the present Conference concerning the proposed World Organisation.

4. that the text of the invitation to be issued to all the nations which would take part in the United Nations Conference should be as follows:

INVITATION

The Government of the United States of America, on behalf of itself and of the Governments of the United Kingdom, the Union of Soviet Socialist Republics, and the Republic of China and of the Provisional Government of the French Republic, invite the Government of ________ to send representatives to a Conference of the United Nations to be held on 25th April, 1945, or soon thereafter, at San Francisco in the United States of America to prepare a Charter for a General International Organisation for the maintenance of international peace and security.

The above named governments suggest that the Conference consider as affording a basis for such a Charter the Proposals for the Establishment of a General International Organisation, which were made public last October as a result of the Dumbarton Oaks Conference, and which have now been supplemented by the following provisions for Section C of Chapter VI:

"C. *Voting*

1. Each member of the Security Council should have one vote.

2. Decisions of the Security Council on procedural matters should be made by an affirmative vote of seven members.

3. Decisions of the Security Council on all other matters should be made by an affirmative vote of seven members including the concurring votes of the permanent members; provided that, in decisions under Chapter VIII, Section A and under the second sentence of paragraph 1 of Chapter VIII, Section C, a party to a dispute should abstain from voting."

Further information as to arrangements will be transmitted subsequently.

In the event that the Government of ________ desires in advance of the Conference to present views or comments concerning the proposals, the Government of the United States of America will be pleased to transmit such views and comments to the other participating Governments.

Territorial Trusteeship. It was agreed that the five Nations which will have permanent seats on the Security Council should consult each other prior to the United Nations Conference on the question of territorial trusteeship.

The acceptance of this recommendation is subject to its being made clear that territorial trusteeship will only apply to (*a*) existing mandates of the League of Nations; (*b*) territories detached from the enemy as a result of the present war; (*c*) any other territory which might voluntarily be placed under trusteeship; and (*d*) no discussion of actual territories is contemplated at the forthcoming United Nations Conference or in the preliminary consultations, and it will be a matter for subsequent agreement which territories within the above categories will be placed under trusteeship.

II. Declaration on Liberated Europe

The following declaration has been approved:

The Premier of the Union of Soviet Socialist Republics, the Prime Minister of the United Kingdom and the President of the United States of America have consulted with each other in the common interests of the peoples of their countries and those of liberated Europe. They jointly declare their mutual agreement to concert during the temporary period of instability in liberated Europe the policies of their three governments in assisting the peoples liberated from the domination of Nazi Germany and the peoples of the former Axis satellite states of Europe to solve by democratic means their pressing political and economic problems.

The establishment of order in Europe and the re-building of national economic life must be achieved by processes which will enable the liberated peoples to destroy the last vestiges of Nazism and Fascism and to create democratic institutions of their own choice. This is a principle of the Atlantic Charter—the right of all peoples to choose the form of government under which they will live—the restoration of sovereign rights and self-government to those peoples who have been forcibly deprived of them by the aggressor nations.

To foster the conditions in which the liberated peoples may exercise these rights, the three governments will jointly assist the people in any European liberated state or former Axis satellite state in Europe where in their judgment conditions require (*a*) to establish conditions of internal peace; (*b*) to carry out emergency measures for the relief of distressed peoples; (*c*) to form interim governmental authorities broadly representative of all democratic elements in the population and pledged to the earliest possible establishment through free elections of governments responsive to the will of the people; and (*d*) to facilitate where necessary the holding of such elections.

The three governments will consult the other United Nations and provisional authorities or other governments in Europe when matters of direct interest to them are under consideration.

When, in the opinion of the three governments, conditions in any European liberated state or any former Axis satellite state in Europe make such action necessary, they will immediately consult together on the measures necessary to discharge the joint responsibilities set forth in this declaration.

By this declaration we reaffirm our faith in the principles of the Atlantic Charter, our pledge in the Declaration by the United Nations, and our determination to build in co-operation with other peace-loving nations world order under law, dedicated to peace, security, freedom and general well-being of all mankind.

In issuing this declaration, the Three Powers express the hope that the Provisional Government of the French Republic may be associated with them in the procedure suggested.

III. Dismemberment of Germany

It was agreed that Article 12 (*a*) of the Surrender Terms for Germany should be amended to read as follows:

> The United Kingdom, the United States of America and the Union of Soviet Socialist Republics shall possess supreme authority with respect to Germany. In the exercise of such authority they will take such steps, including the complete disarmament, demilitarisation and the dismemberment of Germany as they deem requisite for future peace and security.

The study of the procedure for the dismemberment of Germany was referred to a Committee, consisting of Mr. Eden (Chairman), Mr. Winant and Mr. Gousev. This body would consider the desirability of associating with it a French representative.

IV. Zone of Occupation for the French and Control Council for Germany

It was agreed that a zone in Germany, to be occupied by the French Forces, should be allocated to France. This zone would be formed out of the British and American zones and its extent would be settled by the British and Americans in consultation with the French Provisional Government.

It was also agreed that the French Provisional Government should be invited to become a member of the Allied Control Council for Germany.

V. Reparation

The following protocol has been approved:

1. Germany must pay in kind for the losses caused by her to the Allied nations in the course of the war. Reparations are to be received in the first instance by those countries which have borne the main burden of the war, have suffered the heaviest losses and have organised victory over the enemy.

2. Reparation in kind is to be exacted from Germany in three following forms:

(*a*) Removals within 2 years from the surrender of Germany or the cessation of organised resistance from the national wealth of Germany located on the territory of Germany herself as well as outside her territory (equipment, machine-tools, ships, rolling stock, German investments abroad, shares of industrial, transport and other enterprises in Germany etc.), these removals to be carried out chiefly for purpose of destroying the war potential of Germany.

(*b*) Annual deliveries of goods from current production for a period to be fixed.

(*c*) Use of German labour.

3. For the working out on the above principles of a detailed plan for exaction of reparation from Germany an Allied Reparation Commission will be set up in Moscow. It will consist of three representatives—one from the Union of Soviet Socialist Republics, one from the United Kingdom and one from the United States of America.

4. With regard to the fixing of the total sum of the reparation as well as the distribution of it among the countries which suffered from the German aggression the Soviet and American delegations agreed as follows:

> The Moscow Reparation Commission should take in its initial studies as a basis for discussion the suggestion of the Soviet Government that the total sum of the reparation in accordance with the points (*a*) and (*b*) of the paragraph 2 should be 20 billion dollars and that 50% of it should go to the Union of Soviet Socialist Republics.

The British delegation was of the opinion that pending consideration of the reparation question by the Moscow Reparation Commission no figures of reparation should be mentioned.

The above Soviet-American proposal has been passed to the Moscow Reparation Commission as one of the proposals to be considered by the Commission.

VI. Major War Criminals

The Conference agreed that the question of the major war criminals should be the subject of enquiry by the three Foreign Secretaries for report in due course after the close of the Conference.

VII. Poland

The following Declaration on Poland was agreed by the Conference:

> A new situation has been created in Poland as a result of her complete liberation by the Red Army. This calls for the establishment of a Polish Provisional Government which can be more broadly based than was possible before the recent liberation of the Western part of Poland. The Provisional Government which is now functioning in Poland should therefore be reorganised on a broader democratic basis with the inclusion of democratic leaders from Poland itself and from Poles abroad. This new Government should then be called the Polish Provisional Government of National Unity.
>
> M. Molotov, Mr. Harriman and Sir A. Clark Kerr are authorised as a commission to consult in the first instance in Moscow with members of the present Provisional Government and with other Polish democratic leaders from within Poland and from abroad, with a view to the reorganisation of the present Government along the above lines. This Polish Provisional Government of National Unity shall be pledged to the holding of free and unfettered elections as soon as possible on the basis of universal suffrage and secret ballot. In these elections all democratic and anti-Nazi parties shall have the right to take part and to put forward candidates.
>
> When a Polish Provisional Government of National Unity has been properly formed in conformity with the above, the Government of the

U. S. S. R., which now maintains diplomatic relations with the present Provisional Government of Poland, and the Government of the United Kingdom and the Government of the U. S. A. will establish diplomatic relations with the new Polish Provisional Government of National Unity, and will exchange Ambassadors by whose reports the respective Governments will be kept informed about the situation in Poland.

The three Heads of Government consider that the Eastern frontier of Poland should follow the Curzon Line with digressions from it in some regions of five to eight kilometres in favour of Poland. They recognise that Poland must receive substantial accessions of territory in the North and West. They feel that the opinion of the new Polish Provisional Government of National Unity should be sought in due course on the extent of these accessions and that the final delimitation of the Western frontier of Poland should thereafter await the Peace Conference.

VIII. Yugoslavia

It was agreed to recommend to Marshal Tito and to Dr. Subasic:

(*a*) that the Tito-Subasic Agreement should immediately be put into effect and a new Government formed on the basis of the Agreement.

(*b*) that as soon as the new Government has been formed it should declare:

(i) that the Anti-Fascist Assembly of National Liberation (AUNOJ) will be extended to include members of the last Yugoslav Skupstina who have not compromised themselves by collaboration with the enemy, thus forming a body to be known as a temporary Parliament and

(ii) that legislative acts passed by the Anti-Fascist Assemb[l]y of National Liberation (AUNOJ) will be subject to subsequent ratification by a Constituent Assembly;

and that this statement should be published in the communique of the Conference.

IX. Italo-Yugoslav Frontier
Italo-Austria Frontier

Notes on these subjects were put in by the British delegation and the American and Soviet delegations agreed to consider them and give their views later.

X. Yugoslav-Bulgarian Relations

There was an exchange of views between the Foreign Secretaries on the question of the desirability of a Yugoslav-Bulgarian pact of alliance. The question at issue was whether a state still under an armistice regime could be allowed to enter into a treaty with another state. Mr. Eden suggested that the Bulgarian and Yugoslav Governments should be informed that this could not be approved. Mr. Stettinius suggested that the British and American Ambassadors should discuss the matter further with M. Molotov in Moscow. M. Molotov agreed with the proposal of Mr. Stettinius.

XI. South Eastern Europe

The British Delegation put in notes for the consideration of their colleagues on the following subjects:

(*a*) the Control Commission in Bulgaria

(*b*) Greek claims upon Bulgaria, more particularly with reference to reparations.

(*c*) Oil equipment in Roumania.

XII. Iran

Mr. Eden, Mr. Stettinius and M. Molotov exchanged views on the situation in Iran. It was agreed that this matter should be pursued through the diplomatic channel.

XIII. Meetings of the Three Foreign Secretaries

The Conference agreed that permanent machinery should be set up for consultation between the three Foreign Secretaries; they should meet as often as necessary, probably about every three or four months.

These meetings will be held in rotation in the three capitals, the first meeting being held in London.

XIV. The Montreux Convention and the Straits

It was agreed that at the next meeting of the three Foreign Secretaries to be held in London, they should consider proposals which it was understood the Soviet Government would put forward in relation to the Montreux Convention and report to their Governments. The Turkish Government should be informed at the appropriate moment.

The foregoing Protocol was approved and signed by the three Foreign Secretaries at the Crimean Conference, February 11, 1945.

E R STETTINIUS, JR
[V. MOLOTOV]
ANTHONY EDEN

PROTOCOL ON THE TALKS BETWEEN THE HEADS OF THE THREE GOVERNMENTS AT THE CRIMEAN CONFERENCE ON THE QUESTION OF THE GERMAN REPARATION IN KIND

The Heads of the three governments agreed as follows:

1. Germany must pay in kind for the losses caused by her to the Allied nations in the course of the war. Reparation are to be received in the first instance by those countries which have borne the main burden of the war, have suffered the heaviest losses and have organised victory over the enemy.

2. Reparation in kind are to be exacted from Germany in three following forms:

(*a*) Removals within 2 years from the surrender of Germany or the cessation of organised resistance from the national wealth of Germany located on the territory of Germany herself as well as outside her territory (equipment, machine-tools, ships, rolling stock, German investments abroad, shares of industrial, transport and other enterprises in Germany, etc.), these removals to be carried out chiefly for purpose of destroying the war potential of Germany.

(*b*) Annual deliveries of goods from current production for a period to be fixed.

(*c*) Use of German labour.

3. For the working out on the above principles of a detailed plan for exaction of reparation from Germany an Allied Reparation Commission will be set up in Moscow. It will consist of three representatives—one from the Union of Soviet Socialist Republics, one from the United Kingdom and one from the United States of America.

4. With regard to the fixing of the total sum of the reparation as well as the distribution of it among the countries which suffered from the German aggression the Soviet and American delegations agreed as follows:

"The Moscow Reparation Commission should take in its initial studies as a basis for discussion the suggestion of the Soviet Government that the total sum of the reparation in accordance with the points (*a*) and (*b*) of the paragraph 2 should be 20 billion dollars and that 50% of it should go to the Union of Soviet Socialist Republics."

The British delegation was of the opinion that pending consideration of the reparation question by the Moscow Reparation Commission no figures of reparation should be mentioned.

The above Soviet-American proposal has been passed to the Moscow Reparation Commission as one of the proposals to be considered by the Commission.

WINSTON S. CHURCHILL
FRANKLIN D. ROOSEVELT
[I. STALIN]

February 11, 1945.

AGREEMENT REGARDING ENTRY OF THE SOVIET UNION INTO THE WAR AGAINST JAPAN

TOP SECRET

Agreement

The leaders of the three Great Powers—the Soviet Union, the United States of America and Great Britain—have agreed that in two or three months after Germany has surrendered and the war in Europe has terminated the Soviet Union shall enter into the war against Japan on the side of the Allies on condition that:

1. The *status quo* in Outer-Mongolia (The Mongolian People's Republic) shall be preserved;

2. The former rights of Russia violated by the treacherous attack of Japan in 1904 shall be restored, viz:

(*a*) the southern part of Sakhalin as well as all the islands adjacent to it shall be returned to the Soviet Union.

(*b*) the commercial port of Dairen shall be internationalized, the preeminent interests of the Soviet Union in this port being safeguarded and the lease of Port Arthur as a naval base of the USSR restored,

(*c*) the Chinese-Eastern Railroad and the South-Manchurian Railroad which provides an outlet to Dairen shall be jointly operated by the establishment of a joint Soviet-Chinese Company it being understood that the preeminent interests of the Soviet Union shall be safeguarded and that China shall retain full sovereignty in Manchuria;

3. The Kuril islands shall be handed over to the Soviet Union.

It is understood, that the agreement concerning Outer Mongolia and the ports and railroads referred to above will require concurrence of Generalissimo Chiang Kai-Shek. The President will take measures in order to obtain this concurrence on advice from Marshal Stalin.

The Heads of the three Great Powers have agreed that these claims of the Soviet Union shall be unquestionably fulfilled after Japan has been defeated.

For its part the Soviet Union expresses its readiness to conclude with the National Government of China a pact of friendship and alliance between the USSR and China in order to render assistance to China with its armed forces for the purpose of liberating China from the Japanese yoke.

[I. STALIN]
FRANKLIN D ROOSEVELT
WINSTON S. CHURCHILL

February 11, 1945.

Western Hemisphere Security: The Act of Chapultepec, 1945

Throughout the intricate military and diplomatic maneuvering with Churchill, Stalin, and Chiang Kai-shek, the administration did not lose sight of the fact that the Western Hemisphere is both the prime commitment of the United States and the fundamental basis of its defense. Relations within the hemisphere had always been difficult. Canada, with her special commitment to the British Empire, chose to stand aside from hemispheric arrangements. On the other hand, many of the Latin American republics feared the United States and hated Americans for their record of imperialism and intervention. There were overtones of ethnic and cultural prejudice in the attitudes of both North Americans and Latin Americans. And there were nations—notably Argentina—anxious to challenge the overly confident United States assumption of leadership.

All of this was both simplified and complicated during the war. The military threat drove American republics together and moderated some of the difficulties. On the other hand, the regime of Juan Peron which controlled Argentina was closely associated in ideology and sentiment with the Nazis. And some support was gained by Argentine pro-fascist leadership through its cultivation of the concept that Franco's Spain should provide cultural leadership for Latin America.

Yet the war was in general a disciplining rather than a divisive experience. A series of conferences and continuing negotiations led in February, 1945, to the Inter-American Conference at Mexico City. There the states adopted the act printed below which provided the basis for an Organization of American States and which registered general acceptance of the principle of mutual defense in the hemisphere.

The Act of Chapultepec of March 8, 1945, is quoted from Decade of Foreign Relations, *pages 414–421.*

(A) ACT OF CHAPULTEPEC

Whereas:

The peoples of the Americas, animated by a profound love of justice, remain sincerely devoted to the principles of international law;

It is their desire that such principles, notwithstanding the present difficult circumstances, prevail with even greater force in future international relations;

The inter-American conferences have repeatedly proclaimed certain fundamental principles, but these must be reaffirmed at a time when the juridical bases of the community of nations are being re-established;

The new situation in the world makes more imperative than ever the union and solidarity of the American peoples, for the defense of their rights and the maintenance of international peace;

The American states have been incorporating in their international law, since 1890, by means of conventions, resolutions and declarations, the following principles:

a. The proscription of territorial conquest and the non-recognition of all acquisitions made by force (First International Conference of American States, 1890);

b. The condemnation of intervention by one State in the internal or external affairs of another (Seventh International Conference of American States, 1933, and Inter-American Conference for the Maintenance of Peace, 1936);

c. The recognition that every war or threat of war affects directly or indirectly all civilized peoples, and endangers the great principles of liberty and justice which constitute the American ideal and the standard of American international policy (Inter-American Conference for the Maintenance of Peace, 1936);

d. The system of mutual consultation in order to find means of peaceful cooperation in the event of war or threat of war between American countries (Inter-American Conference for the Maintenance of Peace, 1936);

e. The recognition that every act susceptible of disturbing the peace of America affects each and every one of the American nations and justifies the initiation of the procedure of consultation (Inter-American Conference for the Maintenance of Peace, 1936);

f. The adoption of conciliation, unrestricted arbitration, or the application of international justice, in the solution of any difference or dispute between American nations, whatever its nature or origin (Inter-American Conference for the Maintenance of Peace, 1936);

g. The recognition that respect for the personality, sovereignty and independence of each American State constitutes the essence of international order sustained by continental solidarity, which historically has been expressed and sustained by declarations and treaties in force (Eighth International Conference of American States, 1938);

h. The affirmation that respect for and the faithful observance of treaties constitute the indispensable rule for the development of peaceful relations between States, and that treaties can only be revised by agreement of the contracting parties (Declaration of American Principles, Eighth International Conference of American States, 1938);

i. The proclamation that, in case the peace, security or territorial integrity of any American republic is threatened by acts of any nature that may impair them, they proclaim their common concern and their determination to make effective their solidarity, coordinating their respective sovereign wills by means of the procedure of consultation, using the measures which in each case the circumstances may make advisable (Declaration of Lima, Eighth International Conference of American States, 1938);

j. The declaration that any attempt on the part of a non-American state against the integrity or inviolability of the territory, the sovereignty or the political independence of an American State shall be considered as an act of aggression against all the American States (Declaration XV of the Second Meeting of the Ministers of Foreign Affairs, Habana, 1940);

The furtherance of these principles, which the American States have constantly practised in order to assure peace and solidarity among the nations of the Continent, constitutes an effective means of contributing to the general system of world security and of facilitating its establishment;

The security and solidarity of the Continent are affected to the same extent by an act of aggression against any of the American States by a non-American State, as by an act of aggression of an American State against one or more American States;

Part I

The Governments Represented at the Inter-American Conference on Problems of War and Peace

Declare:

1. That all sovereign States are juridically equal among themselves.
2. That every State has the right to the respect of its individuality and

independence, on the part of the other members of the international community.

3. That every attack of a State against the integrity or the inviolability of the territory, or against the sovereignty or political independence of an American State, shall, comformably to Part III hereof, be considered as an act of aggression against the other States which sign this Act. In any case invasion by armed forces of one State into the territory of another trespassing boundaries established by treaty and demarcated in accordance therewith shall constitute an act of aggression.

4. That in case acts of aggression occur or there are reasons to believe that an aggression is being prepared by any other State against the integrity or inviolability of the territory, or against the sovereignty or political independence of an American State, the States signatory to this Act will consult among themselves in order to agree upon the measures it may be advisable to take.

5. That during the war, and until the treaty recommended in Part II hereof is concluded, the signatories of this Act recognize that such threats and acts of aggression, as indicated in paragraphs 3 and 4 above, constitute an interference with the war effort of the United Nations, calling for such procedures, within the scope of their constitutional powers of a general nature and for war, as may be found necessary, including: recall of chiefs of diplomatic missions; breaking of diplomatic relations; breaking of consular relations; breaking of postal, telegraphic, telephonic, radio-telephonic relations; interruption of economic, commercial and financial relations; use of armed force to prevent or repel aggression.

6. That the principles and procedure contained in this Declaration shall become effective immediately, inasmuch as any act of aggression or threat of aggression during the present state of war interferes with the war effort of the United Nations to obtain victory. Henceforth, and to the end that the principles and procedures herein stipulated shall conform with the constitutional processes of each Republic, the respective Governments shall take the necessary steps to perfect this instrument in order that it shall be in force at all times.

Part II

The Inter-American Conference on Problems of War and Peace

Recommends:

That for the purpose of meeting threats or acts of aggression against any American Republic following the establishment of peace, the Governments of the American Republics consider the conclusion, in accordance with their constitutional processes, of a treaty establishing procedures whereby such threats or acts may be met by the use, by all or some of the signatories of said treaty, of any one or more of the following measures: recall of chiefs of diplomatic missions; breaking of diplomatic relations; breaking of consular relations; breaking of postal, telegraphic, telephonic, radio-telephonic relations; interruption of economic, commercial and financial relations; use of armed force to prevent or repel aggression.

Part III

The above Declaration and Recommendation constitute a regional arrangement for dealing with such matters relating to the maintenance of international peace and security as are appropriate for regional action in this Hemisphere. The said arrangement, and the pertinent activities and procedures, shall be consistent with the purposes and principles of the general international organization, when established.

This agreement shall be known as the "ACT OF CHAPULTEPEC."

(B) REORGANIZATION, CONSOLIDATION AND STRENGTHENING OF THE INTER-AMERICAN SYSTEM

Whereas:

The inter-American system and the principles, instruments, agencies, and procedures that give it substance, constitute the living manifestation of the determination of the sovereign American Republics to act together for the fulfillment of their common purposes in the maintenance of peace and security and in the promotion of the well-being of their peoples;

The inter-American system is and has traditionally been inspired by a deep sense of universal cooperation;

The inter-American system, as an expression of the common ideals, the needs, and the will of the community of American Republics, should be further improved and strengthened for the purpose of adjusting and solving inter-American problems;

The inter-American system should, furthermore, maintain the closest relations with the proposed general international organization and assume the appropriate responsibilities in harmony with the principles and purposes of the general international organization,

The Inter-American Conference on Problems of War and Peace

Resolves:

1. That the International Conferences of American States shall meet ordinarily at four-year intervals and shall be the inter-American organ entrusted with the formulation of general inter-American policy and the determination of the structure and functions of inter-American instruments and agencies. The next Conference shall meet in Bogotá in 1946.

2. The regular Meetings of the Ministers of Foreign Affairs shall be held annually upon special call by the Governing Board of the Pan American Union, unless there should be held in the same year an International Conference of American States pursuant to the preceding article. The next regular Meeting of the Ministers of Foreign Affairs shall be held in 1947.

The Meetings shall be charged with taking decisions on problems of great urgency and importance concerning the inter-American system and with regard to situations and disputes of every kind which may disturb the peace of the American Republics.

If, under exceptional circumstances, a Minister of Foreign Affairs should be unable to attend, he may be represented by a special delegate.

3. The Governing Board of the Pan American Union shall be composed of one *ad hoc* delegate designated by each of the American Republics, which delegates shall have the rank of Ambassadors and shall enjoy the corresponding privileges and immunities, but shall not be part of the diplomatic mission accredited to the government of the country in which the Pan American Union has its seat. This provision shall take effect at the expiration of the present period of sessions of the existing Board.

4. In addition to its present functions the Governing Board of the Pan American Union

a. Shall take action, within the limitations imposed upon it by the International Conferences of American States or pursuant to the specific direction of the Meetings of Ministers of Foreign Affairs, on every matter that affects the effective functioning of the inter-American system and the solidarity and general welfare of the American Republics;

b. Shall call the regular Meetings of Ministers of Foreign Affairs provided for in Paragraph 1 of Article 2 hereof, and special meetings, when they are requested, to consider exclusively emergency questions. In the latter case the call shall be made upon the vote of an absolute majority of the Board;

c. Shall supervise the inter-American agencies which are or may become related to the Pan American Union, and shall receive and approve annual or special reports from these agencies.

5. The Chairman of the Governing Board of the Pan American Union shall be elected annually and shall not be eligible for re-election for the term immediately following.

The Governing Board of the Pan American Union shall meet at least once each week.

The seat of the Pan American Union and of the Governing Board shall continue to be in Washington.

The Director General of the Pan American Union shall be chosen by the Governing Board for a term of ten years; he shall not be eligible for re-election, nor can he be succeeded by a person of the same nationality.

In the event of a vacancy in the office of Director General of the Pan American Union, a successor shall be appointed who shall hold office until the end of the term and who may be re-elected if the vacancy occurs during the second half of the term.

The first term shall begin on January 1, 1955.

The appointment and replacement of the Assistant Director shall be made in accordance with the above rules, except that the first term shall begin on January 1, 1960.

It is understood that the Governing Board may at any time, by vote of fifteen of its members, remove the Director General or the Assistant Director, on grounds relating to the efficiency of the organization.

6. Until the Ninth International Conference of American States, in accordance with the procedure provided hereinafter, creates or confirms the various agencies of the inter-American system, the following agencies created by the Meetings of Ministers of Foreign Affairs shall continue to function: The Inter-American Juridical Committee, the Emergency Advisory Committee for Political Defense, and the Inter-American Defense Board.

7. In place of the emergency agency now functioning as the Inter-American Financial and Economic Advisory Committee, there is hereby created a permanent Inter-American Economic and Social Council—subsidiary to the Governing Board of the Pan American Union—the members of which shall be designated by the respective Governments, and which shall be empowered:

a. To carry out recommendations of the International Conferences of American States;

b. To serve as the coordinating agency for all official inter-American economic and social activities;

c. To promote social progress and the raising of the standard of living for all the American peoples;

d. To undertake studies and other activities upon its own initiative or upon the request of any American government;

e. To collect and prepare reports on economic and social matters for the use of the American Republics;

f. To maintain liaison with the corresponding agency of the general international organization when established, and with existing or projected international economic and social agencies.

The Governing Board of the Pan American Union is authorized to organize provisionally the Inter-American Economic and Social Council. The permanent organization shall be established by the Ninth International Conference of American States.

8. The Division of Intellectual Cooperation of the Pan American Union shall be maintained for the purpose of strengthening by all means at its command the spiritual bonds between the American nations.

9. The Governing Board of the Pan American Union, availing itself of all Pan American agencies that it deems appropriate, is charged with preparing, beginning May 1, 1945, a draft charter for the improvement and strengthening of the Pan American system. The Governing Board shall submit the draft to the Governments of the Continent prior to December 31, 1945.

The draft charter shall first of all proclaim:

The recognition, by all the American Republics, of international law as the effective rule of their conduct and the pledge of those Governments to observe the standards enunciated in a "Declaration of the Rights and Duties of States" and a "Declaration of the International Rights and Duties of Man"; these shall serve as the definition of the fundamental principles of international law and shall appear as an annex to the charter, so that, without amending it, the Declarations may be revised from time to time to adapt them to the requirements and aspirations of international life.

For the preparation of the first Declaration, the principles already incorporated into the juridical heritage of the inter-American system shall be coordinated, especially those contained in the "Convention on the Rights and Duties of States" approved at the Seventh International Conference of American States; in the "Declaration of Principles of Inter-American Solidarity and Cooperation" adopted at the Inter-American Conference for the Maintenance of Peace; in the "Declaration of the Principles of the Solidarity of America," and the "Declaration of American Principles" adopted at the Eighth International Conference of American States; in the "Declaration on the Maintenance of International Activities in Accordance with Christian Morality" and the declaration relative to "Reciprocal Assistance and Cooperation for the Defense of the Nations of the Americas," approved at the First and Second Meetings of Ministers of Foreign Affairs, respectively; and in the Declarations on "Continental Solidarity in Observance of Treaties" and "The Good Neighbor Policy," adopted at the Third Meeting of Ministers of Foreign Affairs. The draft declaration on "Reaffirmation of Fundamental Principles of International Law" prepared by the Inter-American Juridical Committee, and any Declaration of Principles that may be adopted by this Conference, shall also be taken into account.

In regard to the second Declaration mentioned above, the text shall be that formulated by the Inter-American Juridical Committee in fulfillment of the request contained in another resolution of the present Conference.

It is the desire of the Inter-American Conference on Problems of War and Peace that there shall be taken into account the Inter-American Commission of Women, which for sixteen years has rendered eminent services to the cause of America and humanity, and that it be included among the organizations which form the Pan American Union, with the same prerogatives and position that have been accorded to other inter-American institutions of a permanent or emergency character that have functioned within or without the Pan American Union.

10. The draft charter shall provide for the strengthening of the inter-American system on the basis of this resolution and by the creation of new agencies or the elimination or adaptation of existing agencies, specifying and coordinating their functions as among themselves and with the world organization.

The draft shall take into account the need of accelerating the consolidation and extension of existing inter-American peace instruments and the simplification and improvement of the inter-American peace structure, and to this end the Governing Board of the Pan American Union shall utilize the services of the Inter-American Juridical Committee. In addition, the draft shall provide for the consolidation and simplification of all other inter-American instruments so that they may be more effective.

11. The American Governments shall send to the Governing Board of the Pan American Union prior to September 1, 1945, all their proposals relating to the preceding articles.

12. The draft charter shall also provide for the establishment of an equitable system for the financial support of the Pan American Union and of all its related agencies.

SELECTION 71

The Charter of the United Nations, 1945

By the time of Franklin D. Roosevelt's death on April 12, 1945, it had become clear that American postwar foreign policy would operate at four interlocking levels. The foundation would lie upon power—massive military potential, and unmatched industrial might. The Bomb was hardly known; it was as yet not thinkable that ravaged Russia, Germany, and Japan could again become major economic forces in the world within ten years of the war's end. Based upon this foundation of power would stand two sets of commitments, for everyone now knew that the United States could not again attempt to live alone. First would be the arrangements for hemispheric solidarity which the State Department had sought to bring from the drawing boards at Mexico City. The United States shared firmly with other American nations the commitment to defend the hemisphere. Beyond this, on another level, it was clear that the world would in large part be ruled by the private agreements of the Great Powers. And finally, if there were to be an umbrella or roof above the structure, it was the United Nations. Despite the misclaimers of later critics, United States foreign policy makers never planned that the nation's entire postwar policy should rely upon the United Nations. Nor were they so naive as to build hopes upon naked power alone.

For better or worse, postwar policy was predicated upon the realities of power. But it was hoped that both the UN and the Organization of American States would moderate issues, disperse tensions, clear up errors and ignorance, channel power, and above all minimize the number of occasions on which it must be used.

The draft of the United Nations Charter had been developed in the late summer and early autumn of 1944 at Dumbarton Oaks, near Washington. Roosevelt, Churchill, and Stalin had undertaken compromises on matters which divided them most sharply—the veto and the number of votes in the Assembly for Russia, Britain, and the United States.

Harry Truman inherited, then, not merely the decision to call the UN Conference and the various arrangements which had been made, all of which he reaffirmed; he also inherited the American intention to deal from power while experimenting with hope. The conference met on Truman's call in San Francisco from April 25 to June 26, 1945. Although the war with Japan was not yet over, no act so clearly delineated the end of an age and the beginning of a new one.

The establishment of the United Nations is discussed in Amry Vandenbosch and Willard N. Hogan, Toward World Order *(1963), and in H. V. Evatt,* The United Nations *(1948).*

The Charter itself is here quoted from Decade of Foreign Policy, *pages 117–140.*

We the peoples of the United Nations determined to save succeeding generations from the scourge of war, which twice in our lifetime has brought untold sorrow to mankind, and

to reaffirm faith in fundamental human rights, in the dignity and worth of the human person, in the equal rights of men and women and, of nations large and small, and

to establish conditions under which justice and respect for the obligations arising from treaties and other sources of international law can be maintained, and

to promote social progress and better standards of life in larger freedom,

and for these ends

to practice tolerance and live together in peace with one another as good neighbors, and

to unite our strength to maintain international peace and security, and

to ensure, by the acceptance of principles and the institution of methods, that armed force shall not be used, save in the common interest, and

to employ international machinery for the promotion of the economic and social advancement of all peoples,

have resolved to combine our efforts to accomplish these aims.

Accordingly, our respective Governments, through representatives assembled in the city of San Francisco, who have exhibited their full powers found to be in good and due form, have agreed to the present Charter of the United Nations and do hereby establish an international organization to be known as the United Nations.

CHAPTER I. PURPOSES AND PRINCIPLES

Article 1

The Purposes of the United Nations are:

1. To maintain international peace and security, and to that end: to take effective collective measures for the prevention and removal of threats to the peace, and for the suppression of acts of aggression or other breaches of the peace, and to bring about by peaceful means, and in conformity with the principles of justice and international law, adjustment or settlement of international disputes or situations which might lead to a breach of the peace;

2. To develop friendly relations among nations based on respect for the principle of equal rights and self-determination of peoples, and to take other appropriate measures to strengthen universal peace;

3. To achieve international cooperation in solving international problems of an economic, social, cultural, or humanitarian character, and in promoting and encouraging respect for human rights and for fundamental freedoms for all without distinction as to race, sex, language, or religion; and

4. To be a center for harmonizing the actions of nations in the attainment of these common ends.

Article 2

The Organization and its Members, in pursuit of the Purposes stated in Article 1, shall act in accordance with the following Principles.

1. The Organization is based on the principle of the sovereign equality of all its Members.
2. All Members, in order to ensure to all of them the rights and benefits resulting from membership, shall fulfil in good faith the obligations assumed by them in accordance with the present Charter.
3. All Members shall settle their international disputes by peaceful means in such a manner that international peace and security, and justice, are not endangered.
4. All Members shall refrain in their international relations from the threat or use of force against the territorial integrity or political independence of any state, or in any other manner inconsistent with the Purposes of the United Nations.
5. All Members shall give the United Nations every assistance in any action it takes in accordance with the present Charter, and shall refrain from giving assistance to any state against which the United Nations is taking preventive or enforcement action.
6. The Organization shall ensure that states which are not Members of the United Nations act in accordance with these Principles so far as may be necessary for the maintenance of international peace and security.
7. Nothing contained in the present Charter shall authorize the United Nations to intervene in matters which are essentially within the domestic jurisdiction of any state or shall require the Members to submit such matters to settlement under the present Charter; but this principle shall not prejudice the application of enforcement measures under Chapter VII.

CHAPTER II. MEMBERSHIP

Article 3

The original Members of the United Nations shall be the states which, having participated in the United Nations Conference on International Organization at San Francisco, or having previously signed the Declaration by United Nations of January 1, 1942, sign the present Charter and ratify it in accordance with Article 110.

Article 4

1. Membership in the United Nations is open to all other peace-loving states which accept the obligations contained in the present Charter and, in the judgment of the Organization, are able and willing to carry out these obligations.
2. The admission of any such state to membership in the United Nations will be effected by a decision of the General Assembly upon the recommendation of the Security Council.

Article 5

A Member of the United Nations against which preventive or enforcement action has been taken by the Security Council may be suspended from the exercise of the rights and privileges of membership by the General Assembly upon the recommendation of the Security Council. The exercise of these rights and privileges may be restored by the Security Council.

Article 6

A Member of the United Nations which has persistently violated the Principles contained in the present Charter may be expelled from the Organization by the General Assembly upon the recommendation of the Security Council.

CHAPTER III. ORGANS

Article 7

1. There are established as the principal organs of the United Nations: a General Assembly, a Security Council, an Economic and Social Council, a Trusteeship Council, an International Court of Justice, and a Secretariat.
2. Such subsidiary organs as may be found necessary may be established in accordance with the present Charter.

Article 8

The United Nations shall place no restrictions on the eligibility of men and women to participate in any capacity and under conditions of equality in its principal and subsidiary organs.

CHAPTER IV. THE GENERAL ASSEMBLY

Composition

Article 9

1. The General Assembly shall consist of all the Members of the United Nations.
2. Each Member shall have not more than five representatives in the General Assembly.

Functions and Powers

Article 10

The General Assembly may discuss any questions or any matters within the scope of the present Charter or relating to the powers and functions of any organs provided for in the present Charter, and, except as provided in Article 12, may make recommendations to the Members of the United

Nations or to the Security Council or to both on any such questions or matters.

Article 11

1. The General Assembly may consider the general principles of cooperation in the maintenance of international peace and security, including the principles governing disarmament and the regulation of armaments, and may make recommendations with regard to such principles to the Members or to the Security Council or to both.

2. The General Assembly may discuss any questions relating to the maintenance of international peace and security brought before it by any Member of the United Nations, or by the Security Council, or by a state which is not a Member of the United Nations in accordance with Article 35, paragraph 2, and, except as provided in Article 12, may make recommendations with regard to any such questions to the state or states concerned or to the Security Council or to both. Any such question on which action is necessary shall be referred to the Security Council by the General Assembly either before or after discussion.

3. The General Assembly may call the attention of the Security Council to situations which are likely to endanger international peace and security.

4. The powers of the General Assembly set forth in this Article shall not limit the general scope of Article 10.

Article 12

1. While the Security Council is exercising in respect of any dispute or situation the functions assigned to it in the present Charter, the General Assembly shall not make any recommendation with regard to that dispute or situation unless the Security Council so requests.

2. The Secretary-General, with the consent of the Security Council, shall notify the General Assembly at each session of any matters relative to the maintenance of international peace and security which are being dealt with by the Security Council and shall similarly notify the General Assembly, or the Members of the United Nations if the General Assembly is not in session, immediately the Security Council ceases to deal with such matters.

Article 13

1. The General Assembly shall initiate studies and make recommendations for the purpose of:

a. promoting international cooperation in the political field and encouraging the progressive development of international law and its codification;

b. promoting international cooperation in the economic, social, cultural, educational, and health fields, and assisting in the realization of human rights and fundamental freedoms for all without distinction as to race, sex, language, or religion.

2. The further responsibilities, functions, and powers of the General Assembly with respect to matters mentioned in paragraph 1 (b) above are set forth in Chapters IX and X.

Article 14

Subject to the provisions of Article 12, the General Assembly may recommend measures for the peaceful adjustment of any situation, regardless of origin, which it deems likely to impair the general welfare or friendly relations among nations, including situations resulting from a violation of the provisions of the present Charter setting forth the Purposes and Principles of the United Nations.

Article 15

1. The General Assembly shall receive and consider annual and special reports from the Security Council; these reports shall include an account of the measures that the Security Council has decided upon or taken to maintain international peace and security.
2. The General Assembly shall receive and consider reports from the other organs of the United Nations.

Article 16

The General Assembly shall perform such functions with respect to the international trusteeship system as are assigned to it under Chapters XII and XIII, including the approval of the trusteeship agreements for areas not designated as strategic.

Article 17

1. The General Assembly shall consider and approve the budget of the Organization.
2. The expenses of the Organization shall be borne by the Members as apportioned by the General Assembly.
3. The General Assembly shall consider and approve any financial and budgetary arrangements with specialized agencies referred to in Article 57 and shall examine the administrative budgets of such specialized agencies with a view to making recommendations to the agencies concerned.

Voting

Article 18

1. Each member of the General Assembly shall have one vote.
2. Decisions of the General Assembly on important questions shall be made by a two-thirds majority of the members present and voting. These questions shall include: recommendations with respect to the maintenance of international peace and security, the election of the non-permanent members of the Security Council, the election of the members of the Economic and Social Council, the election of members of the Trusteeship Council in accordance with paragraph 1 (c) of Article 86, the admission of new Members to the United Nations, the suspension of the rights and privileges of membership, the expulsion of Members, questions relating to the operation of the trusteeship system, and budgetary questions.

3. Decisions on other questions, including the determination of additional categories of questions to be decided by a two-thirds majority, shall be made by a majority of the members present and voting.

Article 19

A Member of the United Nations which is in arrears in the payment of its financial contributions to the Organization shall have no vote in the General Assembly if the amount of its arrears equals or exceeds the amount of the contributions due from it for the preceding two full years. The General Assembly may, nevertheless, permit such a Member to vote if it is satisfied that the failure to pay is due to conditions beyond the control of the Member.

Procedure

Article 20

The General Assembly shall meet in regular annual sessions and in such special sessions as occasion may require. Special sessions shall be convoked by the Secretary-General at the request of the Security Council or of a majority of the Members of the United Nations.

Article 21

The General Assembly shall adopt its own rules of procedure. It shall elect its President for each session.

Article 22

The General Assembly may establish such subsidiary organs as it deems necessary for the performance of its functions.

CHAPTER V. THE SECURITY COUNCIL

Composition

Article 23

1. The Security Council shall consist of eleven Members of the United Nations. The Republic of China, France, the Union of Soviet Socialist Republics, the United Kingdom of Great Britain and Northern Ireland, and the United States of America shall be permanent members of the Security Council. The General Assembly shall elect six other Members of the United Nations to be non-permanent members of the Security Council, due regard being specially paid, in the first instance to the contribution of Members of the United Nations to the maintenance of international peace and security and to the other purposes of the Organization, and also to equitable geographical distribution.

2. The non-permanent members of the Security Council shall be elected for a term of two years. In the first election of the non-permanent members, however, three shall be chosen for a term of one year. A retiring member shall not be eligible for immediate re-election.

3. Each member of the Security Council shall have one representative.

Functions and Powers

Article 24

1. In order to ensure prompt and effective action by the United Nations, its Members confer on the Security Council primary responsibility for the maintenance of international peace and security, and agree that in carrying out its duties under this responsibility the Security Council acts on their behalf.

2. In discharging these duties the Security Council shall act in accordance with the Purposes and Principles of the United Nations. The specific powers granted to the Security Council for the discharge of these duties are laid down in Chapters VI, VII, VIII, and XII.

3. The Security Council shall submit annual and, when necessary, special reports to the General Assembly for its consideration.

Article 25

The Members of the United Nations agree to accept and carry out the decisions of the Security Council in accordance with the present Charter.

Article 26

In order to promote the establishment and maintenance of international peace and security with the least diversion for armaments of the world's human and economic resources, the Security Council shall be responsible for formulating, with the assistance of the Military Staff Committee referred to in Article 47, plans to be submitted to the Members of the United Nations for the establishment of a system for the regulation of armaments.

Voting

Article 27

1. Each member of the Security Council shall have one vote.

2. Decisions of the Security Council on procedural matters shall be made by an affirmative vote of seven members.

3. Decisions of the Security Council on all other matters shall be made by an affirmative vote of seven members including the concurring votes of the permanent members; provided that, in decisions under Chapter VI, and under paragraph 3 of Article 52, a party to a dispute shall abstain from voting.

Procedure

Article 28

1. The Security Council shall be so organized as to be able to function continuously. Each member of the Security Council shall for this purpose be represented at all times at the seat of the Organization.
2. The Security Council shall hold periodic meetings at which each of its members may, if it so desires, be represented by a member of the government or by some other specially designated representative.
3. The Security Council may hold meetings at such places other than the seat of the Organization as in its judgment will best facilitate its work.

Article 29

The Security Council may establish such subsidiary organs as it deems necessary for the performance of its functions.

Article 30

The Security Council shall adopt its own rules of procedure, including the method of selecting its President.

Article 31

Any Member of the United Nations which is not a member of the Security Council may participate, without vote, in the discussion of any question brought before the Security Council whenever the latter considers that the interests of that Member are specially affected.

Article 32

Any Member of the United Nations which is not a member of the Security Council or any state which is not a Member of the United Nations, if it is a party to a dispute under consideration by the Security Council, shall be invited to participate, without vote, in the discussion relating to the dispute. The Security Council shall lay down such conditions as it deems just for the participation of a state which is not a Member of the United Nations.

CHAPTER VI. PACIFIC SETTLEMENT OF DISPUTES

Article 33

1. The parties to any dispute, the continuance of which is likely to endanger the maintenance of international peace and security, shall first of all, seek a solution by negotiation, enquiry, mediation, conciliation, arbitration, judicial settlement, resort to regional agencies or arrangements, or other peaceful means of their own choice.
2. The Security Council shall, when it deems necessary, call upon the parties to settle their dispute by such means.

Article 34

The Security Council may investigate any dispute, or any situation which might lead to international friction or give rise to a dispute in order to determine whether the continuance of the dispute or situation is likely to endanger the maintenance of international peace and security.

Article 35

1. Any Member of the United Nations may bring any dispute, or any situation of the nature referred to in Article 34, to the attention of the Security Council or of the General Assembly.
2. A state which is not a Member of the United Nations may bring to the attention of the Security Council or of the General Assembly any dispute to which it is a party if it accepts in advance, for the purposes of the dispute, the obligations of pacific settlement provided in the present Charter.
3. The proceedings of the General Assembly in respect of matters brought to its attention under this Article will be subject to the provisions of Articles 11 and 12.

Article 36

1. The Security Council may, at any stage of a dispute of the nature referred to in Article 33 or of a situation of like nature, recommend appropriate procedures or methods of adjustment.
2. The Security Council should take into consideration any procedures for the settlement of the dispute which have already been adopted by the parties.
3. In making recommendations under this Article the Security Council should also take into consideration that legal disputes should as a general rule be deferred by the parties to the International Court of Justice in accordance with the provisions of the Statute of the Court.

Article 37

1. Should the parties to a dispute of the nature referred to in Article 33 fail to settle it by the means indicated in that Article, they should refer it to the Security Council.
2. If the Security Council deems that the continuance of the dispute is in fact likely to endanger the maintenance of international peace and security, it shall decide whether to take action under Article 36 or to recommend such terms of settlement as it may consider appropriate.

Article 38

Without prejudice to the provisions of Articles 33 to 37, the Security Council may, if all the parties to any dispute so request, make recommendations to the parties with a view to a pacific settlement of the dispute.

CHAPTER VII. ACTION WITH RESPECT TO THREATS TO THE PEACE, BREACHES OF THE PEACE, AND ACTS OF AGGRESSION

Article 39

The Security Council shall determine the existence of any threat to the peace, breach of the peace, or act of aggression and shall make recommendations, or decide what measures shall be taken in accordance with Articles 41 and 42, to maintain or restore international peace and security.

Article 40

In order to prevent an aggravation of the situation, the Security Council may, before making the recommendations or deciding upon the measures provided for in Article 39, call upon the parties concerned to comply with such provisional measures as it deems necessary or desirable. Such provisional measures shall be without prejudice to the rights, claims, or position of the parties concerned. The Security Council shall duly take account of failure to comply with such provisional measures.

Article 41

The Security Council may decide what measures not involving the use of armed force are to be employed to give effect to its decisions, and it may call upon the Members of the United Nations to apply such measures. These may include complete or partial interruption of economic relations and of rail, sea, air, postal, telegraphic, radio, and other means of communication, and the severance of diplomatic relations.

Article 42

Should the Security Council consider that measures provided for in Article 41 would be inadequate or have proved to be inadequate it may take such action by air, sea, or land forces as may be necessary to maintain or restore international peace and security. Such action may include demonstrations, blockade, and other operations by air, sea, or land forces of Members of the United Nations.

Article 43

1. All Members of the United Nations, in order to contribute to the maintenance of international peace and security, undertake to make available to the Security Council, on its call and in accordance with a special agreement or agreements, armed forces, assistance, and facilities, including rights of passage, necessary for the purpose of maintaining international peace and security.
2. Such agreement or agreements shall govern the numbers and types of forces, their degree of readiness and general location, and the nature of the facilities and assistance to be provided.

3. The agreement or agreements shall be negotiated as soon as possible on the initiative of the Security Council. They shall be concluded between the Security Council and Members or between the Security Council and groups of Members and shall be subject to ratification by the signatory states in accordance with their respective constitutional processes.

Article 44

When the Security Council has decided to use force it shall, before calling upon a Member not represented on it to provide armed forces in fulfilment of the obligations assumed under Article 43, invite that Member, if the Member so desires, to participate in the decisions of the Security Council concerning the employment of contingents of that Member's armed forces.

Article 45

In order to enable the United Nations to take urgent military measures, Members shall hold immediately available national airforce contingents for combined international enforcement action. The strength and degree of readiness of these contingents and plans for their combined action shall be determined, within the limits laid down in the special agreement or agreements referred to in Article 43, by the Security Council with the assistance of the Military Staff Committee.

Article 46

Plans for the application of armed force shall be made by the Security Council with the assistance of the Military Staff Committee.

Article 47

1. There shall be established a Military Staff Committee to advise and assist the Security Council on all questions relating to the Security Council's military requirements for the maintenance of international peace and security, the employment and command of forces placed at its disposal, the regulation of armaments, and possible disarmament.
2. The Military Staff Committee shall consist of the Chiefs of Staff of the permanent Members of the Security Council or their representatives. Any Member of the United Nations not permanently represented on the Committee shall be invited by the Committee to be associated with it when the efficient discharge of the Committee's responsibilities requires the participation of that Member in its work.
3. The Military Staff Committee shall be responsible under the Security Council for the strategic direction of any armed forces placed at the disposal of the Security Council. Questions relating to the command of such forces shall be worked out subsequently.
4. The Military Staff Committee, with the authorization of the Security Council and after consultation with appropriate regional agencies, may establish regional subcommittees.

Article 48

1. The action required to carry out the decisions of the Security Council for the maintenance of international peace and security shall be taken by all the Members of the United Nations or by some of them, as the Security Council may determine.

2. Such decisions shall be carried out by the Members of the United Nations directly and through their action in the appropriate international agencies of which they are members.

Article 49

The Members of the United Nations shall join in affording mutual assistance in carrying out the measures decided upon by the Security Council.

Article 50

If preventive or enforcement measures against any state are taken by the Security Council, any other state, whether a Member of the United Nations or not, which finds itself confronted with special economic problems arising from the carrying out of those measures shall have the right to consult the Security Council with regard to a solution of those problems.

Article 51

Nothing in the present Charter shall impair the inherent right of individual or collective self-defense if an armed attack occurs against a Member of the United Nations, until the Security Council has taken the measures necessary to maintain international peace and security. Measures taken by Members in the exercise of this right of self-defense shall be immediately reported to the Security Council and shall not in any way affect the authority and responsibility of the Security Council under the present Charter to take at any time such action as it deems necessary in order to maintain or restore international peace and security.

CHAPTER VIII. REGIONAL ARRANGEMENTS

Article 52

1. Nothing in the present Charter precludes the existence of regional arrangements or agencies for dealing with such matters relating to the maintenance of international peace and security as are appropriate for regional action, provided that such arrangements or agencies and their activities are consistent with the Purposes and Principles of the United Nations.

2. The Members of the United Nations entering into such arrangements or constituting such agencies shall make every effort to achieve pacific settlement of local disputes through such regional arrangements or by such regional agencies before referring them to the Security Council.

3. The Security Council shall encourage the development of pacific settlement of local disputes through such regional arrangements or by such regional agencies either on the initiative of the states concerned or by reference from the Security Council.

4. This Article in no way impairs the application of Articles 34 and 35.

Article 53

1. The Security Council shall, where appropriate, utilize such regional arrangements or agencies for enforcement action under its authority. But no enforcement action shall be taken under regional arrangements or by regional agencies without the authorization of the Security Council, with the exception of measures against any enemy state, as defined in paragraph 2 of this Article, provided for pursuant to Article 107 or in regional arrangements directed against renewal of aggressive policy on the part of any such state, until such time as the Organization may, on request of the Governments concerned, be charged with the responsibility for preventing further aggression by such a state.

2. The term enemy state as used in paragraph 1 of this Article applies to any state which during the Second World War has been an enemy of any signatory of the present Charter.

Article 54

The Security Council shall at all times be kept fully informed of activities undertaken or in contemplation under regional arrangements or by regional agencies for the maintenance of international peace and security.

CHAPTER IX. INTERNATIONAL ECONOMIC AND SOCIAL COOPERATION

Article 55

With a view to the creation of conditions of stability and well-being which are necessary for peaceful and friendly relations among nations based on respect for the principle of equal rights and self-determination of peoples, the United Nations shall promote:

a. higher standards of living, full employment, and conditions of economic and social progress and development;

b. solutions of international economic, social, health, and related problems; and international cultural and educational cooperation; and

c. universal respect for, and observance of, human rights and fundamental freedoms for all without distinction as to race, sex, language, or religion.

Article 56

All Members pledge themselves to take joint and separate action in cooperation with the Organization for the achievement of the purposes set forth in Article 55.

Article 57

1. The various specialized agencies, established by intergovernmental agreement and having wide international responsibilities, as defined in their basic instruments, in economic, social, cultural, educational, health, and related fields, shall be brought into relationship with the United Nations in accordance with the provisions of Article 63.

2. Such agencies thus brought into relationship with the United Nations are hereinafter referred to as specialized agencies.

Article 58

The Organization shall make recommendations for the coordination of the policies and activities of the specialized agencies.

Article 59

The Organization shall, where appropriate, initiate negotiations among the states concerned for the creation of any new specialized agencies required for the accomplishment of the purposes set forth in Article 55.

Article 60

Responsibility for the discharge of the functions of the Organization set forth in this Chapter shall be vested in the General Assembly and, under the authority of the General Assembly, in the Economic and Social Council, which shall have for this purpose the powers set forth in Chapter X.

CHAPTER X. THE ECONOMIC AND SOCIAL COUNCIL

Composition

Article 61

1. The Economic and Social Council shall consist of eighteen Members of the United Nations elected by the General Assembly.

2. Subject to the provisions of paragraph 3, six members of the Economic and Social Council shall be elected each year for a term of three years. A retiring member shall be eligible for immediate reelection.

3. At the first election, eighteen members of the Economic and Social Council shall be chosen. The term of office of six members so chosen shall expire at the end of one year, and of six other members at the end of two years, in accordance with arrangements made by the General Assembly.

4. Each member of the Economic and Social Council shall have one representative.

Functions and Powers

Article 62

1. The Economic and Social Council may make or initiate studies and reports with respect to international economic, social, cultural, educational, health, and related matters and may make recommendations with respect to any such matters to the General Assembly, to the Members of the United Nations, and to the specialized agencies concerned.

2. It may make recommendations for the purpose of promoting respect for, and observance of, human rights and fundamental freedoms for all.

3. It may prepare draft conventions for submission to the General Assembly, with respect to matters falling within its competence.

4. It may call, in accordance with the rules prescribed by the United Nations, international conferences on matters falling within its competence.

Article 63

1. The Economic and Social Council may enter into agreements with any of the agencies referred to in Article 57, defining the terms on which the agency concerned shall be brought into relationship with the United Nations. Such agreements shall be subject to approval by the General Assembly.

2. It may coordinate the activities of the specialized agencies through consultation with and recommendations to such agencies and through recommendations to the General Assembly and to the Members of the United Nations.

Article 64

1. The Economic and Social Council may take appropriate steps to obtain regular reports from the specialized agencies. It may make arrangements with the Members of the United Nations and with the specialized agencies to obtain reports on the steps taken to give effect to its own recommendations and to recommendations on matters falling within its competence made by the General Assembly.

2. It may communicate its observations on these reports to the General Assembly.

Article 65

The Economic and Social Council may furnish information to the Security Council and shall assist the Security Council upon its request.

Article 66

1. The Economic and Social Council shall perform such functions as fall within its competence in connection with the carrying out of the recommendations of the General Assembly.

2. It may, with the approval of the General Assembly, perform services at the request of Members of the United Nations and at the request of specialized agencies.

3. It shall perform such other functions as are specified elsewhere in the present Charter or as may be assigned to it by the General Assembly.

Voting

Article 67

1. Each member of the Economic and Social Council shall have one vote.
2. Decisions of the Economic and Social Council shall be made by a majority of the members present and voting.

Procedure

Article 68

The Economic and Social Council shall set up commissions in economic and social fields and for the promotion of human rights, and such other commissions as may be required for the performance of its functions.

Article 69

The Economic and Social Council shall invite any Member of the United Nations to participate, without vote, in its deliberations on any matter of particular concern to that Member.

Article 70

The Economic and Social Council may make arrangements for representatives of the specialized agencies to participate, without vote, in its deliberations and in those of the commissions established by it, and for its representatives to participate in the deliberations of the specialized agencies.

Article 71

The Economic and Social Council may make suitable arrangements for consultation with non-governmental organizations which are concerned with matters within its competence. Such arrangements may be made with international organizations and, where appropriate, with national organizations after consultation with the Member of the United Nations concerned.

Article 72

1. The Economic and Social Council shall adopt its own rules of procedure, including the method of selecting its President.
2. The Economic and Social Council shall meet as required in accordance with its rules, which shall include provision for the convening of meetings on the request of a majority of its members.

CHAPTER XI. DECLARATION REGARDING NON-SELF-GOVERNING TERRITORIES

Article 73

Members of the United Nations which have or assume responsibilities for the administration of territories whose peoples have not yet attained a full measure of self-government recognize the principle that the interests of the inhabitants of these territories are paramount, and accept as a sacred trust the obligation to promote to the utmost, within the system of international peace and security established by the present Charter, the well-being of the inhabitants of these territories, and, to this end:

a. to ensure, with due respect for the culture of the peoples concerned, their political, economic, social, and educational advancement, their just treatment, and their protection against abuses;

b. to develop self-government, to take due account of the political aspirations of the peoples, and to assist them in the progressive development of their free political institutions, according to the particular circumstances of each territory and its peoples and their varying stages of advancement;

c. to further international peace and security;

d. to promote constructive measures of development, to encourage research, and to cooperate with one another and, when and where appropriate, with specialized international bodies with a view to the practical achievement of the social, economic, and scientific purposes set forth in this Article; and

e. to transmit regularly to the Secretary-General for information purposes, subject to such limitation as security and constitutional considerations may require, statistical and other information of a technical nature relating to economic, social, and educational conditions in the territories for which they are respectively responsible other than those territories to which Chapters XII and XIII apply.

Article 74

Members of the United Nations also agree that their policy in respect of the territories to which this Chapter applies, no less than in respect of their metropolitan areas, must be based on the general principle of good-neighborliness, due account being taken of the interests and well-being of the rest of the world, in social, economic, and commercial matters.

CHAPTER XII. INTERNATIONAL TRUSTEESHIP SYSTEM

Article 75

The United Nations shall establish under its authority an international trusteeship system for the administration and supervision of such territories as may be placed thereunder by subsequent individual agreements. These territories are hereinafter referred to as trust territories.

Article 76

The basic objectives of the trusteeship system, in accordance with the Purposes of the United Nations laid down in Article 1 of the present Charter, shall be:

a. to further international peace and security;

b. to promote the political, economic, social, and educational advancement of the inhabitants of the trust territories, and their progressive development towards self-government or independence as may be appropriate to the particular circumstances of each territory and its peoples and the freely expressed wishes of the peoples concerned, and as may be provided by the terms of each trusteeship agreement;

c. to encourage respect for human rights and for fundamental freedoms for all without distinction as to race, sex, language, or religion, and to encourage recognition of the interdependence of the peoples of the world; and

d. to ensure equal treatment in social, economic, and commercial matters for all Members of the United Nations and their nationals, and also equal treatment for the latter in the administration of justice, without prejudice to the attainment of the foregoing objectives and subject to the provisions of Article 80.

Article 77

1. The trusteeship system shall apply to such territories in the following categories as may be placed thereunder by means of trusteeship agreements:

a. territories now held under mandate;

b. territories which may be detached from enemy states as a result of the Second World War; and

c. territories voluntarily placed under the system by states responsible for their administration.

2. It will be a matter for subsequent agreement as to which territories in the foregoing categories will be brought under the trusteeship system and upon what terms.

Article 78

The trusteeship system shall not apply to territories which have become Members of the United Nations, relationship among which shall be based on respect for the principle of sovereign equality.

Article 79

The terms of trusteeship for each territory to be placed under the trusteeship system, including any alteration or amendment, shall be agreed upon by the states directly concerned, including the mandatory power in the case of territories held under mandate by a Member of the United Nations, and shall be approved as provided for in Articles 83 and 85.

Article 80

1. Except as may be agreed upon in individual trusteeship agreements, made under Articles 77, 79, and 81, placing each territory under the trusteeship system, and until such agreements have been concluded, nothing in this Chapter shall be construed in or of itself to alter in any manner the rights whatsoever of any states or any peoples or the terms of existing international instruments to which Members of the United Nations may respectively be parties.

2. Paragraph 1 of this Article shall not be interpreted as giving grounds for delay or postponement of the negotiation and conclusion of agreements for placing mandated and other territories under the trusteeship system as provided for in Article 77.

Article 81

The trusteeship agreement shall in each case include the terms under which the trust territory will be administered and designate the authority which will exercise the administration of the trust territory. Such authority, hereinafter called the administering authority, may be one or more states or the Organization itself.

Article 82

There may be designated, in any trusteeship agreement, a strategic area or areas which may include part or all of the trust territory to which the agreement applies, without prejudice to any special agreement or agreements made under Article 43.

Article 83

1. All functions of the United Nations relating to strategic areas, including the approval of the terms of the trusteeship agreements and of their alteration or amendment, shall be exercised by the Security Council.

2. The basic objectives set forth in Article 76 shall be applicable to the people of each strategic area.

3. The Security Council shall, subject to the provisions of the trusteeship agreements and without prejudice to security considerations, avail itself of the assistance of the Trusteeship Council to perform those functions of the United Nations under the trusteeship system relating to political, economic, social, and educational matters in the strategic areas.

Article 84

It shall be the duty of the administering authority to ensure that the trust territory shall play its part in the maintenance of international peace and security. To this end the administering authority may make use of volunteer forces, facilities, and assistance from the trust territory in carrying out the obligations towards the Security Council undertaken in this regard by the administering authority, as well as for local defense and the maintenance of law and order within the trust territory.

Article 85

1. The functions of the United Nations with regard to trusteeship agreements for all areas not designated as strategic, including the approval of the terms of the trusteeship agreements and of their alteration or amendment, shall be exercised by the General Assembly.
2. The Trusteeship Council, operating under the authority of the General Assembly, shall assist the General Assembly in carrying out these functions.

CHAPTER XIII. THE TRUSTEESHIP COUNCIL

Composition

Article 86

1. The Trusteeship Council shall consist of the following Members of the United Nations:

a. those Members administering trust territories;

b. such of those Members mentioned by name in Article 23 as are not administering trust territories; and

c. as many other Members elected for three-year terms by the General Assembly as may be necessary to ensure that the total number of members of the Trusteeship Council is equally divided between those Members of the United Nations which administer trust territories and those which do not.

2. Each member of the Trusteeship Council shall designate one specially qualified person to represent it therein.

Functions and Powers

Article 87

The General Assembly and, under its authority, the Trusteeship Council, in carrying out their functions, may:

a. consider reports submitted by the administering authority;

b. accept petitions and examine them in consultation with the administering authority;

c. provide for periodic visits to the respective trust territories at times agreed upon with the administering authority; and

d. take these and other actions in conformity with the terms of the trusteeship agreements.

Article 88

The Trusteeship Council shall formulate a questionnaire on the political, economic, social, and educational advancement of the inhabitants of each trust territory, and the administering authority for each trust territory within the competence of the General Assembly shall make an annual report to the General Assembly upon the basis of such questionnaire.

Voting

Article 89

1. Each member of the Trusteeship Council shall have one vote.
2. Decisions of the Trusteeship Council shall be made by a majority of the members present and voting.

Procedure

Article 90

1. The Trusteeship Council shall adopt its own rules of procedure, including the method of selecting its President.
2. The Trusteeship Council shall meet as required in accordance with its rules, which shall include provision for the convening of meetings on the request of a majority of its members.

Article 91

The Trusteeship Council shall, when appropriate, avail itself of the assistance of the Economic and Social Council and of the specialized agencies in regard to matters with which they are respectively concerned.

CHAPTER XIV. THE INTERNATIONAL COURT OF JUSTICE

Article 92

The International Court of Justice shall be the principal judicial organ of the United Nations. It shall function in accordance with the annexed Statute, which is based upon the Statute of the Permanent Court of International Justice and forms an integral part of the present Charter.

Article 93

1. All Members of the United Nations are *ipso facto* parties to the Statute of the International Court of Justice.
2. A state which is not a Member of the United Nations may become a party to the Statute of the International Court of Justice on conditions to be determined in each case by the General Assembly upon the recommendation of the Security Council.

Article 94

1. Each Member of the United Nations undertakes to comply with the decision of the International Court of Justice in any case to which it is a party.
2. If any party to a case fails to perform the obligations incumbent upon it under a judgment rendered by the Court, the other party may have recourse to the Security Council, which may, if it deems necessary, make recommendations or decide upon measures to be taken to give effect to the judgment.

Article 95

Nothing in the present Charter shall prevent Members of the United Nations from entrusting the solution of their differences to other tribunals by virtue of agreements already in existence or which may be concluded in the future.

Article 96

1. The General Assembly or the Security Council may request the International Court of Justice to give an advisory opinion on any legal question.
2. Other organs of the United Nations and specialized agencies, which may at any time be so authorized by the General Assembly, may also request advisory opinions of the Court on legal questions arising within the scope of their activities.

CHAPTER XV. THE SECRETARIAT

Article 97

The Secretariat shall comprise a Secretary-General and such staff as the Organization may require. The Secretary-General shall be appointed by the General Assembly upon the recommendation of the Security Council. He shall be the chief administrative officer of the Organization.

Article 98

The Secretary-General shall act in that capacity in all meetings of the General Assembly, of the Security Council, of the Economic and Social Council, and of the Trusteeship Council, and shall perform such other functions as are entrusted to him by these organs. The Secretary-General shall make an annual report to the General Assembly on the work of the Organization.

Article 99

The Secretary-General may bring to the attention of the Security Council any matter which in his opinion may threaten the maintenance of international peace and security.

Article 100

1. In the performance of their duties the Secretary-General and the staff shall not seek or receive instructions from any government or from any other authority external to the Organization. They shall refrain from any action which might reflect on their position as international officials responsible only to the Organization.

2. Each Member of the United Nations undertakes to respect the exclusively international character of the responsibilities of the Secretary-General and the staff and not to seek to influence them in the discharge of their responsibilities.

Article 101

1. The staff shall be appointed by the Secretary-General under regulations established by the General Assembly.

2. Appropriate staffs shall be permanently assigned to the Economic and Social Council, the Trusteeship Council, and, as required, to other organs of the United Nations. These staffs shall form a part of the Secretariat.

3. The paramount consideration in the employment of the staff and in the determination of the conditions of service shall be the necessity of securing the highest standards of efficiency, competence, and integrity. Due regard shall be paid to the importance of recruiting the staff on as wide a geographical basis as possible.

CHAPTER XVI. MISCELLANEOUS PROVISIONS

Article 102

1. Every treaty and every international agreement entered into by any Member of the United Nations after the present Charter comes into force shall as soon as possible be registered with the Secretariat and published by it.

2. No party to any such treaty or international agreement which has not been registered in accordance with the provisions of paragraph 1 of this Article may invoke that treaty or agreement before any organ of the United Nations.

Article 103

In the event of a conflict between the obligations of the Members of the United Nations under the present Charter and their obligations under any other international agreement, their obligations under the present Charter shall prevail.

Article 104

The Organization shall enjoy in the territory of each of its Members such legal capacity as may be necessary for the exercise of its functions and the fulfillment of its purposes.

Article 105

1. The Organization shall enjoy in the territory of each of its Members such privileges and immunities as are necessary for the fulfillment of its purposes.

2. Representatives of the Members of the United Nations and officials of the Organization shall similarly enjoy such privileges and immunities as are necessary for the independent exercise of their functions in connection with the Organization.

3. The General Assembly may make recommendations with a view to determining the details of the application of paragraphs 1 and 2 of this Article or may propose conventions to the Members of the United Nations for this purpose.

CHAPTER XVII. TRANSITIONAL SECURITY ARRANGEMENTS

Article 106

Pending the coming into force of such special agreements referred to in Article 43 as in the opinion of the Security Council enable it to begin the exercise of its responsibilities under Article 42, the parties to the Four-Nation Declaration, signed at Moscow, October 30, 1943, and France, shall, in accordance with the provisions of paragraph 5 of that Declaration, consult with one another and as occasion requires with other Members of the United Nations with a view to such joint action on behalf of the Organization as may be necessary for the purpose of maintaining international peace and security.

Article 107

Nothing in the present Charter shall invalidate or preclude action, in relation to any state which during the Second World War has been an enemy of any signatory to the present Charter, taken or authorized as a result of that war by the Governments having responsibility for such action.

CHAPTER XVIII. AMENDMENTS

Article 108

Amendments to the present Charter shall come into force for all Members of the United Nations when they have been adopted by a vote of two thirds of the members of the General Assembly and ratified in accordance with their respective constitutional processes by two thirds of the Members of the United Nations, including all the permanent members of the Security Council.

Article 109

1. A General Conference of the Members of the United Nations for the purpose of reviewing the present Charter may be held at a date and place to be fixed by a two-thirds vote of the members of the General Assembly and by a vote of any seven members of the Security Council. Each Member of the United Nations shall have one vote in the conference.

2. Any alteration of the present Charter recommended by a two-thirds vote of the conference shall take effect when ratified in accordance with their respective constitutional processes by two thirds of the Members of the United Nations including all the permanent members of the Security Council.

3. If such a conference has not been held before the tenth annual session of the General Assembly following the coming into force of the present Charter, the proposal to call such a conference shall be placed on the agenda of that session of the General Assembly, and the conference shall be held if so decided by a majority vote of the members of the General Assembly and by a vote of any seven members of the Security Council.

CHAPTER XIX. RATIFICATION AND SIGNATURE

Article 110

1. The present Charter shall be ratified by the signatory states in accordance with their respective constitutional processes.

2. The ratifications shall be deposited with the Government of the United States of America, which shall notify all the signatory states of each deposit as well as the Secretary-General of the Organization when he has been appointed.

3. The present Charter shall come into force upon the deposit of ratifications by the Republic of China, France, the Union of Soviet Socialist Republics, the United Kingdom of Great Britain and Northern Ireland, and the United States of America, and by a majority of the other signatory states. A protocol of the ratifications deposited shall thereupon be drawn up by the Government of the United States of America which shall communicate copies thereof to all the signatory states.

4. The states signatory to the present Charter which ratify it after it has come into force will become original Members of the United Nations on the date of the deposit of their respective ratifications.

Article 111

The present Charter, of which the Chinese, French, Russian, English, and Spanish texts are equally authentic, shall remain deposited in the archives of the Government of the United States of America. Duly certified copies thereof shall be transmitted by that Government to the Governments of the other signatory states.

In faith whereof the representatives of the Governments of the United Nations have signed the present Charter.

Done at the city of San Francisco the twenty-sixth day of June, one thousand nine hundred and forty-five.